# CRITICAL FICTIONS

# CRITICAL FICTIONS

## Sentiment and the American Market
## 1780–1870

Joseph Fichtelberg

The University of Georgia Press
*Athens and London*

© 2003 by the University of Georgia Press

Athens, Georgia 30602

Set in 10.5/14 Bulmer by Bookcomp, Inc.

Printed and bound by Maple-Vail

The paper in this book meets the guidelines for
permanence and durability of the Committee on
Production Guidelines for Book Longevity of the
Council on Library Resources.

Printed in the United States of America

07   06   05   04   03   c   5   4   3   2   1

Library of Congress Cataloging-in-Publication Data

Fichtelberg, Joseph.

Critical fictions : sentiment and the American market, 1780–1870 /
Joseph Fichtelberg.

p. cm.

Includes bibliographical references and index.

ISBN 0-8203-2434-5 (alk. paper)

1. American prose literature—1783–1850—History and criticism.
2. Sentimentalism in literature.   3. American prose literature—
19th century—History and criticism.   4. Literature and society—
United States—History—19th century.   5. Literature and
society—United States—History—18th century.
6. Social problems in literature.   7. Middle class in literature.
8. Liberalism in literature.   9. Sympathy in literature.
10. Emotions in literature.   I. Title.

PS366.S35  F53  2003

810.9'353—dc21        2002007564

British Library Cataloging-in-Publication Data available

For my mother and father,
and in memory of Claire Fichtelberg

# CONTENTS

In a book that often examines the debts of others, it is a pleasure to acknowledge my own. Several libraries have aided me in my work. I thank the staffs of the New-York Historical Society, the Historical Society of Pennsylvania, the New York Public Library, Columbia University's Rare Book and Manuscript Collection, the Poughkeepsie Public Library, and the Baker and Houghton Libraries of Harvard University. Hofstra University's interlibrary loan has efficiently filled my numerous requests. Columbia University's Microform Reading Room has been indispensable to this project, as has been its able director, Uday Dhar.

Hofstra has been an ideal place to explore and test my ideas. My colleagues Dana Brand, John Bryant, Tom Couser, Barry Nass, and Lee Zimmerman have helped to clarify my thoughts and have offered invaluable support. Paula Uruburu took time out from a frenetic schedule as department chair to read a draft of the manuscript. Erik Brogger, playwright, has sustained me with his friendship. I have also benefited from a special leave granted by Hofstra University, during which I completed early drafts of chapters 3 and 4.

Other colleagues have been equally generous. Michelle Burnham, Andrew Delbanco, Philip Gura, Sharon Harris, Gordon Hutner, Carla Mulford, William Scheick, Dietmar Schloss, David Shields, and Reiner Smolinski have all read or commented on portions of the book. I am fortunate to have found so many eager listeners among the Society of Early Americanists, whose annual conferences have provided me with opportunities to present my work. Like many in the field, I owe much to the generosity of Carla and David, exemplary scholars and fond friends.

Earlier versions of several chapters appeared in scholarly journals and are reprinted with their permission. In chapter 2, material on Crèvecoeur first appeared as "Utopic Distresses: Crèvecoeur's *Letters* and Revolution," in *Studies in the Literary Imagination* 27, no. 1 (1994), pp. 85–101, copyright © 1994 by the

Department of English, Georgia State University. An early discussion of Equiano was published as "Word Between Worlds: The Economy of Equiano's *Narrative*," in *American Literary History* 5, no. 3 (1993), 459–80, and is reprinted by permission of Oxford University Press. In chapter 3, essays on Martha Meredith Read appeared in two journals. Portions of "Friendless in Philadelphia: The Feminist Critique of Martha Meredith Read" are reprinted from *Early American Literature* 32, no. 3 (1997), 205–21, copyright © 1997 by the Department of English, University of North Carolina at Chapel Hill. Material on Read's feminist essays was first published in "Heart-felt Verities: The Feminism of Martha Meredith Read," in *Legacy* 15, no. 2 (1998), 125–38, and is reprinted by permission of the University of Nebraska Press. A study of Isaac Mitchell is also reprinted from "The Sentimental Economy of Isaac Mitchell's *The Asylum*," in *Early American Literature* 32, no. 1 (1997), 1–19, copyright © 1997 by the Department of English, University of North Carolina at Chapel Hill. I thank the editors and referees of these journals for their unfailing encouragement.

At the University of Georgia Press, two anonymous readers challenged me to think more rigorously about the book's argument and structure. I have greatly profited from their suggestions. Jeanée Ledoux perceptively reviewed the manuscript and saved me from many careless errors. Jon Davies oversaw all details of the book's final preparation. Alison Waldenberg guided the book through two extensive revisions. The project could not have been completed without her enthusiasm, her professionalism, and her tact. I am deeply grateful for all three.

My largest debts are to my family. My daughters, Allison and Vera, have grown up with this book. They have illuminated every day, and every page. My wife, Patti, has been a constant inspiration, the very model of those wise and generous women I take up in the pages ahead. Hers is a debt I can never repay. This book is dedicated to my parents and my grandmother, for their gifts of wisdom, compassion, and love.

CRITICAL FICTIONS

# CHAPTER 1

# Legends of the Fall

ॐ

In the fall of 1837, in a special congressional session prompted by the worst economic crisis in the young nation's history, Senator Robert Strange of North Carolina tried to assess the damage. Trade, he claimed, was "very occult," "scarcely perceptible" even to "the most sagacious mind." Given trade's invisibility, he urged, senators must proceed with caution: "Every attempt to control her, diminishes her freedom; and those who are now beseeching Congress to take her under its special charge, would, if their prayer were granted, ere long discover, that when trade lays herself at the footstool of power for protection, she has deserted her native element, . . . and, having become faint and languishing, will sigh vainly for the return of her health and buoyancy."[1] In that disturbing time, preserving calm was crucial, and what better way than to imagine the unruly market as a delicate female in need of the senators' prudent protection and respect? One did not agitate the feelings of helpless women, panicky merchants, or bankrupt constituents.[2]

Strange's metaphors suggest more than mere distress at the sudden depression. Rather, his imagery exposes a troubling feature of the market revolution through which he lived: its invisible, all-consuming power. Like the senator, this book will try to envision the mysterious, often frightening, economic changes that, from the early republic through the Civil War, transformed American lives. I will argue that sentiment, the language of feeling, was the lens that made those changes visible. Sentiment provided the imagery through which Americans sought to explain and shape the market; in Fredric Jameson's apt phrase, sentimental imagery came to embody the "fundamentally non-narrative and nonrepresentational" stuff of history itself.[3] And the principal agents in these representations of the market, I will argue, were women. With their allegedly unlimited capacity for feeling, women—or their fictional simulacra—secured the American market, not only reassuring in times of crisis, but also figuring the mechanisms of exchange. Long before the antebellum North had been "feminized" by those whom the market ignored, American writers had made the market itself a pageant of feminine feeling.

In making this claim, I am differing from a long-standing scholarly tendency to treat sentimental writing as a refuge, a protest, or an occult expression of the market and its consequences. In her seminal *The Feminization of American Culture,* for example, Ann Douglas sees the cult of sentiment as a rearguard action undertaken by losers in the battle for social power, a retreat by ministers and women to the safety of the parlor while ruthless businessmen reshaped the world out of doors. Those who admire the genre's social power do not escape this sense of marginalization. In a line extending from Nina Baym and Jane Tompkins to recent work by Julia Stern, critical treatments of "woman's fiction" have stressed the protests of economic outsiders overlooked or outraged by the market's effects. For these writers, the central fact of women's lives was their progressive confinement, a condition that domestic fictions both recorded and criticized. Cathy Davidson, whose work on writers of the Revolutionary era has itself revolutionized the field, puts the matter most concisely. "[S]entimental novels in the new Republic," she writes, "are ultimately about silence, subservience, stasis (the accepted attributes of women as traditionally defined) in contradistinction to conflicting impulses toward independence, action, and self-expression"—the entrepreneurial attributes of men. Gender, in these studies, becomes a privileged preserve, an Archimedean point from which to register, from the margins, the perils of those who earned the lowest "wages" in an emerging market order.[4]

Such studies also share a more widespread archaeological impulse to lay bare the hegemonic practices hidden in literary texts. Cultural achievements as complex as the market revolution do not come to pass without a host of coercions and exclusions that social theorists from Karl Marx and Georg Lukács to Antonio Gramsci and Michel Foucault have taught us how to uncover. The critical excavations can be seen in a variety of approaches that tend to treat literary texts as social allegories, epiphenomena of what Julia Stern calls "latent, reprobated social and political impulses" struggling against a dominant code. The very nature of free-market society, in which power is largely "invisible, disseminated throughout the texture of social life," makes *the critic's* penetration crucial. Hence, even those fictions that protest the market are imprinted with what Michael Gilmore calls the shadowy "process of exchange." Ideological criticism of sentimental fiction attempts to uncover the invisible but heavy hand of the market.[5]

Critical excavators have generally exposed three layers of meaning, roughly corresponding to the three principal axes of the market revolution. A primary layer involves the disciplinary ethos of the middle class. Focusing on what Charles Sellers has called the "bourgeois republic," writers like Ann Douglas, Ann Fabian, Richard Brodhead, and Gillian Brown have measured the play of guilt and satisfaction in the antebellum market's fables of love and loss. In these accounts Christian conscience mingles with worldly goods to produce an ambivalent hybrid—both "saint and consumer," legitimating and atoning for success. These are the stories of stern self-discipline celebrated in best-selling novels by Harriet Beecher Stowe, Susan Warner, and others in which Christian submissiveness sanctions prosperity, and property is invested with love. Their pious heroines endorse what Brown calls "sympathetic proprietorship," that "purification of market economy in which commodities are transubstantiated into possessions," infused with intimacy and warmth. Such novels redeem ownership from the general taint of competition. But these are also the stories of antebellum writers themselves who, confronting an unprecedented expansion of the literary marketplace, sought a new legitimation for their roles. Critics who stress such issues are indebted to a rich scholarship charting the effects of consumption on everyday life, the play of "imaginative speculation" and "disillusionment," as Colin Campbell remarks, that helped to shape the middle class. The dialectic of asceticism and ecstatic release that T. J. Jackson Lears associates with the consumer mentality became encoded in the rigorous satisfactions of antebellum Protestant fiction.[6]

A second layer of meaning reveals the self in its new forms of public aggression and artifice. In this drama of what C. B. Macpherson called "possessive individualism," the vulnerable sentimental heroine is a trope for the vulnerable psyche, penetrated and driven by insatiable demands—the "deep internal tensions," as Steven Watts puts it, "of a restless society of self-made men." The popular tales of seduction dominating the early national period demonstrate this new vulnerability, as do the confidence tales of the nineteenth century. In both cases, individuals are imprinted by a money economy that paradoxically amplifies and drains them of meaning—a "fluid, mutable" identity, Terry Mulcaire observes, "whose authority to affirm the social virtue of the self comes at the price of . . . surrendering its psychological autonomy and stability." Indeed, money is a powerful metaphor for the mixture of energy and deception that came to mark a society of actors, parvenus, schemers, and strangers engaged in ceaseless exchange. Feeling, in these dramas of interiority, occupies an unstable middle ground. The sole register of authenticity against the designs of predatory villains, feeling also mimics what Walter Benjamin terms the "empathetic . . . sou[l]" of money, and thus the medium that makes villainy possible. It is no accident that such conflicts are often expressed through the confusions of arousal and seduction, with their loss of self-possession. Tales of ruined heroines, from Charlotte Temple to Eliza Wharton and Leonora Sansay's Laura, betray the impotence of sympathy in a world that trades on feeling. As Watts observes of the injured Constantia Dudley in Charles Brockden Brown's *Ormond* (1799), it was her delusion that "the outward figure [would] also exhibit the internal sentiments" that brought catastrophe. Such figures of commerce are repeatedly disfigured, undone by their treacherous investments of self and feeling. Intimacy itself embodies the market's betrayals.[7]

The third, and perhaps deepest, layer of meaning that critics have uncovered involves Gilmore's "process of exchange." Here the focus is on what might be called systemic metaphors of circulation, with their twin effects of benevolence and passionate excess. Associated, since the eighteenth century, with the benign operation of economies and nation-states, the circulation of feeling came to figure, in Liah Greenfeld's terms, individualistic civic nationalism. Scenes of harmonious feeling made immediately palpable the diffuse operations of the marketplace, like the canals in Henry Brooks's *The Fool of Quality,* which, according to Markman Ellis, "disseminate goods and good feeling . . . by establishing a ramifying network of commercial encounters, . . . polishing social relations and refining the manners." But sentimental spectacles, as David Waldstreicher has shown, could also provide "narratives" of the conflict that economic expansion engendered. Like the civil unrest that often accompanied early national parades, rituals of sympathetic union could reveal a kind of national trauma. Critics like Shirley Samuels and Teresa Goddu have read this doubled meaning in Gothic fictions of the period, whose displays of feeling illuminate the whole vast spectacle of civil oppressions, including slavery, corruption, and epidemic strife. The fine line between ardent sympathy and terror suggests the fragility of a society whose ultimate authority lay in the sentiments of its citizens—what James Madison called the "chords" of national "affection." It made perfect sense, as Shirley Samuels argues, to represent those frailties through narratives of "dead or threatened women," whose trials came to "stand for the state." Ironically, horror, like the sudden turns of the market itself, could also bind the nation's citizens.[8]

In their analyses of class, the self, and the system of exchange, these critical excavations generally expose what might be called, after Slavoj Zizek, the "sublime" elements of ideology. Literary texts, in these appraisals, are symptoms of larger processes whose dark secrets may be glimpsed in an era's discourse. The "traumatic" truths of the marketplace, by contrast, hover just beyond the grasp of authors who can no more comprehend such principles than a coin can understand the laws of supply and demand.[9] I do not wish to deny this significant element of cultural criticism or to argue that historical actors, any more than literary critics, can grasp the full range of their motivations. There remains, however, an important level of *conscious* articulation that few writers on the subject have fully addressed. For the language of sentiment was often used as a means of figuring market relations at the most crucial historical moments, when economic crisis forced individuals to question the very bases of their understanding. At these moments, around which my study will be situated, sentimental imagery did not merely represent the market or record its operation. Rather, the language of feeling was a mode of practical consciousness, a means of thinking through social impasse. To use another metaphor, sentiment, in these critical moments, was not merely the shadowy chemical precipitate of the market deposited on a text's photographic plate. As Robert Strange discovered, feeling could render evocative portraits of the market itself.

In using the term "practical consciousness," I have been influenced by the work of three Marxist scholars who have sought to understand the nature of ideological change. In his discussion of "structures of feeling," Raymond Williams criticized the kind of cultural analysis for which all phenomena were "fixed" and "explicit" ideological effects. What Williams tried to capture was the experience of uncertainty, or possibility, that characterizes all imaginative life and is preserved in literary texts. Often, these "structures" express emergent ideologies, or critiques of dominant assumptions, like the persistent imagery of poverty, illegitimacy, and debt that shadows the Victorian ideal of progress. Such expressions may reveal "an unease, a stress, a displacement" of dominant forms; they may also be the "semantic figures—which, in art and literature, are often among the very first indications that . . . a new structure is forming." The deliberate slipperiness of Williams's language here reflects his desire to oppose the schematic formulations of dogmatic Marxism, for which social process had become a sequence of fossilized modes. The model's attractiveness, for a study of sentimental literature, lies in its sense that even the most idiomatic cultural expressions may be experimental. Over a sufficiently broad period, the critic may discover in such texts "a structured formation which, because it is at the very edge of semantic availability, has many of the characteristics of a pre-formation, until specific articulations—new semantic figures—are discovered in material practice." What Williams calls "cultural work" involves the labor of these evanescent expressions to bring forth new and widely shared attitudes and behaviors—conscious incubations of cultural practice. And those incubations, it should be emphasized, are deliberate. Structures of feeling are collective, conscious creations, the shared work of countless individuals responding to common historical problems. [10]

This cultural incubation, I will argue, can be seen in the work performed by fictions of economic crisis during the long period of America's transition to market capitalism, roughly the period from the Revolution to the Civil War. The corpus of texts each market crisis produced—newspaper essays, congressional speeches, merchants' memorials, credit reports, private letters, novels, short stories, and, especially after 1850, increasingly strident public demonstrations—was both an expression of dominant tendencies and an experiment with alternatives. The results were neither monological nor uniform. Like any ideological production, the sentimental expressions I will be examining demonstrate (to quote Williams again) "not only continuities and persistent determinations but also tensions, conflicts, resolutions and irresolutions, innovations and actual changes." [11] What allows me to treat them as a corpus is their common historical situation. With startling frequency and increasing severity during the nation's first century, Americans endured the disruptive effects of market expansion. They did not lack explanations to account for the recurring crises: moralists and politicians alike fell back on shopworn solutions—jeremiads against extravagance, speculation, or social corruption. But the very persistence of the problem led others to grope for alternate explanations that extended the imagery of sentimental suffering to a new range of meanings. They sought in the inherited imagery a new set of semantic formulations.

In *The Origins of the English Novel*, Michael McKeon provides a model for such innovation through what he calls "microhistories." As English life was being reshaped by the Civil War and the financial revolution, McKeon argues, contemporaries sought new ways to explain shifts in social authority. The experience of instability led individuals to account for "macrohistorical" change by producing microhistorical narratives addressing the corruption of ancient virtue or the rise of the entrepreneurial class. Such narratives were mediatory: they responded to intellectual and social "crisis" by setting forth a range of possible reactions, from celebration of the new mobility to revulsion at its consequences.

In doing so, microhistories converted social instability into fictions of incipient order—ideological attempts to solve "apparently intractable human problems." Microhistories rendered radical change intelligible.[12]

Sentimental narratives performed the same function for American audiences. At a time when conventional explanations of economic change failed to dull its devastations, writers of all kinds appropriated and transformed sentimental discourse to fashion a metanarrative of social process. For the language of sentiment was the currency of crisis, providing a web of meaning intended to resolve a culture's deepest contradictions. Sentimentalism was called on to mediate the complex and delicate transition between premarket and market mentalities, between face-to-face and long-distance economic relations, between the homogeneous village and the heterogeneous republic, between the family and impersonal exchange. Sentimental discourse performed these tasks through an imperialism of feeling. By attempting to extend the reach of affect, it sought to render more intimate and domestic the abstract forces of economy and polity. The sentimental narratives associated with economic crisis were a creative attempt to name, and possibly to control, the pressures that were reshaping lives.

To be sure, these microhistories, as I am interpreting them, differ significantly from those McKeon examines. For McKeon, Augustan social narratives are the culmination of a long cultural process in the West that used epistemological crisis to raise questions about truth and virtue. Hence, his analysis is dominated by a central problematic, and the sense of social experimentation discussed above pales before the iron dialectic of textual representation. McKeon's narratives, moreover, are tied to an English class struggle largely absent in antebellum America.[13] But the microhistories I will examine share with McKeon's examples one important element: the status anxieties surrounding social change. Although McKeon focuses on anxious English aristocrats obsessed with their loss of "honor," the case is similar for anxious American entrepreneurs. For American fictions of the market addressed a critical social contradiction. They sought to accommodate a belief in the power of individual action to the persistent evidence that such action was useless in the face of repeated economic crisis. Such narratives needed to work out a new understanding of personal agency by trying to imagine the individual's place in a system of economic relations that had become increasingly strained and violent. That haunting vulnerability became both critique and resource—a means of attacking the market's excesses, a model for harnessing its possibilities. The new model individual would need to be as supple and fluid as the market itself.

She would have to become a function in an almost mathematical sense, a creature whose inner essence was a kind of relation joining diverse fields. The structure of feeling these narratives elaborated, in short, was a revolutionary pragmatism.

The revolutionary nature of this cultural narrative should not be underestimated. In the hands of a writer like Adam Smith, the sympathetic imagination was a means of instituting prudent, harmonious relations among a diverse field of individual actors. Smith's much-discussed formula for sympathy, in which the observer and the sufferer engage in the reciprocal imaginative pursuit of "concord," allows individuals to regulate their behavior according to a set of normative responses whose goal is approval. The exchange value of feeling ensures a stable moral economy in which "every little circumstance of distress" a sufferer feels induces that individual to "lowe[r] his passion to that pitch, in which the spectators are capable of going along with him."[14] Writers in the sentimental tradition I will examine, by contrast, used the language of feeling to understand conditions of *imprudence,* or social collapse, and turned a provincial imagery of harmonious balance into a means of dynamic accommodation with untamed forces. They converted a vocabulary that shunned excess into a vision of the moral potential of excess itself.

That transition, I will argue, is best understood through an observation of a third Marxist critic, Fredric Jameson. In *The Political Unconscious,* Jameson appropriates a term coined by the French structuralist A. J. Greimas to understand ideological formations. According to Greimas, the elementary structure of signification, or "semiotic square," is a relation of paired oppositions, or semes, in which an abstract pair discloses the logical category expressed by its more literal companion. The analyst may thus discern in each utterance not only its simple meaning, but also its categorical or structural significance. For Jameson, the largely hidden processes of ideology disclose similar structural principles, and the critic's task is to expose that principle, or "ideologeme," contained in each cultural artifact. Conceived in these terms, an ideological formation is a tense balance of opposing forces, not unlike Adam Smith's paradigmatic balance of sympathetic individuals noted above. In Marxist terms, the ideologeme is an "imaginary resolution of the objective contradictions to which it . . . constitutes an active response." But all ideological formations, Jameson argues, contain within them a disruptive moment or pole, the logical possibility that cannot be expressed in the oppositional terms the thought system has established. This moment—the "negative complex term," or the abstract negation of a primary, negative moment—

is the "absence, contradiction, repression, the *non-dit,* or the *impensé*" that has the potential to transform the system of thought, a possibility Jameson associates with "cultural revolution." Marx's labor of the negative is here made part of every utterance, embodying the "innovative" capacity of which Williams speaks. In the right circumstances, even common language can be visionary.[15]

Although my own analysis will be concerned with *conscious* rather than unconscious expressions of culture, the sense of revolutionary potential that Jameson sees in common utterances is vital in assessing a sentimental structure of feeling. Sentimental microhistories provoked by economic crisis repeatedly disclosed this disruptive potential through the trope of boundlessness. Boundlessness was not only the expansive impulse that John Higham ascribes to early national culture.[16] To moralists, boundlessness was also the logical contradiction at the core of rational capitalism itself. It was the engine behind the market's frequent panics and the origin of its most powerful innovations. As such, boundlessness posed an almost insoluble moral problem to conventional market apologists, particularly during periods of economic collapse, when zeal became a kind of contagion. Sentimental narratives groped toward a morally satisfying solution to this problem by reimagining the excesses of the market through limitless feeling and by making sentimental heroines and heroes the only figures who could regulate its excesses. The boundless ability to circulate, negotiate, and sympathize became the mark of a new, more supple morality.

The full elaboration of that morality, the hallmark of the middle class, was the logical goal of the nation's critical fictions. But I want to be careful about invoking the designation "middle class" too early or too often. Since Nancy Armstrong's path-breaking study of sentimental domesticity, critics have routinely read a distinctive class character in the language of eighteenth-century conduct books and novels, which "empower[ed] . . . the middle classes in England through the dissemination of a new female ideal."[17] But the process of class formation, as Williams reminds us in his remarks on structures of feeling, is a halting, often irresolute, and divided one. In a formulation to which I will return, Anthony Giddens provides two terms that help to understand that process. "Class awareness," he writes, is an acknowledgment of similar "attitudes and beliefs," or what Max Weber called "a common style of life." It is a horizontal understanding of class—to be distinguished from the vertical antagonisms of "class consciousness," where individuals perceive their social position as opposed to that of other groups.[18] The particular pragmatism that antebellum critical fictions imagined, I will argue, was an attempt to deny the implications of conflict and thus to preserve the illusion of a society regulated only by individual initiative and rational market rewards—that is to say, by a system in which all life situations were identical. At moments of greatest danger, when panic exposed the irrational nature of markets and incited workers' demonstrations, sentimental fictions shrank from the haunting possibility that Americans were irrevocably divided, and sought solace in the inward spiritual authority of class awareness. These critical fictions sketched the outlines of class, but they shrank from completing the portrait. Only when the language of sentiment could no longer account for the historical problems its readers were facing could writers glimpse the true lineaments of their class position. Ironically, it was the death of sentimental domesticity that gave birth to middle-class consciousness.

In pursuing these large claims for sentimental narratives, I have been mindful of another Jamesonian maxim: "Always historicize!"[19] If the term "structure of feeling" has any usefulness as a critical instrument, it can be established only through close critical readings of historical narratives—both the histories and the stories of each period to be examined. Consequently, I have adopted a textured approach to the literature. Each chapter will provide brief situating narratives of historical issues. These close examinations of problems ranging from the retirement of the national debt to international diplomacy are not intended merely to establish a context for literary analysis. Rather, they are themselves a kind of literary analysis, an examination of the major terms and problems addressed by contemporary creative writers. As the market revolution advances and economic disruptions become more frequent, the two discourses will begin to converge. That is, by the antebellum period through the decade of the 1860s, popular fictions will increasingly take up the cultural work formerly pursued more directly in Congress and the press. That development is but one of the most striking signs of the market revolution whose critical fictions I will consider. The work of assessing them must begin with a reading of market crisis.


## A Culture of Crisis


Reckoning one's life in light of economic crisis is certainly nothing new, either in this or any other modern society. For several centuries now, as what Max Weber called the process of rationalization has gone forward, the West has dramatically transformed its market practices, often with profound human dislocation. Nor, it should immediately be added, would it be accurate to make human crisis the key to all social relations. Most normal people in normal times see their lives through a fund of habitual beliefs and practices that allow them to adjust to most contingencies.[20] Focusing on responses to crisis, and particularly on responses to market shocks, however, may throw those beliefs into sharp outline and thus disclose more wide-ranging adjustments. Moreover, as the nineteenth century progressed, many Americans began to see social experience itself as shaped by periodic economic crises that were structural and inevitable, crises that profoundly influenced how individuals imagined their lives. "The black times have a great scientific value," wrote Ralph Waldo Emerson of the panic of 1837. " . . . What was, ever since my memory, solid continent, now yawns apart and discloses its composition and genesis."[21] By 1870, Americans had endured many black times and had tried to assess their shifting world through the yawning gaps they discovered.

Although one historian has recently characterized the economy of Emerson's day as a relatively stable and productive "equilibrium,"[22] the frequent peaks and troughs in the so-called long wave of prosperity heightened fears for the nation's safety. In an early publication of the National Bureau of Economic Research, Wesley Mitchell identified fourteen depressions between 1790 and 1870—in 1796–98, 1803, 1808–9, 1815–21, 1829, 1834, 1837, 1839–43, 1846, 1848, 1854–55, 1857–58, 1861, and 1866–67—seventeen if the depression of 1785–86 and the panics of 1791–92 and 1825 are included. Even if some of these downturns are too brief or too local to be considered genuine depressions (they did not seem so to contemporaries), there remains general agreement that three of the nineteenth century's six "deep depression[s]" occurred before 1870, those associated with the panics of 1819, 1837, and 1857.[23]

Contemporary observers were quick to note the apocalyptic elements of the business cycle. "Here a deeper gloom hangs over us, than ever was witnessed by the oldest man," wrote a southern essayist on "Political Economy" in 1819. "The late war was sunshine, compared with . . . the deep distress which reigns over us." Blessed beyond any nation, America was selling its soul for a "wild, intriguing, chaffering, subtle spirit of speculation." "Great God!" the writer concludes. "I almost start at the picture I have drawn; . . . is this republican America?"[24] The panic of 1837 induced similar ejaculations. A New Orleans correspondent of Hezekiah Niles ruefully noted the *"anarchie financiere"* that had gripped "all classes of the people." The city seemed consumed by a great fire that would not cease until it had swallowed all and left behind "darkness, doubt, and despair."[25] The refrain was no less urgent in 1857. "It is a gloomy moment in history," lamented *Harper's Weekly*. "Not for many years—not in the lifetime of most men who read this paper—has there been so much grave and deep apprehension; never has the future seemed so incalculable."[26] Henry Ward Beecher mourned that "the Commonwealth lies at length upon the ground, wallowing like one possessed, foaming and rending itself."[27] The very fact that such catastrophes seemed periodic only increased anxiety. Americans, it seemed, had a fatal price to pay for their fragile prosperity.

Such laments resonated with the pronounced strain of apocalypticism that flowed through American life. From the so-called Critical Period under the Articles of Confederation through the political crises of the Federalist era, the populist battles of the Jacksonian period, and the growing sectional crisis of the antebellum years, writers depicted the nation through a language of emergency. The rhetoric Joel Silbey records from the 1840s could have been as readily uttered one or two generations before: "The election of 1840 . . . was 'neither more nor less than a final arbitrament of the great questions.' In 1842, the people were not 'sufficiently awake to the importance of the crisis.' In 1844, the country faced 'the most important Presidential canvass ever held in this country.' In 1848, . . . Ohio Democrats [announced] . . . , 'the crisis has come.' "[28] In 1850, Henry Ward Beecher was sounding the same themes. "A *crisis* is nothing," he boasted in a Thanksgiving sermon. "We have a crisis every month of the year somewhere. They are subject to order." There were sectional crises, temperance crises, religious crises, farmers' and manufacturers' and merchants' crises, and the nearly annual traumas of elections. Indeed, any observer with but "a spice of humor," Beecher declared, "would think a *crisis* to be a jolly thing—nothing more, at any rate, than would be a convenient fainting in some spouse who desires access to her lord's pocket." Having feminized his audience, Beecher converts its weary endurance to a sense of mastery and order. Crisis had become the very pendulum of the republic.[29]

Ideological crises were local as well as national. They were diffused throughout the Union in an innumerable series of small daily adjustments to the strains of modernization. One measure of the strain was the unprecedented mobility of antebellum Americans. It was not uncommon, during the early nineteenth century, for whole regions to empty out and the populations of city neighborhoods completely to turn over in just a few years. The greater mobility meant that families were often less stable, and an increasing number of individuals experienced their lives as a series of distinct breaks with the past. The young man's tear-stained leave-taking from home became a fixture of antebellum imagery. "Departing from his home on the green hill side or in the fertile valley," went the typical scenario, the young man heard "a mother's prayers . . . call[ing] for blessings on the unprotected head of her darling boy; while an affectionate sister . . . clung to his neck, and plead[ed] with him to resist the fatal allurements which encompass a city life."[30] People marked their lives in terms of these everyday crises and may well have seen a continuum between such intimate dislocations and the larger disruptions of national life.

It hardly needs to be added that, despite the accelerating pace of change, anomie did not suddenly seize most average Americans. The restless young were often absorbed by revivalism, which traveled along the Erie Canal to the Burned-Over District of New York as it spread elsewhere, securing workers through moral discipline. In antebellum cities a host of disciplinary institutions arose, from tract societies and Sunday schools to asylums and YMCAs, to invest urban life with moral meaning. Across the country, what Tony Freyer calls the "associational" logic of rural life sought to preserve an illusion of local harmony and control against the more abstract forces of national commerce.[31] Nevertheless, as Charles Sellers and others have argued, by the 1850s the numerous daily adjustments exacted by an expanding market had seriously eroded the world of post-Revolutionary republicanism and replaced it with a colder market discipline.[32] In this wider and more anonymous world, market, like moral, shocks often had to be reckoned as the cost of doing business. As it turned out, the nation's novelists became its prime accountants.

### Accounting for Chaos

Arising in tandem with the market, the popular literature of the young nation inevitably registered its manifold uncertainties. Crisis is basic to most good drama, and it would be foolish to seek market anxiety under every twist of fictional fate. But a significant number of fictions during the period, and nearly all of the texts I will be considering, capture the recurrent crises that were altering so many lives. The sensitive protagonist of J. Hector St. John de Crèvecoeur's *Letters from an American Farmer* (1782), for example, registers the disastrous effects of the Revolutionary War in the forced abandonment of his livelihood. In Isaac Mitchell's best-seller *The Asylum* (1811), a band of Loyalist counterfeiters kidnaps the sentimental heroine and tries to wreck the economy. After the panic of 1837, the concern over business failure became something of an obsession. Dozens of fictions attempted to trace the causes of the unprecedented depression, ascribing ruin to luxury or speculation and prescribing a remedy in the sentimental attachments of family. Even after the long depression passed, it did not take much to revive memories of grinding debt. In her second best-seller, *Queechy* (1852), Susan Warner wove her own experience of the panic into a tale of a country girl forced to sustain a large bankrupt family before she marries a wealthy English lord. Similarly, the tales of young men on the rise that began to appear with increasing frequency toward the end of the 1850s evinced the effects of business failure. Fathers in this fiction die suddenly in hopeless debt; sons migrate to the city and are cheated by employers or con artists; entrepreneurs set up on Wall Street or Pearl Street and are repeatedly ruined. It was an old business adage, preserved in commercial magazines throughout the era, that nine in every ten entrepreneurs failed. Azel Roe, Richard Kimball, and other writers of success stories constantly reminded readers of those very long odds.[33]

These critical fictions, however, were not—to adopt the contemporary economic term—merely registering "revulsion" with the course of affairs. Rather, they were engaged in a complex cultural dialectic, the goal of which was to humanize economic crisis and make it more manageable. The two poles of that dialectic were conspiracy and sentimental union. As Gordon Wood has argued, Americans before the Civil War recurred to conspiracy theory to deny the darker implications of their mechanistic world. The more completely human reason discerned the intricate autonomy of the universe, the more urgent it became to imagine society as a moral economy, a clockwork with a human face.[34] Critical fictions participated in this impulse by turning vast, impersonal economic events into intimate conspiracies—betrayals of moral trust. Such fictions not only reflected popular accounts that blamed depressions on bankers and other rogues, but also gave them substance by portraying a sentimental commerce immune to economic change. True economy could be found only in a genuine exchange of feeling.

But in humanizing invisible forces, these writers were also adopting a powerful discourse that sought to legitimate the market. As I will demonstrate, economic players had long used the language of feeling to represent their experience of circulation, commerce, and trust. Merchants commonly imagined their activities as a republican exchange of feeling. During political or economic crisis, they saw themselves as sentimental heroines and complained of being seduced or raped by predatory opponents. In time sentimental heroines themselves became effective market players, saviors who softened and redeemed all they touched. The market, in this fiction, became a theater of affectionate union. The same revulsion that rejected economic crisis as inhumanly alien, that is to say, could also reinvest that crisis with human significance by adopting sentimental imagery. An economy in which affections circulated as freely as currency could comfort as easily as it could destroy.

By positioning themselves between these alternatives, many popular writers not only reflected current debate but also challenged it. In a manner unavailable to most contemporaries, these writers played off the conspiratorial against the legitimating functions of sentiment. They echoed and transformed readers' fears, used the old tune of republican suspicion in a new, less dissonant key. They made invisible market forces familiar, immediate, and even reassuring. In effect, sentimentalism helped to turn the heartless market into a habit of mind.

## Critical Fictions

In the chapters that follow I will pursue this thesis by surveying a range of popular and political texts from the Confederation era to the Civil War. Chapter 2 examines two early American travel narratives, Crèvecoeur's *Letters from an American Farmer* and Olaudah Equiano's *The Interesting Narrative of the Life of Olaudah Equiano* (1789), to discern the logic behind an emerging structure of feeling. Both texts attempt to manage the boundless potential of a world impelled by a revolutionary economic force: the drive to consume. That drive, unleashed in the United States by the Treaty of Paris and encoded in the practices of Atlantic slavery, clashed with older disciplinary impulses—republican restraint, Protestant asceticism, democratic competency. Each writer responds to the conflict by attempting to reconstitute a threatened ideology. For Farmer James, the collapse of his rural life amid revolutionary violence signifies the failure of a republican determination to restrain excess. As he circulates through the colonies, James records the increasing appetite for power and property evident in his earliest paeans to his farm. His laments over southern slaveholders and British regulars are merely the final stages of a process his narrative meticulously records, one in which an old ideological structure is inescapably transformed. Ironically, at the end of the process, as James depicts the simpler life of an Indian village, he carries with him a reliance on feeling and the imagination that is the hallmark of what Colin Campbell calls the "spirit of modern consumerism."[35]

In far different circumstances, but more nimbly and more urgently, Equiano wrestles with the same effects. Forced to refashion himself in the image of British consumer society, Equiano must seek out, identify, and somehow balance the contradictory elements of a rapidly maturing market culture. Like Crèvecoeur's text, Equiano's narrative displays warring attitudes: a critique of luxury and a desire to consume, a celebration of enterprise and a guilt over the isolation it engenders. As he works through these contingencies, Equiano, too, arrives at a visionary threshold—the celebration of merchant capitalism in Africa that seems to threaten his earlier defense of African simplicity. Indeed, the ideological struggles of both authors signify a pregnant moment in the Atlantic world, when writers began to see their lives as reflections of market forces. Their very circulation represents a desire to bind together experiences rendered suddenly and permanently vulnerable from afar. Sentiment circumscribed their narratives, as it measured both the disruptive force of the market and of their own restless desires.

But the critical attitude both writers adopt—as sojourners and captives—also suggests the resistance to market practices felt by many contemporaries. For the sensibility of the captive, during the Confederation period, was put to very specific ideological uses. During the depression of 1785–86, a debate flared over the propriety of consumption, as the country was suddenly swamped by British goods. Essayists and politicians urged rational restraint and often likened unrestrained consumption to the behavior of savages. As Crèvecoeur and Equiano entered this rhetorical field, they, too, tried to strike a balance between desire and control. Their travel narratives, conducted in the shadow of the captive, offer highly literal, complex versions of the public debates. Desiring mobility but condemning excess, rejecting confinement yet longing for discipline, they internalized the political controversies and invested them with a language of feeling. That language would be decisive in later attempts to confront the market's imperatives.

Although the first thirty years of the republic were a period of prosperity, they were punctuated by sharp sieges of doubt, when market crises forced the nation back on first principles. The opening two decades of the nineteenth century— roughly from the British attack on the American frigate *Chesapeake* in 1807 through the panic of 1819 and its aftermath—presented repeated emergencies that stimulated sentimental responses. The language of sentiment, as I demonstrate in chapter 3, provided a crucial counterweight to the sense of helplessness and alienation that many contemporaries felt. But sentiment also allowed writers to explore the problems of distance and dispossession, appropriation and intimacy, that Crèvecoeur and Equiano had used to figure market relations. Significantly, by 1807 these were no longer purely literary fancies. Merchants and impressed sailors harmed on the high seas adopted the sentimental imagery of threatened heroines to dramatize their plight. Conversely, threatened heroines, in the popular fiction of the period, came to figure the trials of those who sought to master unruly markets. The peculiar mixture of frailty and resistance so common to early national market players was embodied in the era's sentimental narratives.

The chapter explores how three best-sellers adapted and extended the critical concerns of the era. In Martha Meredith Read's *Margaretta* (1807), the heroine circulates through the Atlantic world in a course that takes her from sexual dependent and virtual commodity to wealthy heiress and mistress of an American estate. But the conventional tale of virtue rewarded poignantly captures a wider array of Jeffersonian anxieties. As a feminist and wife of a prominent Philadelphia banker, Read was uniquely positioned to explore republican doubts over free trade and moral autonomy that the embargo crisis exposed. Margaretta's circulation through the Atlantic world defies British injustice, yet she does so by adopting the feminized imagery of merchants who claimed to be raped by British privateers. Her boldness, however, exacts a heavy price. Running through the tale of this assertive but pliant heroine is an insistent imagery of incest, as if the very exposure to the market and its perils evoked a vulnerability too horrible to contemplate. Both the vitality and the exposure, I will argue, become hallmarks of the sentimental apprehension of the market, an apprehension that novelists like Read helped to make familiar.

Americans during this period were preoccupied with international trade. To the popular mind, political economy was largely the science of distant markets, and the disordered state of those markets made the imperiled adventurer or trader an irresistible figure. Three additional texts I examine in chapter 3 demonstrate that fascination and suggest how critical fictions often doubled as economic thought. Isaac Mitchell's best-selling *The Asylum,* composed in two installments bracketing the embargo crisis, attempts to weave a tale of European disorder into a narrative of American sentimental economy. The novel's lovers, Alonzo

Haventon and Melissa Bloomfield, must each confront the ripple effects of market disruption—Alonzo by trying to dig out from his merchant father's bankruptcy, Melissa by facing down British counterfeiters in a Gothic Connecticut castle. But the novel also seeks to intervene in contemporary policy debates by echoing and extending their sentimental premises. In wide-ranging controversies aired in the public sphere, orators and essayists examined the fundamental principles of the market, the structure of promises and contracts now rendered vulnerable by British deceivers. Mitchell, a newspaper editor intimately attuned to the controversy, sensed its underlying theme: a determination to maintain an intelligible and orderly political economy through an insistence on sentimental ties. His novel functions as a kind of aesthetic dynamo, converting the latent power of popular appeals into the explosive emotions of his characters.

The desire to deploy feeling in the service of orderly international markets reached a terminus of sorts after the War of 1812. The long conflict convinced Americans that they could far more prudently fashion a world unto themselves, sheltered from economic derangement. The vision of an orderly domestic asylum, celebrated at the end of Mitchell's novel, soon became a shibboleth. But such optimism received a sharp challenge in two best-selling pamphlets commemorating the war. *The Female Marine* and *The Surprising Adventures of Almira Paul,* both published anonymously in 1816 and running through many editions, use cross-dressing to make a patriotic point. Lucy Brewer, an American runaway, disguises herself as a sailor and wins merit aboard the *U.S.S. Constitution.* Almira Paul, her British counterpart, meets ignominy aboard the *Guerrière.* But in almost every other way, *The Female Marine* challenges received opinion. As a seduced prostitute who finds military success, Lucy is both victim and entrepreneur, soiled and saintly. Rejecting the false comforts of a home that failed to defend her, she becomes cosmopolitan, retaining her military guise even after she returns home victorious. Her history thus unsettles the self-gratulation that attended the war's conclusion, as it crucially extends the imagery of the enterprising heroine claimed by American merchants. Such a figure, the pamphlets seem to be saying, could no longer afford to see her activities through the blurred lens of republican propriety. Even as Americans claimed victory in the second war of independence, critical fictions suggested that moral autonomy paled before the market's sovereign demands.

Chapters 4 through 6 explore the decisive moment in this ethical shift, when popular writers used sentimental tropes to define a new pragmatism. The story begins in the Jacksonian era, as financial turmoil led Whigs and Democrats alike to fear for their autonomy. Beneath the partisan attacks and party rhetoric, however, which often pitted virtuous producers against avaricious speculators, there remained significant consensus. "Post-Revolutionary" Americans, concerned that their fathers' virtue was slipping away, sought new sources of intrinsic value in this unstable environment, an impulse widely explored in the critical fictions emerging from the panic of 1837. Merchants, too, participated in this process. Their overtly sentimental responses to the panic—including dead faints and passionate tears—suggest their desire to retreat to the refuge of domestic security. But there were other voices during this period that sought in sentimental imagery a more energetic response to market shocks. By insisting on the plastic, transparent nature of feeling, on the ability of sympathetic souls to yield to others and yet remain morally pure, many writers began to fashion a more supple virtue, one ideally suited to the shifting demands of an unpredictable market.

In chapter 4, I trace the intellectual source of that impulse to Ralph Waldo Emerson. Himself saddled with debt during the period and reluctant to touch his substantial investments, Emerson used his vulnerability to fashion a professional stance that suited the market. As he incurred debt to save his brother William from bankruptcy, Emerson struggled to find a model for the lecturer and essayist he hoped to become, one who would expose himself to the uncertainties of trade, disseminate his vital spirit through diverse audiences, and yet remain sound. His financial habits provided one model, as he attempted to transform money relations into bonds of affection with William, Thomas Carlyle, Bronson Alcott, and others. But another important influence, I argue, was Anna Barker, wife of his protégé Samuel Ward, who appeared at a critical moment in his career to offer Emerson a model of pure but vigorous sympathy. Barker's pragmatic ability to adapt herself to any situation without losing her innate goodness became a type of the sincerity and transparency that Emerson found admirable in merchants and scholars alike. In his essays of the period, virtuous pliancy became a new measure of moral autonomy, a theme I explore in popular writers of the 1830s and 1840s. In the fiction of T. S. Arthur, Eliza Follen, Susan Warner, and others, what I call (after the essayist Elizabeth Oakes Smith) the "characterless" woman emerges as a new ideal. Seizing the reins from their failed husbands, the resourceful women of these narratives manage to make money and maintain innocence. In doing so they figure a new kind of market virtue, one in which the very sacrifice of autonomy through sentimental accommodation is the sign of entrepreneurial purity.

More than any other writer, Walt Whitman, the subject of chapter 5, translated characterlessness into national ideology. His poetry provided an enduring imagery of supple yet sympathetic democrats warmly embracing experience. That breadth of appeal was rooted in republican rhetoric—but a particular strain of republicanism that reasserted itself in the early 1850s. The first two editions of *Leaves of Grass* (1855, 1856), I argue, directly responded to the brief yet vigorous surge of New York labor activism between 1850 and the panic of 1854. After years of desuetude following the panic of 1837, New York workers widely organized in the early 1850s amid renewed prosperity. In schemes ranging from socialist co-operatives to benefit societies and land reform associations, they transformed the language of artisan republicanism to meet new market conditions. The rhetoric of sympathy dominated their debates, reflecting a widespread need for the kinds of social and professional bonds that the panic jeopardized. Whitman was attentive to the range of these languages, and after the movement collapsed, he preserved and fused them in his poetry.

Linking sympathy and exchange, spontaneous feeling and negotiated value, Whitman suggested how shocks like the repeated panics laborers faced could be overcome through a principled accommodation. The poet was not only the heroic male, plunging his seminal muscle into the landscape, but also the "characterless" woman, adapting to any contingency. By seeing "precision and balance" in national life, Whitman ratifies and deepens the sentimental imagery through which his culture assessed social change. Those notions of sympathetic balance, descendants of the moral harmonies envisioned by Adam Smith, make the poet a regulator and reflector of society, able to sense and express the emotions of every reader and render them an orderly whole. In advancing this vision, he became what Antonio Gramsci called an "organic intellectual," embodying a new liberal order. Feeling and "prudence," Whitman believed, would sustain this republic of compliant souls.

Whitman was not alone in using economic uncertainty to fashion cultural response. In chapter 6 I examine how bankruptcy fictions of the 1850s and 1860s helped to shape the self-perception of an emerging middle class. Although the 1850s were relatively prosperous, and the panic of 1857 was far milder than its Jacksonian predecessor, tales of failure remained in great demand. What made these later fictions distinctive, however, is that bankruptcy was now often divorced from dramatic calamities like bank failures or mercantile collapse. Rather, failure had become almost routine, the inevitable price of doing business in an untamed market. This wider tolerance—or at least greater expectation—of failure shifted popular attitudes about business probity, as mere survival became a kind of moral distinction. Anecdotal evidence from Lewis Tappan's Mercantile Agency confirms what many readers must have felt: that the wily pragmatist ought to be accorded the same credit as the prudent entrepreneur. In an environment where all were vulnerable, adaptability had become a moral necessity.

This shared vulnerability, I argue, emerged as one of the most powerful markers of middle-class awareness. But while popular novelists continued to measure, and often to censure, the sacrifices success demanded, they took two additional steps that mark the final rapprochement between sentiment and the market, as they help to forge a distinctive middle-class consciousness. Uncomfortable with the moral instabilities of commerce, writers before and after the Civil War reimagined the entrepreneurial figure of the characterless woman as a feminized and sensitive male. Often in his late teens, the same age as his Jacksonian sisters, this rising clerk combined sentiment and Christian resolve with a pragmatism that allowed him to smooth over moral ambiguities on his way up. In effect, Whitman's androgynous hero had become a model businessman. But an opposite impulse, arising during the same period, also signaled the decisive appropriation of this rhetoric by the middle class. Attending the growth of urban vice, many city novels of the era portrayed this group as under siege from the predatory poor, who could not even aspire to the dignified failures of their betters. The masses in these novels must be viciously suppressed as a means of preserving a fragile middle class that identified itself through its ability to share refined feeling. Popular novelists of the period thus decisively shifted the nationalist sympathy espoused by Whitman and converted it into an instrument of exclusion. Ironically, it was the failure of sentiment to account for the increasing complexities of the market that turned it into a means of social distinction. Affection could no longer be wasted on the poor.

What survived after the Civil War, again prefigured by Emerson, in *The Conduct of Life* (1860), was a radically different sympathy, one I briefly examine in the concluding chapter. The successful man, Emerson now claimed, was one for whom sympathy meant an essential harmony with the larger designs of fate. The individual's pragmatic power was his ability to adjust to that higher law in which we move and find our being. For Emerson, there was a clear, if attenuated, link between this rhetoric and the transcendentalism of an earlier era. The individual who could soar above convention to perceive spiritual law could also be counted on to sense the shaping force of necessity. But the higher laws that contemporaries like William Graham Sumner now detected in nature had little use for the determinations of individuals, and the characterless figure soon became a mere effect of the structure that figure had helped to raise. Sentiment yielded to process, the dim reflection of abstract systems. Amid the ungoverned flux of the industrial economy, sensitive souls could only observe, gamble, and endure.

From the more distant perspective of the twenty-first century, however, the sentimental narratives that faded with the Civil War may nonetheless offer a different lesson. They provide us with an intimate register of the market, a means of measuring both its idealism and its strains. Through what Emerson once called the harsh "discipline" of debt and panic,[36] antebellum Americans relentlessly insisted on the human dimensions of their world. They clung to the local and affective, even as everyday life was transformed beyond recognition. The narratives they produced thus offer tantalizing glimpses, perhaps the only still available, of a lost cultural ideal. For if a benign economy exists nowhere else, it survives in these old, largely forgotten texts. In the critical fictions that occupy this book, I will try to recapture that vanished American sensibility.

# CHAPTER 2

# Captives of the Market

When Americans stepped back to admire their revolution in the mirror of history, they often saw themselves clad in the grand robes of eternal law. American history was prophecy, or rather the fulfillment of prophecy—the inevitable measure of human progress. This was particularly true of the nation's commercial prospects. American trade, declared Ezra Stiles in 1783, would exchange commodities for the wisdom of nations, which, "being merely digested and carried to the highest perfection, may reblaze back from america [*sic*] . . . and illumine the world with truth and liberty."[1] American consumers would refine the mere products of trade, transform them through republican alchemy into the very principles of civilization. As Drew McCoy has shown, this widely shared optimism united agrarians and neo-mercantilists, republicans and protoliberals. To all but the most spartan patriots, the nation's economy promised to expand indefinitely, bestowing abundance on all. Indeed, American prospects seemed to ratify the tenets of a "commercial humanism" that linked consumption with the refinements of culture. Commerce, to these enlightened republicans, was not merely the handmaid of democracy: it was the moral register of the race.[2]

But if republican consumption welcomed the new world of market goods, it was no less true that many consumers remained rooted in the past. Schooled in a psychology of "competency" that stressed the moderate pursuit of wealth, and committed to a morality of discipline and restraint, most middling Americans paused well before the threshold of prosperity. While they welcomed the new self-fashioning that their political revolution had bestowed, they acted, as Joyce Appleby notes, "without a coherent social theory to explain" the changes they experienced.[3] More accurately, they had several competing theories and attitudes, a bundle of strategies for responding to the rapidly changing conditions of the new nation. Gordon Wood has argued that the inflationary stimulus of the Revolution acted with irresistible force to break down the remaining barriers restraining liberal capitalism.[4] But the air of national crisis pervading the 1780s suggests that the transition was anything but smooth. At moments of doubt, Americans of all mentalities did what most people do when facing emergency: they fell back on well-worn beliefs. Anxious over the new nation's economic problems, they sought refuge in a republican rhetoric that stressed caution, prudence, or outright hostility to the revolutionary force of the market.

In light of these mixed motives, the practical problems of fashioning republican consumption in the new nation took on added urgency. How could individuals make unfettered choices that would not threaten the polity? How could a market that allowed nearly boundless pursuit of interest restrain the individual passions that fueled that pursuit and threatened competency? In the uncertainty of the Critical Period, the answers to those questions were by no means assured. The severe fiscal legacies of the Revolution—a punishing national debt, pent-up consumer demand, and an overheated market that produced the nation's first depression—caused economic and political fears quickly to converge. The double dose of bankruptcies and Shays's Rebellion produced dire calls for national repentance. But soul-searching alone could not quell anxieties about the activities of a mixed multitude whose volatility, by 1786, seemed to resemble the market itself. Indeed, in the minds of many social critics of the Confederation era, consumption was the root cause of the crisis. The "common experience" of consumer goods that had helped forge national union now seemed to be tearing the nation apart.[5]

It was in this context that the two principal texts I will examine in this chapter, Crèvecoeur's *Letters from an American Farmer* and Equiano's *Interesting Narrative,* performed their cultural work. These writers bracket the social crisis—Crèvecoeur warily assessing, before abandoning, the world of colonial abundance, Equiano embracing that world and fashioning a rationale for its operation. Both writers explore what might be called the "deep structure" of consumption, the peculiar play of energy, restraint, and longing that many Americans felt during the period. Both writers sought to assess themselves against the new world of goods that had the power to reshape lives. And both texts did so by offering synoptic travel narratives that attempted to provide, from the perspective of the alien observer, the "coherent" vision that Americans themselves lacked. In effect, the two texts used the cultural materials at hand to sort out the antinomies of abundance.

Chief among those materials, I will argue, was a narrative of captivity, a microhistory, that precisely captured the era's contradictory attitudes toward consumption.

The figure of the captive became a means of assessing the feelings of impotence, the demands for repentance, and the deep longing for stability that many felt in the 1780s. For both writers, the captive stimulates powerfully ambiguous responses. Crèvecoeur's caged slave in Letter 9 provokes a savage critique of consumption that prompts Farmer James to long for the savage state himself. His imagined sojourn with the Indians in Letter 12 amounts to a voluntary captivity for the purpose of cleansing his own material possessions. Equiano's course is precisely opposite. Himself a captive, he attains freedom by mastering the inner life of commodities, which he associates with the discipline of Christian feeling. Yet he ends his text with an imperial vision of Africa that turns Christian restraint into a means for the unlimited appropriation of goods. Both texts struggle to formulate a version of republican desire that will be as rigorous and expansive as Ezra Stiles's grand vision of trade. But the figure of the captive complicates the vision, suggesting the hidden costs of consumption to individual and polity alike. Abundance, it seemed, could both liberate and enslave.

At the heart of the problem was the continent's overpowering fecundity, stimulating American passions in contradictory and unpredictable ways. As foreign travelers gazed into the American mirror, they employed a language of feeling to convey the unprecedented temptations inhabitants faced. Passionate behavior, they contended, was endemic to America, as native as the wild landscape with its still wild people. It was against these arraignments of native feeling that Crèvecoeur, Equiano, and the defenders of commercial humanism took their stand, attempting to replace illicit passion with generous sentiment. But amid the uncertainties of the 1780s, the border between licit and illicit feeling was elusive, if not treacherous. In their surveys of America, foreign observers traced and frequently crossed Stiles's line dividing mere digestion from the perfections of history. Their analyses will help to frame the ideological clashes of the Critical Period.

## Consuming Interests

In the 1780s, European observers were often the most sensitive registers of the new forces abroad in America. Postwar travelers were quick to record the global picture that, they charged, eluded natives. To the most hostile observers, the American Revolution wrought not an outburst but a collapse of civility, a surrender to instinct and excessive feeling. But even sympathetic writers were forced to admit that dangerous new passions had arisen since the war. To almost every European commentator of the 1780s, America took an unprecedented toll on feeling. Abbé Robin, following the New World antipathy of Georges Louis Leclerc, comte de Buffon, set the tone early in the decade by questioning American spirit. If the Americans drank tea and milk and moved about in the moist atmosphere of primeval forests, was it any wonder that they lacked "natural sensibility" and seemed more "indolent" and "passive"?[6] The rude environment depressed competitive fires more common in older societies, a condition that would disappear only as the landscape was cleared. John Smyth, whose account of hair-breadth escapes during the Revolution is by far the most heart pounding, gives the keenest portrait of this oppressive environmentalism. He has often wondered, he confesses, if other European travelers shared his experience of primal terror in the wilderness—the sensation of confinement "within narrower compass than the mind requires" and the "universal gloomy shade, rendered dismal by the intermixing branches of the lofty trees."[7] No wonder if feeling is aroused in exact proportion to the overbearing landscape.

If the American environment wreaked havoc with the body, it also stimulated the senses in unaccountable ways. Smyth recalls a sojourn on the Kentucky border with the Bailey family, whose fifteen-year-old daughter was so alluring that she aroused a passion nearly fatal to his enterprise. Only the greatest resolution allowed him to leave, yet once separated, he "was seized with a kind of languor, or carelessness of my fate, my mind and spirits being enervated and softened down with an inexpressibly painful sensibility," so that he was soon quite bewildered (1:269–70). Thomas Anburey narrowly escapes a similar fate when he is invited to bundle with the young daughter of a host, and perseveres only by imagining the consequences of her seduction.[8] Even the staid fictional narrator of *The European Traveller in America* (a text most likely written by an American) confesses that his attachment to the country has become all too sensitive: "When I first perceived the connection I was forming with America, and how inseperably [*sic*] my affection was united with her interest, I was not insensible . . . to what a vicissitude of passions I was fated. The idea at first startled me; but I at length freely submitted, to what my love had made irresistible."[9] Yet this passionate admirer, not unlike Crèvecoeur's Farmer James, is soon forced to retreat to a wilderness plantation— beyond the lure of the city but exposed to an equally perilous frontier. Whether the environment or custom held sway, these writers were saying, America made extraordinary demands on the feelings that cried out for regulation.

But what kind of regulation would accord with the new society? In the absence of a directing aristocracy, even conservative travelers were not quite sure. Moral restraints were not reliable in a country whose lush abundance and native population tempted whites to stray from civility. A telling example of this confusion was Smyth's experience among the Indians. Moonstruck over young Bailey, he ventures into Kentucky during an Indian disturbance, stumbles upon a war party, and spends a pleasant afternoon with them. Only when he reaches a white outpost is he denied admittance to what proved to be "an abandoned set of miscreants" rioting in "every species of iniquity" (1:283–84). The whites, threatened with anarchy on the edge of settlement, turned anarchic themselves. And yet, where the weakening of civil conduct threatened good order, the exertion of further control imposed perils of its own. This is nowhere more clear than in the *European Traveller*'s antidote to luxury. Expressing the typical republican fear of social climbing among the masses, the narrator wishes instead for more effective bookkeeping: "Every member of the community should reduce his affairs as near as possible to a system, like the well bred merchant methodise all his domestic business, compute the necessary expence of his family, . . . and annually plan and execute his business accordingly" (26). Strict accounting of income would no doubt make families more frugal, but it would also allow them to be more efficient consumers, thereby reigniting the passions that the narrator hopes to quell. The problem, as this writer dimly sensed, was that social discipline was imperceptibly meshing with market discipline, making the goal of subduing an explosive dynamism ever more elusive. The conservative foreign observers of the Confederation period sought internal principles of order, but they were stopped by an aggressive new sensationalism that was not to be denied.

In the postwar era, however, Americans were roused by passions that most travelers ignored. Insulated from the marketplace, these independent men of means could not have understood the profound stimulus of trade—a stimulus that Crèvecoeur and Equiano alone would grasp. In the new nation, market forces could have momentous consequences. For the first time, during the postwar consumer boom and bust, Americans had to confront their passion for imports without the defense of revolutionary nationalism or the consumer boycotts that helped sharpen their resistance to imperial Britain. Newspapers throughout the country, both before and after the financial crisis of 1785–86, ran double-column advertisements crammed with consumer goods. In early 1786, for example, the

*Charleston Morning Post, and Daily Advertiser* displayed the wares of John-Daniel Kern, who sold not only the usual assortment of clothing and china, but also bird cages, mirrors, Dutch quills, brass candlesticks, anvils, shoe buckles, steel-spring snuffers, spices, and "a variety of other articles too tedious to enumerate."[10] Since merchants offered both "unlimited credit" and goods in exchange for produce, such merchandise was suddenly available to almost anyone.[11]

The effects were immediate and profound. In an article reprinted in several Pennsylvania papers, "A Farmer" marks the course of one typical experience. Although he had once provided for many of his needs at home, his wife and marriageable daughters proved irresistibly enterprising. After each shopping excursion they return with a lengthening list of goods—"a callico gown, a callimanco petticoat, a sett of stone teacups, half a dozen pewter teaspoons and a teakittle [*sic*] . . . and a hundred other things, . . . besides all sorts of household furniture unknown to us before." Whereas he had once marketed only the surplus of his farm, now "the wheel goes only for the purpose of exchanging our substantial cloth" for consumer goods.[12] Another harried husband, complaining that the advertisements set his wife "on fire," stopped getting newspapers altogether, only to discover that she had catalogs sent from the warehouses instead. Her inability to pass up a good buy has filled his house with twenty featherbeds, six clocks, and so much furniture that "[t]he servants can scarcely creep to their beds."[13] Humorous or not, these writers were pointing to a bold and troubling new absorption in the market.

When the inevitable collapse of credit struck, spokesmen reacted in a variety of ways. Many were stunned by the depth of the depression, which left wharves idle, businesses shuttered, and farmers in debtors' court. "I dare appeal to the oldest merchant among us," wrote "A Friend to Commerce" in 1785, "whether this country was ever in such a deplorable state. . . . the whole prospect will forcibly convince every one that our trade is in the last stages of a decline."[14] "Jonathan of the Valley" was even more gloomy, calling the whole "commercial circle . . . violently agitated," and wondering whether American freedom itself were jeopardized.[15] More than an economic event, of which contemporaries had a fairly clear understanding, the depression challenged national character, and in the months before the calling of the Constitutional Convention, writers tried to address the passions that consumption exposed.

One prominent response was to stress the virtues of contentment. In Boston, James D. Griffith's *Continental Journal, and the Weekly Advertiser* made the issue a crusade. A writer in 1786 cautioned against "the over desirous vehemence, with which men are actuated in the chace [*sic*] of felicity," and urged the rejection of "those numerous luxuriances and refinements" that offer illusory happiness.[16] Another writer struck at the heart of the problem when he warned against the "strange variety of passions" that the market causes "daily [to] distract the human mind" and diminish its powers.[17] Such commentators clearly understood what Jean-Christophe Agnew calls "threshold psychology," the sense, in a market society, that every encounter holds the possibility for infinite gain and infinite loss.[18] Lulled into a kind of "[u]nconscious[ness]" by the market's constant lure, claimed one writer, "we grasp at objects difficult to come at: and which, if we chance to obtain we soon let go, for the same endless pursuit of others."[19] And yet, just as the *European Traveller* lacked specific antidotes to luxury, many of these writers could more easily attack the market than imagine an alternative. An essayist on "The Inconsistency of our Desires" captures the dilemma: "We should consider this world as a great mart of commerce, where fortune exposes to our view various commodities, riches, ease, tranquility, fame, integrity, knowledge. Every thing is marked at a settled price. Our time, our labour, our inginuity [*sic*], is so much ready money, which we are to lay out to the best advantage."[20] Although the essayist counsels making a purchase and resting satisfied, his metaphor suggests that everything is always up for grabs and the process never ending. As Americans suffering through the depression well knew, there were no settled prices.

Traditionalists continued to urge discipline, reason, and order. "Jonathan of the Valley" warned that there was only one solution to the threshold mentality, a recollection that "the depravity, or imperfection" of human nature would inevitably ruin all hedonistic pursuits.[21] Other, more enlightened writers stressed the "order, beauty and . . . regular movement" of society as it reproduced the eternal "oeconomy of the heavenly bodies."[22] But such rhetoric did not entirely prepare readers, particularly those in New England, for the shock of Shays's Rebellion. As farmers in western Massachusetts marched on courthouses and engaged in sporadic encounters with the state militia, essayists began thinking in naked class terms once reserved for the British. "Since the war," charged one writer to the *Connecticut Courant,* "blustering, ignorant men, who started into notice during the troubles and confusion of that critical period, have been attempting to push themselves into office."[23] "Camillus" argued that the Regulators' attacks on *"great men"* were "proof of a seditious purpose," and he feared that backwoods Machiavellis had "excited . . . and stimulated" the passions of the unthinking mob.[24] One writer even went so far as to imagine a biblical parable in which a "passionate and headstrong" multitude spurned both the "wise men of the land" and their "sober Prince," inviting universal ruin. Even monarchy seemed preferable to such "disorder, anarchy and rebellion."[25]

Of course, the traditionalists were answered in kind—and the responses point to a larger ideological impasse of the Confederation period, one that the Constitution did not fully resolve. It was a fairly simple matter to attack merchants and other monarchs for their abuses in debtors' court. A writer to Isaiah Thomas's *Worcester Magazine,* for example, described the "fealing [*sic*]" of a youth who sees his "Elder Brother clothed in Purple and fine Lining [*sic*]" while he must toil in rags, stung by the knowledge that both "belong to the same family."[26] Indeed, it may well have been family resemblance that prevented a truly radical solution to the deep divisions the crisis exposed, for neither side seemed to be able to break free of the rhetoric it had inherited. One "Member of Convention" demonstrated the impasse by precisely duplicating the language of the Boston Selectmen he opposed. Where the Selectmen railed against "*habits* of luxury" and the thirst for imports purchased on "unlimited credit," the Member urged the wealthy to forgo "every extravagance in dress, living, importation, and government" and return to the people.[27] Republican rhetoric actually impeded analysis by referring to an ideal community that was visibly eroding, if it had ever existed at all.

But if attempts to impose republican discipline rang hollow, so too did some efforts to look past the threshold, to a truly liberal polity. An essayist offering "Thoughts on Good Times" captures the dilemma. Although the writer invokes the Calvinistic truism that our wishes for better times are illusory, his approach is actually quite shrewd. The source of better times, he implies, is not beyond human control: our *thoughts* may themselves generate the desires that shape the world. But desire, it turns out, is only a limited engine. When we "fix our eyes on the whole" of society, the numerous desires of its constituents breed mutual loss. The farmer's desire for high prices hurts the city dweller, the merchant's desire for great profits hurts the farmer, and so on. "[B]y taking a review . . . of all ranks of people," the "wise man" can easily see that any object of individual felicity will mean "a great loss for the whole community; where one is a gainer, there are ten losers." That was an accurate appraisal of American fortunes in 1786, but it was also an admission of intellectual failure. "[I]magination" may well motivate individuals, but there seemed no direct route from this consumer psychology to a synoptic view of a dynamic economy.[28] When one began with the obvious fact of consumer tastes, the ideal of Newtonian balance quickly dissolved into a self-canceling chaos.

In short, the problem these writers confronted involved an inadequacy of expression. Although they understood the social difficulties, their ideological tools did not fully permit them to offer a solution. With what amounted to a class war in Massachusetts, talk of republican unity was fatuous at best. But if social discipline was failing, neither was it evident how the vast desires unleashed by the consumer revolution could be controlled. It was in this context that the imagery of Indian captivity emerged as a powerful means of addressing social division and individual desire. Because captivity narratives explored the frontier of civilized behavior, references to captivity could be used to imagine the passions that consumption had generated, while at the same time providing a means to reject those passions. What was most disturbing about American prospects could be projected elsewhere, upon the Indians or their accomplices. Often the targets were Loyalists and British agents, or "factors," an internal enemy "scattered throughout the whole country" that would "unite tomorrow with any banditti . . . sufficiently powerful" to defeat us.[29] Arrayed in their "gay tinsels of Britain . . . too captivating to be resisted," worried "A Friend to Commerce," Americans made willing victims, *"fluttering for a season in their funeral plumes"* before being led to some savage sacrifice. Even more humiliating, British creditors seized property almost before payments were due, achieving through commerce what they had failed to do through arms. Such agents were *"fatning* on the calamities of their countrymen, and . . . with unrelenting rapaciousness would sacrifice the families of their own friends, to execute the mandates of a *British employer."*[30] To any witness of the late war, such language made unmistakable reference to Britain's Indian allies; yet the same language could be applied to American insurgents as well. That "Tribes of angry politicians, groaning under the weight of the poll-tax," have attacked *"great men,"* "Camillus" charged, is itself "proof of a seditious purpose."[31] Party rage became Indian rage, commercial passions became Indian passions, and all became un-American.

It was far from fortuitous, therefore, that at the height of the depression there appeared in a number of newspapers "A Narrative of the Captivity and Escape of Mrs. Francis Scott, an Inhabitant of Washington County, Virginia."[32] The brief account may be best seen as a microhistory, a narrative attempt to refashion the contradictions besetting contemporary readers. At first glance, the tale seems to recount the ruthless suppression of worldly attachments. Her husband having carelessly forgotten to lock the front door after seeing off a band of Kentucky settlers, Scott is forced to watch in "Astonishment and Horror" as her family is massacred—first the "impruden[t]" (8) husband, who staggers dead across the threshold; then her three youngest children; and finally her eight-year-old daughter, whom her mother's "deepest Anguish of Spirit . . . [and] Flood of Tears" cannot save (9). The Indians then lay claim to the Scotts' property—not only the "four good Rifles well loaded" that the family failed to discharge but also "a great Quantity of Cloathing and Furniture" with which Scott, too, is borne away (10). There in the wilderness, Scott endures severe penance for her family's carelessness. "[W]ithout any Provisions, having no kind of Weapon or Tool to assist her in getting any, and being almost destitute of Cloathing" (13), she is gradually reduced to "a mere Skeleton" (16). Only the juice of "Cane-Stalks, Sassafras-Leaves, and some other Plants she did not know the name of" (18) sustained her. Indeed, when she had the chance to steal the meat of a fawn freshly killed by a bear, she resolved against it, for fear of being similarly attacked. Scott's tale would thus seem to convey a brutal asceticism—a message driven home by a telling detail. When bitten by a "venomous Snake," the writer reveals, Scott miraculously survives. There was so little left to her body, worn down by "Fatigue, Hunger and Grief" (16), that the poison simply could not take hold. Hardship, it would seem, had inoculated her.

Yet that inoculation fails to preserve her from the very deepest sources of infection. For despite the text's manifest message that God alone sustains, the narrative does not present an unambiguous story of pious submission or triumph over evil. Rather, Scott's deprivation seems to deepen longing and intensify dangerous, even self-destructive, desire. To be sure, when she narrowly misses being recaptured by the raiding party, Scott feels "excited" by "Emotions of Gratitude and Thankfulness to Divine Providence" (13), but these feelings pale before the mental agonies of her ordeal. She is tormented by the "painful Sensations" of hunger, haunted by the horrible "Beings" (14) who pursue her, driven to such despair by the terrible solitudes in which she wanders that she throws herself from a cliff. Even after her return home she "remains inconsolable" (18), a ruined monument to catastrophe. "Return unto thy Rest, O my Soul," reads one of the editor's prefatory psalms, "for the Lord hath dealt bountifully with me." Francis Scott's tragedy seems stubbornly to resist such pious sympathy.

By focusing the reader's attention on Scott's physical sensations, the captivity narrative attempts to mediate the deep cultural fissures that the political crisis exposed. Wandering in the Kentucky frontier that had seen so much racial warfare sparked by acquisitive whites, Scott seems a warning against avarice. After the initial scenes of cruelty, however, the Indians quickly fall away, and the drama becomes one of psychological and physical endurance in which hunger dwarfs all other concerns. The writer's concentration on the sufferer's hunger works to resituate desire in the heart of the "bloody ground." It is as if the captivity narrative had isolated and purified the acquisitive instinct, converting it into naked need in a landscape where it could not possibly be satisfied. The narrative both denies and restores the need to consume. In performing this double function, Scott's microhistory gives a vivid version of the threshold psychology dominating public discussion of the depression and Shays's Rebellion. Captivity served as a powerful metaphor for the critical impasse facing the new nation.

In the largest terms, the conflicting messages of Scott's narrative were the signs of an ideological transition, one that Enlightenment notions of balance and reason would find increasingly difficult to master. Although James Madison, in the most far-reaching response to the problem, would envision American politics as an equilibrium of numerous oppositions, his tacit assumption was that the contest would be controlled from above, regulated by those best able to gain a view of the whole. Scott's microhistory defied that vision and thrust to the fore a competing version of American life, one driven from below, actuated by feeling, and impervious to satisfaction. To the commanding vision that would dominate the Constitutional Convention, Scott's narrative opposed what Sir William Temple, in a passage widely reprinted at the time, called "A certain restlessness of mind . . . inseparably annexed to our very natures and constitutions, unsatisfied with what we are, or what we at present possess and enjoy, still raving after something past or to come, and by griefs, regrets, desires or fears, ever troubling and corrupting the pleasures of our senses, and of our imaginations."[33] But if Scott's captivity narrative lacked the imaginative means to cross the threshold it conveyed, the accounts of other wanderers did not. Indeed, an obscure "farmer of feelings" had already done so, in a text American readers best knew through the image of a caged slave. In *Letters from an American Farmer*, Crèvecoeur would transform the captive into an instrument of ideological reflection.

### Facing the Frontier

At first glance, J. Hector St. John de Crèvecoeur makes a poor candidate for social analyst. Branded a "trimmer," a "monarcho-anarchist," a Loyalist who fled the

Revolution and returned a booster, he seems either too cagey or too conflicted to speak with much authority.[34] At times naïve or sentimental, feigning ignorance of the obvious or wonder at the commonplace, he lacks the penetration of his great successor, Alexis de Tocqueville, for whom America was a hard fact, a standard for aristocratic Europe. Crèvecoeur's America often does fulfill that function, heaping scorn on an Old World in which people "were as so many useless plants . . . mowed down by want, hunger, and war."[35] But there is also a profound horror lingering about his portrait, as if he were an eighteenth-century Kurtz discovering hidden savagery. Some of that sensibility doubtless stems from Crèvecoeur's own experience during the war, when he was forced to flee the country, with the loss of his wife and farm. But that very distance and vulnerability may have put him in touch with other elements of American life, elusive yet powerful by 1782, when the book was published in England. Although there is much that remains to be answered about the text of *Letters from an American Farmer*—how much rewriting his English editor(s) performed, how the twelve sketches were selected, and who was responsible for arranging them—it is clear that Crèvecoeur ultimately used his marginality to make a powerful statement about American life itself, an ideological critique that admirers like Jefferson either missed or ignored. For Crèvecoeur, the position of the captive became the fulcrum allowing him to balance America's prospects against the passions they excited. He turned the language of feeling into an ideological tool.

Letter 2 of Crèvecoeur's text presents this critique schematically and repeatedly. After a brief introduction in which James contrasts himself to European peasants, he makes his first reference to "our negroes" (22). The fact that the European poor are as "industrious . . . as we are" (22) makes their lot even worse than that of American slaves, who at least are not offered a sham independence. The association with slavery causes James to think back to a time when he felt his own independence threatened. Years before he had "entertained some thoughts" of selling the farm, imagining that it offered "but a dull repetition of the same labours and pleasures." To be so thoroughly bound may well have proved a more than European confinement, but James is saved from himself by reflecting on his heritage. "Why should not I find myself happy . . . where my father was before" (22), he asks himself, as he lists the charms of the family farm, concluding that he has but "to regulate my little concerns with propriety" to merit full contentment (24). Warming to his subject, James ends the two-paragraph meditation with a telling remark: "these are the grand outlines of my situation, but as I can feel much more than I am able to express, I hardly know how to proceed" (24). Taken together, these elements constitute what Fredric Jameson calls an ideologeme, an irreducible structure of political thought. An individual, fearing enslavement, longs to wander through the "wide world" (24) but is checked by patriarchal authority. He learns to circumscribe his wants within the "bounds" (24) of his farm—to regulate his actions—but his feelings, the source of his erstwhile discontent, refuse to be bound. They remain inexpressible, beyond the power of language, and thus beyond rational control. On the frontier between desire and duty, James remains linked to the restive, expressionless slaves.

The pattern appears repeatedly in the chapter. When James's first son is born, he realizes once again the wisdom of boundaries. "I ceased to ramble in imagination through the wide world," he confesses; "my excursions since have not exceeded the bounds of my farm" (24). And yet in one respect he remains restless. Nominating himself "the farmer of feelings" (24), he recurs to the inexpressible, writing that he "cannot describe the various emotions . . . which thrill in my heart, and often overflow in involuntary tears" (25). Of course, Crèvecoeur may well be using the excessive feeling to underscore James's sincerity, an ingenuousness designed to win over the reader. But the insistence with which James evokes boundaries—protesting that his son calmed his wanderlust after he has already claimed to dispense with the feeling—suggests that the urge did not fully leave him. It was merely sublimated, made part of (un)conscious expression. Much the same effect recurs in a passage later in the paragraph, where imagination and boundary, desire and limit, all jostle for control: "When I play with the infant, my warm imagination runs forward, and eagerly anticipates his future temper and constitution. I would willingly open the book of fate and know in which page his destiny is delineated; alas! where is the father who in those moments of paternal extacy can delineate one half of the thoughts which dilate his heart? I am sure I cannot; then again I fear for the health of those who are become so dear to me. . . . Whenever I go abroad it is always involuntary" (25). The strict demands of fate and sickness portrayed in this passage strain against those of ecstasy and imagination, making the farm less a safe repository of paternal care than the site of an intense struggle between propriety—the eighteenth-century term for property, rule, and character—and desire. Avidity, in this instance, submits to be bound, but only at the cost of a muteness that betrays its power (he cannot express himself). Self-mastery leaves an inexpressible residue of desire.

James's conscious attachment to the patriarchal world of balance and order is pointed, if vulnerable. Turning philosopher for the benefit of his patron, Mr. F. B., he professes that "nothing exists but what has its enemy, one species pursue and live upon the other" (28). Later he applies that wisdom in winter quarters. Seeing the greed with which some of his animals attack their fodder, he becomes "a bridle and check to prevent the strong and greedy, from oppressing the timid and weak" (31). Here the order of his barnyard republic appears to reflect the order of nature, but the desired balance is achieved only through an incomplete suppression.

Crèvecoeur makes that clear in the numerous twists of his tall tale about the resurrected bees. Sensing an imbalance in nature, James concludes that the king-birds on his farm have "increased too much" (28) and resolves "to kill as many as I could" (29) before they exterminate the insects. Before he can strike the first blow, however, nature intervenes, as a threatened swarm of bees severely stings one antagonist. The bird is merely stunned, though, and once recovered, pursues its attackers and "snapped as many as he wanted" (29), before James becomes the aggressor, killing the bird and disgorging the bees—171 in all—of which 54 revive and fly home. The well-known tale seems to accord with James's later talk of political resurrection in America, but the reflections across species establish a different resonance none too flattering to him. Is his eagerness "to kill as many as I could" different in principle from the bird's desire to snap "as many as he wanted"? When he does finally kill the bird, is he acting through wisdom or avarice? And when he affects nature in this impassioned way, is he promoting or impeding order? Many of those questions seem to be present in James's conclusions about his farm animals. "Could victuals thus be given to men without the assistance of any language," he writes, "I am sure they would not behave better to one another, nor more philosophically than my cattle do" (31). On the surface this statement reflects good Enlightenment doctrine, relying on reason to subdue unruly passions. Yet James's repeated willingness to test the limits of language in expressing his feelings suggests that, once again, there are legitimate and powerful human motives that do not always serve the ends of authority. There remains a subliminal, wayward desire here that James is not willing to check or renounce.

For James, the ground uniting discipline and desire is, of course, nature itself, the incredible fecundity of the Pennsylvania landscape. And it is against that abundance, and the desire to consume it, that one may understand the subtlety of Crèvecoeur's analysis. James presents himself as a subsistence farmer, content to produce what he can on his paternal farm and to barter for what he cannot. But the episode of the kingbird demonstrates that such discipline always strains against other, more destructive motives. A parallel example, once again employing bees, will demonstrate how following nature's order is linked in this text to its violation.

Bees, to James, are a symbol of natural discipline. He prizes them on his farm, goes out every year to get more, and endlessly contemplates "their government, their industry, their quarrels, their passions" (33). When he needs a phrase to describe the sober inhabitants of Nantucket, he can do no better than to compare them to a "fruitful hive constantly send[ing] out swarms, as industrious as themselves" (182). Yet these exemplars of industry are marked by a kind of avarice that James adopts through an elaborate ritual denoting boundaries and their violation. When he goes bee hunting each year—a venture he finds more "profitable" than hunting game (34)—he establishes a base on some flat stones, distributing wax, honey, and vermilion to attract his quarry. James is certain that their fondness for "preying on that which is not their own" will lead them to the spot and that, once satiated and marked, the bees will lead him to their "republics" (35). Then it is a simple matter of getting help, cutting down the tree, and transferring their home to his. The point of the description is not that James has an apian fondness for taking what doesn't belong to him; indeed, he discusses the solemn duty of every bee hunter to secure permission of the landowner and divide the profits. Rather, the more striking analogy involves the bees' greedy "preying" on the spots of honey, and James's appropriation of the hive. "[I]t is inconceivable what a quantity of honey these trees will sometimes afford," he comments (35), once again invoking the inexpressible, the level beneath language, that he earlier used to discuss his avaricious cattle. Here what cannot be expressed is the boundless desire to consume, stimulated by nature's own fecundity.

A final example, more brutal than the rest, may serve to illustrate the underside of James's benevolent discipline. Twice a year, he imparts, Carlisle farmers have the "pleasure" of trapping pigeons. Everything about these creatures is prodigious: they arrive in such "astonishing" numbers as to obscure the sun; they fly "with the celerity of the wind," from regions over five hundred miles away (37). Such numbers are bound to stimulate prodigious appetites, and James confesses that he himself has caught as many as fourteen dozen. The reverse logic of the marketplace makes them almost worthless, for they arrive in such quantities "that for a penny you might have as many as you could carry away" (38); yet, reinforcing the theme of pleasure with which he began the discussion, James pronounces them excellent. A final remark identifies this sequence with the chapter's other ideologemes: the "pleasure" James derives from the songs of birds is "superior to my poor description" (38). Superior, astonishing, inconceivable: these are the markers for a fund of satisfaction that cannot easily be contained. What makes the present example more sinister is the manner in which Crèvecoeur links it to a later, crueler instance of destructive avarice. Like the caged slave of Letter 9, one pigeon, "made blind, and fastened to a long string" (37), is used to attract the flocks. "Every farmer has a tame wild pigeon in a cage at his door all the year round, in order to be ready whenever the season comes for catching them" (38). The passage does not so much convict James of cruelty to animals (although his sentimental excesses over unhatched eggs might suggest that possibility) as expose the always unstable boundary in this text between reason and avarice. The ingenuity that traps pigeons is little different from the ingenuity that locates bees or operates a farm. All assume a discipline that rewards virtue, but nature always presents another face, one mediated by desire. If James is often incapable of imagining that other face in Letter 2, he may well recognize it in the hollow eye sockets and bare cheekbones of the martyred slave concluding Letter 9.

James ends the chapter by offering a provisional solution to the problem of desire: when passion threatens, retire to the farm. Property imposes its own discipline, its own discretion. Thus, although he vows never to be done recounting "the many objects which involuntarily strike my imagination . . . and spontaneously afford me the most pleasing relief" (43–44), he checks imagination, expression, and spontaneous pleasure as he buries himself within his family. Domestic happiness depends upon the unfolding of his children's reason, a goal for which he must devise little punishments and rewards, as he did for his cattle. But these measures, too, James finds inexpressible, "being domestic mysteries adapted only to the locality of the small sanctuary wherein my family resides" (44). His inability to keep pace with pleasure is put to rest at home, where silence reinforces, rather than frustrates, order. When James confronts the problem of social heterogeneity in Letter 3, he will try to project that solution upon America itself.

The numerous temptations, impulses, and desires James surveys in Letter 2 suggest a further disciplinary problem. Just as individuals are challenged by abundance, so the society at large is challenged by its promiscuous immigrant population, a mass whose sheer number and diversity defy any simple reduction to order. Given the many tensions he has exposed, his solution is ingenious and elegant. Relying on social models advanced by Montesquieu and Raynal, he offers an array of influences to explain this scattered society, suggesting, as he did with his farm, that land is the final determinant, the force that confirms character. With this flexible model in place, Crèvecoeur can then address the vagaries that so threatened discipline in Letter 2. Individuals may be driven to America on impulse, but the land will guarantee order.

The central assumption appears early in the letter. "We are nothing," James asserts, "but what we derive from the air we breathe, the climate we inhabit, the government we obey, the system of religion we profess, and the nature of our employment" (53–54). Each one of these factors will come under his scrutiny. European peasants, long crushed by despotism, become flourishing American plants. Those, like Andrew the Hebridean, who have nothing to work for in Europe will find their industry profitable here. And to those, like Abbé Robin, who worry that American character will suffer in the absence of established religion, James offers an apparently liberal response. The real problem is not indifference but zealotry, the unchecked religious passions that thrive in Europe. Change the continent, and people may be zealous or indifferent as they please—in the few moments they can rescue from their labor. Even the most ardent sectarian "raises good crops, his house is handsomely painted, his orchard is one of the fairest in the neighbourhood" (60). Where property is the all-absorbing interest, the impulses that stir the landless masses of Europe will be effectually quelled. There will be no crusades in America.

Indeed, the largest source of social distress, the extreme passions produced by despotism, here finds a new equipoise. If the difficulty for aristocratic observers like Mr. F. B. lay "in the manner of viewing so extensive a scene" (46), Crèvecoeur's solution lay in the efficiency with which the land itself became an emotional topography, selecting, sorting, and absorbing individuals in a process of natural equilibrium. Twice during the first half of the letter, James describes the means whereby the vicious are drawn to the frontier, the bold to the seacoast, and the prudent to the middle settlements. For immigrants, the passage "from oppression . . . into the unlimited freedom of the woods" (65) is the most traumatic, since the backwoods settlers have neither law nor property to restrain them. Appropriately, James devotes most of his attention to demonstrating how they are controlled, both by the pressure of more civilized settlements encroaching on them and by the natural competition for game that keeps them solitary. Similarly, excesses in the middle colonies produce their own self-regulating responses. "That rich, that voluptuous sentiment" (64) occasioned by the ownership of land creates a corresponding jealously, a litigiousness that makes the courts a great leveler. There need be no aristocracy to subdue these people; Americans will do it themselves.

Yet although this social mechanism has the Newtonian balance later associated with the Constitution, it is not quite the liberal vision of a self-regulating system. The giveaway lies in an almost incidental example of American largesse, the discussion of a redeemed captive. This homegrown metaphor, the final piece of evidence before James begins the narrative of Andrew the Hebridean, offers an appropriate summary of Crèvecoeur's position. The captive is freed from despotic control, brought back from the "frontiers of Canada," and allowed to flourish in Albany, the middle region. Even after an absence of many years, the change transforms him so that he is able to live a long life and leave a large estate to a family "all well settled." Whatever passions he had accumulated on the frontier were checked by his means of liberation, the "gentleman" who both "purchased" him and generously "bound" him to a tailor (86). Gratitude, rank, and contract reabsorb him into the host community; he is given property and made property in an act that reinforces the same benevolent authority that James found in contemplating his father's farm. The transformation is thus rendered at once radical and modest, the anxieties of the captive contained by the filial devotion of the "person who was but twelve years old" when taken away (86).

Andrew's profound gratitude follows the same course. Although captive in Scotland, a landless subject of his all-powerful "laird," he is reinvigorated through the loan of tools and the rental of land, all presided over by the ever-watchful James and his prosperous friends. Against the emotional background of Letter 2, Andrew's deferential response is resonant. After he is first bound to Mr. P. R., "honest tears of gratitude fell from his eyes . . . and its expressions seemed to quiver on his lips." "Though silent," James adds, "this was saying a great deal" (99). Here strong passion reinforces social bonds through a deference that is not inexpressible but mutely eloquent. Even the Indians, those specters of American passion, become rude symbols of social order. Roughly invading P. R.'s parlor, they terrorize Andrew, who leaves them "masters of the house" (104) as they help themselves to the provisions and warm themselves by the fire. By attempting to defend his patron's property, Andrew proves himself worthy of his calling, just as the Indians, by awaiting their trading partner P. R., confirm their own regard for property. Indians, master, and apprentice are all bound by the same potent law.

When, at the end of the letter, James offers the audit of Andrew's estate, he has apparently solved the problem of liberated social passions. Because his attainments are so saturated with obligation, Andrew has reduplicated James's filial dependence, even though the Scot's father is overseas. Just as filiopietism checked James's wanderlust, so gratitude checks Andrew's rudeness—indeed, the rudeness of thousands of his fellow immigrants. "He could say nothing," James writes of Andrew's response to his house raising, but "with thankful tears" shook hands with his neighbors (111). The united effects of innumerable such incidents occurring all across the land, James implies, will have the same influence as the heterogeneous actions of climate, religion, and geography. All will allow long-suppressed energies to emerge, but the energies will be bound.

On the seacoast, James tells us in Letter 3, lie the greatest social energies. Constant contact with the "boisterous" sea makes the inhabitants "bold and enterprising": they love trade, rove the world, and "converse with a variety of people" (54). But the same traits that render them prosperous also make them vulnerable. It is not wealth alone that James fears will transform American prowess into European luxury and despotism; it is a false relation to property. If land is literally invested with social power, then those who make their living from the sea ought to be powerless, adrift on a frontier as savage as the inland forests. That is why, in a book ostensibly about farmers, James spends almost half his time on Nantucket, where farmland doesn't exist. Nantucket is the logical next step in Crèvecoeur's territorial survey, a test of how the most boisterous social elements may thrive. In his five-letter account of the region, Crèvecoeur gives his most incisive portrait of a republican order capable of managing its impulses.

The discussion of the island is as sophisticated as it is intricate. Intending to trace the islanders "throughout their progressive steps, from their arrival here to this present hour" (117–18), James begins the chronological account with the 1671 patent. Since the island was "universally barren and . . . unfit for cultivation" (126), the proprietors immediately marked off small home lots and held the rest in common. If property is truly salvific, this was a perilous step, made all the more dramatic by the founders' extraordinary assessment of the commons. Computing the number of sheep and estimating the reserve acreage, they issued shares of ideal *"sheep-pasture titles"* (127), still circulating in the island's economy a century later. James stresses three aspects of the titles: their ideality, their control, and their uncertainty. Because the value of all possible tracts could not be known when the shares were first issued, and because no specific plots were assigned to any share, the ownership is purely imaginary—"an ideal, though real title to some unknown piece of land, which one day or another may be ascertained" (127). Moreover, the indeterminate status created instant market imbalances, since the initially equal shares were distributed across land that may have been widely varying in quality. All of this is a formula for fluctuating value, sharp competition, and speculative bubbles—in short, credit, that nemesis of republican economy.

But Nantucketers did not succumb. Instead, they evolved a "council of the proprietors," a control board that judged whether "some peculiar spot" was "adequate to [a title's] value" (128). Market fluctuations and social conflict could thus be forestalled by a just price—yet another ideal figure, but one reached by a consensus of elders. And lest the reader feel that there is something despotic in allowing anyone to impede the market, James offers a shrewd rationale. The shares of ideal land are meant to counterbalance "misfortunes from their sea adventures" (127): "and this is the reason that these people very unwillingly sell those small rights, and esteem them more than you would imagine. They are the representation of a future freehold, they cherish in the mind of the possessor a latent, though distant, hope, that by his success in his next whale season, he may be able to pitch on some predilected spot, and there build himself a home, to which he may retire, and spend the latter end of his days in peace" (128). It is all an elaborate illusion, the pieces of paper representing ideal land, offsetting imagined voyages promising distant income. And in the movement from imaginary property to the council's judgment to the anticipated voyage, we can see—in reverse order—the ideologeme James explored in Letter 2: the desire to wander is checked by patriarchal authority and returns through an instrument whose value cannot be expressed. But the presence of the elders secures that value, making any recourse to the market unnecessary. Thus a landless island is invested with scores of prosperous acres, and social order is secured.

To see the genius of this solution, one need only recur to the original inhabitants, the Indians who preceded the Quaker settlers. Unlike the whites, who conscientiously purchased the land and then made its preservation a kind of secular devotion, the natives, who enjoyed such ready abundance that "there could be no jealousy" (139), engaged in a Hobbesian "perpetual war . . . founded on no other reason, but the adventitious place of their nativity and residence" (140). At the very verge of extinction they finally made their peace and the warring groups retired to opposite ends of the island, only to face a greater threat from European smallpox that all but eliminated them. Since they are originally vicious and passionate, the "accidents" (141) of association with whites seem less a calamity than a natural order, the land's ultimate punishment of frontiersmen. English notions of property quite literally changed the island's prospects, without altering its physical appearance much at all.

But the island's real nemesis is not the internal pressure of scarce land; it is the ocean and the commerce it demands. Unable to produce their own necessities, Nantucketers are forced upon the market, procuring everything from lumber to linen at great expense. Even if James were serious about the subsistence-surplus model in Pennsylvania, he could find no prospect for it here. And although the council of elders might restrain the passion for ideal land, the competitive pressures of seafaring would seem to impose their own kind of rudeness and savagery. Once again, James must confront prodigies and the appetites they unleash. Nantucketers must sail "an immense distance, and with Herculean labours" gather the sea's "riches," the "huge fish" whose almost unimaginable bulk fueled one of America's most profitable industries (121). "It is astonishing what a quantity of oil some of these fish will yield, and what profit it affords" (167), he writes, offering a page of commercial statistics on the animals, their yield, and the steady progress of the Nantucket fleet. And beyond the moral effects of such uncertain wealth lies the treacherous sea, belittling human security much as the American forest disturbs James, but also evoking balance and order. The boisterous wind may cause shipwrecks and "extensive desolations" (209), but it also cools American fields; it churns up tributaries but also deposits food. The sea contains a terrible beauty and a promise of natural order that shrewd navigators understand. Nantucketers made that promise the basis of their own natural economy.

Once again, we must approach James's analysis through the ideologeme. Just as the ocean's rhythms bring abundance and destruction, so the island's economic rhythms are a succession of excesses and lacks, preserving a moral balance. Whereas in Letter 2 James posed the problem of restraining natural appetites, here appetites are restrained by necessity and by a community attuned to natural signs. Nantucket's condition provides the first lesson. The island, James avers, "furnishes the naturalist with few or no objects worthy [of] observation" (128). It has "neither wolves nor foxes" (133); a "steril[e] . . . soil" (120); few trees; indeed "nothing deserving of notice but its inhabitants" (121). What is more, its northern latitude exposes it to extremes—"extremely pleasant" summers but winters whipped by northwest winds that make the island "bleak and uncomfortable" (134). But the long string of negatives, or lacks, is counterbalanced by a natural exuberance—the "great plenty of clams, oysters, and other fish" (138) that "multiply so fast, . . . they are a never-failing resource" (135). In a passage reminiscent of the pigeon gathering of Letter 2, James details how islanders breach the sandbars protecting tidal pools and "with proper nets catch as many [fish] as they want" (129). But there is no hint of depravity here, since the tide itself provides the rhythm that the fishermen exploit. Sterility and abundance now yield a rewarding mediocrity.

Because Nantucketers depend on the sea for survival, they have transformed the natural rhythms into a moral order. Like the sea they generate abundance, and like the sea they cleanly dispense it. "[D]eprived as they are of every necessary material, produce, &c.," they still "live well, and sometimes . . . make considerable fortunes" (173). But the great cost of importing goods from the mainland, combined with Quaker simplicity, prevents wealth from turning poisonous. What elsewhere may be termed "opulence" on Nantucket merely intensifies community—"an increase of business, an additional degree of hospitality, greater neatness in the preparation of dishes" (205)—just as the profit motive itself is distributive on whaling voyages. "They have no wages," James explains; "each draws a certain established share in partnership with the proprietor of the vessel; by which oeconomy they are all proportionably concerned in the success of the enterprise" (163). And when the successful sailors come ashore, they check the natural appetites that a long voyage stimulates but that nature itself subdues. Because they are all married, they avoid the "debauchery" that too often "compensate[s] for months of abstinence" (170), allowing their families to "absor[b] every other desire" (171). In a paradigmatic passage, James captures the finely wrought tensions of the sailors' moral lives: "The motives that lead them to the sea, are very different from those of most other sea-faring men; it is neither idleness nor profligacy that sends them to that element; it is a settled plan of life, a well founded hope of earning a livelihood; it is because their soil is bad, that they are early initiated to this profession. . . . The sea therefore becomes to them a kind of patrimony" (171). Excess and lack, the rhythms of exchange that Richard Halpern calls "the ideologeme of the economic,"[36] here resolve themselves in a perfectly balanced acceptance of patriarchy.

In effect, Nantucket is Crèvecoeur's answer to Max Weber's Protestant ethic, a locale where discipline yields profit without excess. "It is but seldom that vice grows on a barren sand like this, which produces nothing without extreme labour" (148), James remarks. So great is the cost of business, though, that the islanders' enterprise must produce either "temperance" and "equality" (148) or "the most abject misery" (148–49). Indeed, in a final irony, Nantucket makes Europe itself appear on the fringes of civilization. Import European manners, James contends, and, "like an epidemical disorder they would destroy every thing," turning the islanders into Indians (149). It is not discipline alone that saves Nantucket; it is discipline, manners, religion, climate, land—the combination of influences sketched in Letter 3, conspiring to limit growth on a barren outpost of capitalism. "Here . . . human industry has acquired a boundless field to exert itself in" (212), James concludes his sketch, but the field is as narrow as the title to imaginary land.

Writers on Crèvecoeur have often noted the decisive effect of Letter 9 on James's sensibilities. Whatever his own complicity in holding slaves (he intends, finally, to free them), the dramatic recognition of this American cancer darkens his portrait, making him aware of other kinds of despotism that lead to his own experience of powerlessness in Letter 12.[37] What is less often recognized is how his ravings actually promote the very conditions he seems to despise. Without accusing James of hypocrisy, I would like to argue that his global empathy with the slave is a last-ditch effort to save his schematic program, his ideologeme, from its own internal pressures. The outpouring of emotion, that is to say, the inexpressible excesses that he contemplated on his farm, can now be contained in imagination only through recourse to an equally severe authority, an excessive patriarchal discipline that makes despotism appear not only universal but also necessary. In this sense slavery is not an aberration of the luxurious South; it is an imperative for the entire system, the only way to preserve order, and James's recognition of that fact pushes him to an imaginative frontier. Ironically, both positions in the dilemma, slavery and residence with the Indians, ultimately reinforce the logic of consumption that Crèvecoeur wants to evade.

As James himself indicates, the most convenient point of departure for assessing Letter 9 is the caged slave—or rather, James's responses to the slave. "I found myself suddenly arrested by the power of affright and terror," he writes; "my nerves were convulsed; I trembled, I stood motionless, involuntarily contemplating the fate of this negro, in all its dismal latitude" (234). The last remark is indeed quite literal, as James projects from this solitary misery a general review of human suffering in every climate and latitude. "[I]f we attentively view this globe," he argues, "will it not appear rather a place of punishment, than of delight?" (228). Even mild climates, which to "the geographical eye" should appear earthly paradises, are home to "the most wretched people in the world" (230). Although such outbursts have led many readers to accuse James of sentimentalism, his conclusions are actually irresistible, given the initial jolt he has experienced. Just as the sublime apprehension of nature, for conventional writers, was the window to finitude, the slave, for James, represents the limits of a disciplinary worldview. And the discovery of those limits, as he recognized in Letter 2, lay through the feelings.

Once the encounter has forced James to breach the carefully nurtured restraints on feeling, he uses slavery to vent all the sensations he found inexpressible in Letter 2. Here, by contrast, nothing is held in reserve. Slaves, James imagines, are subject to "the most acute, the most pungent . . . afflictions" (219). Not only do they suffer from the "anguish" and "despair" (220) of the Middle Passage, but if they survive they will feel "all the passions . . . of inveterate resentment, and . . . revenge" (223), of awe and fear. These are the very feelings James himself indulges in his planetary review, as he recounts the "boiling matter" creating immense subterranean graves "wherein millions will one day perish!" (229), the "delirium of tyranny" (231) subduing with "lawless rage," the "tears" and "groans" and blood and ruin (230). And just as his sensibility destroys his former modesty, so the slaves' dire fate destroys his filiopietism. How many slaves have cursed their paternity, he asks, when they discover that to have children is to ensure despair? So, too, James curses nature. Can "[t]he same sublime hand which . . . preserves the arrangement of the whole with such exalted wisdom and paternal care," he asks " . . . abandon mankind to all the errors, the follies, and the miseries, which their most frantic rage, and their most dangerous vices and passions can produce?" (225). Nature had once seemed "indulgent, . . . a kind parent" (228); now it appears a devouring tyrant threatening the globe itself with "dissolution" (230). One by one, each element of the supple ideological structure James announced in Letter 2 has crumbled. If he was once bound to his farm, now he roams the globe, constrained by neither duty nor propriety. The slave has paradoxically liberated something powerful in James, and its expression is terrible to behold.

What he has grasped, however, is more than simple compassion or the gnawings of conscience. For slavery reveals to him the irresistible drive toward accumulation, toward excess, that he failed to see at the pigeon-shoot. It is easy enough to convict white southerners of this sin. Charles Town lawyers have long committed it, acquiring "[t]he whole mass of provincial property" (215) as they undermine the character of the region. But his identification with the slave forces James to see the inner logic of the system as he has never seen it before—that the instruments of infinite profit are subject to infinite loss. Day after day these victims "are obliged to devote their lives, their limbs, their will . . . to swell the wealth of masters" who consider them lower than animals (218). So, too, the globe itself displays its "spontaneous riches" only to produce "the most wretched people" (230). James has not, and will not, identify himself with the slave master responsible for evil, but he has established a crucial point of contact. So vast were the demands unleashed by American abundance, so dangerous to patriarchal order, that only an equally vast repression could contain them. That paradox cut to the heart of republican discipline. If consumption, passion, and profit menaced colonial harmony, James would seek a refuge from the tyranny of desire.

The last three letters chart James's approach to that desired state, his attempt to cross over into new territory with some of his old baggage intact. As he does so, he is preoccupied by the theme of transformation, of how individuals may change all their circumstances, all the elements that define them, and remain themselves. The intensity of his concern brings him face to face with the most subtle and troubling aspect of the consumer's behavior, the pragmatic and mutable search for happiness.

The process begins back on James's farm, where a strange assortment of creatures alters the landscape. Snakes and other reptiles indigenous to the South have made their way to Pennsylvania, where they signify an uncanny confusion of species. Men, James tells us, turn into snakes. A "poor wretch" (236) stung by a copperhead suddenly turns venomous: "his eyes were filled with madness and rage, . . . he thrust out his tongue as the snakes do; he hissed through his teeth with inconceivable strength" (237). Snakes turn into cats, like the *"tamed,"* defanged one who loved to have his back stroked (238). Hummingbirds attack with the ferocity of lions; snakes slither with the speed of horses and stand half erect, almost like humans. Propriety and self-will also fall victim to the confusion. James tells of a slave-owning Dutch father and son both fatally poisoned by the same fangs embedded in the same boots—the venom no respecter of property or persons. Lesser victims go to their deaths with a curious rapture: a snake's prey "seems to be arrested by some invincible power; it screams; now approaches, and then recedes; and after skipping about with unaccountable agitation, finally rushes into the jaws of the snake, and is swallowed" (241). Here James's close observation reminds one of his identification with the slave, as if, once again, he has felt the essential violence of the world. What appears uncanny in the violence of Letter 10 will strike home with redoubled force in Letter 12.

Appropriately, then, the return to James's farm does not present another vision of wise restraint, but one of rabid appetite. Crèvecoeur's most striking emblem of that change is the hummingbird, a creature that might scandalize any republican neighborhood. Its gaudy livery, more exquisite than the palette of the "most luxuriant painter" (242), its eyes like "diamonds" (243), and its "majestic" (242) head seem to make it an interloper, one that James has trouble assigning to his normal categories. On the one hand it feeds like bees, hovering around flowers to extract their nectar. On the other hand, it harbors an unaccountable rage and "will tear and lacerate flowers into a hundred pieces" (243). The paradox it presents is identical to the anguish of Letter 9, writ small. "Where do passions find room in so diminutive a body?" James wonders, answering himself by assigning responsibility to "our great parent" (243). But the explosive fury can no longer be contained by appeals to a higher order. The farm now more resembles a market than a republic, a naked contest of wills in which the passions prevail.

That is the message of the letter's chilling final vignette, the battle of the two snakes. Although this animal tale might be no more trustworthy than his other yarns, it captures James's apocalyptic fear in the image of the aggressive black snake lacerating its paler opponent—the two "biting each other with the utmost rage" (244), their eyes "on fire" (245), their bodies "convulsed with strong undulations" (245). All of the farmer's anguish over repression, race, consumption, and desire is compressed in the haunting image of the "two great snakes" entwined in hemp stalks and "mutually fastened together by means of the writhings which lashed them to each other" (245). Any separation of the antagonists, any attempt to restore a former order, seems too radical to contemplate. The effort would pull up roots and all.

By contrast, Letter 11 presents a deliberate naïveté, an isolated preserve all the more poignant for its dreamlike impossibility. Of all the letters Crèvecoeur selected for his volume, this one seems the most formulaic—a sketch rather than a chapter in his protagonist's experience. And yet, by depicting the good Quaker botanist in the manner of other travel narratives, Crèvecoeur seems to be deliberately pointing to an ideal whose artificiality must now be beyond question. With his mild and efficient intelligence, John Bertram precisely represents the ideology of republican discipline. A student of Linnaeus, he has managed to botanize throughout the colonies, acquiring "a pretty general knowledge of every plant and tree to be found in our continent" (261)—an American exponent of what Mary Louise Pratt calls planetary consciousness.[38] Like James, he cultivates restraint (when we first see him he is engaged in erecting banks to contain the Schuylkill), and like James he comes to his avocation through soul-searching. "I could not resist the impulse" (261) to study nature, he admits as his wife warns against exchanging honest labor for brain work. So, too, James's wife had insisted that "it is not by writing that we shall pay the blacksmith, the minister, the weaver, the tailor, and the English shop" (18). And yet even the parallels disclose a poignant difference. For Bertram's enterprising yet simple life, his extensive operations employing dozens of hands, seems to be tethered to the demands of abstract principles that have almost nothing to do with the marketplace. It is a freed slave who faithfully transacts all Bertram's "business" in Philadelphia (263), but the agent's sales and purchases are overshadowed by his employer's rational benevolence. The Carlisle farmer, by contrast, must find money for the "English shop"—the consumer purchases that so sharply stimulated desire. Significantly, then, James is nowhere to be seen in this letter, which is narrated by the ghostly presence of Mr. Iw——n Al——z, a Russian traveler. The farmer of feelings, vainly clinging to his property, senses himself already transported to the frontier.

But if republican order now seems an insubstantial dream, what possible orientation can save James? If writers like Clifford Geertz are correct, no one, not even those witnessing profound cultural upheaval, approaches crisis innocently. As old certainties erode, individuals may be expected to improvise, arranging cultural materials in ambiguous or compromised ways, like the funeral rites Geertz describes in Sukarno's revolutionary Indonesia.[39] As the ideologeme we have been tracing collapses under the pressures of Revolutionary America, we might expect James to adapt by retrieving fragments of the old vision of balanced order and embedding them in a new context, where he can retain the illusion of control. In the new regime, he must yield to desire without succumbing to it, abandon property while retaining it, seek discipline in the face of tyranny. If John Bertram had codified America's flora, James was about to portray its emerging inner life.

In many respects, Letter 12 merely sharpens the tone of Letter 9, giving its general anguish a local habitation and a name. Here the locale is the Pennsylvania frontier, and the tyrant's name is Britain. What James finds inconceivable is that the metropolis, "that once indulgent parent" (286), could send its emissaries to butcher his family. Indulging this metaphor, he imagines King George as a blind but affectionate father, possessor of "the most numerous, as well as the fairest, progeny of children, of any potentate now in the world" (281). And yet the patriarch has no concern for his more distant offspring, destroyed by "monsters, left to the wild impulses of the wildest nature" (283). Just as nature's balance erodes in Letter 9, so the break in this chain of authority has wrecked all virtue, all discipline. "[I]n vain I exert my authority" (274) to silence his family's fears, James confesses; their wildest nightmares become omens, regulating action in place of reason. Once the world had seemed ordered, and society an equilibrium in which "the weakness of each [member] is strengthened by the force of the whole" (271). Now, when Pennsylvania suffers from the Hobbesian atavism of Nantucket Indians, balance is a mere pretense, a story that men with too much power tell about themselves. Accordingly, James subjects the old disciplinary paradigm to withering criticism. Mr. F. B., the aristocratic English traveler, now strikes him as little more than a "cool, . . . distant spectator" (280) who can have no idea of American perils. Such an observer may issue balanced pronouncements about justice and duty; but let him "tremble with us in our fields, shudder at the rustling of every leaf" (281), and the world would look quite different. "[C]ould they be transported here, and metamorphosed into simple planters as we are," the arbiters of planetary consciousness would "feel and exclaim as we do" (284). The metamorphosis James foresaw on his farm has now, at least in imagination, reached to the very center of world power, and all authority has shifted with the change.

What James needs is a new perspective more sensitive to his own obscure distresses, and he finds it by recourse to long-suppressed feeling. Calm reasoners cannot possibly know the extent of his own evils, he claims, since "no relation can be equal to what we suffer and to what we feel" (274). Consequently James permits himself to plumb the depths of his feelings, however excessive. When he realizes he is connected in misery to all the sufferers of this war, he exclaims, "I am seised [*sic*] with a fever of the mind, I am transported beyond that degree of calmness which is necessary to delineate our thoughts. I feel as if my reason wanted to leave me" (272). Bursting the bounds of reason, he reveals the most "afflictive sensations" (275)—"despair" (283), impiety (287), "sorrow" (287), vengefulness (285), "despondency" (274), the "keenest regret" (298), the most "tumultuous sentiments" (299). Let the observer "come and reside with us one single month," James writes; " . . . let him pass with us through all the successive hours of necessary toil, terror and affright, let him watch with us . . . through tedious, sleepless nights, his imagination furrowed by the keen chissel [*sic*] of every passion; . . . let his heart, the seat of the most affecting passions, be powerfully wrung by hearing the melancholy end of his relations and friends" (280–81)—then, and not until then, can one truly know the sorrows of the American farmer. With such knowledge, James implies, one cannot help being transformed.

But transformed into what? If James is quite clear about the breakdown of the old order, he is less certain of its alternative. Conscious, perhaps, that his own suppressed desires may reflect those of his persecutors, he makes his distress the grounds of denial. Like the slave masters of the South, the bloody British tyrants lay claim to the most rapacious needs. Already "masters of two thirds of the trade of the world; who have in their hands the power which almighty gold can give" (286), they continue to consume land and lives, turning all their subjects into victims. By contrast, the contemplated flight to the Indian village will automatically cure him of excess. Already deprived of "appetite" (273), he foresees Indian life as a combination of "bread, safety, and subsistence" (288), an inland version of Nantucket. "[W]ithout salt, without spices, without linen and with little other clothing," what difference to him "whether we eat well made pastry, or pounded àlagrichés; well roasted beef, or smoked venison; cabbages, or squashes. . . . whether we sleep on featherbeds, or on bear-skins?" (292–93). This is more than James's attempt to cheer himself up; it is the necessary result of the text's ideological tensions, an enforced curb to appetites that the continent, for all the fine talk of balance and discipline, seems to incite.

To underscore the "great transmutation" (290), James announces that he will impose his own kind of frontier discipline, in violation of everything that land, climate, and religion ordain. Since hunting is deleterious, he vows to give a homemade mill "to every six families" (307). He will clear as much land as he can; regulate the natives' trade so that they are insulated from British agents, "those pests of the continent" (307); inoculate them; plough with them; and hope his "example . . . may rouse the industry of some, and serve to direct others in their labours" (307). Even the accommodations he will have to make with Indian manners will only serve to underscore his salvation, as if wigwam and deerskin were cultural signs not for savagery but for temperance. The frontier would be a haven from luxury.

All well and good; but what has come of James's earlier scheme that placed all license on the frontier? It will not do to say that he has abandoned that perspective through overwhelming necessity; his preoccupation with discipline is evidence enough that the old prejudices survive, albeit in attenuated form. But James's very pragmatism, his scrambling for any elements that will make sense of the world, may tell us something important about the frontier he faces. For it must not be forgotten that, by Letter 12, he no longer considers his farm to be anchored to the middle region at all. Exposed to the mountains, open to the forests and to Indian attack, he has long since identified himself as a "poor defenseless frontier inhabitan[t]" (279), transporting the farm and its rational order to the very seat of chaos. I have suggested that this new identification largely represents the liberation of that wayward desire barely contained on the paternal farm—a desire widely associated, in the 1780s, with consumption. But the "metamorphos[is]" (308) also relates to another facet of the new consumer mentality, its absorption in imagination.

Buried feeling, scholars have argued, drives the consumer revolution. Consumption, as Joyce Appleby notes, "requires that emotions dominate individual consciousness"—emotions rooted in "Protestant piety and its peculiar form of sentimentality, individualism, escape, melancholy, and fantasy."[40] Colin Campbell locates those feelings in the imagination. Through daydreams, he argues, modern consumers exert emotional autonomy in their lives, using goods to construct ideal versions of themselves.[41] Imagining his own frontier, James seeks a similar autonomy. Through daydreams, James can shed his status as victim and enjoy that tenuous freedom he so highly prizes. Appropriately, Letter 12 is studded with references to the power of the imagination to alter the world. Like avid readers, James's family is obsessed with tales of Indian massacres that, "told in chimney-corners, swell themselves in our-affrighted [sic] imaginations into the most terrific ideas!" (273). Imagination is "chissel[ed]" by "every passion" (280), alarms them into feverish activity, turns dreams into omens. But it is imagination, too, that may ultimately save James by allowing him to "gil[d]" the "distant prospect" of his wilderness retreat (313). "These vague rambling contemplations . . . carry me sometimes to a great distance; I am lost in the anticipation of the various circumstances attending this proposed metamorphosis!" (313). Imagination alone allows him to control his intolerable anxiety, to construct a world of more generous rewards.

Chief among those rewards is the very mechanism Nantucketers discovered to regulate their economy—with one important difference. No matter how diligent James might be in maintaining order in the wilderness, he knows that the unfamiliar setting and Indian influences will weaken his authority, hence, his scheme of credit. Although his wants on the farm were modest and the work hard, he had been stimulated by the promise of "solid wealth" (310). Since the lure of "future riches" would disappear in the interior, James will have to turn accountant. "I will keep an exact account of all that shall be gathered," he imagines, and give to his children "a regular credit for the amount of it to be paid them in real property at the return of peace" (310). Their diminished wardrobes will also be repaid, to ward off murmuring over their blankets and moccasins. Just like the Nantucket sailors, who remain tied to their elders by the hope of future gain, James has apparently found a market solution that does not sacrifice control. But there remains a crucial difference. For the Nantucketers, discipline was concentrated in a council of elders issuing shares; their authority counterbalanced the imaginary nature of the instruments. James, by contrast, must share his authority with the Indians, inventing fictions that hunting and fishing are mere "pastime[s]" (310), face-saving devices to show that whites belong in the neighborhood. Because James will be immersed in a foreign element, his ability to direct fantasy, to dominate credit in the manner of the Nantucketers, is circumscribed. Any credit he issues will be riskier, driven by a new combination of forces beyond his control. He will be subject to the more potent market imperatives of negotiation and exchange.

In this sense, James's contemplated withdrawal is both a discovery and a rediscovery. Beset by a sense of bad faith, the feeling that the terrors and oppressions he saw through the caged slave were really his own, he attempts to return to principle on unfamiliar ground. He wants to discover a cleaner discipline, a purer desire, by divorcing himself from the source of all hated power, both British and Revolutionary. Yet the frontier also fulfills its initial, passionate purpose, at least in imagination. By allowing James to daydream, it exposes a power far more threatening to republican order than the rapacious British. There, far removed from Indian traders, Crèvecoeur had discovered the inner workings of consumption.

## Word between Worlds: Equiano's Interesting Narrative

Farmer James's domestication of the frontier seems a long way from Ezra Stiles's vision of trade. For Crèvecoeur, the clergyman's boundless republic, expanding indefinitely in space and time, becomes a nightmare of acquisitive desire—the landscape of Francis Scott's narrative writ large. Toward the end of the decade, however, a bolder account of consumption appeared. Like *Letters from an American Farmer*, Equiano's *Interesting Narrative* provided what might be called a "structural" account of consumer desire, an interior rendering of the market's logic. But where Crèvecoeur exposed the contradictions of republican consumption, Equiano offered the inner life of commodities themselves. The commodities, of course, were slaves, and Equiano's extraordinary account of his passage to freedom and Christianity suggests a determined search for the intrinsic value that a dehumanizing enslavement denied him. But the dialectical course of that search—from the use values of Africa to the exchange values of Europe, and from the fulfillments of freedom to the terrors of Christianity—suggests that Equiano could not completely embrace the logic of the marketplace he served. His endless circulation through the Atlantic economy allowed him to simulate the market's transforming power, but he could not preserve himself from its stubborn contradictions. Like Crèvecoeur, Equiano stood at the threshold of consumption, where restraint collided with desire. His attempts to reconcile the two offer the most trenchant eighteenth-century prospect of the market revolution yet to come.

The structural source of the contradictions may be glimpsed in a brief comparison of two arresting passages. In the first, appearing in one of the text's most vivid chapters, Equiano catalogs the abuses of Caribbean slavery—the "scandalous" rapes and beatings, the mutilations and hangings, the fearfully short lives of plantation workers, who are treated little better than beasts. Small wonder, then, that slavery's excesses generate its downfall:

> No peace is given
> To us enslav'd, but custody severe;
> And stripes and arbitrary punishment
> Inflicted—What peace can we return?
> But to our power, hostility and hate;
> Untam'd reluctance, and revenge, though slow.
> Yet ever plotting how the conqueror least
> May reap his conquest, and may least rejoice
> In doing what we most in suffering feel. [42]

The passage is an ominous warning to slaveholders about the paradoxes of power. Ruthless suppression, Equiano implies, breeds righteous revolt; slavery promotes its own undoing. Yet that moral stance is upset by the darker resonances of the passage. For the rebellious speaker is John Milton's Beelzebub, who refuses to accept Mammon's plea to rest satisfied with the "Gems and Gold" of hell. [43] Given this provenance, how righteous is the rebellion, how edifying the pursuit of wealth? Even if Equiano intends to show the perversions of a slave economy, distortions that would dissolve in a system of free trade, he cannot banish Mammon, who thrives in such a system. A logic of exchange, in short, subverts the antislavery stance precisely as the rebellious slaves subverted their masters. All moral certainty suffers in this hellish system wrought by the lure of commerce.

The second passage offers an apparent antidote through a vision of commercial humanism. Appealing to his English readers to hasten the abolition of slavery, Equiano sees trade as the engine of culture: "Population, the bowels and surface of Africa, abound in valuable and useful returns; the hidden treasures of centuries will be brought to light and into circulation. Industry, enterprize, and mining, will have their full scope, proportionably as they civilize. In a word, it lays open an endless field of commerce to the British manufactures and merchant adventurer. The manufacturing interest and the general interests are synonymous" (2:190). Equiano's appeal to the general interests of manufacturers invokes the most enlightened sentiments of his day. For the muzzles and whips of slavery he would substitute the effects of civilization, including the saving influences of Christianity. But the taint of exchange that suborned the antislavery passage is not eliminated here, for the apparent benevolence masks a troubling imbalance. Africans can receive enlightenment only by forgoing the pastoral blessings that, as Equiano put it in chapter 1, allowed them to remain insulated from the "debauch[ing]" "refinements" of foreign luxuries (1:9). It is this new element of compulsion, all but invisible to eighteenth-century advocates of commercial humanism, that has so disturbed modern readers. Even if, as Houston Baker suggests, the appeal was progressive in an era long before widespread colonization of Africa, the passage remains curiously divided, as if the intrinsic values Equiano once saw in his homeland have little utility on the world stage. Once again, exchange shatters the symmetry of the text's moral project.[44]

These instabilities of subversion and benevolence, of money and charity, are the dialectical core of Equiano's narrative. Starting with a nostalgic portrait of republican simplicity in Africa, one stressing the intrinsic values of compassionate community, Equiano struggles to master a different code that assigns value according to extrinsic relations in distant markets. Goods that were once saturated with social meaning become mere instruments of trade, the profits of which yield self-ownership. But commercial mastery does not replace the aboriginal compassion. Rather, Equiano's wide experience represents the effort to graft an earlier intimacy onto the new, extrinsic relations of trade. His commitment to commercial humanism—to the exchange of republican feeling for commodities— involves him in an endless circulation, as if he were attempting to preserve the face-to-face world of his African past. But his longing for intimacy cannot quite

overcome the anonymity and domination of the Atlantic market, and his efforts to
fashion a truly spiritual economy remain compromised. Religious feeling alone,
his narrative demonstrates, cannot undo the market's double binds.

Such ambiguities, in turn, reflect the complicated attitudes toward consumption held by many of Equiano's readers. As Charlotte Sussman demonstrates,
British antislavery activists saw colonial produce as seductive poisons. In their
eyes, the tea, sugar, coffee, and rum that so stimulated consumer demand invited
cannibalism, since the commodities were purchased through the blood and bodies of slaves. But that "consuming anxiety" did not provoke a rejection of trade.
Most British opponents of slavery, Sussman argues, were commercial humanists,
republican advocates of free trade who fashioned a revolutionary vision of consumers as "powerful individuals who controlled the conditions of production in
other parts of the world." That compassionate embrace of commerce, however,
was counterbalanced by an equally powerful fear of contagion, the desire "to
keep their own culture pure of disgusting items, as well as of disgusting peoples
and practices."[45] As an African engaging in colonial trade, Equiano both eased
and aroused such consuming anxieties. His efforts to define a purified exchange
attempt to satisfy the contradictory demands of his republican audience.

Significantly, Equiano's principal tool for confronting such contradictions is
an accounting procedure. "Alligation," the last accounting term the author uses in
reporting on his business studies in London (2:64), is the operation for combining
ingredients of different values to yield a product of a specified purity or price. The
*OED* calls alligation " 'The Rule of Mixtures': the arithmetical method of solving
questions concerning the mixing of articles of different qualities or values." In
light of Equiano's extraordinary career, however, alligation is no merely neutral
function of trade. Rather, it is a metaphor for the constant adjustments of an Anglo-
African Christian adventurer striving for purity in a field of shifting values. At
moments of greatest conflict, Equiano makes his most determined adjustments—
alligations that strive to smooth over the text's double binds. But it is a sign of the
narrative's commercial restlessness that no adjustment is definitive, and Equiano
must constantly retrace the circles he has squared. *The Interesting Narrative* is a
record of Equiano's dialectical progress through this broken field, a progress as
restless and divided as the market he so vigorously served.

Perhaps Equiano's most formidable adjustment involved his initial portrait of
Africa. His challenge here was twofold: to present his origins sympathetically

and to suggest their linkage to the ideological world of which he became a part. In his capacity as travel narrator, moreover, he would have to measure his authority against the accumulated weight of observers' reports, many of them commissioned by state-chartered trading companies and thus bearing official status. The composite image of the African that emerges from these accounts is not only of a primitive, but of an economic primitive—one who lacks the skills to participate in a free-market economy. Almost all travelers, for example, found Africans lazy. In his standard eighteenth-century travel compendium, Thomas Astley reported of Guinea males that only the "wretchedly poor worked," the rest preferring to "lay the whole Burden of their Work on their Wives and Slaves." Among the Mandingo "Self-Preservation" alone provoked a "Spirit of Industry" lasting for the brief two-month harvest season; "All the rest of the Year they do nothing but gossip from House to House."[46] The same portrait emerged in more sympathetic accounts. To John Corry, the African was a noble savage, "his wants . . . supplied without laborious exertion, his desires . . . gratified without restraint, [so that] his soul remains in peaceful indolence and tranquillity, and his life glides on in voluptuous apathy."[47] Equally suspect was African thievishness. A popular anecdote depicted how Africans traded with their hands while they filched with their toes, drawing an object to their ankles and seizing it behind their waist. Indeed, so adept were the natives of Whydah, that a Frenchman complained, "they understood the Art of Thievery better than the Cutpurses and Pickpockets of *Paris*," and when challenged, provokingly ask "whether you can imagine they would work for such small Wages, without the Liberty of stealing."[48] Such people violated the two principal tenets of bourgeois conduct: industry and respect for property.

Understanding the motives behind this hostile composite, Equiano had to absorb its criticisms before he could refute them. If the perverse and child-like Africans were ripe for exploitation because they ignored market discipline, Equiano would need to demonstrate that they were above the market—not only pastoral but almost Christian in their simplicity. Among the most prominent features of this counterassessment, largely borrowed from Anthony Benezet's *Some Historical Account of Guinea* (1771), is Benin's serene virtue—diligent, modest, corporate. The land promoted a calm, almost unconscious harmony in which the self dissolved into the timeless cycles of communal life, an order Equiano captures in his description of a family compound. At the center of the compound stands the master's house, surrounded concentrically by those of his wives and slaves, who in turn have families of their own. Each fenced compound, then, presents "the appearance of a village" within the larger structure of village life (1:11–12). Slaves, too, are treated like family members, and when any house is erected, "the whole neighbourhood afford their unanimous assistance" (1:12–13), so that family and village coincide. Agriculture is pursued in common, and rituals of love and war, illness and worship prescribe the fixed principles of a communal life. To republicans struggling with the irrationalities of trade, that life must have seemed nothing short of benign.

Essakan incorporation, however, does not demonstrate mere ignorance of the market and its demands. Rather, Equiano makes clear, Essakans have been shrewd observers of commercial life and have absorbed from its practices only what can be morally justified. His chief evidence is their treatment of *"Oye-Eboe"* (1:13), or Aro traders, involved in the Atlantic economy. The villagers barter their wood and potash for guns and gunpowder but will not allow the traders free passage before they can certify their most valuable commodity, slaves. Those dealing in kidnapped slaves, rather than in slaves condemned through war or crime, presumably merit punishment. But Equiano's term for the traders—"red men living at a distance" (1:13)—also suggests his larger design, to demonstrate a principled *opposition* distancing the villagers from such commerce. Thus not only do the Igbo satisfy most of their needs indigenously, they hardly have money at all: "As we live in a country where nature is prodigal of her favours, our wants are few, and easily supplied; of course we have few manufactures. . . . But these make no part of our commerce, the principle [*sic*] articles of which . . . are provisions. In such a state, money is of little use; however we have some small pieces of coin, if I may call them such. They are made something like an anchor; but I do not remember either their value or denomination" (1:13). It may well be, as Adiele Afigbo suggests, that Equiano was simply too young when he left Benin to have remembered such details—or that, as Vincent Caretta implies, he merely manufactured them—but his distortions remain significant. In fact, Benin had a thriving commerce, extensive markets, and widely circulating currency— in short, a well-established system of exchange. Equiano's decision to discount these features (which, Afigbo notes, he could have easily discovered from fellow Igbo slaves) is consonant with the ideological perspective he had adopted.[49] His Africa, like the dreams of a republican America revived by market crisis, remains the antithesis of competitive individualism.

In Marxian terms, a system without money is one in which use-value predominates, individuals enjoy an unmediated relation to things, and goods retain an intrinsic value untarnished by exchange. The same sense of the intrinsic can be seen in Equiano's discussion of a social sign he calls the "Embrenche," the ceremonial scar marking Igbo nobility. By peeling away a layer of skin on the forehead, one could become quite literally a marked man, distinctive as a ruler or judge, but equally a marker, one taking his place in a series of those similarly distinguished. Like all goods in Benin, such men were at once communal and immediately identifiable, their social designation unambiguous. The fact that Equiano's account of the Embrenche confuses Igbo scarification, *igbu ichi*, with a designation for elders, *Ndicichie*, [50] only reinforces its social function. His Benin is stable, communal, and rigorously precommercial.

And yet, in a key adjustment of values, Equiano also stresses the industry of these precapitalists. Africans, he remarks, are "habituated to labour from [their] earliest years," and since diligence procures wealth, they have "no beggars" (1:15). Far from being lazy, Essakans are the very model of diligence, a point Equiano underscores in one of his first significant instances of alligation. "The West India planters," he asserts, "prefer the slaves of Benin or Eboe, to those of any other part of Guinea, for their hardiness, intelligence, integrity, and zeal" (1:15). The challenge to interpretation here, similar to that in the passages on British manufactures and slave rebellions mentioned above, involves a clash of perspectives that Equiano intends to harmonize. By invoking the diligence of his countrymen, Equiano continues the account of their pastoral superiority. Even when pressed into slavery, Essakans summon their native dignity and resourcefulness. But the words "hardiness, intelligence, integrity, and zeal" can have little meaning when attached to the murderous efficiency of the sugar trade, which killed up to half of its newly imported slaves within three years. [51] Viewed from the narrator's mature perspective, slavery might well seem an apprenticeship in self-reliance, but the zeal belonged exclusively to the absentee owners and overseers who worked their slaves to death. In part, the claim is a shrewd move to stimulate his readers' benevolence by making Africans more like themselves—in the same way that Equiano claims biblical status for Essakans. But the statement also shows how the text's key terms circle back on themselves, undoing their cultural work. The industry of a pastoral laborer can scarcely be comprehended in terms of the systematic exploitation that characterized slavery in the Atlantic world. The logic of exchange subverts the purity of his abandoned home.

During the long passage from Essaka to the Atlantic, pastoralism is decisively replaced by a more enduring identity: the consumer good. As he makes his way to the coast in chapter 2, Equiano faithfully notes every encounter. In Tinmah, after being separated from his sister, he first tastes sugar cane (1:44); later he would note the "iron pots, and . . . European cutlasses and cross bows" common in a more remote region (1:47). On the slave ship he tastes his first liquor (1:51), and on the Campbell plantation in Virginia he is transfixed by a watch and a portrait, among the eighteenth century's most prominent signs of status. Even before he could speak his captors' language, Equiano was absorbing the language of trade.

Along with his first slave position comes a heightened awareness of the wider commerce in which he figures. As Equiano notes the price that Michael Henry Pascal paid for him, he also discusses the "fine large ship, loaded with tobacco" (1:67) on which they return to England. Each initiation into a wider realm of experience is greeted with a similar expansion in commodities. Aboard the *Royal George*, "the largest ship I had ever seen," Equiano is greeted with "shops or stalls of every kind of goods, and people crying their different commodities about the ship as in a town" (1:83, 84). Once baptized and with the Mediterranean fleet, he registers his familiarity with the English world through his own ability to command commodities—from the "various fruits in great plenty" (1:97) he buys in Gibraltar and Barcelona to the sugar and tobacco he purchases for a shipboard patron, Daniel Queen (1:122), to the prize money he boldly demands of James Doran. If T. H. Breen is correct in arguing that the ability to make choices in the marketplace conferred a measure of autonomy even to marginal participants like colonial women,[52] then Equiano's epic account of his manumission is doubly significant. Not only is it the record of a subaltern mastering a repressive apparatus, as Houston Baker argues;[53] it is also a testament to how the market can confer that "industry and zeal" that are so great a part of Equiano's self-fashioning, as if the very ability to direct commodities imposes an integrity of its own. So, too, the emphasis on consumption helps explain one of Equiano's greatest initial fears, that Europeans would kill and eat him. If the control of goods helps to bring Gustavus Vassa into being, then his own disposition as a commodity is tantamount to annihilation. Much of the text's drama involves Equiano's negotiating between these alternatives.

But Equiano's absorption in the market exposes another one of its principles, capable at all times of overturning that hard-won integrity. While the activity of trade may promote autonomy, the accidents of trade, its essential fluctuation, may crush the individual. Chief among those subversions is the instability of market signifiers, each of which confirms his status as object upon which others confer meaning. The most powerful is the writer's changing name. Originally named Olaudah, which signifies "fortunate" or "having a loud voice" (1:22), he is renamed Jacob by an early master, then renamed Gustavus Vassa against his will. He is even beaten into acceptance of the new name, an economic sign forcibly proclaiming the exchange value others have delegated. With his variety of names, Equiano comes to signify nothing so much as the very principle of commerce. But this local exchange is merely part of a more comprehensive ambiguity in which all signs are relative. On a campaign against Louisbourgh his ship encounters what were thought to be confederates, until the opposing ship hoists French colors and attacks (1:88–89). Sometime later he is conducted to a woman who looks a great deal like his sister; but "on talking to her, I found her to be of another nation" (1:98). Other signs are simply inexplicable: in Gibraltar he sees a soldier hanging by his heels (1:98); in Savannah he attends the deathbed of a reputedly rich man who turns out to be impoverished (2:8). Even as a freeman he is often betrayed, cheated in transactions and threatened with imprisonment or enslavement, like the free black carpenter he knows who, seeking payment for work, is thrown in jail, accused of arson, and deported (2:18).

Such ambiguities are more than the perverse marks of racism: they suggest the logic of consumption itself. "Could commodities themselves speak," Marx suggests, "they would say: Our use-value may be a thing that interests men. [But i]t is no part of us as objects. . . . In the eyes of each other we are nothing but exchange values."[54] Exchange splits the unitary object into a "double existence . . . in which . . . it is a mere symbol, a cipher for a relation of production," measured by an equally empty sign. Gold, the mercantilist standard, Marx argues, is useful not "because it alone expresses *an authentic value,* but because as money it does *not* express *value at all,* but . . . merely carries its own quantitative definition on its forehead."[55] Equiano's Embrenche has thus been replaced by a sign of vacancy, an economic cipher in a sign system in which all meaning is mutable. In this universe there are no distinctive marks; rather, Equiano himself becomes a mark in a savagely symbolic economy. If he is to survive and make sense of these predatory values, he will need to peel away illusory skins and invest them with intrinsic meaning.

The most important element in this countercurrency is feeling. With a self-fashioning vigor akin to his market activity, Equiano uses sentiment to mark his transformation. Like Farmer James, measuring the marketplace through depths of inexpressible emotion, he begins the process of change with an almost inarticulate violence. The horrors surrounding his enslavement strain his powers of speech. When his sister is taken from him, he feels a "distraction not to be described" (1:36). Removed from an early, kind African master and returned to the uncircumcised coffles bound for the coast, he is thrown from a "state of bliss" into a scene of "inexpressible" torment (1:46). There is a direct link between these inarticulate torments and Equiano's inability to speak alien languages. In Virginia, he is "exceedingly miserable" and feels himself worse off than fellow Africans, "for they could talk to each other, but I had no person to speak to that I could understand" (1:64). The most haunting instrument of torment he records is a muzzle that locked a slave's mouth "so fast that she could scarcely speak" (1:65). The enforced silence makes him wish for death. Aboard his first ship, Equiano's inability "to talk much English" increases his terror that he will be sacrificed to the sea (1:72). Significantly, even well after he assures us that he has mastered language, feeling, and the torments of displacement, Equiano does not lose sight of these primal impulses. Wandering in the alien territory of Christian doctrine, he once again confronts "unspeakable" horrors and "uncommon commotions within, such as few can tell aught about" (2:111, 113). Such riotous feelings remain in marked tension with the global benevolence he later professes, suggesting the fragility of his search for self-mastery. The alien will need to find a new language to express the burdens he has assumed.

In his role as native entrepreneur, mastery is a process of replacing emotion with reason, the overpowering sensations of enslavement with the neutral descriptions of the world traveler surveying and cataloging experience. Accordingly, almost every aspect of Equiano's experience follows the same design. An initial period of shock, when his astonishment is so profound as to threaten annihilation, gradually fades as he acquires more knowledge. His diligence eventually allows him to master the alien code, whereupon he turns his mastery upon the white world, professing shock at any violation of the rational structure he has discovered. In this manner, Equiano not only saves his readers from their excesses, but also claims a personal stake in their salvation. Single-handedly, he vaults from the position of captive to that of disciplinarian, a leap made more secure by his own widely varied experience.

The most vivid example of this change involves Equiano's mastery of his culture shock. In his passage from Essaka through Benin to the slave ship, he is often "amazed" (1:47), "filled . . . with surprise" (1:60), "beyond measure astonished"

(1:48). Much of this language, with its naïve repetitiveness, is intended to evoke sympathy for the untried boy as he confronts Europeans. But the text also indicates how his old self must be extinguished and reconstituted before he is able to survive. One early sequence may suggest the subtlety of the pattern. Aboard the slave ship bound for Barbados, Equiano first sees sailors using the quadrant and is suitably astonished, whereupon the sailors allow him to look through it. "The clouds appeared to me to be land, which disappeared as they passed along," a phenomenon that heightens his "wonder" and persuades him that he is "in another world" (1:59). Soon, however, he is confined below deck, convinced that he "should be eaten by these ugly men" (1:59). He reemerges in a Barbadian merchant's yard, where the houses and horses "filled [him] with surprise" (1:60), so different was this world from that of Africa. Surprise thus functions as an instrument, much like the quadrant, for registering things from afar, but surprise also makes the experience less threatening. The very repetition of the formula renders the encounter more intelligible, capable of being plotted and endured. The radical shifts in perspective disclosed by the quadrant are already part of a pattern that measures the relations between objects, encodes an exchange.

Equiano uses the same terms to assess other alien discourses he eventually masters, including Christianity, for which the believer's awestruck reverence becomes the means toward acceptance. On board the *Etna,* he relates, Daniel Queen taught him many scriptures he "did not comprehend" (1:121). But astonishment restores Equiano's perspective: "I was wonderfully surprised to see the laws and rules of my own country written almost exactly here; a circumstance which I believe tended to impress our manners and customs more deeply on my memory" (1:121–22). Even as he severs himself from tribal ritual, Equiano imagines recovering Africa through the Bible, as the uncertainties surrounding him begin to acquire a new symmetry.

But the route from uncertainty to self-mastery is a dialectical one, marked by the renewed need for alligation and the shadow of servitude. Two symmetrical instances will reveal Equiano's constant, often tenuous adjustments. His first moments on the slave ship, he tells us, threw him into a dead faint, so horrified was he by the menacing environment. The shaggy-haired whites, the copper cauldron, the hold he is soon thrust into, with its riot of noxious odors, force him into one of the captive's most familiar attitudes, as he is deprived of all sensation. Here, once again, is Equiano's record of the inexpressible, the point at which the intensity of his emotion defies all available language. Later on, the same scene becomes a typological drama designed to illustrate self-mastery. Now a free sailor aboard the *Nancy*, Equiano appropriates the authority that whites abandon and delivers slaves languishing in the hold. But the market's encrypted logic subverts his authority and disturbs the parable he has constructed. The *Nancy* episode reveals the enduring ambiguities of Equiano's position.

The details of the episode are well known. In an ill-advised trip during a bad storm, Captain William Phillips resigns himself to fate. Allowing the sloop to drift toward some rocks, he refuses to take charge until it is too late, orders the ship abandoned, and directs the crew to nail shut the hatches to prevent a "cargo" of slaves from swamping the lifeboats. Equiano vigorously protests and saves the slaves as well as the white sailors too weak or drunk to abandon the wreck. Acting as "a kind of chieftain amongst them" (2:36) in the absence of white authority, Equiano conducts the evacuation to a nearby island, then leads the search for a relief ship that returns for the castaways. The passage is a telling indictment of white men, who did nothing to save themselves, "but lay about the deck like swine" (2:35). Equiano alone had the full humanity to assume command.

That command, though, is qualified by both God and Mammon. As a parable of Christian conduct, Equiano's actions have an almost prophetic power. The wreck, he is convinced, was his responsibility. Having thoughtlessly "Damn[ed] the 'vessel's bottom out' " (2:29) in a fit of rage, he is horrified when the oath comes true. The moral irony only heightens his guilt, which becomes unendurable when he hears the captain's order to sacrifice the slaves. "I thought that my sin was the cause of this," he remarks, "and that God would charge me with these people's blood" (2:32). It is at this point that Equiano faints, recapitulating the earlier moment when he first realized the consuming power of slavery. Now, however, the soulless sacrifice of bodies is invested with a deeper feeling, as Equiano seeks to redeem his "sin" by saving the ship. The drama thus demonstrates the humble egotism of the Christian seeker who, struck with the high importance of his struggle, projects it on the world. God has arranged the episode to clarify Equiano's self-control. And yet his salvific role here does not entirely free him from sin, since he is still tethered to the slave trade, which provides the ironic platform from which he launches his parable. In becoming a kind of chieftain among them, Equiano has not so much surmounted the whites as adopted their position, using the slaves to measure his own purity. Christian mastery, at this point in the text, is measured through lost souls.

A parallel instance registering the contradictions of mastery occurs in the much-discussed trope of the talking book. Equiano marks every stage of his literacy, from the instruction the Guerin sisters give him to the lessons he receives aboard the *Etna*. Circumscribing those incidents are strikingly parallel scenes. In the first, Equiano admits to having "often taken up a book, and . . . talked to it, and then put my ears to it, when alone, in hopes it would answer me" (1:75), confessing his disappointment at the book's silence. As Henry Louis Gates Jr. suggests, this action is the mark of an oral sensibility,[56] and Equiano's inclusion of it underscores the initial confusion of Western signs, the mastery of which will confirm cultural authority. His struggles with the legacy of this moment mark his emergence from mere astonishment to highly articulate feeling. Late in the text, however, in one of Equiano's most dubious ventures, the same image becomes the sign of a complex and compromised power.

Having accompanied Dr. Charles Irving to Nicaragua to attempt to establish an English beachhead in that strategic region, Equiano is forced to confront an unruly crowd of natives. Although the neighboring Indians are so modest as to remind him of Essakans, the visiting governor and his party soon spark a riot by their officious behavior. As in the *Nancy* episode, white authority fails. Irving absconds, and left alone, Equiano must improvise. Recalling "a passage I had read in the life of Columbus, when he was amongst the Indians in Mexico or Peru, where . . . he frightened them, by telling them of certain events in the Heavens," he threatens to "take the book (pointing to the Bible), read, and *tell* God to make them dead" (2:140–41). The stratagem works "like magic" (2:141), and the Indians soon disperse. In this scene the book does indeed talk, and it is Equiano's voice it enunciates—a voice, however, in which Christianity and the imperial vantage coincide. By engaging in the stratagem, Equiano protects innocent neighbors from persecution. But he does so by (mis)appropriating the figure of God to preserve the colonial subjection of slaves. Here, Beelzebub's argument is fairly turned on its head: the subaltern assures his conquest by invoking the arbitrary power of God, sanctifying a commerce menaced by riotous appetite. The rational calculation of Europeans purifies the base instincts of natives, even as the natives figure forth the desires driving the colonists themselves.

The episodes on the *Nancy* and in Nicaragua suggest the continuing difficulties Equiano faced in maintaining a balance between severely conflicting imperatives.

Having embraced the self-interest of the marketplace, he both reviled and reiterated its tactics. But the lost integrity of his homeland survived in two larger movements the text traces, one toward the spiritualizing of commerce, the other toward the economizing of God.

One of the most obvious yet most impressive of Equiano's adjustments is his bold association of free trade with the principles of Christianity. If, as a Protestant heritage informed him, a saint's increase in store denoted an increase in grace, then any violation of that equation ought to summon God's wrath. In a manner his American readers, many of them industrious artisans,[57] could easily understand, Equiano lovingly marked the former half of the equation, allowing righteousness to march in lockstep with money. In Santa Cruz, for example, his attempt to sell fruit fails when whites steal the entire consignment. "Thus, in the very minute of gaining more by three times than I ever did by any venture . . . before, was I deprived of every farthing I was worth" (1:170). But as he sees his freedom vanishing he pursues the men, retrieves two bags, and calls on God to preserve him—whereupon he is able to resell the fruit for a profit. "Such a surprising reverse of fortune in so short a space of time seemed like a dream, and proved no small encouragement for me to trust the Lord in any situation" (1:171). Later, Thomas Farmer offers the free Equiano two bullocks to trade in the West Indies but at the last minute substitutes turkeys to save room. When a storm overtakes the ship and brings on the deaths not only of the bullocks but of the captain himself, Equiano rejoices that both he and his produce survived. Noting that he cleared a 300 percent profit, he calls the episode "a particular providence of God" (2:26). Just as trade could be rendered rational, so virtue was measurable, and Equiano duly recorded every entry.

One of the strengths of this theism, and a comfort to readers battered by economic disruptions of their own, was that accident could be personalized. Like the Americans who, suffering from postwar recession, blamed their problems on British merchants and Indians, Equiano could use his own dramatic experience to account for the market's irrationalities. If the market functioned according to providential law, then any violations of that law were either satanic plots or accesses of madness. In rapid succession late in the text, Equiano provides two examples. After quitting Irving's Nicaragua plantation and contracting with the owner of a ship for passage to Jamaica, he discovers he has been tricked into serving as a common sailor and demands his freedom. The owner refuses, suspends him above the deck, and threatens to sell him into slavery, blaspheming all the while.

"I trust I prayed to God to forgive this blasphemer," Equiano remarks (2:149), as he assumes the Christ-like role of martyr for the sanctity of contract. But as if Nicaragua exerted a gravitational pull, he is faced with an even greater challenge once he escapes this master and finds passage on another ship. This time the captain, after promising to sail to Jamaica, heads south instead, persecuting the crew and whipping one man so severely that he almost dies. When the captain's wrath turns on Equiano, he beats him with a burning stick, fetches a barrel of gunpowder, and for more than an hour threatens to blow up the ship. Once again, Equiano has recourse to prayer, and his providential survival helps the reader to see the injustice of an irrational system that permits sadists "to pay free negro men for their labour in this manner" (2:160). Madmen may tyrannize, but they may also be exposed.

Conversely, Equiano could treat the inevitable contradictions in his own economic activity as spiritual crises, tests for which the measure of success was not necessarily profit but endurance. One such contradiction involved the gratitude that, as Orlando Patterson notes, often motivated the freed slave.[58] When his patron, Dr. Irving, asks Equiano to serve as a factotum, gathering slave labor and material for the Nicaragua venture, Equiano does not hesitate, but vows "to be an instrument under God, of bringing some poor sinner to my well beloved master, Jesus Christ" (2:130). His target is a Musquito prince whom the adventurers bring back with them from England to legitimate the enterprise. Taking every "pai[n]" (2:131) to enlighten the youth, even exhibiting a favorite copy of Fox's *Book of Martyrs,* Equiano makes some progress, but then stalls when the prince himself points out the contradictions his instructor has known all along: English technological superiority did not eradicate frightful abuses. As with the hostile captains, Equiano's solution is to imitate Christ. Descending from a church with the prince one Sunday, "we saw all kinds of people, almost from the church door for the space of half a mile down to the waterside, buying and selling all kinds of commodities: and these acts afforded me great matter of exhortation to this youth, who was much astonished" (2:134). Equiano assumes the role of Jesus among the money changers, whose half-mile American bazaar underscores the ambivalence beneath the African's gratitude. His diatribe, hidden from the reader, allows Equiano to express his most profound reservations about the abuses of exchange, even as he supports those abuses. Indeed, for the moment, he merges with the prince, who as outsider registers the astonishment that Equiano once felt for the white world. To the pious reader, such astonishment is entirely justified:

one could not remain a good Christian and reject the message behind this imitation of Jesus.

But the tactic also suggests the rigors of alligation, Equiano's continued need to adjust the components of his contradictory experience. Like his earlier remark that Igbo slaves are industrious, this appropriation of Christ allows him to criticize the very principles of a colonial endeavor to which he contributes. Both here and in the subsequent identification with Columbus, Equiano interprets all political subjection as subjection to sin, offering the pious hope that if all could be spiritually enlightened, the vicious abuses would end. And yet they did not, as he discovers when he determines to quit the venture. Although he is invaluable to Dr. Irving, he reluctantly concludes that his soul is imperiled by the "heathenish form" (2:145) of Nicaraguan life, and procures his discharge. There ensue the further series of difficulties with irrational captains, each of whom attacks Equiano's status as independent agent. And once bound for Jamaica, Equiano is confronted with the ultimate irony—that after his discharge a cruel overseer so persecuted the slaves he had procured that "every one got into a large Puriogua canoe, and endeavored to escape; but not knowing where to go, or how to manage the canoe, they were all drowned; in consequence of which the Doctor's plantation was left uncultivated, and he was now returning to Jamaica to purchase more slaves, and stock it again" (2:159–60). If Equiano feels any responsibility for this catastrophe, he does not record it. Indeed, his own sense of fleeing, like Bunyan's Christian, from the region's corruption may be fully vindicated in the episode. But the deaths also challenge his corporate responsibility, the lost communalism of an African world now distorted by slavery. Ironically, he has been returned to the position of Milton's Beelzebub, doubly bound by a trade he reviles.

Facing that contradiction is the burden of Equiano's conversion crisis, in which, as Robert Allison notes, he comes closest to addressing his own continued participation in the ambiguities of commerce.[59] After a free black shipmate, John Annis, is forcibly returned to St. Kitts and enslaved despite the legal efforts of Granville Sharp, Equiano lapses into a despair he blames on "villains in the late cause" as well as on his own spiritual poverty (2:93). But though a sojourn in London brings astonishment at the piety of some fellow Christians, he is forced to return to sea, only to be overwhelmed anew by the continued pressures and compromises of the market. Three times he asks the captain to discharge him, preferring "to beg my bread on shore rather than go again to sea amongst a people who feared not God" (2:108). Only after religious friends urge him to pursue his "lawful calling" (2:108) does he feel some relief, and he soon experiences a vivid vision of Christ relieving his sin: "Now every leading providential circumstance that happened to me, from the day I was taken from my parents to that hour, was then in my view, as if it had but just then occurred. I was sensible of the invisible hand of God, which guided and protected me, when in truth I knew it not. . . . When I considered my poor wretched state I wept, seeing what a great debtor I was to sovereign free grace" (2:111–12). Equiano's conventional formulas for grace, with their mild evocations of both debt and the invisible hand that Adam Smith would transform into economic principle, suggest how this leap of faith was designed to serve as the ultimate alligation. Just as Christ absorbs all sinners, so Christianity can absorb all sinful contradictions, relieving Equiano of his guilt over Annis as it turns his roving life into a search for grace. If the world of the market was one of fragmented and ambiguous signs, then faith alone could confer unity. In Montserrat—a demonic parody of corporate Essaka—a single plantation "might serve for a history of the whole" (1:159). Now Equiano's history, stripped to its bare spiritual essentials, could serve as a model for all true believers. Piety had rationalized the market.

How fully Equiano depended on that adjustment may be seen in the final sequence of events he narrates, those surrounding his failed appointment as a missionary and the more disastrous colonization scheme for Sierra Leone. Given Equiano's failure in the matter of Annis and the Irving plantation, his desire to "be of service in converting my countrymen to the Gospel faith" (2:165) is entirely understandable. Missionary work would allow him to exploit both the corporate and the antiauthoritarian dimensions of his faith in this essential service to imperial enterprise: he could invoke a community of believers while holding its disposition of Africans to a higher standard. Appropriately, then, the official documents thicken here, with the correspondence between him and British emissaries meant to portray this activity as the culmination of Equiano's mastery—the convergence of his literacy, his freedom, and his faith. Although the bishops decline to ordain him, he soon agrees to participate in another benevolent enterprise, as he becomes commissary for the Sierra Leone effort. Here the reader senses the intensity of Equiano's inner conflict, for the venture should have answered every one of his spiritual demands. Returning the poor to Africa under the guidance of presumably benevolent administrators, the colony should have reversed all the errors of Nicaragua. But Equiano remains suspicious, concerned over the continued involvement of "slave dealers" (2:175) and outraged by the peculations of government agents. Although he severs himself from the enterprise, at "a considerable loss in my property" (2:179), he still must read of emigrants "so wasted by their confinement [in ships] as not to survive" (2:180). Equiano duly publishes his outrage, attempting to reassert mastery by appealing to conscience, but avarice has once again usurped benevolence. Denied this final consolation, Equiano, like Farmer James, takes refuge in sentiment.

For Equiano, the answer to these double binds lies in the soaring affirmations of feeling. Having emerged from the status of a commodity to a master of commodities, he reimagines world trade as a righteous exchange of sympathy. Thomas Haskell has plausibly argued that one spur to the English abolitionist movement was the internationalism stimulated by eighteenth-century commerce. The sense of involvement with distant enterprises made merchants susceptible to other appeals, including the distress of slaves. [60] For Equiano, such sentimental commerce reunited England and Africa. "Every feeling heart," he would insist in 1814, " . . . sensibly participates of the joy, and with a degree of rapture reads of barrels of *flour* instead of *gunpowder* . . . *implements of husbandry* instead of *guns* for destruction, rapine, and murder." [61] With their crucial support, he was convinced, "[i]n a short time one sentiment alone will prevail, from motives of interest as well as justice and humanity" (*Narrative* 2:190–91), giving *"heart-felt pleasure"* to all true advocates (2:186). By imagining a sentimental union of artificers and tradesmen—a union securing the entire African continent—Equiano reconstitutes the communal ethos of his childhood on the world capitalist stage. It is a final alligation, purifying trade even as it reconfigures the boundless, all-encompassing desire that had dispersed Africans throughout the Atlantic world. Sentiment did not replace the lost intimacy, the intrinsic use-value consumed in exchange. Sentiment was a simulacrum of immediacy, an imagined substitution that gestured toward an interior state. It transformed and preserved the consuming anxieties of trade.

Although a New York edition of *The Interesting Narrative* was published in 1791, and subscriber lists indicate it had a keen artisan audience, there is little evidence that the anxious essayists of the early national period turned to Equiano for comfort. Rather, the text's significance lies in its precise formulation of the issues and the aversions that would increasingly preoccupy American market players. Confronting, as Equiano did, the market's many double binds, caught between a nostalgia for immediacy and a longing for boundless possession, writers would seize on the figure of the sentimental wanderer who exploited opportunities and united hearts. Sentimental activity, for these heirs to Equiano, became a substitute for market activity that sought to equal or better the market's profits. But sentiment alone could not eliminate the anonymous and brutal shocks, panics, and distresses that all too frequently belied the unity of commercial feeling. In the fiction of the new republic, confronting that contradiction would be the work of the nation's most sensitive entrepreneurs: its women.

CHAPTER 3

# Lovers and Citizens

§◆.

Late in 1797, as French attacks threatened American shipping and the nation's economy slid into depression, the *Philadelphia Minerva* ran a "moral tale" that captured the sense of crisis. Set in England and modeled after Henry MacKenzie's *The Man of Feeling,* "The Impressed Seaman" limns the complex associations between sentiment and international commerce that would engross Americans before the War of 1812. The protagonist, Henry Randolph, sees his plans for worldly success disrupted as he is torn from his family and made the passive instrument of British aggression. In a scene often repeated in the coming decade, the moment of impressment transformed Randolph from self-interested agent into lachrymose victim: "Instantly they seized upon their defenceless prey, and notwithstanding the bitter cries of his wife, the little Harriet and her companion, hurried him away from a home of peace and comfort. . . . In vain did he entreat for a little time, to reconcile his Nancy to the bitterness of her fate; strangers to humanity, . . . it [*sic*] did not belong to the horrid business of these protected plunderers to attend to the wailings of the wife and child."[1] As the officers pursue their "horrid business," Randolph becomes both a casualty of war and a victim of seduction, whose vain entreaties could not prevent the plunder of his body. Sentiment has turned heroism into rape, forever robbing Randolph of his prowess.

But Randolph's is not the tale's most striking transformation. After returning from the war to find his wife dead and his daughter eloped, he abandons himself to beggary and highway robbery before sinking into decrepitude. On a friend's farm, he is reunited with his daughter, who has in the interim resisted temptation, won the heart of a virtuous lord, and inherited his estate. While the broken father has amply illustrated the author's injunction to "posses[s] a heart ready to burst on the relation of human misery,"[2] it is the daughter who has literally saved the family fortune. The tale has used a sentimental currency to convert male impotence into female enterprise.

This chapter will trace that conversion through the public debates and critical fictions of the early national period. I will argue that the language of sentiment, long used to imagine a virtuous polity, was increasingly strained when called on to account for severe economic disruptions at home and abroad. A discourse that saw feeling as the expression of enlightened self-control suddenly had to represent abstract or predatory economic forces that denied self-control. The assault on republican autonomy had two dialectical effects: a preoccupation with languishing, sentimental men on the order of Henry Randolph, and a groping toward an alternative imagery of sentimental and pliant circulation whose chief exemplars were women. Rooted in the links between feeling and commodities explored by Equiano, this second strain used the exquisite sensibility of females to comprehend the erratic nature of commerce. By circulating without succumbing, pliant women like Harriet Randolph could attempt to restore commercial propriety.

In the largest sense, these critical fictions sought to rescue the founders' vision of republican prosperity by conceiving commercial relations in sentimental terms. Accordingly, I begin the discussion by examining how economic pressures forced men like James Madison to recur to a language of sentiment to hold together an increasingly diverse polity. Ideals of affectionate union, however, became difficult to sustain during ensuing economic crises, as merchants, robbed of autonomy, cast themselves as sentimental victims of predatory foreigners and a callous federal government. The debates they stimulated in Congress will frame my consideration of four fictions that responded to market disruptions by imagining new uses for the imagery of feeling. In *Margaretta,* Martha Meredith Read sends her heroine throughout the Atlantic world in quest of a compromised purity. Like Equiano, she longs to preserve intrinsic merit, yet she must do so in an environment that punishes rigid adherence to virtue. Read's character points to a new mood of market pragmatism stimulated by the travails of the merchants whose movements she paralleled. The figure of the circulating sentimentalist reappears in Isaac Mitchell's *The Asylum,* in which a bankrupt lover demonstrates his constancy by ranging widely across the Atlantic, staving off catastrophe through an ardent display of feeling. Here, what Adam Smith disparaged as effeminate indulgence in sensibility comes to serve the higher ends of economic prudence. In a final pair of best-selling pamphlets, *The Female Marine* and *The Surprising Adventures of Almira Paul,* female *imprudence* becomes a means of salvation, as the anonymous author turns a fallen woman into a military hero. In all of these critical fictions, the plasticity of feeling, long used as a metaphor for market activity, allows writers to see sensitive women as economic saviors. Beleaguered men battered by market distress could console themselves through these tales of sympathetic entrepreneurs.

In a discussion of *The Theory of Moral Sentiments* (1759), John Dwyer argues that Adam Smith had little use for naked sentiment. Mere feeling, which Smith termed "humanity," sapped manly spirit, he thought, turning men of action into "indolent and irresolute" figures of "little self-command." "Humanity," Smith maintained, "is the virtue of a woman."[3] To rise to the level of principled action meant exercising a different faculty that Smith called "sympathy." Sympathy was the ability to moderate feeling, to control one's responses so as to achieve the precise balance, the perfect pitch, that would secure social concord. Unlike "humanity," sympathy was not opposed to selfishness; indeed, the exercise of sympathy helped to convert self-interest into ethical conduct. It was precisely because the "weaker passion," as Dwyer puts it, "the desire for fellow feeling," could never displace human egotism that Smith stressed the prudent effects of sympathy. The prudent man thus learned "the fundamental lesson of an ethical life": the self-command that turned vital selfishness into vigorous cooperation. "Although there may never be unisons," Smith insisted, "there may be concords."[4]

Dwyer's emphasis on the relation between self-command and fellow feeling helps to frame early national approaches to economic crisis. Rooted in ideals of republican community, sympathy also allowed spokesmen to imagine elite control through an imagery of self-command. In emergencies, however, even the most disciplined republicans often sought refuge in the more primitive feelings that Smith termed "humanity." Indulging in ardent feeling for its own sake became a way of acknowledging the breakdown in self-command without sacrificing the hope of ultimate authority. It was the tension between sympathy and humanity that increasingly characterized public responses to economic crisis during the years leading to the War of 1812. Those responses, in turn, were involved in a crucial problem that sentimental fictions addressed: the representation of diffuse economic effects in immediately apprehensible terms. Humanity domesticated the abstract forces of an emerging free-market society. Sympathy offered the distant prospect of control.

The problem had been raised early in the debate over the Constitution, as theorists sought a formula for social adhesiveness. Antifederalists like "Brutus" worried that national representation in Congress implied an unconscionable sacrifice of intimacy. His sense that a mere sixty-five men could not possibly "hold the sentiments, possess the feelings"[5] of countless citizens urges the claims of local experience as a means of national union. Native humanity, the immediate exchange of feeling, could best secure the commonwealth. A countervailing sympathy characterized the paternalistic vision of Nicholas Collin. "A well-ordered political society," he declared in 1787, "is a theatre for . . . the best feelings of the human heart." Only the most "enlightened and exalted minds" could inspire the "respectful affection" and "grateful esteem" of the many.[6] With the "diabolical outrages"[7] of Daniel Shays's mob so fresh in mind, it was imperative that commoners learn deference, participating in "the sympathetic passions of hopes and fears, grief and joy, admiration of worthy members, [and] dislike of the bad" that would secure order.[8] A properly regulated sympathy, Collin assured his readers, could bind the most contentious union.

Characteristically, *The Federalist* sought a middle course between these positions. Common citizens, Hamilton argues in Number 35, will naturally select their social betters to represent them, men whose broad experience would compel their performance as "patron and friend."[9] The commanding sympathies of rank would inevitably produce reciprocal obligations. "Duty, gratitude, interest, ambition itself," he argues in Number 57, "are the cords by which they will be bound to fidelity and sympathy with the great mass of the people" (2:156). But the attachments could also be more visceral, the binding cords more voluntary. "Hearken not to the unnatural voice which tells you that the people of America, knit together as they are by so many chords of affection, can no longer live together as members of the same family," pleads Madison in *Federalist* Number 14 (1:84). Were the nation to be threatened by faction, it could seek refuge in the supreme fiction of a universal affective bond.

And yet, the very attempt to imagine a unity of feeling was inherently compromised by the breadth of the enterprise. With Lockean rigor, Madison exposed the difficulties in envisioning an almost boundless constituency as diffuse as nature itself. "Every man," he wrote in *Federalist* Number 37, "will be sensible of this difficulty, in proportion as he has been accustomed to contemplate and discriminate objects, extensive and complicated in their nature." With so many "departments" in natural and social life, it was difficult, if not impossible, to trace the "distinctive characters" of each "province," the "delicate shades and minute gradations" that conceal their elusive "boundaries" (2:5). Although Madison's strategy here is concessive, raising these taxonomic fears to allay them, his comments suggest the underlying anxiety of a mind suddenly confronted with a heterogeneous mass of phenomena, a "complexity of objects" (2:6) almost boundless in their variety. The problem was how to retain control in the face of a diffuse, recalcitrant mass. Smith's "humanity," in this case, became an apt metaphor for the fluid uncertainties of republican life, dissolving the boundaries between individuals and threatening to erase the distinctions between leaders and the led. Sympathy sharpened the political equation by offering a model for control, but humanity exposed the polity's innumerable and shifting variables.

In the narrow sense, these were the concerns of an elite struggling to share power—issues that would gradually fade as Federalists and Jeffersonians gave way to Jacksonians in the nineteenth century.[10] But in broader terms, Madison's survey suggested the difficulties involved in confronting what J. G. A. Pocock has called the "moving objects" of a new commercial order.[11] To master that order, as Madison implied, one had to define it; but how was it possible to define an inchoate, ever-shifting mass? The problem intensified as spokesmen tried to imagine their place in an "extensive and complicated" national economy where class boundaries and the relations among individuals were more volatile. The debates surrounding three policy issues in the early republic—the national debt, the panic of 1797, and Jefferson's embargo—suggest that spokesmen remained divided in their responses to economic crisis. While they clamored for control, Republicans and Federalists alike recurred to a language of feeling that expressed their sense of "irresolute" (and womanly) humanity, the only means of representing the crisis. As international pressures intensified and curtailed commercial activity, merchants increasingly portrayed themselves as suffering victims in a national seduction narrative that assessed their reversals through raw feeling. But that collapse of self-command spawned an opposite imagery of resolute and circulating women who rose above seduction to conquer market problems—a rhetoric that the era's best-selling fictions amply explored. These figures did not solve the problem of how to maintain autonomy in an environment that savaged self-control. Rather, they suggested a shift in the principle of autonomy itself, a fusion of sympathy and womanly humanity. It would be left to a succeeding era to reclaim that fusion for men.

The origins of the change can be seen in the nation's earliest economic emergency, when Washington became the sympathetic savior of his languishing nation. By 1790, the national debt had ballooned to almost forty-two million dollars, imperiling both political and economic stability.[12] To establish federal credit and to maintain orderly securities markets, Alexander Hamilton proposed redeeming government certificates, issued to Revolutionary soldiers and suppliers in lieu of funds, at slightly depreciated rates. For years the paper had been nearly worthless, but with the establishment of the federal government and the news of Hamilton's plans, it had considerably appreciated—to the regret of the original holders, who had overwhelmingly sold it at steep discounts. The Treasury Secretary's proposal became an early test of the government's policy toward a commercial elite as against the claims of commoners, and elicited arguments that would become more heated and numerous in the ensuing years. Beyond the economic issues, however, loomed Madison's problem of representing a boundless field of market activity. To reward original holders meant, as the Federalist Elias Boudinot argued, chasing down every ghostly transaction in the long chain each certificate had undergone. How, he asked, could one stamp identity on such an anonymous medium? "Not from the name on the face of the paper, because it is the name of the clerk in office, the mere agent of the public. . . . Other certificates were taken out of the loan-office, by persons who were not concerned in making the loan; many neighbors sent money by one hand, who went and took out certificates in his own name, which he afterwards returned to the real lender."[13] So diffuse was the market that at no point but the present, evanescent moment could one find a foothold. All boundaries and distinctions dissolved in the continuous circulations of the certificates; the emotional investments of the original purchasers could not be recovered. For Boudinot, prudence meant abandoning local attachments in the interests of national resolve.

Into this conceptual vacuum, the proto-Republicans rushed with a tide of feeling. Madison, who led the fight for discrimination (recognition of original claims), grandly asserted that "the sufferings of the military part of the creditors can never be forgotten, while sympathy is an American virtue" (1193). Humanity, though, was not merely a political ploy, a means of striking out against Hamiltonian speculators. In an urgent sense, it was a way of making the ghostly economy visible. One finds dramatic evidence of this in Pelatiah Webster's *A Plea for the Poor Soldiers* (1790). Webster, a political essayist known for his strong advocacy of free-market principles, also clung to republican notions of a virtuous polity. Although time and market forces had scattered the original community the certificates represented, Webster proposed to recapture it by imagining the entire army once again assembled before its grieving commander. How animated, Webster exclaims, "how alive would be every *fine sensibility* of that great man, how dilated his *whole heart,*" could the original holders be located. "With what a *suffusion of pleasure,* would he *hasten* to find out these *noble spirits* in their retreats of *obscurity and distress,* extend to them *welcome relief,* and sympathize in their *joy and gladness.*"[14] Here, in what Jay Fliegelman has called the national family,[15] the bonds of affection can still hold sway. Draw aside the veil of Federalist rhetoric, and the warm, beating heart of the republic still drove economic affairs.

In Webster's scenario, Washington serves a mediatory function, one that will resonate in popular fiction through the Civil War. As embodiment of national purpose and command, the figure of Washington has the power to ease market anxieties and reassert central authority. Yet he diffuses that influence through an imagery of immediate feeling reminiscent of "Brutus's" Antifederalist "humanity." A hybrid figure, he succeeds through circulation, energetically searching for every sufferer and sharing his trials. In this manner, Washington seems both subject and sovereign, suggesting a mastery of hard economic facts that have subdued almost all his comrades. In this narrative, exchanging feeling is itself a market mechanism, an attempt to make the primary links in the transaction immediately visible and intelligible. To promote fiscal virtue, wrote Webster pointedly, we must "strain every nerve,"[16] a task superbly met by his sympathetic general. Webster's Washington thus fulfilled an ideological task that would have been almost unimaginable only three years before. His domestic economy turned Antifederalist intimacy into the exercise of Federalist command.

Seven years later, however, in the year Washington left office, a different senti-mental sufferer suggested the decay of the general's sovereignty. John Swanwick—merchant, poet, member of Congress—sent a circular to his constituents apol-ogizing for his bankruptcy. The sixteen-page document, studded with ledgers and correspondence, patiently explains how even one who traded "more ex-tensively . . . than any other merchant in the United States" could become so suddenly vulnerable.[17] The raids of French privateers had interrupted "all com-munication" (1) with his overseas agents, freezing American funds and forcing the London houses to call in their loans. Americans, "distan[t] from the scene of action," found themselves defeated "by circumstances on which they could have had no right to calculate" (1). Even the normally safer West Indies trade was interdicted because Swanwick could not get insurance, and though he "ex-erted every nerve" (3), he lost more than seventy-five thousand dollars. Now the nerves do not subdue but echo the forces that produced the crisis. Speculators are "ruin[ed]" by the panic, bankruptcies cascade, and "the state of doubt, in which our situation with the belligerent powers involved us, compleated [*sic*] the destruction of confidence" (2). Succumbing to vastly superior powers, Swanwick records his downfall as a firestorm of anxiety sweeping the whole Atlantic world. Like a sentimental victim of seduction, he has been ruined by raw feeling.

That sense accorded with a new national mood that would intensify during Jefferson's administration. "Have not our citizens lost several millions of money by unprecedented depradations . . . both by French and English?" asked a writer to the *Weekly Oracle* with typical anxiety. "Has not a great stagnation of business taken place all over America, on this account?"[18] "When we send a ship to sea," complained Swanwick in Congress in 1796, "we cannot possibly know at what port she will arrive; so uncertain is our trade."[19] Financial uncertainty lent itself to a new language of feeling that eluded sympathetic control. To languishing merchants like Swanwick, market shocks were shocks to the nerves, setting hearts fluttering with every palpitation in trade. An essayist on discrimination, for example, writing in 1792, long after Congress had decided the matter, argued that the wily creditor "instantly feels" even slight changes in value and would infect the entire economy with his "impulsive and stimulating" behavior.[20] Similarly, a satirical piece on "The Disadvantages Which Have Attended the Introduction of Nerves," published around the time of Swanwick's circular, traces the widening circles of infection. Claiming that he has noticed a marked increase in sensibility, the writer links the problem to consumption of caffeine and alcohol. "It is with great justice," he claims, " . . . that nerves are reckoned no part of the ancient human body, but a modern addition drawn from the sugar cane and sundry other foreign vegetables by means of fire." No wonder that ladies and gentlemen who imbibe the stuff are apt to become agitated by the slightest domestic incident.[21] Both merchants and their customers were increasingly caught up in an erratic and feminizing system of international trade that dissolved moral autonomy.

These anxieties reached a climax in a third set of critical responses to Jefferson's embargo. With Britain and France engaged in their epic clash of empire, American shipping suddenly became more vulnerable, and a flood of petitions from merchants, ships' captains, and insurers descended upon Congress. Seeking to cut off French supplies in the year before Trafalgar, British cruisers began seizing American merchant ships carrying produce between the West Indies and Europe. An older decision in England's Admiralty Court had allowed such commerce, so long as the ships first returned to a neutral port; but beginning in 1805, the court reversed itself, claiming that these so-called "broken voyages" had become shell games, allowing colonial provisions to reach France. As in the Revolutionary period, when British taxes spurred colonial boycotts, the House debates, widely reprinted in local newspapers, centered on nonimportation. But if the opponents remained the same, the political motives had shifted, as republicans responded to the mounting ironies of world trade. The result was an outpouring of wounded feeling.

Although Jeffersonians forced the nation to curtail Atlantic trade, they were not anticommercial ideologues. Indeed, they defended international market speculators because the tariffs they generated were paying off the national debt. Like their Federalist opponents, however, Jeffersonians were most disturbed by the prospect that Americans were no longer masters of their republican fate. "What!" shouted the merchant congressman Jacob Crowninshield. "Shall a neutral ship and cargo be captured and condemned because it was the owner's intention to send the produce to Europe to a better market than his own country afforded him? The principle is monstrous. . . . It sets reason and justice at defiance."[22] The Virginian John Jackson put the matter more succinctly and more plaintively: "nothing is safe, everything is afloat, and no man knows to whom any property belongs" (725). Commerce had come to seem violently irrational, eluding all virtuous resolve.

Other features of the controversy proved even more unsettling. In addition to interdicting supplies, the British also impressed American sailors into service on British warships. Reports abounded of Americans presenting their papers to English officers, only to see the papers thrown back at them as forgeries. Since Americans looked and acted like the English, it was impossible to assert personal identity, and once on the warship, the resisting American entered a world of arbitrary punishment and unbridled passion. Just as John Randolph of Virginia had caustically asked how it was possible to discriminate "between those products which are, and those which are not the property of an enemy" (772), so American sailors were themselves reduced to commodities and robbed of self. The delegates' response, widely repeated throughout 1806, was to insist on identity through the language of domesticity and sentiment. Dragged from their "homes"—for, maintained Andrew Gregg, "his ship is a seaman's home" (540)—such unfortunates were exposed "to the most outrageous ravages of the daring and unprincipled,"[23] "degraded," and "subject . . . to . . . disgraceful and mortifying obligations of gratitude,"[24] which were "aggravated by unprecedented circumstances of insult, oppression, and barbarity."[25] The scene was repeated in the sufferings of families like the fictional Henry Randolph's—elderly parents leaving an only son "with tears and blessings [at] the water's side," never to see him again; the "disconsolate widow, bathed in tears, surrounded by helpless orphans," or "manacled and confined in the cold damp cells of a lunatic hospital."[26] Merchants also used this language, claiming in their memorials that they were worried sick— penetrated by "mingled feelings of indignation," "commiseration," and "anxious solicitude."[27] By portraying themselves as sentimental victims, these petitioners were invoking the language of "humanity" that sought to depict irrational and distant affairs in immediate and visceral form. Such dramas of suffering, which Toby Ditz has also found among eighteenth-century merchants, literally brought the crisis home.[28]

But there is a difference between these evocations of sentimental suffering and those Ditz examines. Colonial Philadelphia merchants who portrayed their "ruin" as seduction narratives used the rhetoric to regain self-command. By describing their sentimental weakness, they could evoke the power of sympathy to distance and control painful experience. Their writing, Ditz argues, "was a reconstitution of self."[29] For Jeffersonian sufferers facing an irrational market, there was no prospect of command. Indeed, commerce seemed as volatile as a sentimentalist's overstimulated nerves. As G. W. Campbell proclaimed, "Our commerce . . . is more vulnerable than any other portion of our possessions. . . . Every impulse that is given, will be first felt by commerce, and through its medium by every other occupation in society."[30] Even more revealing is the remark of South Carolinian David Williams, an opponent of the nonimportation measures. Commercial interests, he declared, "run parallel with the other great interests of the community, and are so intimately connected that the vibration of a stroke on one, is sensibly felt by all the rest."[31] Here, the language of sentiment is made to do the work of the capricious marketplace, and it is but a step from this imagery to the treatment of merchants themselves as sentimental heroines who, in circulating for the national good, claimed that their "defenceless and unprotected state" had exposed them "to the most outrageous ravages . . . and most wanton cruelties." "[D]aring and unprincipled" foreign aggressors could not resist the "temptation to rapacity" the merchants presented and mercilessly made them "the prize of violence."[32] Trade, as one writer later put it, had become "the *sensorium of our national sensibility.*"[33] The merchant, in short, like the sentimental heroine, occupied a shifting middle ground. Both active and passive, mercenary and selfless, chaste and compromised, he figured the ideological travails of a commercial society groping for mastery. The conventions of sentiment provided a narrative for his calamities.

These appeals to sentimental suffering, however, were offset by another seduction narrative captured in the experience of Harriet Randolph. In these accounts, seduced and sentimental victims transformed themselves into invigorated heroines and entrepreneurs capable of self-command. In 1797, for example, a piece in *The New-York Weekly Magazine* followed the fortunes of Maria, who, exhausting her funds as she vainly awaits her lover, decides to go off on her own and seek work as a kitchen servant. "The wages were liberal, and . . . I endeavoured to give satisfaction to my employer."[34] Only the birth of a son and her subsequent illness force Maria to accept charity. A more striking instance of redeemed virtue appeared in *The Universal Asylum* in 1791. After Clarinda succumbed to her seducer, "[s]he did not . . . abandon herself to despair," but "summoned that resolution, which too often her sex, in similar circumstances, is incapable of exerting." Selling all her property and loaning the proceeds, she manages to live on the interest, buy a country home, and raise her child in piety.[35] A novel entitled *Sincerity,* serialized during 1803–4 in the *Boston Weekly Magazine,* takes a somewhat different tack, following Sarah Darnley as she flees a callous husband and finds work as a governess in Ireland. "I am resolved to go," she declares; " . . . to be treated either like a child, an ideot [*sic*], or a slave, is what I cannot, will not submit to."[36] The feminist Martha Meredith Read creates an equally determined heroine in her first novel, *Monima; or The Beggar Girl* (1801). Forced continually to seek work to support her bankrupt and ailing father, Monima seems vulnerable to the plots of a rejected lover. Yet through all her fainting she, too, seeks out work and manages to wound and deter the persecutor who had been secretly employing her. In these instances, sentiment propels the heroine into the wider commercial world, where she can both register and oppose its evils. The experience of subjection summons a new moral authority.

These circulating heroines do not entirely shed their vulnerability, nor do they spring forth as full-blown saviors of an economy at risk. But they do suggest an attempt to use sentimental discourse to work through the challenges to autonomy that the Atlantic conflicts had forced on all Americans. Because the sentimental heroine was presumed weak and dependent, she did not have to confront the "moral anxiet[ies]"[37] that Ditz associates with ruined men. Instead, her struggle was often one of reconstitution, the reestablishment of a stable home abandoned or undermined by failed or deceitful fathers and lovers. The moral authority she managed to recover did not erase her weakness, any more than ruined Jeffersonian entrepreneurs could easily preserve their masculine independence. But the texts to which I will now turn—Read's *Margaretta,* Mitchell's *The Asylum,* and Nathaniel Coverly's pamphlets, *The Female Marine* and *The Surprising Adventures of Almira Paul*—do suggest how popular fictions used sentimental imagery to rethink the commercial problems of the era. Their resolute women infused chastened feeling with the rigor of self-command.

## Incest and Enterprise

Conventional as it appears in many respects, Read's second novel has a radical core. In her "A Second Vindication of the Rights of Women" (1801), published in Isaac Newton Ralston's *Ladies' Monitor* along with the first several chapters of *Margaretta,*[38] Read echoed Mary Wollstonecraft in arguing that "to remedy any wide-spread evil . . . is to grasp at the root" (19). But unlike Wollstonecraft, whose radical critique extended to all of European intellectual culture, Read's fragmentary essay focused on the ambiguities of what she calls "custom"—a term that embraces both social and business practice. Custom involves unreflecting behavior and the everyday conduct of families as well as the habits of commerce. Mothers indifferently reared endanger "their daughter's temper" (19). So, too, parents moved by "mercenary" interests rather than love will ruin daughters (34), as will fathers who refuse to extract even a little time from "business" to "impress . . . daughters with a knowledge of the dignified sphere they were intended to move in" (19). The center of that sphere is what Read calls the "qualities of the heart" (19), those intrinsic values unaffected by "corroding" (20) social practices. "If nature were taken as guide to all our actions," Read declares, "the world would be one system of excellence, for in love is comprised every quality that can conduce to the purest happiness, but custom is substituted for nature, and many infringements to the indignity of human nature are sanctioned by her arbitrary sway" (35). Heart affections are thus the true measure of humanity, eclipsing the claims of reason and sordid interest.

Read's overlay of feminism by sentiment creates an interesting and important tension. Her opposition of heart and head, nature and custom, proclaims a need, like Equiano's, to defend intrinsic value against all incursions from without. The family itself is radically bifurcated in this manner, with social custom and business practices distracting from the authentic duties of love. And yet even this gesture toward purity remains compromised. Twice in the fragment, intended to appeal to "the hearts of fathers" (20), Read raises the specter of incest. Arguing that it is "natural" for men to be insinuating in courtship, she faults both schools and families for their want of institutional restraints. Even "fathers have been guilty of [seduction] . . . toward some youthfully innocent daughters" (34). Similarly, when she argues that husbands ought to treat wives with dignity, she appeals to an insinuating, almost prurient interest. Were a bright, capable daughter to be mistreated by her insecure husband, "can a father brook such treatment . . . with placidness and composure?" (20). So much more should fathers honor their own wives. Read's hypothetical question, implying either an inability to modify parental ties or an unseemly involvement in the marital affairs of one's children, suggests the difficulty she faced in finding a safe haven from custom. The heart may prompt reform in everyday practice, but the heart remained immersed in that practice, vulnerable to its intrusions and violations. It was this sense of embattled virtue that made *Margaretta* a sensitive register of the era's economic stresses. Like the merchants familiar to her husband (who helped negotiate the Jay Treaty and later headed the Philadelphia Bank), Read made a harried purity the center of her heroine's experience. Her attempt to imagine a cleansed custom not only fashioned a role for Read's modest feminism, but also tried to restore moral autonomy amid the era's poisoned trade. Margaretta's virtuous vulnerability made her an emblem of commercial sympathy.

Modeled in part on Frances Burney's *Evelina* (1778), *Margaretta* tells the story of a beautiful young foundling who seeks out her rightful, aristocratic place in society.[39] At the heart of both novels is the conflict between vulgarity and virtue; but whereas Evelina's biggest worries involve how her social gaffes will affect her reputation, Margaretta's experience is more harrowing. Forced to leave her rural home after the attentions of high-toned suitors anger her reputed father, the seventeen-year-old is adopted by a series of caretakers, all convinced that her beauty will make her fortune. The plot links her social rise to the fall of William De Burling, who renounces his shrewish but wealthy fiancée, Arabella Roulant, and his own fortune for the chance to earn a competency as a merchant, and Margaretta's hand. Hoodwinked by the enraged Roulants, Margaretta endures humiliation and seduction on a slave plantation before she is rescued by another, older suitor, Edward Montanan, with whom she later travels to England. There she resolves to marry Montanan before discovering that he is her real father, and reunites him with her real mother, the Lady Montraville, who had been ostracized for marrying a commoner and was presumed dead. As these complications are resolved, the impoverished De Burling reappears and proves himself worthy at last, the whole clan removing to republican America, where "equal rights . . . between man and man" (398) prevail. By gathering the principal characters about her, Margaretta preserves the community's virtue, as well as her own.

On one level, the novel presents the old ethical problem of how to reconcile passion and reason. In a final word to the reader, for example, the author retraces ground covered in *The Theory of Moral Sentiments,* arguing that although the desire for wealth is "one of the ruling passions of the human heart" and "gives rise to our greatest activity," these desires must be balanced by other "laws of men" so that "reason" prevails (418). So, too, the novel's dedication seeks to play off fears of exposure to the literary marketplace against the desire for fame, claiming that sympathy for the "indigent sufferer . . . is the only compensation a generous heart aspires to" and is the author's own "rich reward" (iii). The desire for wealth is no more blameworthy here than it is elsewhere in America; all actions must be weighed in the balance. De Burling's "industry, and . . . active spirit" (137) thus redound to his credit because he labors for love, whereas his father's desire to see De Burling "the richest man" around (121) sacrifices honor to wealth and must be condemned. The crucial difference involves sympathy, the ability to temper one's own desires through compassion for others. "Love all free; all unblemished; untainted with any sentiment of a mercenary nature," declares De Burling, is " . . . the offerin[g] my soul thirsts for" (47). The novel's display of sentiment is thus a kind of higher education in the moral laws of the market.

During the nonimportation crisis, however, the market was far from ideal, and aggressive but victimized merchants used the language of sympathy in contradictory ways. *Margaretta* tries to thread through these contradictions by creating a scale of benevolence. At the bottom of the scale are those characters whose compassion for the heroine is excited by selfish or mercenary motives. These include some of Margaretta's most vocal champions. A wealthy benefactress named Miranda Stewart, for example, early confesses that the girl's charms "have so roused every tender feeling of my heart" that she must show off Margaretta before Philadelphia society (8–9)—a move that will enhance Stewart's reputation as much as it will imperil Margaretta's. De Burling's early attentions have the same quality. As he moves from outright passion to sober reverence, each crisis in his affections is marked by a new outburst of fervor. Thus, when Margaretta is almost kidnapped in Philadelphia, De Burling exclaims that he "never knew, 'till [that] moment . . . how much my soul was devoted to you" (75), and, passionately catching her to his breast, resolves to be Margaretta's protecting brother. Significantly, the novel sees this almost incestuous act as the first flowering of true love, and it is repeated at a higher level when the more sober Montanan takes Margaretta in his arms, vowing that he would reject "all that the world calls magnificent and great . . . for such exquisite happiness" (209). At its highest level, the desire to help Margaretta becomes piety itself, as when a character named Vernon rescues her from the Roulant plantation. Alone at night on a moonlit river, the two discover "a congeniality in our sentiments . . . interesting to the heart. We seemed to be of one mind and one soul," yearning for "a blissful hereafter" (254). This true exchange of sentiments propels the characters beyond passion, to that realm of "perfect propriety" that Adam Smith defines as the highest good. Pure commerce creates harmony by showing the indivisibility of human interests—a link that is ultimately spiritual.

By supporting such spiritual commerce, *Margaretta* extends and perfects the political claims of the merchants. Just as the three regions involved in the political dispute were the U.S. seaports, the West Indies, and London, so, too, the text is set, successively, in Philadelphia, the West Indies, and England, before its final return to America. Through these regions Margaretta circulates much as the merchants did, promoting harmony through her complete candor. For if Americans somewhat guiltily protested that their intentions were the target of unjustified scrutiny by English warships seeking to cut off trade with France, the novel presents a heroine only too willing to disclose what she thinks. Anything "mysterious" in the conduct of a young woman, Montanan warns Margaretta, "depreciates her worth" (207) and destroys society by substituting "a cool reserve, or unbecoming haughtiness" for the "happiness refined society have a right to expect from one another" (286). By contrast, Margaretta's heart is "unadulterated, honest, and open" (307), giving her every action such "unaffected simplicity" (24) that even rakes are forced to drop their seductions. The novel's solution to British charges of duplicity is thus to offer a sanctified commerce of the passions from which nothing is withheld. As one character remarks of Margaretta and a friend, "they intend to make *the best* market of themselves" (268, my emphasis).

But just as the best markets could prove treacherous, so the contradictions *Margaretta* attempts to resolve often threaten to cancel one another. By far the deepest contradiction involves the novel's almost universal cupidity—the manner in which, in a market culture, nearly everyone is driven by the need to possess and dominate. The most sympathetic male characters, De Burling and his patron, a sea captain named Waller, initially try to remove Margaretta from circulation, to make her a kept mistress untouched by competitors. Old M. Roulant and Montanan have similar reactions—as do four or five other suitors—all of them professing their love. "[H]er heart . . . is a prize worthy of regal honors," Miss Stewart warns De Burling (93); and when De Burling finally agrees, his confession to Margaretta remains soulfully selfish: "You are mine," he exclaims, " . . . by the fiat of God himself.—*He* has implanted that sympathy in our nature which we call love" (102). Similarly, when Vernon rescues Margaretta from the lascivious Roulant, his immediate impulse is to pursue her, crying, "game; game" (231), mistaking her for a quarry. Facing this onslaught, Margaretta cannot escape without herself being rendered a kind of commodity—a thing, like the impressed sailors, deprived of identity and independence. When she travels from Philadelphia to Haiti in order, she thinks, to prevent De Burling from ruining himself for her, she is taken under the protection of a supercargo, who "saw me placed in the family to which his bills of consignment directed" (174), as if she were part of the shipment. On the Roulant plantation she becomes a virtual slave and must plead with Vernon "to dispossess this gentleman of me, whose rightful claim to me is no more than to you" (246). And in England she is tricked into consorting with prostitutes, on suspicion that Montanan was no more than her "keeper" (309). Such difficulties reflect the subversions of custom during the embargo period, when even able seamen could suddenly find themselves slaves. But they also undermine Margaretta's search for autonomy since, as a mere commodity, she is subject to the unpredictable whims of commerce.

The ambiguities of possession in a fluid and treacherous market encouraged, in turn, a dialectical stress on transparency. In *The Origins of the English Novel,* Michael McKeon has argued that one of the social impulses giving rise to the early novel was the "question of virtue," the anxiety that a gentleman's status was no longer visible merely through the insignia of social esteem. The conservative novel of virtue was intended to reassert the intrinsic value of its noble subjects. [40] During the embargo crisis, market uncertainties similarly threatened republican virtue, committed at once to commercial expansion and to conscientious restraint. In *Margaretta,* the implicit demand that intrinsic merit be visible results in a pervasive surveillance. Virtually no letter passes without some reference to individuals gazing or avoiding gazes. Margaretta's great beauty makes her a cynosure wherever she goes, and whether the attention is curious or lascivious, there is always the sense that her extraordinary gifts create extraordinary demands. Thus Stewart, like Margaretta's later guardian, Edward Montanan, scrutinizes her with an expression that "wished to penetrate the inmost recess of my soul" (110; cf. 203), and when Margaretta appears at Bath in the company of two prostitutes attempting to suborn her, she is "regarded by the gentlemen with the utmost scrutiny, and by the ladies with scorn" (308). Margaretta thoroughly understands and accepts such scrutiny. When she is introduced to the woman later revealed as her mother, she protests that if she were really immoral, her "eye" could not "thus dwell on you"; rather, "a blasted character, a contaminated conscience" would make her blush with shame, and she "never could venture in [Lady Montraville's] presence" (317). Conversely, when Margaretta is made a prisoner in the Roulants' Cape François mansion, subjected to the constant scrutiny of Arabella's aunt and father, she manages to terrorize the former by so "fix[ing]" her eye that the aunt "ran screaming" (183). The power of truth gives to such penetration a brazen authority.

Allied to this scrutiny is the technology of modesty. Like the gaze itself, Margaretta's blushing is both a response to and an assertion of power. Thus when she first senses De Burling's "penetrating scrutiny," she immediately blushes (4), a performance she repeats when he promises her immense wealth (22). But modesty can also curb sexual aggression, as Margaretta's "genuine modesty" and "dignified reserve" (34) overcome De Burling's wish to kiss her. Other marks of sensibility serve the same end. When she is imprisoned and threatened with rape by the drunken Roulant, she apparently saves herself by fainting—one of at least twenty occasions in the novel when she is overcome. And her frequent attacks of pallor, weakness, illness, and nerves compel compassion from even her harshest assailants.

Margaretta's genuine authority, even over rakes like De Burling and Roulant, arises from her unambiguous demonstration of intrinsic value. In a milieu in which all property had become unstable, she suggested an unassailably constant worth. Her instantaneous reactions are windows on the soul. As Anthony Ashley Cooper, earl of Shaftesbury, had argued, to sensitive natures beauty and taste—the admired object and the aesthetic response—were reflections of virtue, spontaneous indications of nobility.[41] So Margaretta's instinctive "taste" (9), her rare beauty that inspired all observers to possess her or imagine her wealthy, reveals the possibility that in an embattled republic, custom still conformed to virtue, extrinsic values to inner worth. "[He] would for ever doubt Lavater's doctrine of physiognomy," one of Margaretta's protectors declares, "if the countenance of such an angel could deceive him" (239). Another suitor underscores how Margaretta's transparency becomes a kind of social authority. "The face . . . would be a deceiving index indeed," remarks Lord Orman, "if your heart be not the seat of every better passion" (333). Without a way to measure every better passion, the aristocrat's claim to honor itself might be in jeopardy. As De Burling maintains, Margaretta's "soul . . . [is] the true seat of honour and modesty" (40).

But despite these evident virtues, there remain numerous signs that intrinsic merit is increasingly threatened by the very republican milieu it was intended to serve. One of the most prominent symptoms of that jeopardy is the ubiquity of slander. If transparency, the spontaneous testimony of inner worth, is the sign of social purity—a purity enforced by the critical gaze—then slander, the obfuscation of value by arbitrary judgment, is a sign of social decay. From the opening pages of the novel, in which an innkeeper attacks Margaretta as "none of the best of characters" (3), intrinsic merit is viciously perverted. The pattern is almost comic in its frequency. No sooner does Margaretta arrive somewhere than she attracts universal regard, whereupon ardor turns to envy and nearly murderous competition ensues, for which she is invariably blamed. On the road to Philadelphia, for example, the rake Archibald Custon encounters her in the company of De Burling and vows to possess her "at the risque of life and fortune" (69). Accordingly he sabotages the coach, kidnaps her, and is apprehended and insulted, whereupon he determines not only to defame Margaretta and De Burling, but to inform Arabella, who exacts vengeance on both.

In Santo Domingo the costs of slander are even more severe. Adopted by a succession of protectors, Margaretta is admired, spurned, and defamed by each in turn. During her passage to the island the supercargo, Welton, vows "to protect [her] from insult" (176), thereby mortally offending Arabella's aunt, to whom he is engaged. Margaretta then excites old M. Roulant, who risks his reputation to kidnap her, and is severely censured after her escape. Retreating to Fort Dauphin on the other side of the island, she endures the same fate by residing with homely Marien Duchamp and attracting her fiancé, who soon breaks off *his* engagement. In every case what excites the worst propensities is the spectacle of a beautiful, solitary young woman, out in the world as if she were out on the town— her "loose conduct confirm[ing] the belief . . . that [she] was a lost abandoned creature" (227). Ironically, the pure young woman becomes a kind of cancer, infecting all around her with corruption. Not even the blameless Lady Montraville, Margaretta's actual mother, is immune. When her daughter, at Bath, becomes the object of scandal for living with Montanan and associating with prostitutes, Montraville risks her own character by merely talking to the girl. The guardians of custom who so extravagantly value transparent innocency are thus exposed by the very rigor of their own surveillance. Purity, in this instance, breeds defilement.

The most critical sign of this inner tension is the frequency with which Read raises the specter of incest. Several writers have recently discussed this theme, so prominent in American and English novels of the period, as an indication of status anxiety: the horror attending such promiscuity suggests the uneasiness associated with the relaxation of class or other communal boundaries.[42] In *Margaretta*, those anxieties are trained on the exposure of republican virtue to international predation. Merchants, too, were heroines, whose embrace of custom might ruin them. Each of the novel's three settings—America, Santo Domingo, and England— brings together Margaretta and a paternal or fraternal figure whose pressure threatens to overwhelm her. In America the figure is De Burling, whose rakish ardor impels him to declare himself her "enamoured brother" (114), and who in that capacity imagines her his mistress in Santo Domingo. That island's menace, though, turns out to be Roulant, whose "silvery locks" (227) and "fatherly" (230) appearance do not prevent his taking "indecent liberties" (196). But while Roulant comes closest to consummating the crime, it is Montanan who inspires the most dread. His desire for this woman who so resembles his lost wife is irrepressible, playing havoc with his health and with her sensibility. Yet although Margaretta submits to his importunity, she remains "revolted" and overcome by a "secret horror" (301). Along with the acute sensibility that allows her to avoid crime, her loathing also reveals a desire to hold herself inviolate, proof, finally, against the novel's innumerable attacks. But this time her modesty is cold comfort, since only a series of accidents preserves her from the most horrid crimes.

Viewed in these terms, Margaretta's exposure to the capricious world is almost total, with no possibility of preserving any pure source of value. Unable to secure herself against the treacheries of her protectors, she seems as vulnerable as a trader attacked by his former partners. But if Read evokes all the conditions for commercial and sexual treachery, she does not allow Margaretta to languish in them. Although Margaretta's modesty achieves a qualified power through silence, and although she can occasionally wield the silent authority of the gaze, her most vigorous and convincing actions are uniformly associated with speech. This authority, exercised by a woman who so seamlessly fits her era's conventions for shrinking virtue, is the most arresting of Margaretta's contradictions. Read uses her outspokenness to enact almost all the novel's critical transitions. What begins to transform De Burling from a manipulative rake to a self-sacrificing lover are

Margaretta's "sentences" that betray "a feeling heart: a mind intelligent" (20). Her "simple, yet powerful" (35) speech discloses a "heaven-illumined" "wisdom" (31, 24) captured in the perfect propriety of her sentiments and the elegant periods of her thought. And lest the reader mistake De Burling's praise for passionate hyperbole, Read repeats the performance in Santo Domingo. Although the silent acceptance with which Read appears to treat most references to slavery is not the least of the novel's disturbing elements, there can be no doubting the power of Margaretta's republican ardor. Imprisoned on Roulant's plantation and labeled "hysterical" and subject to "fits" in order to blunt her appeals, she nevertheless brands her captor a "tyrant, [who] has robbed me of my liberty" (236). When Custon, who shows up at the retreat to curry favor with the old man, assails her, she confronts her persecutor "with a firmness of thought of which, at any other time, I should have believed myself incapable" (241). And although she cannot entirely renounce modesty, vowing that "I should not thus plead my own cause, had I one friend to vindicate me," her very solitude compels her "to speak for myself" (242), upholding spurned "rules of honor, truth, and integrity" (241).

Her boldness proves a turning point in her own development, one that frees Margaretta to speak her mind whenever she feels her liberty threatened. In England, when Montanan becomes too ardent, she coldly repulses him by remarking, "I hate your fervour" (290). And when Lady Montraville, still clinging to slanderous report, questions her fondness for her guardian, Margaretta vows to "retire" rather than hear "even . . . the indirect abuse of his character"—a response that her listener immediately calls "spoken with American independence" (320). Even before her suitor, the powerful Lord Orman, is revealed to have seduced a village girl, Margaretta abruptly announces, during a ball in her honor, that she "hate[s]" him (397), and when he is finally exposed she calls him a "CRIMINA[L]" (401). Perhaps the boldest assertion she makes, though, bears the tension evident in all of the novel's ideological postures. Now installed as heiress to the Barton fortune, Margaretta is nevertheless abducted by her rakish uncle, who takes her for an impostor. When he declares that she will be his lover but not his niece—once again introducing the possibility of incest—Margaretta responds, "Then, . . . setting nature out of the question, there is a law for women, which will, independent of her voice, plead for me" (365). By adverting to an independent law to which women can appeal exclusive of their "nature," she reasserts the power of a transcendent, republican value immune to international betrayal, a fact not lost on Sir Henry, who sardonically reminds her that she is "not in America" (365). Although her power to enforce her speech remains limited—it is Lord Orman who saves her—she has nevertheless laid claim to a critical element of public discourse, one that allows her to identify honor, integrity, and custom as her own.

In their 1806 memorial, the New York merchants made a prescient claim. Far from being held accountable for their initial intentions in shipping goods, they held they must not be looked into. Their plans are "necessarily revocable," they argued, since all intentions "are liable to be affected by circumstances not to be foreseen or controlled."[43] The intermediary who would link disparate markets must yield to occasion; he cannot dictate terms. At his limit, the merchants might have added, such an individual would have no firm intentions at all, but would be infinitely plastic, perpetually differing from himself as he yields to the demands of the world. Yet the merchants were also representing American virtue, the offended modesty of republicans beset by foreign predators. It was that sinuous mixture of motives—aggression and principle, outraged innocence and shrewd calculation—that gave their protest its distinctively national accent. Arising from that moment of national crisis, Read's novel attempted, however tenuously, to resolve these ideological tensions. By offering a transparent virtue continuously compromised and a submissiveness that could rise to radical assertion, *Margaretta* sought to reclaim virtue amid the custom that so thoroughly violated it. Against all odds, she strove to "make the best market."

But despite her heroine's vigor, Read was no more successful than the merchants in resolving the contradictions of custom. Indeed, in a final ideological turn, she comes to prefigure a troubled national policy by transporting the best characters—Margaretta's mother and father and De Burling—now titled and fabulously wealthy, to a rural retreat in America. Here they will practice virtue in a restricted sphere, shielded from both passion and interest. "I would have the wife to have a vivid understanding, with a correct taste," Margaretta declares, "and the husband, to have sense enough to know how to appreciate their value" (404). In this sequestered community, value is measured by the exchange of sentiments, and noble intentions guarantee harmony. That the novel's solution predicted the embargo, anathema to most merchants, is both significant and ironic. With their claims to both an inviolable integrity and a virtue easily menaced, republican spokesmen like Jefferson allowed notions of principled retreat to determine national policy. Republicans, too, had begun to confront the market, but they did not yet know how to live in it.

## *Order in* The Asylum

In a discussion of Isaac Mitchell's *The Asylum,* Cathy Davidson has pointed to the disparity between its lovers' roles. Whereas Alonzo Haventon is a feckless sentimentalist who plays "only a minor part" in the novel, Melissa Bloomfield shows resolution and "verve" in confronting a host of gothic horrors. After losing touch with his betrothed, Alonzo languishes, moping about Europe and New England as he mourns Melissa's apparent death. Melissa, by contrast, asserts her will against persecutors, tests her lover's resolve, and reforms her avaricious father. The novel is "*her* forthright story," Davidson argues, one in which Melissa "proceeds alone."[44]

For Davidson, Melissa's discipline of unruly men provides a message to her culture. The Gothic castle where her father immures her and British counterfeiters torment her is intended to warn readers that their avaricious market practices are turning America's republican asylum into a prison.[45] But by focusing on how the heroine rises above the sentimental suffering of her gothic sisters, Davidson misses a crucial element of Mitchell's design. Far from rejecting commercial practices, *The Asylum* is deeply embedded in them. An ardent republican and newspaper editor who published the second half of the novel in 1804, at the start of the prewar crisis, and completed an expanded version by 1811, Mitchell was absorbed in the commercial and political struggles of the era. His novel, like Read's *Margaretta,* responds to the economic crisis by imagining an energetic woman whose sympathetic resolve allows her to discipline unruly market players. But her superiority to distress is only half the story. For the action is sustained by her sentimental lover, whose melting moods and restless circulation recall the vulnerable merchant "heroines" besieging Congress. The novel's design fuses these motives, uniting Alonzo's suffering to Melissa's distant mastery, his humanity to her sympathetic control. The result, as in the case of *Margaretta,* is a hybrid that attempts to resolve the nation's urgent commercial problems. To appreciate Mitchell's mastery of those problems, it is necessary to take a closer look at the fight over the embargo.

To read through the controversial literature of the years during which Mitchell was presumably revising *The Asylum* is to grasp the full force behind the title of his short-lived journal: *Republican Crisis.*[46] Although Republicans were firmly in control of the White House and Congress, there was a nagging sense that they were not in control of national destiny. The period between 1809 and 1811 was particularly bewildering. In early 1809 England's minister to the United States, David M. Erskine, offered to settle several long-standing disputes between the two nations in a move, prompted by Foreign Secretary George Canning, to exert more pressure on Napoleon. In a general agreement Madison endorsed on 19 April, Britain would pay reparations for its unprovoked 1807 attack on the American frigate *Chesapeake* and would suspend its Orders in Council of the same year, which blocked American trade with the continent. In return America would reopen full trade with Britain. The agreement brought "riotous celebrations,"[47] as long-hindered merchants poured their goods upon the sea. But by mid-July, the euphoria had become outrage: Canning peremptorily overturned the agreement, declaring (not without reason) that Erskine had exceeded his authority. Britain's Orders remained in effect, the ships were seized, and the newspapers were full of attacks on England, on the administration, and on its supporters.

French diplomacy was even more capricious. Responding to the threat he perceived from a relaxed American-British trade, Napoleon, in July 1810, teased American negotiators by overturning the Rambouillet decree, which mandated seizing all American ships in French ports—this in addition to earlier decrees blocking trade with Britain. Concurrently, though, he imposed another order placing prohibitive duties on imports, exploiting that same pent-up demand. Although a steady flow of American goods continued to cross the Atlantic, the confusing array of offsetting decrees profoundly disturbed many Americans, who felt their honor, as well as their income, imperiled. "After all our efforts to obtain redress," complained the Philadelphia *Aurora* in 1810, " . . . it is painful to find ourselves in a situation as hopeless as when we began. . . . Our remonstrances are now scarcely thought worthy of notice, at best are shuffled aside by diplomatic management, and deprived of their strength and effect . . . till a fresh act of injustice claims a fresh discussion. Orders in council, and decrees at first issued with some plea of reason . . . are now become a mere matter of course, . . . as if they were mere municipal laws."[48] Perhaps never since the Stamp Act had so many felt so wronged yet so impotent.

The political response took a variety of forms. Congressmen, buffeted by constituents' outcries but lacking clear directives from the White House, struggled to find a way to stand up to the powers without declaring war. Shortly after Madison's inauguration they voted to repeal the disastrous embargo—months before the administration desired—replacing it with a nonintercourse act that both prohibited American calls by British and French warships and offered to drop all restrictions on the first power to restore full commercial rights. That regimen was succeeded, in the following year, by Macon's Bill #2, a weakened compromise that dropped all trade restrictions but still held out the promise of favored trade to the first accommodating party. What had become clear to everyone was that the nation lacked the political will to impose an order of its own. "[T]he spirit of the nation is evaporated," William A. Burwell declared in 1809, "and . . . I despair of taking any measure . . . which would not meet with such opposition as to make it useless."[49] Nathaniel Macon was even more despondent. "The Lord the Mighty Lord must come to our Assistance," he wrote to a correspondent, "or I fear we are undone as a nation."[50]

Acute as the political crisis was, however, there were other motives fueling such pessimism. Jeffersonians had come to power professing an Enlightenment faith in free trade as the means to world order. National interests could be counterposed, secured by treaties, so that a predictably benevolent balance would prevail.[51] The Erskine affair—followed months later by Madison's dismissal of his replacement, the abrasive Francis Jackson—proved a profound shock to that sensibility. It is doubtless true, as Bradford Perkins argues, that the interminable debates in the House were a symptom of Madison's hands-off policy, his refusal to provide an agenda.[52] But from another angle, the weeks of tedious discussion of diplomatic correspondence, the endless hermeneutic dissection of Erskine's motives, Canning's implications, and Madison's resolves were means of taking collective bearings in a commercial world gone profoundly awry. Once again, economic crisis had forced many Americans to examine their most cherished assumptions.

Perhaps most shaken was the faith in rational markets. One of the delegates' most immediate concerns, for example, was that contract, the soul of commerce, had been violated. Madison himself, in his annual message to Congress, had complained of the "refusal of the British government to abide by the act of its Minister Plenipotentiary,"[53] and others soon took up the charge. The Republican Richard M. Johnson painted the dilemma in highly sentimental terms. While Americans were imagining a golden age of renewed trade, he charged—"at a time when the farmer had prepared his grain for market, and promised his impatient creditor speedy payment; when the mechanic expected an additional reward for his labor; when the flag of the honest trader floated in the winds of every region, and the seamen exulted with joy at the return of better times . . . the disavowal of that arrangement was announced to blast our hopes, and to put down our pretensions to credit."[54] But the disease affected American leaders as well. Is it possible, thundered Samuel W. Dana, that our ministers could "solemnly announce to the world a pledge to call into action the whole force of the nation, and yet that it can be all idle words? That in fact they intend to do no such thing as they promise?" Of such broken promises, declared Jonathan Fisk, Americans could well be making "a shroud for our national sovereignty."[55] For with the collapse of national credit went the whole structure of rational self-interest on which American policy had been predicated. "We now . . . discover," grimly declared the *Aurora* early in 1810, " . . . that in state logic, the conclusion rarely follows the premises; that reasoning is but a poor defence [*sic*] against power."[56] Passion, not reason, seemed to govern world affairs.

Indeed, the national drift of which the delegates complained was itself symptomatic of this loss of credit. In a variety of ways, some melodramatically underscoring party loyalties, others merely plaintive, orations of the period disclosed their sense of impasse through an imagery of wounded or outraged feeling. "Your government has led the nation to the very verge of the precipice," warned Martin Drake in 1809; "another step, in the same course, and we plunge into an ocean, of blood."[57] Other writers beheld a "dreadful gulf of unfathomable uncertainty," "a state of most *disgraceful* jeopardy," "national suicide."[58] Beneath their hyperbole, these statements express a genuine concern that the world had become dangerously unpredictable, almost random in its violence. Federalists feared that "the thousand frauds and forfeitures," both here and abroad, would undermine "all authority, laws and habits."[59] Republicans lamented that the entire world seemed "curtained with darkness," and God's charter abrogated.[60] Within memory of the Revolution many wondered if the republic itself would survive.

The malaise affected merchants as well. Risk takers by nature, they foresaw great profits if they could find some way to serve needy Europeans; but the risks, they often had to acknowledge, were simply too great. The constant and unpredictable disruptions of trade played havoc with insurance rates, keeping their vessels in port. Like the politicians, they responded to their loss of control through an outpouring of feeling. So few were the opportunities that the New Yorker Robert Hartshorne Bowne felt compelled to dun correspondents for even small sums, claiming that "we are in fact in a dreadful state," with a volume of failures that "would astonish and confound thee."[61] To their English contacts, merchants often put on a brave front, reiterating Republican slogans about domestic manufacture and national honor. So the Philadelphian William Jones boasted to a London firm that America "is flourishing in the highest degree," and warned that it was up to Britain to cultivate "that harmony and good understanding" on which commerce depended.[62] But in less florid moments, as when Jones pleaded with the Bank of the United States to extend a loan, he could flatly bemoan "the perilous State of our commerce with Europe, aggravated by the stagnation of trade and declension of confidence."[63] At their bleakest, even merchants who remained in business betrayed that declension. Lamenting the grievous state "of the Commercial world thro out the Universe," Edward Gernon, brother of Philadelphia merchant Richard Gernon, succumbed to despair: "all hopes of seeing once more the human race happy and comfortable have left me. . . . if at times particles of hopes [*sic*] break thro' this much confused state of nations, they as soon are lost, and what may appear practicable one day is entirely out of the reach of man the moment after—so great are the follies of men!!!"[64] "[A]ll is confusion & disorder," Gernon wrote after the failure of Erskine's initiative, "and God knows how all will terminate."[65]

In an essay on capitalism in the age of sensibility, Thomas Haskell has examined the sources of such fears. As the market took hold in the West, he argues, it wrought vast changes in the predictability of the world. The calculating behavior that Max Weber studied suddenly made it possible for individuals to measure and adjust their daily performance. As a result, the market nurtured what Haskell calls promise keeping and recipes—the inclination to rely on the bond of strangers engaged in transactions and the consequent ability to plan extended undertakings in order to keep one's word. In effect, these networks of sympathy, which first came to prominence in the late eighteenth and early nineteenth centuries, created a "stabilized environment" based on "long chains of will" that were literally bound to be realized.[66] Humanitarian sensibility was possible, Haskell claims, precisely because individuals felt in control of their world, and the distant affairs of others became suddenly meaningful. Underlying this ethos was a sense that the world was orderly, rational, predictable—the arena of measured and sympathetic exchange that Smith envisioned in *The Theory of Moral Sentiments*. The distress Madisonians felt over broken promises and over their inability to act suggests their keen awareness of these issues; but Americans also found more pragmatic ways to deal with their malaise—adjustments that would influence Mitchell's work.

If vast gulfs suddenly yawned beneath them, if their governing assumptions were being challenged, then one recourse was to deny the severity of the challenge. Thus, many spokesmen attempted to reassert control by insisting that promise keeping and following recipes were as useful as ever. Americans had simply been hoodwinked, taken in by predatory disguises. Josiah Quincy charged, for example, that the Erskine reversal was all the fault of Francis Jackson, who schemed "to excite dissensions among the people through false and fallacious disguises."[67] Once Quincy's rhetoric had penetrated that disguise, the threat would presumably end. Others attacked Jefferson as the arch deceiver, whose every move was meant "to mask his real designs."[68] Madison came in for the same treatment. Congressman Jacob Swoope claimed that the administration was full of impostors "whose intrigues were covered by a veil" he alone could lift,[69] and a writer to the *Alexandria Daily Gazette* vowed to "expose the machinery" of Madison's deception. Using the theatrical language that Jean-Christophe Agnew has associated with the market, the author of "The History of Our Times" proposed to "view the system that moves the *puppets,* and see the transactions behind the curtain."[70] In all of these instances authority is reclaimed by tearing away the curtain, removing the disguise before it is too late, before reason itself is compromised. A contemporary warning in the *Columbian Centinel* suggests the full dimensions of the threat. Masquerades are contemptible diversions, claims the essayist: "Any characters may be assumed and represented; and any manners and sentiments will be tolerated, which agree with these characters. None of the company will be considered as speaking in their own persons; some will be able to conceal themselves effectually from all their associates; under such circumstances, what may not be said; what may not be done?"[71] The concern with the mechanics, the system, the exchange of deception devolves upon a threat to language (what may be said), the essence of promise-keeping behavior. People who cannot be trusted to be themselves cannot be trusted to act in the orderly, predictable ways the market demanded. The obsessive unmasking of disguise, long a fixture of republican discourse, thus becomes a way to reclaim a vital power and attribute of market behavior. As Mitchell himself claimed in the inaugural issue of *Republican Crisis,* the sole antidote to anarchy was to tear away the "specious and imposing garb" of deceivers.[72]

Another widespread antidote was to blame the malaise on foreigners. If France and England had hobbled our economy, then America alone could right it. Although the embargo and nonintercourse acts demonstrated our hostility to Europe, more radical proposals had been circulating since at least the *Chesapeake* incident. Reviving Richard Price's 1785 maxim that the American states were a "world within themselves,"[73] entrepreneurs began lobbying for government support of domestic manufactures. With its diversity of climates and resources, its extensive rivers and nascent internal improvements, America could mount a formidable economic challenge, they claimed, with almost no risk. Often this impulse was expressed in pastoral form. "The mountains," declared Benjamin A. Markley, " . . . will yield the vine and the olive; the fertile vallies [*sic*] . . . will cloathe themselves in golden harvests; and the streams . . . will aid the toil of man." The new world was simply too young to pursue the promiscuous pleasures of trade, which would "introduc[e] . . . the luxuries and vices" of Europe.[74] Charles Glidden Haines sought a similar security. "No," he proclaimed, " 'when the day is overcast, when the tempest lowers and the lightnings play,' we seek an asylum from the threatening danger, and wait till the elements spend their fury."[75] The pastoral calm he craves points to the essential conservatism of this solution. Despite the promise of dynamic economic growth, the asylum these writers imagined was one that exempted Americans from troubling contingency. In such a balanced, orderly realm, recipes could be minutely observed, promises scrupulously kept. The vision was one of a cleansed commerce in which Americans still mastered their world.[76]

It is worth repeating that the topoi I have been discussing—promise keeping, recipe, disguise, and asylum—were not the property of either political party, but were ideological in the broad sense of worldview or cultural orientation. Behind the partisan rhetoric, spokesmen sensed a genuine challenge to what was still a very fragile American commerce, and their use of these ideas demonstrates what Michael Gardiner (after Mikhail Bakhtin) describes as the true function of ideology—as a focus for the shifting, often radically conflicting perceptions of a shared milieu.[77] Isaac Mitchell's contribution was to give these tensions dramatic form in a narrative that melded commercial anguish and sympathetic command. His heroine, Melissa Bloomfield, would teach her lover how to turn raw feeling into virtuous resolve.

Although *The Asylum* is set during the Revolutionary period, there is ample evidence that it is very much of its own time. It seems significant, for example, that when Mitchell needs a plot device to disrupt or hasten the action, he often turns to contemporary economic problems. The novel's principal reversal, severing Melissa from Alonzo, involves the "sequestrat[ion]" of his merchant father's ships in both England and the West Indies (2:13). When the father's partners abscond and he is left alone to face his creditors, Colonel Bloomfield sequesters his daughter, and the novel's gothic effects begin. Similarly, when Alonzo learns of Melissa's supposed death, another mercantile venture intervenes to remove him from America. A convoy was gathering "for the protection of our European trade" (2:139)—an undertaking that never occurred during the Revolutionary War but that was often urged before the War of 1812—and Alonzo takes refuge in action. And when Mitchell needs gothic villains he turns to "a gang of *Illicit Traders*," Loyalist counterfeiters who, like many illicit traders during and after Jefferson's embargo, conduct "secret and illegal commerce" with the British and sell imported goods at "extortionate" prices (2:258). In each case, plot reversal accompanies economic threat, which the novel seeks to overcome in the manner of the Fourth of July orators cited above, who discern national perils in order to dissolve them in native virtue. The drama thus registers the tensions of its uncertain time.

When one considers the economic shocks as structural effects, however, another aspect of Mitchell's art becomes puzzling. In a preface to the novel, he defends his decision to insert the long interpolated tale of Selina Bergher, who narrates her hazardous elopement across Europe, by appealing to his readers' need for repose. To burden the text with cross-cutting scenes or simultaneous narratives would create "a wilderness of intricate mazes, from whence, with extreme difficulty and embarrassment, the chain of events leads . . . through . . . impenetrable obscurity" (xiii). His novel is designed, rather, for those "who prefer connexion and regularity to disorder and interruption" (xxvi). Mitchell must have already feared the response of his numerous readers, who often dispensed with the Bergher narrative for the more compelling tale of Alonzo and Melissa. But his insistence on order and regularity makes sense in light of the tortuous plot. In Selina's inset, the beautiful young woman, compelled to marry the sinister Count Hubert, prefers the dashing Colonel Herman Bergher instead. Learning of her plans to elope with Bergher, Hubert tricks her, abducts her, and is overtaken by Selina's brother, whence, in the ensuing skirmish, all three are separated. Bergher later seeks out Hubert, wounds him in his drawing room, and is imprisoned, but escapes with the help of a loyal soldier. Then, regaining and marrying Selina, Bergher sets out, chased across Europe by both the state and the agents of Hubert, who has miraculously survived. The two hide in copses and crevices, are captured and released by banditti, and take up residence in Paris and London, only to be surprised at every turn by a wanted poster or gendarme from whom they must precipitously flee.

Ironically, they are not safe even in America. After assuming anonymity in Boston, Bergher is spotted by a foreign agent and must remove to the interior of

Connecticut, where he finally becomes a tenant and manager for Melissa's aunt, Martha Bloomfield. Only much later does he learn that the warrant had long been lifted, and that much of his flight was unnecessary. Melissa is only slightly less peripatetic, leaving her father's estate for the notorious Gothic castle on Long Island Sound, where she is the victim of strange contingencies, and thence to New London and Charleston before she reunites with Alonzo, who has been jailed in England as a prisoner of war, employed at a bookseller's in Paris, and shipwrecked off South Carolina in the interim. Even after one acknowledges the popular appetite for what Mitchell calls "variety" (xiii), this is still a formidable array—one that makes the tension between disorder and regularity all the more striking. In a fundamental sense, the novel is precisely "about" that tension.

Some of Mitchell's more noteworthy shocks closely parallel the apocalyptic imagery of popular debate. In the plot contrivance that brings together the two lovers, added to the 1811 version, Melissa suddenly loses control of her carriage and hurtles toward a cliff. "[S]he saw herself on the verge of a tremendous precipice, ready to be plunged, and dashed to pieces, among the rocks below" (1:49), when Alonzo appears to divert the horses. The almost casual boundary between life and eternity impresses Melissa "with sensations not to be obliterated" (1:49). Indeed, the scene recurs in a premonitory dream Melissa has before her imprisonment, when, at the brink of "a deep, horrid chasm," she sees the drowning Alonzo (2:9). When Melissa is later isolated in the castle, this sense of the arbitrary intensifies. Strange apparitions, icy hands, deathlike masks assault her, topped off by the inevitable thunderclap so loud that "[i]t seemed nothing less than the crush of worlds sounding through the universe" (2:93). Mere reason alone, the ultimate solace of gothic novels, is insufficient here, as Mitchell suggests in a later incident involving Alonzo. In Paris, despondent over Melissa's presumed death, he is assisted by the eminent Dr. Franklin, who dispenses sage advice. "Exquisite sensibilities are ever subject to exquisite inquietudes," Franklin urges. "Counsel with correct reason; . . . and the triumph of fortitude and resignation will be yours" (2:183). But reason cannot prevent cataclysm. No sooner is Alonzo in sight of America, having returned home through Franklin's agency, than the ship "struck upon a reef with [a] tremendous crash. All was alarm and confusion. The darkness of the night, the raging of the wind, the roaring of the sea, mingled with the despairing cries of men, women and children, formed a scene beyond description terrible" (2:189–90). Chasms, crashing worlds, engulfing seas: these were also the images of a society struggling for its own version of rationality in a treacherous world.

It is in this cultural context, perhaps moreso than in the psychological terms that Davidson explores, that the novel's gothicism makes most sense. The irrational is so threatening precisely because it prevents characters from fulfilling their obligations, acting out their market roles. Alonzo, after Franklin's sermon, finds he has a patriotic obligation to his country, as well as an obligation to restore to his father the lost property that Franklin has helped to secure. The storm intervenes, with sensations not to be obliterated. Baron Du Ruyter promises Selina she can choose her husband, but the irrational avarice of her stepmother, who is "passionately fond of deep play" (1:65), leads him to impose Count Hubert. And the gothic terrors of the castle, the work of disruptive economic agents, stand in the way of Melissa's marriage vows. On the other side of the Atlantic, the counterfeiters' compatriots act to similar effect. When Alonzo's father ventures his all in one last investor's play, acting "on a fair calculation of liberal and extensive profits" (2:13), the whole is cataclysmically seized—defying all calculation. His creditors exact an awful penalty, and the afflicted family, in language reminiscent of Melissa's accident, is "hurled in a moment from the lofty summit of affluence to the low and barren vale of poverty" (2:16). What truly terrifies in these scenes is the uncanny nature of a disrupted economy, where the familiar suddenly turns frightening and nothing is secure.

It is appropriate, then, that Mitchell's text is studded with broken promises. Franklin may ultimately be wrong about the relative authority of reason, but there is no denying that individuals add to their woes by not upholding a rational code. A case in point is Count Hubert, whose sense of honor, cynically perverted in his brokered deal for Selina, further betrays him when he finds it necessary to fight three successive duels. Severely wounded in the first one, he yet hopes to face his other opponents when death intervenes. Colonel Bloomfield also perverts promise keeping, crediting his tenants with advances he knows they cannot return in hopes of seizing their land. When he applies the same mentality to his daughter, Alonzo gets to the heart of the matter by charging that Bloomfield "heedlessly" breached "a most solemn contract" (2:103). Perhaps the most perverse of all violators, though, is the bandit Nimrod, who briefly detains Bergher and Selina. An Italian noble betrayed by political enemies, Nimrod considers that broken faith a license to plunder, claiming that although the world could not restore his honor, still it "owed me a support" (1:156). And yet Nimrod is courteous, efficient, and, within certain limits, equitable—a mirror image of Mitchell's commercial world.

It is not without reason that he is termed a "rational maniac" (1:164). But virtuous characters also struggle with tortured promises. Although Melissa acknowledges her father's cruelties, she cannot bring herself openly to defy him, even when she is imprisoned. Paradoxically, the same "principles of truth and justice" (2:33) that make her resist her father's marriage choice cause her "extreme agitation" (2:105) as she plans her escape, and she can void the contract only by staging her own death. If destruction looms behind every gothic menace, Mitchell seems to be saying, then only a fierce adherence to contract can redeem.

Melissa's artifice in publishing her own obituary captures Mitchell's divided response to his era's distorted credit. On the one hand, like the numerous controversialists he followed and reported on, Mitchell was quick to attack the artifice of disguise. The most telling example of his hostility is the Illicit Traders, who not only dress up as corpses to scare away Melissa but also circulate counterfeit bills to wreck New England's currency. Colonel Bloomfield, similarly, likes to assume "only, the appearance of a plain Connecticut farmer" (1:32) while he amasses enormous wealth. Count Hubert disguises himself as an attendant in order to kidnap Selina, aided by Selina's maid, who disguises her loyalty; and Nimrod sends his spies to "every quarter," disguised as peasants (1:157). The most curious instance of disguise in the novel is an interpolated tale conveyed to Alonzo while he is imprisoned in England. A condemned murderer named Henry Malcomb recounts how his inability to perceive a counterfeit led him to murder his sister and his fiancée. After returning from a long voyage and receiving a note that his lover was unfaithful, he surprised the two and shot them, learning too late that the whole scene had been contrived to try his jealousy. Adrift amid specious signs, Malcomb destroys the most enduring sources of value—an act utterly typical of his distorted time.

Against these examples of perverse or delusory disguises, Melissa's management of her marriage is all the more compelling. Relying on an uncanny resemblance between herself and a cousin with the same name, she travels to the latter's Charleston home and discloses her plight to her uncle, who agrees to publish *her* death when his own daughter dies. When Alonzo lands in Charleston and is at last conducted to the house, he finds a woman elegantly adorned and wearing a green veil, who reveals herself as Melissa. Pages of explanation ensue, whereupon the two return to Connecticut and play the same trick on a contrite Colonel Bloomfield, who has allowed Alonzo's wedding to a veiled woman to be conducted in his home. Thus, disguise can either prevent promises or redeem them—provided one knows the truth. As in the newspaper debates, it was all a matter of seeing behind the veil.

The motifs I have been discussing suggest Mitchell's general use of his era's received ideas; indeed, since he was an editor shaping public opinion, it would be hard for him to do otherwise. But how, specifically, does *The Asylum* contribute to the debate over America's commercial policy? In what specific ways does it attempt to address the sense of powerlessness besetting so many readers? The answer to those questions seems to be mixed. Although an ardent Republican (and staunch opponent of New York's Clintonians), Mitchell was not a war hawk—this despite his setting the novel during the Revolution. War, in *The Asylum,* is almost an afterthought, a metaphor for the disordered state of the grieving Alonzo, who spends more time desponding in prison than he does engaged in battle. The real source of Mitchell's political wisdom lies elsewhere—not on the high seas or the treacherous highways of Europe, but in the pastoral haunts of Connecticut. Mitchell's evocations of landscape, which he vigorously defends in the preface, seem intrusive to the modern reader, a kind of pious natural history that burdens the action. But for Mitchell that is precisely the point: amid so many artificial disruptions there lay an infinite natural economy, a vision of perfect order. In one typical passage, the lovers view Long Island Sound in midsummer—the moon rising above the glassy calm, the air fragrant with flowers and lively with the sounds of birds and music from the village. An impending storm only adds to the charm: far off "hung a pile of brazen clouds . . . over which the crinkling red lightning momentarily darted, and at times the long peals of thunder were faintly heard" (1:213). Although the storm, at the end of Book 1, foreshadows the couple's troubles, it also counsels in how to overcome them. The predominant message, here and elsewhere in the text, is to preserve a wise silence in the face of unkind fortune. The world is a complex harmony beyond the grasp of any mortal. As Alonzo puts it, "[t]empests are succeeded by calms; war ends in peace; the splendours of the brightest morning arise on the wings of blackest midnight" (2:35)—a sentiment echoed by Franklin, who advises Alonzo that "the all-wise, dispensing hand of Providence" (2:182) orders the world.

That sense of ultimate harmony finds its way into more conventional images of political economy as well. When Alonzo and Melissa select the property they will call the Asylum, they are attracted as much by the natural harmony of the village as by the landscape: "The inhabitants of this new Avernum were principally farmers;

they were mild, sociable, moral and diligent; the produce of their own flocks and farms gave them most of their food and clothing; to dissipation they were strangers, and the luxuries of their tables were few" (1:263). Here we are indeed on familiar republican ground, a vision of a peaceable American world within itself. The novel's principal narratives generally conform to this theme. The Berghers, for example, trapped by the cynical codes of a corrupt aristocracy, gradually part with Selina's jewels in order to survive, until they arrive in America virtually destitute and must support themselves as farmers. Similarly, Alonzo's father, cut off from the deep play of international commerce, learns to value the simple pleasures of rural retreat, where he may "realize the blessings of health, comfort and contentment" (2:117). In this fashion, Mitchell offers a frank, conservative, republican anodyne to his troubled readers: curb your appetites, leave off aggressive commerce, and a mild prosperity will be yours.

But there is another, countervailing strain in *The Asylum* that modestly challenges this received wisdom. The contradiction is most evident in what should be the novel's moral center, the counsel of Benjamin Franklin. Advising Alonzo to quit moping and to take his place in the world, Franklin, like his contemporary, Adam Smith, comes down hard on "inordinate passion": "If my reasoning be correct, the ardency of your passion must have expired with the pursuit. . . . [O]n your part, indifference would consequently have succeeded; on that of your partner, disappointment, jealousy and disgust. . . . [H]ow few among the sentimentally refined are even apparently at ease, while those insusceptible of what you term tender attachments . . . plod on through life without ever experiencing the least inconvenience from a want of . . . pleasures" (2:181–83). This is the unsentimental, calculating Franklin of Weber's caricature, the rational man with a vengeance. But it is not Alonzo, and Mitchell, after all his hero's struggles, makes sure the reader will reject it. Franklin succeeds only in substituting the passion of patriotism for that of love—not in overturning sentiment. His observations are in one sense undeniably true. Alonzo does engage in all the extravagances of sentiment, prostrating himself after Melissa's presumed death, dressing in high mourning, reverencing her miniature, even having a good cry over her (cousin's) grave in Charleston. But Mitchell, tutored, perhaps, by sentimental merchants, did not reject such displays. Rather, he sought to demonstrate that feeling—even the "womanly" feeling that Smith called "humanity"—*was* action, and economic action of the most pointed kind. Not only did sentiment impel Alonzo into the world, but it also underscored the need for sympathetic union amid national crisis.

To abandon feeling, as Franklin advised, was, then, to abandon society to the very anarchy that so many of Mitchell's contemporaries feared. Feeling, circulating through the deranged Atlantic market, had the power to order the world.

Indeed, Alonzo's experience is a primer in how to convert feeling into sympathy, suffering into resolve. The formula, which becomes a kind of structural device in the novel, demonstrates how prudence and resolute action arise through uninhibited sentiment. A good example of this balance occurs after Alonzo's compassionate prison interview with Henry Malcomb, during which the criminal would "frequently . . . burst into tears" (2:157). When Alonzo then learns that he is to be transferred to a yet more wretched prison, he shreds his clothes to make a rope by which he escapes and, wandering naked through the streets, is overtaken by the benevolent English sailor Jack Brown, who commiserates, shelters him, and gives him ten guineas for the passage to France. Feeling begets action, and action begets sympathy. A more involved example of the same effect occurs in Paris, where Alonzo finds work through Franklin's agency. Walking the streets one morning, he spots a silk purse with some money and a miniature he recognizes as Melissa's. Thanking God for pitying his "sufferings," he soon locates the owner—none other than Edgar Bloomfield, Melissa's brother—and the two engage in a melting interview in which they "mingle [their] tears" (2:174). There follows the astringent meeting with Franklin; the voyage and shipwreck off Charleston, from which Alonzo preserves his father's fortune restored by Franklin; and the long sojourn in town, Alonzo's bosom forever "swell[ing] with mournful recollection" (2:195). Reduced to its essentials, the plot is an almost schematic repetition of economic shock and passionate compensation. If there is radical disruption, there is also unfailing, affectionate order.

That balance applies even to the most luxuriant of Alonzo's excesses, his prostration over Melissa's presumed death. Slowed, in his pursuit of her, by nervous fatigue, he has himself bled at Killingworth and waits a few weeks before proceeding to New London. There he comes across Melissa's obituary and yields to "stupifying agony" (2:134) from which he even more slowly recovers. Yet the long rest is merely a prelude to his long-deferred military service, prefaced by a last visit to that point above Long Island Sound where he once sensed nature's all-encompassing order. If the desperation of grief propels him into war, Mitchell suggests that both responses are part of a divine economy, overseen by Alonzo's transcendent love. And it may be this sentimental confidence that accounts for the novel's success. By enlisting his readers so thoroughly in Alonzo's plight, Mitchell guarantees that they will embrace all aspects of his experience—the combat as well as the retreat, the prostrated sentiment and the passionate command. Not only was this balm for nervous contemporaries on the brink of war, it was also a prescription for sympathetic order. For the crosscurrents of feeling, like economic ripples, would ultimately balance in a grand, self-regulating design. In the midst of the most deranged markets the nation had yet witnessed, Mitchell imagined an ultimate harmony. He had created an affective equilibrium.

In presenting Alonzo's sympathy as the answer to America's economic woes, Mitchell was less an innovator than a shrewd observer of the cultural scene. On the eve of a war that would answer their prayers but also turn the country decisively inward—toward domestic manufacture and Manifest Destiny—he was articulating a vision all the more poignant because it was fading. Just as Alonzo repays Jack Brown by rescuing him from an American prison (commemorated in the name Brown later gives to his English pub, The Grateful American), so some Republicans still hoped for an enlightened future in which Madison's "chords of affection" would unite economic opponents in a rational world order. But even as James Monroe proclaimed a postwar Era of Good Feelings, it was evident how fully sectional tensions and the business cycle were taking their toll. The panic of 1819 would throw half a million people out of work, precipitating a "deeper gloom . . . than was ever witnessed by the oldest man,"[78] while antislavery Federalists and Clintonians openly spoke of disunion. Even Jefferson was brought under, forced to make good on a friend's debt that would distress him for the rest of his life. Perhaps that is why Mitchell's novel endured so late into the century. Like all works of ideological art, it sought comfort in the very conflicts it portrayed. Dispelling its gothic nightmare, *The Asylum* made republican crisis dissolve in eternal accord.

## Of Marriage and Marines

The *frisson* of novels like *Margaretta* and *The Asylum* stemmed from the tension between propriety and experiment, between autonomous virtue and random vulnerability. Margaretta's fate is interesting precisely because she can be so easily threatened, exposed to corruption in ways that even well-wishers are all but powerless to prevent. That same threat becomes palpable in Mitchell's Connecticut castle and in the numerous shocks to Alonzo's peace of mind. The clash between rational principle and accident made these novels important ideological tools, as

readers confronted the new and often frightening prominence of market forces
in their own lives. By offering protagonists who surmounted debility through
feeling, these texts used cultural anxieties to fashion parables of control.

After the war and the commercial anxiety had ended, however, many spokesmen sought a new rationale for economic behavior, one that imagined a purified,
protected commerce. American theorists turned inward, seeking the divine balance of market forces within the safety of their own shores. And to secure that
purity the president himself engaged in sympathy, transforming the displays of
bereaved feeling so prominent before the war into a ritual of national resolve. Cel-
ebrating an Era of Good Feelings, he would circulate through the Union, allaying
sectional controversy through an outpouring of sentiment. At last, sympathy
seemed the true register of national affairs.

But although the nation appeared to have resolved its economic problems,
difficult cultural work remained. As I will argue in the next chapter, the insistence
on republican purity became increasingly strained as economic crises multiplied,
belying the fantasy of sympathetic control. The greatest intrinsic purity could not
defend against market disruptions, and an ideology of self-control only multiplied
the occasions for self-blame. But while republicans sought refuge in a cleansed
domestic economy, two remarkable pamphlets, appearing in 1816, suggested a
different course. Despite their obscurity, *The Female Marine* and its counterpart,
*The Surprising Adventures of Almira Paul,* are significant cultural documents.
Drawing on the rhetoric of seduction and sentimental suffering common before
the war, the two pamphlets transform patriotism into a model for pragmatic
virtue. With an almost impudent grasp of popular feeling, the pamphlets work
dialectically to convert virtuous retreat into patriotic, world-traveling prostitution.
Purity, in this account, becomes another name for the frank embrace of experience;
prudence is the celebration of risk. Read against the economic prescriptions of the
era, Coverly's pamphlets suggest a new element in the culture's structure of feeling.
A brief consideration of the political milieu will indicate their subversive impact.

Jefferson's conduct of the embargo is often considered a watershed event, a defensive reaction fraught with unintended consequences. While contemporary critics
charged that the embargo stymied trade and ruined prosperity, hindsight suggests
that it may ultimately have served to promote a kind of primitive accumulation
by stimulating domestic manufactures. [79] Jefferson himself bought merino sheep,
wore homespun, and boasted that Monticello was spinning its own cloth; and he

often urged "that we should encourage home manufactures to the extent of our own consumption of every thing which we raise the raw material."[80] With high moral seriousness, he contended that England had sowed "a field of lawless violence . . . no longer regulated by the laws of reason or morality."[81] And if England had destroyed trade, it was up to Jefferson to restore it, to reconcile, in the words of one correspondent, "the Passions and temporary emoluments of the Citizens of the U.S. with their permanent Interests."[82] Significantly, Jefferson wanted to accomplish this goal by turning away altogether from aggressive accumulation. His pronouncements on domestic manufactures stressed balance, order, and a due proportion "between agriculture, manufactures & commerce,"[83] and he urged state governors to make trade strictly conform to local needs. If European interest ruined free trade, American protection would restore it.

Jefferson's most perceptive critic understood the ideological stakes in this argument. In *An Address . . . upon Foreign Commerce* (1809), Charles Brockden Brown pointed out that the laws of the marketplace made no exceptions. What drove trading nations was raw desire, the need to "enrich and aggrandize themselves, by all the means in their power."[84] American interests were no less avaricious than Britain's; we, too, would one day "gain our ends by force over neighbors, whose weakness will have nothing left them, but remonstrances and syllogisms" (48). To Brown, the estate of commerce was a state of war, whose outcome was no more assured than that of a lottery (72), no more stable than the ocean on which it was conducted (71). And to the Jeffersonian vision of a balanced marketplace, Brown opposed the contentious "equipoise" (62) of hostile powers, each "constantly swelling and enlarging his hulk both by sea and land" (62). The "encroachments" of powerful states and the acquiescence of others—these "constitute a scene of perpetual fluctuation" (43) that is the market's only certainty. In Brown's Hobbesian critique, accumulation, contingency, and irrational desire were thus the sole basis of commerce—a critique of American as well as European affairs.

Postwar pronouncements on American economic prospects, however, generally followed Jefferson's lead. The best way to deny the market's irrationality was to blame Europe for the problem. In 1816, for example, a House subcommittee on the tariff claimed that peacetime Europe was even less inviting and more dangerous to Americans. Despotism and ambition had ruined their markets: "Every moment is looked for with tremulous, anxious, and increased solicitude; hope languishes, and commercial enterprise stiffens with fear."[85] If foreign commerce aroused familiar anxieties, it also touched off uncertainties long the preserve of sentimental fiction. A reliance on international trade, John Calhoun claimed, would make Americans slaves to "contingency,"[86] just as overseas merchants, wrote Virginian Thomas Newton, must remain "exposed to the 'shafts of fortune.' "[87] By contrast, domestic commerce was a tranquil preserve where a free market could flourish as nature intended. "[H]ere is ample scope for all the various branches of industry,"[88] proclaimed Selah North in 1819. The home market, suggested the House Committee on Agriculture in 1824, "would prove . . . at once various, in point of demand, but sure, steady, and unchanging."[89] Such claims were all the more urgent as sectional tensions increased. As Jonathan Maxcy hoped in 1819, "our mutual, though opposite interests [would be] reconciled and promoted; and what at first appeared like a source of discord, may be converted into a bond of union."[90] Manufacturing, agriculture, and internal commerce would promote a stable, sensible prosperity.

That impulse received a powerful enactment after the war in James Monroe's tour. Ostensibly a private survey of defensive preparations, his progress soon became something much more, as virtuous republican citizens poured forth their spontaneous veneration. Monroe shrewdly spent most of his time in New England, where Federalist opposition had been strongest, indulging in an elaborate series of military reviews, factory tours, formal repasts, and public celebrations. Significantly, although he was officially depicted as a father blessing his family, the real force of his actions involved playing the role of an Alonzo who united through exchange of affection. "I have not the pretension, to arrogate to myself, the emotion of the sentiment my presence awakens," he told the citizens of Hanover, New Hampshire. But he saw in the display "that national feeling" so crucial as a "means of union."[91] Even cranky opponents wondered to see "the entire face of society changed, and all hearts united in a lasting friendship."[92] In Baltimore his inspection of the harbor quickly gave way to an "interchange of sentiments and feelings";[93] and in Salem, his genuine warmth evoked affections similar to those that greeted Margaretta herself. "We believe if the human countenance can be depended on as a correct criterion," wrote one journal, "that the President was much gratified . . . ; and surely he must have read in the delighted eye, the pleasure which his presence infused."[94] Under this benign influence, Americans would redeem the sordid interests of the marketplace. "[T]here is but one common interest," Monroe contended. "We are all, equally, interested, in preserving our present republican . . . institutions, in their utmost purity."[95]

By circulating sentiment rather than capital, he had single-handedly restored a republican balance.

Steven Watts has argued that the War of 1812 marked a seismic shift in American economic behavior. Before the war the nation's elite reacted with a mixture of energy and guilt to new economic possibilities. Self-made men were breaking old ties and forging new worlds, yet they paid for success with a rigid self-discipline only sharpened by their anxiety. These tensions finally broke during the war, Watts maintains, to be submerged in a new rhetoric of militant national union that wed expansiveness and discipline, aggression and virtue. By the war's end, the old republican guard had given way to a new wave of unembarrassed liberals.[96] But the drive for sympathetic concord culminating in Monroe's tour suggests that the war did not mark an unambiguous transition between merchant capitalism and liberalism, as Watts contends. Rather, liberal spokesmen, struck by the same market irrationalities that the novels of virtue revealed, tried to soften or deny their fears by staging a strategic retreat similar to that at the end of *Margaretta* or *The Asylum*. In its most extreme form, this impulse attempted to appropriate Adam Smith's notions of equilibrium while attacking Smith himself. A common postwar refrain, for example, was that the United States was a world within itself, one "blessed with all the combined resources that can render our nation independent and happy."[97] The origin of these claims, Richard Price's 1785 tract *Observations on the Importance of the American Revolution*, argues that although trade generally softens manners and elevates societies, it would damage America, which could be corrupted only by "foreign frippery."[98] Smithian free trade might apply to European economies, but America was its own law.

A similarly mixed impulse marked America's first economic treatise, Daniel Raymond's *Thoughts on Political Economy* (1820). Disturbed by continuing shocks from the panic of 1819, Raymond argued, much like Brown, that Smith's theories failed to account for the way nations really behaved. All states sought monopolies, and should seek them, for the international marketplace was the site of an unrestricted competition whose goal was always domination and advantage. The domestic market, however, was another matter. Here ideals of fairness and justice ought to prevail, and the best way to promote that justice was to enforce absolute balance: "The principal, or at least one of the principal objects of government, should be to preserve the body politic from the disease of *accumulation*, not by stifling industry, or preventing production, . . . but by making effectual provision for the complete consumption . . . of the whole product of industry."[99]

Surpluses destroyed balance and were dangerous; an orderly market would nec-essarily insulate itself from its own tendencies. And America was the only place where such economies would succeed.

Dorothy Ross has argued that the rise of American social science in the late nine-teenth century was closely tied to fears of European disorder. American monopoly capitalism would thrive only if it avoided the twin threats of socialism and class conflict. The solution, embraced widely across disciplines, was to contend that American society was an exception, "an unchanging realm of nature, that had left behind the structured, changing European past."[100] Clearly, Jeffersonians early in the century anticipated this response—in part by appropriating tropes that had been circulating in contemporary novels. But certain texts published during the period continued to demonstrate the shaping force of sentiment in subsuming the market's excesses. It was left to a best-selling pamphlet to show how risking everything could be a form of virtuous control.

Like their cross-dressing heroines, both *The Female Marine* and *The Surprising Adventures of Almira Paul* are actually amalgams of literary disguises.[101] The frontispiece of *Almira Paul* presents the reader with an attractive sailor gesturing to a sloop and the legend, "A YOUNG WOMAN, who garbed as a Male, has . . . actually served as a common Sailor, on board of English and American armed vessels, without a discovery of her sex being made." The disguises for *The Female Marine* are even more elaborate. An early edition announced *The Adventures of Louisa Baker,* only to claim, a few months later, that *Lucy Brewer* was the real adventurer, having assumed a protective pseudonym. Shaw and Shoemaker list the work under those two names, but also under the names Lucy West, Mrs. Eliza (Bowen) Webb, and Nathaniel Coverly Jr., the Boston publisher. Even the texts' provenance is often in doubt, with editions purporting to have been published in Portsmouth, New Hampshire; Boston; Hartwick, New York; and New York City. Indeed, the best scholarship suggests that most of these names and places were part of an elaborate literary hoax so shrewd that it has taken in even a modern editor.[102] Coverly probably wrote the texts or had them written, concocted publication sites outside of Boston to boost sales, and continued to issue installments of the tale until its craze died down.[103] Although *Almira Paul* had modest sales, there may have been as many as nineteen printings of the Baker/Brewer/Webb/West story between 1815 and 1818, in parcels Coverly advertised "by the gross, dozen, or single."[104] Those quantities, as Daniel Cohen observes, probably made the tale one of the most widely circulated pamphlets in postwar Boston, if not in the nation at large.

What made these texts so popular? Part of the appeal undoubtedly lies in their prurience. Lucy Brewer purports to give the reader an inside look into the brothels of West-Boston Hill. The heroine, after having been betrayed by a merchant's son, leaves her parents' farm in shame and takes refuge in the heartless city, where a madam literally takes her in with false kindness. After the crisis of a stillbirth she is forced to remain a prostitute for the better part of three years, during which she is nightly subjected to "terrific . . . disturb[ances] . . . not perhaps equalled by those of the numerous hordes of the wild inhabitants of the Ganges" (34). A third installment of the tale, *The Awful Beacon*—nominally a tract against vice—gives case histories of the young and restless ruined by "the detestable Beldams of the Hill, and by them devoted to a state of wretchedness" (35). Almira Paul follows a similar path. After knocking about the Atlantic, parting with her money at every port, and even duping a widow into marrying her, she finds a less demanding outlet for her talents in the dockside haunts of Baltimore and Boston, ending her narrative in "Boston Goal" (24). As in many novels of sentiment, the announced intention to expose vice allowed the novelist to savor its every nuance.

But the tracts' larger appeal undoubtedly lay in their ability to link these transgressions with patriotism. Daniel Cohen has plausibly argued that Boston readers, haunted by their opposition to the "second American Revolution," snapped up *The Female Marine* for its tale of vice redeemed. When the Brewer texts are linked to their British counterpart, the political message is all the more compelling. Almira's tale is one of British corruption. As a young wife in Halifax, she is led to enlist by a desire to avenge her husband's war death but soon finds that the outgunned Americans are dangerous opponents. Forced to surrender after her very first engagement, with the *Constitution,* she soon realizes that her husband had been killed "in fair and equal comba[t]" (9), and spends the rest of the war skirting naval action aboard merchantmen or sneaking around in port until her final imprisonment. Brewer's tale makes a neat counterpoint. After a first lieutenant jokes with her about life at sea, she decides to try it. With the real-life Revolutionary example of Deborah Sampson before her, she excels in service. She wields a musket in close combat, once succeeding in the arduous feat of loading and firing nineteen straight times; falls overboard and is rescued (to the imminent risk of her disguise); and participates in "three severe engagements, and never absented myself from my post in time of danger" (48). After three years at sea—from early 1813 to the war's end—she returns to civilian life and to forgiving parents. What British corruption could engender, the texts seem to be saying, American virtue would redeem.

Beyond the obvious political celebration, however, both texts relied on cross-dressing to pose serious questions about the larger mercantile aspects of the war, questions that could be posed in no other way. In the case of Almira Paul, the problem involved the alleged rationality of the market itself. The original passion for vengeance that forced her to sea is quickly supplanted by a more powerful urge, the desire for money. Having no other source of income, Almira continually accepts hazardous voyages, only to face a series of misadventures, including severe injury and capture by an Algerine pirate, that continually bankrupt her. Having entered this treacherous world in the grip of a passion for vengeance, Almira soon sounds the depths of irrational avarice and accident, literally succumbing to her urges. Once attempting a reckless climb in the rigging, she is thrown to the deck, fractures her skull, and remains so affected that she is nicknamed "Ratling Jack" [*sic*] (11). That inability to steady herself becomes a metaphor for her perilous circulation in a mercenary world, one in which she gains favor only by allowing others "to pick my pockets" (16). Not only is it fitting that this British adventurer end her tale in a brothel; it is all but inevitable.

Almira's foreign experience makes Lucy's American life all the more poignant. Adopting the conventional trappings of the novel of virtue, the author of *The Female Marine* soon turns the tale into something else entirely. At her country home, Lucy is seduced by "the son of a respectable trader" (8), who steals a possession "of inestimable value . . . that . . . did not enrich the monster, [but] made me poor indeed!" (7–8). Her young heart "glowing with sensibility," she succumbed, she realizes, to "specious appearance" (10), and adopts the wandering role of the sentimental victim. But as Lucy prepares to leave for Boston, she begins to shed these parallels. Shamed by her ruin, she is goaded into activity, entertaining "[a]n hundred different projects" (11) before she escapes to Boston. It is not the first time she projects; the "advertisement" on the first page notes how she "formed the curious project" of turning marine—an ironic echo, perhaps, of Franklin's "bold and arduous project" of achieving moral perfection. An activist, Lucy is not content to adopt the submissive stance of the conventional heroine; and although the epigraph to the second edition of *An Affecting Narrative of Louisa Baker* quotes *Charlotte Temple*—"She was her parents' only joy:/ . . . / But ah! the cruel spoiler came"—the seduction has already changed her. To remain rigid, passive, suffering her fate in moral purity or avoiding further compromise is beyond her. Instead, she becomes a kind of trader herself, as deceptive in the cause of virtue as her seducer had been for vice. More than any other heroine we have considered, she becomes a manipulator with a conscience.

She has good need of those qualities. In Boston, as at home, her native sensibility sharply clashes with a nakedly mercenary ethos. While she is once again attracted by the sham generosity of a madam who appeals to her "open" and feeling heart (22), she is soon initiated into the colder motives of the most selfish of trades. The "arch hags" with whom she must now work "value nothing but money, and value not how they obtain it," cajoling, flattering, and plotting to gain the "cargo" of their customers (30). And although Lucy is silent about her own participation, it is clear that she has mastered the art practiced by her peers, of "disguis[ing] themselves as much as possible . . . with the aid of paint, patches, false teeth and hair" (31). Significantly, the narrative in this part of the text is static, as if Lucy, her sensibility shattered by such gross deceptions, can no longer circulate as do conventional heroines. But the confluence of profit and disguise eventually works to her advantage. Hearing from a customer that "had he been born a female, his disposition would have been the same to rove about and see the world" (35), Lucy determines to put her skills to better use. Deception now becomes the means toward heroism, as the woman of sensibility forgoes profit for travel—first in the city and along the coast, and then in the navy itself. Suddenly she is pliable for the right cause.

In most conventional accounts of the transition to capitalism, the adoption of disguise is seen as a fatal flaw. Whereas the older, precapitalist world valued authenticity and unity, the modern world enforces what Steven Watts, after Max Horkheimer, calls "personae"—a "pluralistic personality structure" that defies authenticity. Constant fluctuations of markets create constantly fluctuating personalities and a longing for a forsaken unity of feeling lying somewhere in the cultural past.[105] Clearly, *The Female Marine* does not fit this model. Lucy's escape into the larger world represents a flight from shifting domestic interests, with their confusions between commodity and virtue, to a more stable international order, where duplicity is rewarded amid mutual destruction. Through her actions she seems fully to have achieved what Fredric Jameson calls a "squar[ing]" of ideological circles, amalgamating clashing motives in a manner that seems to make perfect sense.[106] The key, as in older novels of sentiment, is virtue; but unlike the static notions of virtue that Jeffersonians used to define American order, Lucy's virtue is as subtle and pliable as that of any English competitor. She is both corrupt and saved, passive and active, an abused innocent and an aggressive materialist, who has left behind the profit motive but has absorbed the lessons that profit has to teach. In this way she can manage to be *both* an aggressive international competitor *and* one who upholds the superior virtues of modest retirement. Almost incredibly, her own conclusion points up the charms of domesticity and restraint: "If what I have exposed to public view is sufficient to induce youths of my sex never to listen to the voice of love, unless sanctioned by paternal approbation, and to resist the impulse of inclination, when it runs counter to the precepts of religion and virtue, then, indeed, have I not written in vain" (51). Having so spectacularly succeeded by yielding to inclination and interest, Lucy may well speak with the authority of a new model virtue—one that underscores her consummate ability to play off cultural roles. Retiring to the home, she remains utterly independent of it, adrift now, even as she renounces adventure. Indeed, she refuses to remain there, but takes another tour in military guise, during which she outfaces an opponent in a duel, returns to her old brothel, and marries a better businessman than the one who seduced her. Unlike Almira Paul, who remains imprisoned by the viciousness of trade, Lucy Brewer has thoroughly mastered her mercantile world.

What is most remarkable about Lucy's pliant virtue is that in the very year when Monroe himself appropriated the sympathetic attitude of the virtuous heroine, her best-selling text had left the president far behind. While the Era of Good Feelings proclaimed an all too temporary harmony of republican sentiment and market desire, Lucy turned virtue on its head. In effect she adopted the prewar claim of the New York merchants that intentions should remain as pliable as the market they served—a claim that threatened all notions of virtuous stability. But if Lucy's chameleon virtue marked the end of republican orthodoxy, it also marked the beginning of a new liberal pragmatism that would soon find its moral spokesman. "Place yourself in the middle of the stream of power and wisdom which animates all whom it floats," Ralph Waldo Emerson counseled in "Spiritual Laws" (1841), " . . . and you are without effort impelled to truth."[107] Emerson's dictum, as David Robinson argues,[108] imagined an action that was at once surrender and assertion, a formula for both fixity and constant change in perfect keeping with the commercial world. For by surrendering oneself, the new moralist would discover the more comprehensive order of higher laws, "whose waters ebb and flow with perfect balance . . . swallowing up all relations, parts and times, within itself."[109] That those laws are also the laws of the marketplace suggest how fully Lucy herself had entered that wider world, in which surrender and aggression were one.

# CHAPTER 4

# Exchange Values

The sentimental language shaped by early national novelists, merchants, and politicians was a language of survivors. Confronting sudden shocks to domestic ease, sentimental heroines, like impressed sailors or harried traders, used the language of feeling to restore moral order. To Jeffersonians, the political currency of feeling suggested an ideal market conduct, and even when that ideal failed, the adaptable virtue of heroines like Margaretta Wilmot and Lucy Brewer could inspire a principled resourcefulness. But such resources, and the optimism that fueled them, would be sorely tested by the late 1830s, when the nation was rocked by severe financial strain. Between 1837 and 1843, an unprecedented depression forced thousands into bankruptcy. Moralists saw the wave of failures as the shadow of a larger contest between reason and passion, punctuated by panic, dead faints, and tears. But to tradesmen, investors, and laborers suddenly left holding worthless paper or locked out of shuttered banks and stores, a lapse in reason could not entirely account for the problem. Many were forced to confront a haunting possibility: that by midcentury the old moral economy was beginning to slip away. If sentimental idealism could soothe in such an emergency, it would need to match the heartless conditions of a new market order.

A significant number of fictions in the late thirties and early forties took on that ideological challenge. Popular writers recurred almost obsessively to the central experience of sudden and unmerited impotence brought about by market collapse. For many conservatives, the lesson of the panic was quite clear: retrench, repent, reform. The excesses of the midthirties—the poisons of gambling and speculation—needed to be expelled before the body politic could be restored. But other writers, both men and women, sensed a more powerful change in these circumstances that no mere assertion of reason could forestall. With insolvency, these writers saw, an older vision of the autonomous self was also waning, and newer conceptions of a more plastic, deft, market-molded individual were demanded. It was in this context that the circulating heroines of an earlier era emerged as a potent cultural force. Such figures simultaneously demonstrated sincerity and suppleness, inner constancy and shrewd responsiveness. Collectively, they helped to shape an awareness, shared diffusely by many contemporaries, that the liberal market order Americans were creating could no longer be guided by the strident republicanism of the Jacksonian era. The critical fictions I will examine in this chapter attempt to find a middle ground between an old moral autonomy and a new market heteronomy, a nostalgic self-sufficiency and a more vigorous commerce. They do so by insisting on a more supple virtue, a sentimental enterprise that saves the market itself from its worst offenses.

In one sense, the outpouring of feeling by victims of the panic was an extension of a cultural impulse stemming from the Revolution. In both periods, sentiment allowed republican citizens to imagine diffuse and distressing social conditions in reassuring terms. A rhetoric of feeling sustained the illusion that Americans, taxed by market pressures, were united by intrinsically meaningful bonds impervious to injury or distress. Fictions like *Margaretta* or *The Asylum* wove that message into plots that traced the ascent from sentimental abjection to sympathetic mastery. By yielding to market forces, readers were promised, they could reclaim a threatened autonomy.

But the increasingly frequent panics inaugurated by the Jacksonian era challenged that article of faith. It was impossible to assert prudence or to achieve competency when currency values spun wildly out of control, suspending all economic activity. Insisting on intrinsic value proved meaningless in such a climate, just as maxims of moral restraint seemed to falter. The very desire to envision the crisis through bonds of affection collapsed: the problem was too big, too opaque, many contemporaries thought, to be grasped at once, or at all. From this cultural impasse, two important responses emerged. The first, fashioned during the panic years by Ralph Waldo Emerson, sought to rehabilitate a threatened masculine autonomy through a more vigorous affection. Figuring his own considerable indebtedness as an ever-widening circle of attachments—to his brother William, his family dependents, professional associates, and, finally, his lecture audiences—Emerson redeemed the debts through an imagery of sympathy and sincerity. He aspired to be a transparent medium, an affectionate general equivalent like money itself, trading on feeling. It was a capacity, he insisted, that he shared with all true souls. All could rise above contingency in a sincere exchange rooted in the behavior of the marketplace.

Emerson's response to the crisis in male autonomy was echoed and extended by a second impulse, largely pursued by women. In dozens of microhistories, writers responded to the impasse by imagining what a contemporary called "character-less" women—resourceful figures who resisted domestic confinement. Unlike their Jeffersonian predecessors, these sympathetic actors did not have to bear their fate alone. They were not thrust from home through imprudence or malevolence, forced to recoup a lost intimacy in sentimental circulation. Rather, they most often replaced failed fathers and husbands, whose excessive feeling marked their bewilderment in a new environment where affection alone did not solve social ills. What was demanded was a more pliable prudence, one compounded equally of feeling and transparency, integrity and the ability to yield. Theirs was the sinuous virtue of a Lucy Brewer cleansed of its abjection and risk. This cultural narrative, present in dozens of popular fictions during the period, emerges most fully in Eliza Follen's *Sketches of Married Life* (1838) and Susan Warner's *Queechy* (1852). Collectively, these "woman's fictions" complete the work that Emerson begins. They elaborate a new structure of feeling that sought to dispel panic through a reinvigorated sympathy.

## The American Way of Debt

Although scholars have recently played down the panic of 1837 and its aftermath, calling it a deflation rather than a depression,[1] Jacksonians themselves took a different view. To be sure, Democrats were quick to dismiss the contraction in credit as a necessary reaction to financial imbalances brought on by their political enemies, while Whigs blamed the reckless policies of Jackson. Virtually all spokesmen feared the era's rampant speculation, the boom psychology that profit and confidence were limitless. When the boom faltered, many reverted to republican warnings against market corruption and urged a return to simplicity and virtue. These conservative voices often harked back to a "truly" republican world in which market relations were rooted in face-to-face encounters, and virtue was as legible in conduct as in currency. "There must, above all, be a rigid attachment to the dictates of the moral sense," warned one monitor in 1840, a resolve that would "answer as a perfect protection from the attacks of avarice and sensuality."[2] Exercising republican virtue was like gazing into a mirror: positing a moral sense, one discovered it in the world. And outer harmony, in turn, was a sign of inward mastery. Through such appeals, anxious Americans imagined not only that the crisis had a clear and simple solution, but also that they remained autonomous agents capable of restoring order to a world gone awry.

But not everyone agreed. Just beneath the surface of these calls to order there often lay an uneasy fascination with an unpredictable market poised for a capitalist takeoff that ignored the moral world. In the same journals, sometimes in the same articles as the appeals to reason, could be found glimpses of another world—not exactly irrational, but so complex and alien as to elude attempts to grasp it or to see it whole. A writer in J. H. Hunt's *Merchants' Magazine and Commercial Review,* for example, admitted that currency fluctuations had become so "palpable and astonishing" as to "dizzy the head most calmly employed in observing it. . . . [A]nd as to the scrutiny of every particular wheel or spring that is set in motion, while all are in such constant action, the attempt is vain and fruitless."[3] The clockmaker's mechanisms that provided a central metaphor for classic republicanism seemed to be yielding to a new, more diffuse machine. Others saw the problem as a want of moral or physical constraints. "Nobody has much faith in the stability of any thing," complained one writer at the end of 1839, "for the reason that little or no stability has yet been shown any where."[4] Merchants feared being swept away in a tide of debt—an anxiety captured in Edgar Allan Poe's "A Descent into the Maelström" (1841), where salvation lay in abandoning oneself to the whirlpool, whose "gleaming and ghastly radiance" was magnified by "the bewildering rapidity with which [it] spun around."[5] A volatile market had made relations between all elements of society more shifting, treacherous, and uncertain.

Intimately tied to these struggles with the financial elements is the metaphor of the panic as a vast, intimidating, but opaque spectacle that few observers could penetrate. The metaphor appears frequently in congressional debates on the crisis. The Democrat Francis Pickens, for example, maintained that the banking system "is as hidden as the air we breathe, and penetrates unseen, but, alas, not unfelt, into the most retired scenes of society."[6] Daniel Webster lamented that while currency fluctuations were understood by plutocrats, such "operations are a little out of the sight of other classes of the community."[7] The mysteries of credit, with their manifold contradictions between appearance and reality, needed to be exposed so that autonomous reason could reassert control. What was demanded, wrote "A Democrat in Earnest" to the *Richmond Enquirer,* was that "the whole world see" the politics and consequences of banking. Both stockholders and the general public would then "look to their own interests,"[8] and the magic of the market system would do the rest.

But few polemicists saw the full depth of the crisis. Democrats read the panic as a plea for laissez-faire. Their article of faith was that unfettered private enterprise produced the greatest public good, and yet unfettered interest had also led to the speculative mania that fueled the panic. Merely break the "unnatural fetters" and allow universal, local, and popular credit, contended one writer for the *United States Magazine and Democratic Review,* and the *"intrinsic* value" of currency would be reinforced by the intrinsic virtues of Americans.[9] Like his Jeffersonian predecessors, he sought a principle immune to market change. But the imagery with which this essayist describes the diseased and the healthful operation of the system is nearly identical. When one tries to trace the corruptions of credit, he soon becomes lost amid innumerable influences that "ramified out to myriads of minutest fibres" (112). Yet the same ramifications would magically solve the credit crisis by allowing unfettered local interests to "determine, with an unerring instinct, the proper proportions" (118) of specie and credit. The unrestrained excess of a system awash in credit would somehow be checked by the unrestrained activity of virtuous yet credit-hungry farmers, land agents, country storekeepers, factors, commission merchants, local banks, and consumers. The threats to moral restraint are thus magically neutralized by an opaque mass of innumerable activities, even as such activities are condemned as the root of the problem. Once again, a boundless polity seemed to elude ready control.

To Whig writers, the economic crisis exposed a yet more terrifying blindness, a moral opacity that could not be diagnosed or cured. One of the most revealing sketches, appearing during the darkest months of the panic, detailed the fortunes of Harry O'Blank.[10] In a tale that incorporated all the cultural elements noted so far—the emphasis on sight, the preoccupation with uncertainty, the desire for autonomy, and the wisdom of laissez-faire—O'Blank is depicted as a cynosure and a thief. An attractive college student turned prosperous merchant, O'Blank is laid low by the embargo of 1807 and escapes to the West. Years later word comes of a pleasure palace he had built for himself, and of his parading about the area "fashionably and richly dressed" (253). But when a dead man turns up in the mansion and a search is made, authorities conclude not only that O'Blank has been killed while attempting to commit burglary, but also that his basement conceals a nest of dungeons and storerooms containing the loot from various crimes. When the secret comes to light, Harry's wife reacts in kind, hanging herself in her fashionable silk robe, "profusely decked with jewels" (255). The tale thus seems to capture the uncertainties of the period by focusing on the seductive yet subterranean influences of the market.

But the tale also strikes at many of the comfortable assumptions Jacksonian readers made—assumptions about their own moral hold on the market and their ability to manage change. The Whig writer, broaching the contradictions scouted by the Democratic author of "The Moral of the Crisis," suggests that laissez-faire simultaneously prevents and provokes the destructive effects of "CHANCE" (250). Jefferson's "wicked" embargo (250), he charges, squeezed the life from the eastern seaboard and provoked a depression. "Then came the breaking up of the elements of community," as families scattered in search of food and clothing (253). Ironically, the dispersion brought on by a bankrupt policy sharpened an O'Blank family trait. For no one was really home at the O'Blank household. It was a parental maxim that chance governed families as well as the world, so that even a simple dinner was likely to end in "a general breaking up of the family elements . . . [in] uproar and riot" (250). The "absence of all parental authority" (251) had thus schooled young Harry to thrive amid conditions of chaos. When the embargo triggered depression, he felt entirely at his ease.

But even though the tragic conclusion to the tale visits justice on moral and financial rogues, its focus on the implications of chance raises other questions not so easily settled. On the one hand, the Whig emphasis on family authority and government from above seems vindicated in this account. The failure to assert moral and paternal responsibility at home creates the chaotic conditions in which rogues thrive. Conversely, the abuse of paternal authority by a president increases chaos abroad, allowing for a perfect fit between loose men and hard times. On the other hand, the tale also suggests that the older model of rational and moral restraint may be equally threatened. Increased mobility and market fluctuation might well make any exercise of control largely impossible and moral autonomy a mere illusion. The very conditions of chance seemed to open a new set of disturbing possibilities sharply upsetting to Whig notions of disciplined economic development in a protected marketplace. Not only was the economic villain of the tale a confidence man, but he also mimicked the conditions of chance itself by becoming literally Blank—both infinitely adaptable and inscrutable. Like his underground hoard, he could not be seen into.

The moral problem posed by the panic came down to this: could one leap boldly into a rapidly developing market requiring a radical restriction on positive freedom, on the ability to define one's own moral economy? As John Ashworth argues, that question motivates a wide range of political expression during the postpanic years.[11] For Democrats, the panic struck at a fundamental article of faith. Convinced that the only check to an aristocratic abuse of power was its diffusion among a multitude of self-interested individuals, they confronted an economy that turned that liberal formula on its head. Their attacks on the market abuses of moneyed aristocrats were an expression of a deeper fear that the economic system of moderate but unrestrained competition they envisioned was threatened. Panic, complained Senator Robert Strange in 1837, "has a tendency to make us a nation of gamblers, by the constant stimulus to that spirit which finds a place in almost every bosom, from the savage to the sage. . . . [T]he frequent and sudden reverses to which every man is exposed . . . must, in process of time, engender all that loose morality which characterizes the professed worshippers at the shrine of fortune."[12] Such pronouncements, as Michael Rogin and others have argued, look simultaneously forward and backward—forward to the capitalist enterprise of the postbellum years, backward to a more orderly world of limited market penetration.[13] It was a formula that attempted to claim an uncertain middle ground in a rapidly shifting terrain.

Yet the explosive politics generated by this threat was not confined to Democrats. Whigs, too, after 1840 often evinced a mood of pessimism approaching despair. With their ability to impose their legislative will checked by such insurgencies as the Dorr rebellion in Rhode Island and widespread antibanking sentiment, as well as by the sudden death of William Henry Harrison and the intransigence of John Tyler, Whigs after 1837 felt a heightened sense of crisis, captured by the brooding Philip Hone. The "tyranny of public opinion," he wrote in his diary, referring, in part, to Jackson's manipulation of the electorate, " . . . has destroyed that proud and manly personal independence which was heretofore the characteristic of my countrymen."[14] The precipitous drop in prices caused by the panic had not only crippled him but also turned him into a debtor, since he had cosigned loans made to family and friends. Long after recovery had taken hold, Hone remained in debt. "There must be a recuperative principle in this great country to restore things some time or another," he wrote bitterly in 1842, "but I shall not live to see it" (2:139). Although he continued to enjoy the life of a patrician power broker, even receiving an appointment as naval officer for New York from Zachary Taylor in 1849, he remained distressed by the market's excesses. The stigma of debt had challenged his sense of autonomy.

Hone's anxieties over the loss of independence received national attention between 1840 and 1842, when Congress debated and passed a bankruptcy act. Like most other economic issues of the day, this second attempt to establish a constitutionally mandated "uniform" bankruptcy code (the first had been instituted in 1800 and had lasted for three years) was sharply partisan. But the measure also marked a common recognition that the cherished republican ideal of competency was fading. "What . . . can an honest debtor do?" asked petitioners to Congress in 1840. "He is compelled to abandon the business for which his education and habits have fitted him, or submit to work for hire as a clerk, and thus earn a pittance for the support of his family, without a hope of bettering his condition." [15] His independence shattered, the bankrupt became a testament to an illogical and vindictive legal system that punished bad luck. The panic had proved that even prudent citizens could be ruined.

While many Democrats attacked those "desperate" speculators who plunged recklessly into ruin (463), others resorted to an imagery of feminized suffering that evoked the full depth of the bankrupt's impotence. "Without a measure of this kind," asserted John Norvell, the bankrupt becomes "an outcast and a reproach in the world; mortified, humiliated, shunned by others, and degraded in his own estimation" (464). The debtor's shame is reminiscent of the seduced victim's response to pregnancy, a link that Henry Hubbard echoed by warning that "a long subsequent life of purity would not be sufficient to wipe away the deep stain, with which [the debtor's] moral character would be tainted" (485). [16] Even Whigs, who generally supported the code, could not escape the sense that social barriers were eroding. Why distinguish between the commercial bankrupt and the larger pool of insolvent farmers, wondered Oliver Smith? "All classes of our citizens contract debts . . . [and] may be placed in the condition of bankruptcy" (837). Congress could, and did, limit the merchant's liability, but could it provide the water to wash away his stain? Debtors throughout the 1840s found no easy answer.

For both Whigs and Democrats, however, the deepest challenge the panic posed was ideological. Faced with an ever more complex economy and polity, they struggled to adapt their republican heritage to more exacting demands. George Forgie has argued that the antebellum generation was "post-heroic," acutely conscious of its duty to a Revolutionary past, yet uncertain how to maintain that legacy. [17] As different elements of classical republicanism gradually gave way— the elitist emphasis on leisure, the expectation of modest economic activity, the condition of rough equality—what remained was the stress on independence in a morally intelligible world. Whigs cherished a familial model of autonomy in which powerful fathers ordered the lives of inferiors, and they bristled when powerful executives like Jackson suborned that model themselves. Democrats clung to the yeoman ideal of Jefferson and John Taylor of Caroline, even as market uncertainties threatened the average man's ability to order his affairs. The nation's core belief itself was yielding to the pressures of change. Responding to these pressures, many writers would seek a middle ground by reimagining market behavior not as a process of taint and seduction but as the desire to be immersed in the economic currents. Virtue was no longer the capacity to resist fluctuation but to incorporate it, to make variation an aspect of the sensitive soul. Central to that reorientation was the work of one of the era's most gifted debtors, Ralph Waldo Emerson.

## *Ralph Waldo Emerson, Bookkeeper*

Toward the close of 1839, a year that saw him take on large risks both as a debtor to Massachusetts banks and as a lecturer seeking ever wider audiences, Ralph Waldo Emerson had an anxiety dream. Imagining himself, a few days before Christmas, at Harvard's library, he noticed "a man reading . . . and one who stood by said, 'He readeath advertisements,' meaning that he read for the market only & not for truth. Then I said,—Do I read advertisements?"[18] The answer to that question was, strictly, Yes. For the previous two years, Emerson had been his own impresario—renting lecture halls, writing advertising copy, distributing tickets—all with mixed results. Never commanding more than fifty dollars per lecture, and sometimes as little as ten dollars, he had been able, nevertheless, to derive a modest income while he honed his transcendentalism and shaped the material for his essays. By the end of 1839, however, he was facing new pressures. He had borrowed thousands of dollars to help his brother William and was paying hundreds in interest each year. Although the town of Concord rated him a man of means, most of his property was tied up in stocks whose dividends could not cover his expenses. As the waves of the nationwide depression washed over Boston, he had increasing trouble paying his bills and took out dozens of loans just to stay even with the scores of creditors—day laborers, dry goods merchants, cooks, stage coach operators, booksellers, coal porters, asylum keepers—with which his ledgers abound. The "anchorite"[19] who would soon declare to the

Boston Mechanics' Apprentices' Library Association that "the general system of our trade" was one of "perjury and fraud"[20] was very much in the market. Indeed, there were times he must have dreaded that the market would flatten him.

That Emerson was forced to confront the market is an issue many scholars have discussed.[21] What has rarely been explored, though, is the connection between the anxieties of these panic years and Emerson's fashioning of a distinctive stance toward the marketplace, a stance that would have profound significance for an emerging middle class. For Emerson, during this period, market uncertainties became linked to questions of value. Just as the moralist urged his countrymen to retain their hold on the immutable Ideal, so he was forced to confront the daily uncertainties of a world unusually mutable and fragile. Declaring the need for self-reliance, he remained deeply in debt. Attacking the falsities of speculation, he depended on credit for his very survival. From this dialectic of ideal and actual, Emerson gradually developed a market persona that managed to be sympathetic, shrewd, and sincere. By redefining this behavior as a variant of friendship, he imagined friendly activity as a means of restoring intrinsic value while allowing that value to be shaped by others. In doing so, Emerson gave intellectual depth to the panic and helped to define popular responses to radically new market conditions that deeply influenced his most productive years.

The decade from 1837 to 1847—roughly the years between his delivery of "The American Scholar" before the Phi Beta Kappa Society at Cambridge and his departure for England—is the most critical in Emerson's career. During these years he publicly and decisively broke with Unitarianism, gave up his preaching in East Lexington, and turned to lecturing and writing. During the first half of that period, the immediate years of the panic, he published the first collection of his *Essays,* delivered the lectures that made his name, and established *The Dial.* He attended periodic meetings of Hedge's, or the Transcendental Club; patronized a widening circle of intellectuals; and published American editions of Thomas Carlyle's works. It was during this period as well that he began accruing a formidable debt. Throughout the decade, his account books show, Emerson's income never quite met his expenses.[22] In 1837 alone, as the panic deepened, he spent or loaned $700.72 more than he took in, and although the balances varied during the decade, he was never able to turn a profit. From 1837 to 1842, his loans and expenses overshadowed his income by $3,627.17; for the decade 1837–47, the figure was $7,487.62. To put these figures into perspective, Emerson's total loss for the decade was about twice the value of his Concord home. If today's dollar is taken to be worth roughly fourteen times the value of a dollar in the 1840s, Emerson's deficit for the period was almost $105,000.[23]

The ledgers alone, of course, do not tell the whole story. As in all facets of his life, Emerson's accounts suggest that he held much in reserve. In 1839 the Concord assessors estimated his net worth (stocks and real estate) to be about $23,000—roughly $320,000 in today's terms—so that he could well afford to lose a few thousands.[24] The ledgers also teem with evidence of his far-flung obligations, everything from the support of his sister-in-law, Lucy Jackson Brown, to loans to Bronson Alcott and Henry Thoreau. Meticulously and democratically, Emerson recorded all such transactions, however minor, until the pages devoted to expenses swelled his double-entry account books and he was forced to skip over dozens of blank pages to keep his income ledgers in tandem with his outgo. Such obligations, including the largest he incurred for his brother William, were not so much expenses as expressions of benevolence by an unusually conscientious steward. If Emerson were both banker and debtor, then God was the primary creditor. Nevertheless, as Emerson sat at his desk recording his expenses and his ruminations, the stock funds often retreated into the distance and he was haunted, as in his dream, by the pressures of the moment. He could not sell the stock, he could not live on the dividends, and he could not afford his obligations. The result, for Emerson, as for thousands of others in these years, was ballooning debt.

Although there is no simply causal relationship between Emerson's finances and his thought, his fashioning of a vocation during these years and the aims he imagined for his writing were profoundly conditioned by his daily and monthly accounts. Emerson's monetary activities over the decade can be divided into three general periods. The years 1837-39, when the shock of the panic was most profound, were years of heavy loans, principally to William. By the end of 1839 the loans to William amounted to $6,400—the majority of which Emerson raised by taking out loans of his own. The years 1840-43 were years of consolidation, when Emerson tried to digest the debt through modest repayment and refinancing, principally by selling off stock. The final period, 1844 to his departure for England in October 1847, was one of investment. As the economy revived, Emerson bought land and built houses. Although he continued to depend on loans, he was more certain of his prospects. By then, Emerson had come to terms with the market and had discovered new ways to imagine moral stability. As his land purchases suggest, he had come to ground his market transactions in the natural world.

On or about 12 December 1836, William sent his brother an anguished message. The Wall Street lawyer had bought property on Staten Island, financing the purchase with a series of loans. Land values in the New York area had been steadily rising in the midthirties, and William apparently deemed the property a shrewd investment. But by December, following "unusual pressure on the money market,"[25] William was caught short. He owed $2,150 immediately, with another two notes totaling $2,348 due in four months. Emerson's initial response was to deplore his brother's "anxiety," but to confess that "I have not the means of aiding you" (*L* 2:50). But if he did not have that much cash on hand, Emerson knew where he could get it. Borrowing from Lidian, Lucy Jackson Brown, and the Globe Bank, he soon sent William a draft for $2,900 (LDG 1.14; *L* 2:53). So began a complex series of transactions that would, within two years, funnel nearly all of the $6,500 William said he "want[ed]" in his first anxious letter of December 1836.[26]

Most of the succeeding loans were much smaller, with Emerson helping William meet a variety of bank deadlines. From April through August 1837, for example, Emerson scraped together $700 for his brother (LDG 1.156; *L* 2:86–87, 91, 93). In May 1838 he sent him another $300, the following September he sent almost $200 more, and throughout 1839 there were numerous small loans. Most of these sums Emerson obtained from several area banks, including the Concord, Atlantic, and Globe Banks, and the Middlesex Institution for Savings. Some of the money also came from investments. A ledger entry for 4 April 1837, for example, records the receipt of $250 from Pliny Cutler (LDG 1.18), the lawyer representing Emerson in the probate case over the will of his first wife, Ellen Tucker Emerson. This sum may have represented a semiannual payment Emerson received from the Tucker estate—a sum he sent to his brother at the end of the month. And at the beginning of August 1838, Emerson used a "dividend of one hundred percent of the capital stock owned by Lidian E."—eleven shares in the Boston Marine Insurance Company (LDG 1.30)—to pay down part of the initial $2,900 loan to William (LDG 1.93), thus shoring up his credit for future loans. Although Emerson had help with many of these transactions, relying on the advice of his banker friend Abel Adams, his widespread activities during the period reveal him as an adept and resourceful borrower.

A number of features emerge from Emerson's ledgers and correspondence during these years. Most striking is his position as an engaged, often skittish spectator of a national tragedy. Although William's dilemma did not exactly retrace the popular story of the speculator caught in his own web, it was close enough to produce some uncomfortable moments. When Emerson, in search of funds, consulted William Sohier, a lawyer in the Tucker case, he was forced to listen to a lecture on the "judiciousness" of New York investments and the integrity of New York lawyers. "I told him," Emerson wrote William, "that the attitude in which he now saw you, was wholly unjust to your character & habits, for you were never before a speculator, & probably never would be again, but were the most discreet & honest of men." Abel Adams was no less skeptical, and Emerson had to endure more criticism as his old friend "expatiated on the same string" (*L* 2:86). But if William did not seem the classic speculator, he developed the classic symptoms. By July 1837, Emerson was lamenting that his brother had become "invalid," and urged him "Please to consider firstly & lastly that we shall never get on if your health fails" (*L* 2:89). "Do not be sick," Emerson implored the following week. "That would be giving too much importance to this land-trap" (*L* 2:92). Even after he recovered his health, William was often subject to anxiety, confessing wryly in May 1838 that he was "as craving as Regan or Goneril in the play"[27] as he sought more funds. The references to stock characters allowed both brothers to identify and rise above their problems, which appeared as familiar as Shakespeare, yet remote as the actors on a stage. The frightening financial scenes were all scripted, but William imagined he retained the freedom to avoid tragedy.

Emerson, however, while playing savior in this family drama, was not entirely immune to his brother's anxieties. In June 1837 he resisted William's request to endorse a loan. Most of their transactions had been secured through a variety of collateral, including mortgages, life insurance policies, and other securities. But a large "new obligation," especially given Emerson's own "feeble health," was a risk that his modest income "does not justify me in signing" (*L* 2:83). Emerson was forced to adopt a similar tone about a year later when William again needed funds. "Your last letter troubled me somewhat because I supposed you had before fully understood the narrow limits of the aid I had just now offered," he lectured William, reminding him that Emerson could not extend a loan beyond July "because it is my household purse for bread & meat & shoes" (*L* 2:132). Indeed, on occasion Emerson seemed as needy as William. In August 1839 he thanked William for a check for $125, "as I had exhausted if not my credit yet certainly my estimate of my credit, & so of course my power to ask for more" (*L* 2:217). Now the pressure was coming from a different quarter—the obligations Emerson incurred in printing Carlyle's *Critical and Miscellaneous Essays,* for which Emerson laid out all expenses against future profits. Although he was eventually reimbursed, Emerson had as good a reason as William to bemoan his financial fate. "I am no very good economist," Emerson lamented early in 1837, complaining that despite "a large income . . . I seem to be no dollar the better" (*L* 2:64). The confession must have become something of a standing joke in the family, for his sister-in-law recalled the remark almost two years later, lamenting to William that the two "were own brothers." Both had to learn how to be "more wise & more economical."[28]

Emerson's private response to the panic had the same mixture of pity and fear, as he sought to take the full measure of the spectacle. The same day that he drew up a detailed account of his assets in the hope of locating funds for his brother, he lamented his own impecunious labors over Greek and German. In these times, the timid scholar was as unskillful as the "merchant who should invest his money at three per cent," far below the prevailing return rate of 6 percent. Without the faith that his scholarship had some more "general . . . advantage," Emerson ruefully concluded, "we might shoot ourselves" (*JMN* 5:296). Yet he was not therefore willing to jump into the marketplace. In his journal he likened himself to a scientific spectator of a great calamity, observing for the first time the fault lines that produced the earthquake (*JMN* 5:333). A series of entries he wrote on 14 May 1837, after he commiserated with William about the financial crisis in New York, captures his ambivalence. "Yesterday afternoon I stirred the earth about my shrubs & trees & quarreled with the piper-grass," he recorded. "The humblebee & and the pine warbler seem to me the proper objects of attention in these disastrous times" (*JMN* 5:327). Better to quarrel with tangible vegetation than with intangible credit. Yet, revisiting the thought somewhat later, Emerson had a change of heart. "When I see an evil," he now declared, "it is unmanly to hide my head in the flowering bushes & say I will hunt the humble bee & behold the stars & leave this sorrow for those whom it concerns" (*JMN* 5:330). The real thing was to embrace calamity and work his way toward the Ideal.

In taking this approach, Emerson was strongly tempted to turn the panic into one more metaphor for Compensation. Debt was a stern preceptor, he had declared in "Nature" (1836), the discipline imposed by Spirit. So, too, the "universal calamity" that had "checkmated" (*JMN* 5:331) his neighbors taught him a lesson about society. People were mere appendages—"the treadle of a wheel," or worse, mere "money chest[s]" craving some higher duty. "Let me begin anew," Emerson heroically declared. "Let me teach the finite to know its Master. Let me ascend above my fate and work down upon my world" (*JMN* 5:332). The trouble was that the market was not as remote as State Street, the Divinity School, or other institutions that drew his fire. It had infiltrated Concord and worked its way into the Emerson home. There is a poignancy to Emerson's stubborn insistence in 1838, as his debt load steadily rose, that his "acciden- tal freedom by means of a permanent income is nowise essential to my habits" (*JMN* 7:71). Accidents of the marketplace had continued to erode the freedom that Emerson's income bestowed, and had turned even his investments into illiquid liabilities not to be risked in the panic. There was thus ample warrant for his reflection later that year that "you must pay your entire expense. Uncles & Aunts, fathers & elder brothers . . . may stand for a time between you & justice; but it is only postponement[—]you must pay at last your own debt" (*JMN* 7:144– 45). Only by working through the marketplace could one hope to rise above its demands.

As the credit crisis around Boston gradually eased, Emerson took steps to pay his debts. Throughout the late thirties, when money was tight, he took out short-term loans, generally for two to three months at 6 percent. Often he paid off these loans by taking out new ones, creating elaborate genealogies of debt. In two transactions on 3 May and 1 June 1838, for example, Emerson borrowed $300 and $200 from the Concord Bank and sent the money to William (LDG 1.26; *L* 2:128). The $200 was a long-term loan: an entry for 18 June 1840 shows that he was still paying interest on it (LDG 2.18). The $300 loan fell due in three months, and he paid it off by taking out another loan of $500 from the Concord Bank (LDG 1.32, 95), sending the remaining $200 (minus interest) to William (*L* 2:159).[29] Three months later, when the new loan fell due, Emerson repaid it by borrowing yet again, this time from the Middlesex Institution for Savings (LDG 1.34, 103). Eighteen months after that, he was still paying 6 percent interest on this loan (LDG 2.18). By early 1840, such debt kiting had begun to take its toll. "I suppose that now I am at the bottom of my wheel of debt," Emerson wrote William, "& shall not hastily venture lower" (*L* 2:283–84). This sense of exposure must have contributed to a series of debt consolidations over the next three years. Although the new activity did not break the cycle of deficit spending, Emerson was eventually able to take advantage of more favorable interest rates and thus to reduce his payments.

Significantly, many of these new transactions involved the sale of stock. Throughout the late thirties, Emerson's investment counselor, Abel Adams, refused to let him sell off his holdings, reminding Emerson that he would have to take a loss. But when stock prices rebounded in 1840, Adams decided it was time to act. The first step, on 15 August 1840, was to transfer his $3,500 mortgage, outstanding since 1835, from the Boston Provident Institution for Savings to Globe Bank. To do so, Emerson borrowed a fresh $3,500 from Globe (LDG 2.7), paid off Provident (LDG 2.22), and retired part of the new Globe debt by selling ten shares of Massachusetts Bank stock (part of his legacy from Ellen Tucker Emerson) for $2,479.52 (LDG 2.7). Now he had two large loans from Globe, one for $1,040 (originally $1,140) (LDG 1.158; 2.18), outstanding since January 1837, and the second for $1,020.48 (LDG 2.26). In the ensuing months he would pay down some of this principal, so that his indebtedness was $1,940 (LDG 2.26). Still he was paying 6 percent interest. Continued repayments of principal would reduce his total indebtedness to Globe to about $1,300 by April 1843 (LDG 2.36, 112). By then, however, his engagements elsewhere had begun to creep up again. In addition to the Globe loan, he owed money to the Massachusetts Fire and Marine Insurance Company and to the Concord and Middlesex Banks—a total of $3,567.99, much of it borrowed for William (LDG 2.128). To reduce this burden, Adams arranged for a new loan from Globe for $3,500 at 4 percent, allowing Emerson to pay off these more costly debts (LDG 2.37; L 3:242). His interest payment to the Globe Bank now amounted to $140 annually, and his deficit for all of 1843 was $734.93.

Although Emerson relied on Adams for market timing during this period, he nevertheless demonstrated a deft, often breathtaking ability to manage a web of complex transactions. In addition to his loan activity, he was also handling investments, payments, and ledgers for others. He kept track of Lidian's investments and rental income from Plymouth properties as well as of the modest investments of Lucy Jackson Brown. He paid for his brother Bulkeley's upkeep at a variety of institutions around Concord (William reimbursed Emerson for half the cost) and managed funds for the care of the indigent Nancy Barron in a Concord asylum. He sponsored his nephew, Frank Brown, at Brook Farm, as he had paid tuition for the son of a deceased friend, George Sampson, at Alcott's school. He bailed out *The Dial* from time to time and loaned money to friends and relatives. He oversaw the publication of Jones Very's poetry and kept meticulous records for

Carlyle, arranging for transatlantic couriers and currency exchanges. Above all, one gets the sense from Emerson's ledgers of a man for whom finance was not merely a means of survival but a mode of affiliation. His loan activity, in part, made palpable the long lines of influence and concern his essays would trace through the world.

As the country emerged from the depression in 1844, Emerson used better times to cement some of those bonds. In January 1844, he paid off the Globe debt by selling thirty-six shares of City Bank stock (inherited from Ellen) for $3,456 (LDG 2.45). A year later, feeling more prosperous, he began to make his presence felt in Concord. He paid $500 for the land on which Alcott would build his house, and acted as his agent for a loan (LDG 3.8). In June and July 1845, he borrowed heavily once again, using $1,020 to pay for a new house for Lucy Jackson Brown and financing the building by selling another fourteen shares of City Bank stock (LDG 3.13, 15). In December 1845 he bought a forty-one-acre woodlot on Walden Pond for $1,239.56, paid for by a bank loan and the sale of Atlantic Bank stock (LDG 3.17). From 1844 to 1847, Emerson took out more than $4,000 in loans—most, it should be noted, paid off not from income but from sales of assets. Yet he had also managed to expand his land holdings and increase the permanent members of his Concord circle. By any measure, his debts remained formidable. But as for so many of his contemporaries, Emerson's debts became so numerous as to be nearly indistinguishable from the fabric of living itself. As his ledgers abundantly indicate, the debt practices of the Jacksonian economy had been thoroughly domesticated in Emerson's Concord retreat.

Emerson's shift from anxiety to affiliation marks a broader rapprochement with the marketplace. While he continued to attack the harsher aspects of capitalism, he also made trade more intimate by associating it with benevolence and friendship. This move allowed him to see his personal and family crisis in larger terms that made money management itself a higher calling. To read advertisements with one hand on his heart was a means of urging all Americans to engage in what John Winthrop once called "familiar Commerce."[30]

Emerson's anxieties over market participation, many writers have noted, reflected concerns over his own vocation. Having left the ministry and cultivated a wider, more anonymous audience, he embarked on this new career at the precise moment when social relations seemed to be driven askew by the currency crisis. His pronouncements of the period suggest a heightened sense of vulnerability as he sought to take the measure of the remote pressures shaping his new calling, so that the panic became almost a metaphor for his personal fortunes. Throughout the early years of the decade, when the depression was most severe, Emerson continued to echo Jacksonian attacks on predatory capitalism. Immense new prosperity, he argued in his "Address on Education," delivered on 10 June 1837, "overpowered in the farmer the still religious tendencies of his primitive employment" and substituted a "fever," detectable as well in both scholar and clerk. All were seduced by "this excessive sensual life."[31] Like other critics of paper money, Emerson longed for intrinsic value. The worst aspect of trade, he argued in early 1838, was its utter aimlessness—"bubble built on bubble" and blunder upon blunder until greed brought down the whole structure (*EL* 2:363). Credit itself was treacherous, a "dangerous balloon" (*EL* 2:242) waiting to wreck all those willing to build on its thin and plastic surface. But of most concern was the infectious spirit of commerce, shoving aside the state, the family, and faith itself in pursuit of profit. "It encroaches on all sides," Emerson worried in December 1839. " 'Business before friends' is its byword" (*EL* 3:191). At a time when he was struggling to sustain friends and meet payments, the mechanisms of credit must have seemed particularly sinister indeed.

Running through Emerson's objections to the market, as through the objections of his contemporaries, was a nostalgia for unassailable worth. That longing took pragmatic as well as symbolic forms. When William was most desperate for cash, in July 1837, Emerson tried to anchor their discussion in brute facts. "If 20 shares of Bank stock shall be worth next year to me $2000," he reasoned, "it would seem unwise to sell them for $1800, or perhaps much less." To do so would be to act, "as the seamen say, 'by main strength & ignorance' " (*L* 2:90). Battered by the uncertain currents of the market, he refused to take more than his share of losses. Prudence demanded adopting the long view, resisting the panic selling that was sweeping the nation. But there was also an element of almost wistful resolve in Emerson's refusal to accept anything less than full value for his securities. As he held onto the stocks for years after they had depreciated and failed to pay dividends, he continued to insist on an ideal value immune to actual decay. Par value was real value, he stubbornly maintained, an intrinsic (or transcendental) identity that no accidental commerce should alter. "This is the causal bankruptcy," he wrote in late May 1837, " . . . that the ideal should serve the actual. . . . Then first I am forced to inquire if the Ideal might not also be tried" (*JMN* 5:332). The psychological risk of abandoning that ideal standard may well have been more serious than the financial risk of hanging on to depreciated securities. Like many Jacksonians, Emerson was not ready to renounce moral certainty for the dangers of chance.

But the times demanded quick thinking, and gradually Emerson began to reconcile his desire for intrinsic value with the instabilities of the market. As his experience with William amply demonstrated, he could ill afford to act on the most severe of his oracular pronouncements. It may have been true that the "present generation [wa]s bankrupt of principles," incapable of perceiving the Ideal (*JMN* 5:332), but banknotes continued to fall due, and avoiding insolvency demanded a stern attention to all the meaner virtues of "Pride, Thrift, & Expediency" (332). Hence, Emerson began to seek a middle way between prudence and protest, in a manner that reinvigorated market behavior. An early sign was his positive review of mercantile activity. Side by side with the pummeling he gave soulless speculators was the praise he heaped on the honest merchant whose very trade seemed the expression of higher power: "In every corporation meeting, in every conversation, almost in every passing salute in the street, he feels his own and his neighbor's measure. He looks upon a man's property as a medal of skill. . . . He knows that Moral considerations give currency every day to notes of hand. . . . This man during the land fever bought no acre in Maine or Michigan. His notes of hand have a better currency as long as he lives" (*EL* 2:239). The good merchant was natural cousin to the good debtor, the individual who could sign over his property to bankers without becoming subject to the whims of the banking system. In his very fluency, the good merchant functioned like Intellect itself, as a kind of ideal currency that "pierces the form and overleaps the wall, detects the intrinsic likeness between remote things, and as a menstruum dissolves all things into a few principles" (*EL* 2:249–50). His career had a moral as well as a material clarity.

Emerson's meditations on the merchant in the winter of 1837 had much to do with his own career path. Like a speculator borrowing large sums in the hope of large profits, he felt both invigorated and terrified by the prospect of depending so heavily on anonymous and unpredictable audiences. A man who can find his pleasure anywhere, Emerson wrote in 1838—in the barroom as well as in the schoolhouse—"is so alive to every presence that the approbation of no porter, groom, or child is quite indifferent to him" (*JMN* 7:51). The philosopher's charisma, he confidently assumed, would turn the common opinions of porters and students into applause. But the public speaker was also a marked man. "As soon as he has once spoken or acted with eclat, he is a committed man, watched by the sympathy or the hatred of hundreds, whose affections must now & will enter into his account" (*JMN* 7:66). Ironically, to mount the speaker's platform meant to risk swelling one's accounts until the long ledgers of approval and disdain threatened to become overwhelming. By 1839, however, at the moment when he had begun to cultivate a national audience, Emerson seemed suddenly inspired by the very promiscuity of the lecture form. "[H]ere everything is admissible," he wrote, "philosophy, ethics, divinity, criticism, poetry, humor, fun, mimicry, anecdotes, jokes, ventriloquism. . . . highest lowest personal local topics, all . . . may be combined in open speech; it is a panharmonicon" (*JMN* 7:265). Such heterogeneity could well be liberating, Emerson imagined, but could also be daunting. How could he tap his listeners' experience without exposing his message to the undisciplined influence of the multitude, whose random enthusiasms had so clearly marked his era as one of "bankruptcy" (*JMN* 5:331)?

One answer was to insist on sentiment. "I am to fire with what skill I can the artillery of sympathy & emotion," he wrote in October 1839. "I am to console the brave sufferers under evils whose end they cannot see by appeals to the great optimism" lying in all (*JMN* 7:271). As the effects of the economic depression deepened, Emerson found himself well practiced in both consolation and optimism, the very elements that structured his financial relationship with William. The reference to sympathy here, as a source of inspiration to those casualties of "the mechanical philosophy" (271), anticipates the responses of other writers on the panic, who used Christian sentiment to soothe weary spirits and made commiseration a form of command. What made Emerson's use of the concept unique was the authority, care, and insistence with which he advanced sympathy as an ethical standard for market behavior. With a boldness few writers of the period were willing to risk, Emerson affirmed an equivalence between feeling and commerce. "[P]roperty in the possession of the heart," he came to maintain, "is brave as innocence" (*EL* 2:285).

We can see the roots of this attitude in his relationship with Carlyle. Ever since his return from their initial meeting at Craigenputtock in 1833, Emerson had conducted with the Scotchman a correspondence touched by the conventional affections of the era. With an intimacy not possible in his exchanges with William, Emerson and Carlyle played a full range of sentimental roles. "It is ten days now—ten cold days," wrote Emerson early in 1838, "—that your last letter has kept my heart warm,"[32] a sentiment echoed across the Atlantic. Significantly, when Emerson sent the first receipts for *The French Revolution,* Jane Carlyle was moved by a " 'pathetic feeling,' which brought 'tears' to her eyes" (*E&C,* 193). At other moments, both writers played the blushing beauty. "I am ashamed," wrote Emerson of his "Poor little pamphlet," *The American Scholar* (191), to which Carlyle responded in kind. "I declare I blush sometimes," he wrote concerning the sales of *The French Revolution,* "and wonder where the good Emerson gets all his patience" (248). Like Jeffersonian merchants, the writers reckoned their commerce through bonds of affection.

Such sentiments seem all the more remarkable when placed beside the sharp accusations from Margaret Fuller that Emerson confronted during the same period. The intense Concord associate and editor of *The Dial* was pressing Emerson for ever greater intimacy and was deeply disappointed when he did not respond. Emerson, she maintained, "always seemed to be on stilts" and was so frigidly correct that no real affection could emerge from the "porcupine impossibility" of his conduct. Emerson shined, said Fuller, only at his lectures; and yet, as Emerson mused, in one who aspires to "so vast an elevation," was it "not a little sad to be a mere mill or pump yielding one wholesome product at the mouth in one particular mode but as impertinent & worthless in any other place or purpose as a pump or a coffee mill would be in a parlor or a chapel?" (*JMN* 7:301–2). The ideal posture of the sympathetic friend—even sympathetic business manager— seemed to break down in more intimate settings, as Emerson struggled to adopt a vocabulary of the parlor to the town square, and the elevation of the pulpit to the levity of the sitting room.

Fuller's comments hit home because they were echoes of self-criticisms Emerson had made many times before. After concluding his course of lectures "On the Present Age" early in 1840, he confessed that he felt "little pleasure" in recalling his performance. "I have not once transcended the coldest selfpossession [*sic*]," he wrote. He had imagined his lectures as intellectual revival meetings, and they had turned out to be mere museum pieces. "Alas! alas! I have not the recollection of one strong moment," he lamented, no point at which he saw "the cheek blush, the lip quiver, & the tear start" (*JMN* 7:338–39). Significantly, in assessing his poor performance, Emerson blamed himself for his failure to be sufficiently intimate. The average audience, he noted, was around four hundred persons. To satisfy such divergent listeners, to be deeply inspiring to that crowd of strangers, he would have had to be dozens of times the man he was. "I ought to be equal to every relation," he bitterly reflected. "It makes no difference how many friends I have & what content I can find in conversing with each if there be one to whom I have not been equal" (339). Could he have devoted sixty hours a week to writing each lecture, the sum of his forces would still not stir or inspire. He needed to reach directly into each individual soul. Then "I should hate myself less," he concluded; "I should help my friend" (339). The most serious charge he confronted was that he was too "pruden[t]"; he "economize[d]" (339) when he should have spent lavishly, even if it meant going into debt, dividing his powers. To be equal to all the personal demands buried in this mass audience, he must reinvent himself. The advertiser must also be a friend—but a friend whose intimacy would embrace multitudes.

Emerson found inspiration in a stirring friend he first met in early October 1839. Anna Barker was a New Orleans socialite—beautiful, ingenious, intelligent, charming—who had entered the Concord circle through Emerson's protégé, Samuel Gray Ward. Emerson was captivated by her manners but more greatly moved by the ways in which her behavior seemed to solve his prickly dilemma of distance and intimacy. In a journal entry on 7 October 1839, he assessed her character:

> She is not an intellectual beauty but is of that class who in society are designated as having a great deal of Soul, that is, the predominating character of her nature is not thought but emotion or sympathy . . . she is so perfect in her own nature as to meet these [women I have admired] by the fulness of her heart, and does not distance me as I believe all others of that cast of character do. She does not sit at home in her own mind as my angels are wont to do, but instantly goes abroad into the minds of others, takes possession of society & warms it with noble sentiments. Her simple faith seemed to be that by dealing nobly with all, all would show themselves noble, & so her conversation is the frankest I ever heard. She can afford to be sincere. The wind is not purer than she is. (*JMN* 7:260)

Barker's allure lay in her frank circulation. Like a Jeffersonian heroine, she could extend herself, open herself to the influences of others and make them feel the freshness of her interest, yet never sacrifice her innocence and charm. Promiscuous as the wind, she remained chaste as the Muses, unmarked, despite her universal sympathy, by those with whom she engaged. Each new friend must have felt with her, as Emerson did, a sense of self-discovery. Four days after he recorded these impressions, Emerson wrote his enthusiastic account of the lecture form, in whose "breadth & versatility" "everything is admissible" (*JMN* 7:265).

Barker's adept friendship may well have inspired him with a new professional enthusiasm.

The connection between friendship and "advertisement" was probably strengthened by Emerson's wide-ranging obligations. In his exchange with Carlyle, the language of commerce mingled freely and frequently with terms of endearment. Early in 1837, for example, Emerson gratefully acknowledged receiving Carlyle's *The Diamond Necklace* and his essay on Mirabeau, along with "the olive leaf of a proofsheet" (*E&C*, 160). These leaves of friendship made out "the sum of [a] debt" that Emerson could acknowledge only through an affectionate letter. Later, in 1840, when Carlyle was haggling with his English publisher, James Fraser, over an edition of his *Miscellanies,* he cursed trade as the devil's instrument, then turned his eyes gratefully toward America, from which he had just received royalties "by decidedly the noblest method in which wages could come to a man." "Without friendship," Carlyle concluded, "there had been no sixpense [*sic*] of *that* money here" (263). Indeed, so frequent and favorable were their business dealings that Carlyle was almost willing to embrace the ideal of affectionate commerce. Combining the notions of literature and their own familiarity, Carlyle asked, "why should not Letters be on business too? Many a kind thought, uniting man with man, in gratitude and helpfulness, is founded on business" (221). From such affectionate debts running through his ledgers, Emerson began to construct a public persona as effective as the private philanthropist.

He did so by merging an accounting metaphor with Anna Barker's openness. To business associates, faithful accounts were transparent accounts. Hence Emerson thanked William in 1840 for rendering their complicated ledgers "true & transparent as usual" (*L* 2:283), the precise words he used in correspondence with Carlyle a day later (*E&C*, 268). To Emerson's imagination, however, the phrase provided more than a convenient shorthand. It was linked with an idealizing view of the marketplace as a field transformed by affection. This attitude is most forcefully conveyed in a maxim he wrote down for another friend, Caroline Sturgis, in 1841. Arguing that conventional lovers were egoists, he concluded that "right Love & transparent Dealing are two names for our God before the heavens were bro't forth" (*L* 2:416). Love, truth, and transparency all revealed the divine essence, whether that essence was manifested in business "dealing" or in benevolence. And transparency, in turn, was linked with the ideals of genius and correspondence that run through all of Emerson's writing of the period. Thus, in 1837 Emerson could write both of the mind as containing, within its "transparent chambers," the categories that structure the world (*EL* 2:201) and of the broker as one who "could foresee & transpierce" a complex transaction from a few simple entries (*L* 2:89). The individual who ascends to the transparency of Mind is free to circulate, much like Anna Barker, in mixed companies without sacrificing essential truth. Indeed, such an agent would be able to assert truth without reserve, becoming the transparent medium through which all can share in the truths of nature. "[O]ver all men and through all men," Emerson maintained, "is diffused an affection. . . . [that] is present to all and like electricity entire in every part" (*EL* 2:281). The object of every man, as of every lecturer, is *"to make daylight shine through him"* (*JMN* 7:195).

What saves such pronouncements from being the mild truisms of transcendental piety is the way in which they satisfy an acute social problem. Faced with proliferating debt and the demands of swelling audiences, Emerson had to find a way to embrace the very disorder of the panic years without sacrificing inner command. His solution leaned heavily on sentimental tropes. The successful orator, like the victorious heroines of domestic fiction, would venture forth, absorb and be absorbed into his auditors, but sacrifice nothing of his intrinsic merit. Like the deeply indebted, he would yield to the demands of the marketplace while insisting that, should his obligations consume "what money I have, I should live just as I do now" (*JMN* 7:405). He would express his indebtedness in waves of "sympathy" (271) that would even all accounts. And crowning all such relations was another trope that, for more conventional minds, served to isolate polite behavior from the mores of the market: the ideal of sincerity.

To Emerson, sincerity was the natural effect of sympathetic exchange, the sign and seal of a saintly economy. Just as "property acquired with constant sympathy with the human race" is ennobling (*EL* 2:285), so knowledge acquired from a sympathetic lecturer can transform the world. "I am to fire with what skill I can the artillery of sympathy & emotion," Emerson wrote of his lectures in 1839. "I am to try the magic of sincerity" (*JMN* 7:271). Sincerity was the "religion" of genius (*EL* 3:81), the true mark of the ideal man. And yet its mark was no mark at all, but a transparency that allowed Emerson to imagine an intense engagement with his audience at the same time that he maintained an infinite reserve. "Why insist on these rash personal relations?" he wrote in 1840. "Leave this touching & clawing. . . . A message, a compliment, a sincerity . . . —*that* I want" (*JMN* 7:370). The same kind of measured transparency he achieved through his "letter[s]" (370) and ledgers, Emerson sought to weave into his public performances. By insisting on the common medium of truth that united all paying customers, he was able to reconceive loss of independence as personal power. To be indebted to banks or friends, to lecturers or correspondents, was to yield to a new kind of authority, one Emerson associated with the sincere conduct of domestic heroines. The domestic scholar was fully at home in the world.

Emerson's essays and lectures, to be sure, did not dramatically touch the promiscuous audience he had envisioned. Despite his constant touring on an ever-expanding lecture circuit, he never reached the legions who read T. S. Arthur, Sarah Josepha Hale, Eliza Follen, and Susan Warner, all of whom treated the panic. Nevertheless, the conflict between Emerson's debt and his obligations brought into sharp focus the era's anxieties, and his recourse to sympathy helped to define an innovative response. By imagining market activity as transparently sincere, Emerson could claim to be preserving an old autonomy in a new medium. The market still revealed moral order, but it was the revelation of a prism rather than a mirror, changing according to one's position and angle of vision. The more volatile times demanded greater diversity, like refracted light whose range of colors bespoke an essential unity. Emerson's sympathetic scholar pointed the way toward a new harmony.

## The Wages of Sincerity

By requiring the American scholar to be sincere, Emerson was adopting one of the badges of popular gentility. In her study of the period, Karen Halttunen has shown how antebellum writers responded to ideological challenge through the cult of sincerity. Sincerity was a medium between the excesses of domestic consumption and the hostility of an alien urban world, asserting autonomy by cultivating feeling. In the controlled environment of the parlor, a precise code of dress and conduct could enforce at least the appearance of openness, honesty, and unaffected simplicity. These Victorians could thus convince themselves that they were greeting the market order on their terms. "Sincere" fashions suggested spontaneous, unaffected feeling and the desire in treating others to avoid the elaborate confidence games of the street or the marketplace. Sincerity was thus a covert protest against the jangling uncertainties of the public sphere, a protest that placed the home and its demands at the center of an emergent bourgeois code. But Halttunen also shows how the cult of sincerity played a mediating function by allowing the demon excess to plant one foot at the parlor door. For sentimental rules of appearance and conduct quickly became so elaborate as to stimulate the very mannered "theatricality" they were trying to suppress. And with an increasing acceptance of the theatrical nature of all social relationships came an ever greater tolerance for theatrical fashions and the fortunes they served. Sincerity thus admitted and denied its fascination with commodities and the instabilities of the market.[33]

In much the same manner, sentiment played a mediating role in coming to terms with new market demands. For one thing, the inherited sentimental language of suffering and sojourning in a hostile world made the genre ideal for portraying the pressures brought to bear on innocent or erring victims of financial excess. Almost every senator who spoke on bankruptcy, for example, gave lip service to the plight of desperate families. Is there a more poignant scene, asked Daniel Webster, the author of one bill, than the imprisoned debtor depending on "some relative, perhaps almost as poor as himself—his mother, it may be, or his sisters, or his daughters—[who] will . . . make beggars of themselves, to save him from the horrors of a loathsome jail"?[34] John Calhoun, who opposed the bankruptcy act, nevertheless asked his colleagues to remember the "thousands on thousands, not shadows, but real, sensitive human beings" prostrated by debt.[35] News accounts also relied on sentimental discourse. At the height of the panic a report from New York detailed the suffering of John Fleming, president of the Mechanics' Bank, who was found dead of "apoplexy." In a scenario that would be widely repeated in contemporary fiction, the president, "a kind and obliging man," did his best to save the bank before it failed. Then, like William Emerson, he "repaired to his affectionate family, . . . much oppressed in mind," where his deep sorrow proved fatal.[36] Market updates, too, often read like weather reports of the soul. "The heavy and desponding feeling with which the last week closed has increased," lamented the *Morning Courier and New York Enquirer* in 1837. Such "pecuniary afflictions . . . are sensibly felt" by all economic sufferers.[37] These pathetic accounts had the double function of expressing widespread fears and making hidden financial currents intelligible and immediately visible. The language of sympathy offered a way to domesticate an alien marketplace.

Occasionally, sentimental suffering and redemption also provided more direct plots for abstruse financial affairs. Perhaps the most dramatic casualty of the panic was the J. L. and S. I. Joseph trading house of New York, which precipitated the crisis. Flooded with depreciated notes from New Orleans merchants, the Josephs scrambled to meet their ballooning obligations until the balloon burst and the house closed owing over four million dollars. To defend their credit, the failed merchants published a letter from a New Orleans correspondent, detailing the default. As reported in the *New York Herald,* the affair had theatrical poignancy. "The whole community demanded information of the facts," claimed James Gordon Bennett in defense of the Josephs: "In a matter that concerns the general credit of our commercial community, we do not beg, we demand information, and will dash through all obstacles to reach it correctly. If the Josephs in publishing the letter of Baretta & Co. invaded the sanctity of private life, the whole commercial community of New York are involved in the same guilt." Indeed, when the younger Joseph received the letter, "so great was the excess of joy . . . that . . . he burst forth—'we will resume'—'we will resume,' and immediately fainted away like a child overcome with the gush of his excited feelings."[38] The account readily adapts themes popularized in the conduct books and sentimental fiction of the day. To New Yorkers, private life is public property—a financial sincerity that is reflected in the guileless joy of the principal merchant, who plays the role of the fainting heroine. Sentimental fiction surrounding the panic, drawing on the same imagery, would approach the problem from the other side. The Josephs brought private life to Wall Street. The fictions of the panic brought Wall Street into the private heart.

The Josephs' experience, however, also reveals how Emersonian prescriptions alone could not readily serve as a popular narrative of the panic. Although Emerson advocated an athletic sympathy capable of subduing all experience, he clung to a certain solitude. His sincerity was the deliberate projection of a contemplative soul forced to confront the world. Emerson's sentimental commerce was an act of *self*-assertion, as if in rebellion against the hostile conditions that influenced his thought. His extended encounter with debt represented a rejection of his brother's position. William may have been caught flat footed by the panic; Emerson would rise above it. In this sense, if in no other, Emerson's responses to economic crisis accord with David Leverenz's view that American Romantics sought a form of manhood that resisted both the demeaning competitiveness of business and the suffocations of the home.[39] Although he did not rigorously reject all feminizing effects of the market, Emerson did attempt to preserve a commanding position from which to assess its operation. His sympathy, like Adam Smith's, remained largely a male preserve.

Such a response could not cope with the profound disorientation of bankruptcy. While canny entrepreneurs recognized that repeated failure was often the price of ultimate success, the social effects of far-flung credit relations, the lifeblood of a rapidly expanding economy, were more difficult to master. Any number of distant strangers could set off a chain of events that ended in ruin. Mobile or Lexington could precipitate a banking crisis in New York or New Orleans. That sense of helpless exposure could not be dispelled in the study or from the lecture platform, but it could be imagined through the conventions of sentimental fiction. A popular literature depicting the struggles of vulnerable women lent itself to a vulnerable economy that still depended on sentiment to figure forth its increasingly anonymous transactions. Sentimental heroines could help to make sense of economic jeopardy. And, like the Josephs, they could also suggest how weakness was the prelude to recovery.

Panic fictions of the 1830s and '40s generally used sentimental heroines in two ways. Many narratives sought to reassure anxious readers by portraying Christian heroines whose reserves of feeling sustained them through any loss. Such women stood by their man, salved his wounds, and thanked God for their humility. Their sympathy displaced panic. But some texts in the corpus of "woman's fiction" that Nina Baym has explored actually promoted economic change.[40] Through sympathy and sincere circulation, these more enterprising heroines sought not to withdraw from the marketplace, but to redeem it. Like the childlike merchant who faints in the street, they profited without being stained.

One of the most remarkable statements of this experimental mentality appeared in *Graham's Magazine* in 1842. In a short essay titled "Characterless Women," Elizabeth Oakes Smith, journalist and feminist, expressed her impatience with fictional treatments of women that confined them to a single, sentimental character. The new heroine, Smith asserted, "must be one equal to all contingencies, whose faculties or powers are developed by circumstances, rather than by spontaneous action." Such a figure cannot be dominated by simple impulse or predictable response. "Weakness as often imports character as strength. Any one attribute, in excess, imports a distinctive characteristic. We talk of vain women, coquettish, masculine, sensible, dull, witty, &c., running through all the defective grades of character. Now a true woman must, as circumstances warrant, exhibit something of all this; for she is a 'creature of infinite variety.' "[41] Such an infinitely varying character, Smith implies, does not sacrifice virtue or dissolve into moral ambivalence. Rather, her many-sided pragmatism is a mark of a new, more supple sincerity that becomes the standard of virtue. To register, record, and respond to change while retaining one's moral tone is to be "characterless"—beyond the restrictions of an arbitrary identity. A characterless variety is the precise counterpart of market heterogeneity, yet moral character is not compromised. Rather, a characterless heroine shows uncommon strength, as well as the ability to retain an intrinsic value in the face of rapidly shifting demands. She becomes a kind of cultural currency. Smith's virtuous figure is the fictional foil to Harry O'Blank. Her very ability to adapt and change is the register of her sincere soul.

On the broadest level, this move from character to characterlessness reflects a change (as Baym argues) in sentimental writing itself, a change that has profound links to the new ways in which market culture was attempting to conceive itself. Under the rubric of Smith's "character," we might place those fictions in which a woman, reduced by moral treachery, succumbs to guilt or wanders, forlorn, in the world. While not entirely rejecting this scenario, fictional responses to the panic used it to define one aspect of their complex position. Sentimental victims, in this fiction, often represent the loss of autonomy. Their fate figured the death of that innocent assumption that a rigid independence is possible or necessary. Interestingly, the chief exponents of "character" in these tales were men, forced to endure the stain upon their honor brought on by the market's excesses. Against this vulnerable sentimentalism, the fictions often presented a more supple response, one defined by adaptable, "characterless" women who met market contingencies by yielding without sacrificing their essential selves. Such heroines, altered to meet the market conditions of the panic, actually had their roots in sentimental heroines like Margaretta Wilmot and Lucy Brewer, who in turn looked back to Samuel Richardson's Pamela Andrews: active, engaged, vulnerable figures capable of encountering and braving the world. When Americans met this figure in scores of fictions after the panic, they were reassuring themselves that adaptation did not mean defeat. Republican virtue might yet be saved through the efforts of these faithful emissaries.

Popular writers often expressed the era's commercial anxieties. In orthodox fashion, their fictions imagined the market as the abode of obscurity and deception, where open exchange was darkened by selfish desires. As L. E. Penhallow put it in 1838, "The commercial horizon was . . . obscured by so dense a cloud" that even shrewd merchants "found it impossible to penetrate."[42] The nation, according to the more doctrinaire moralists, was paying the price for its fascination with paper worth. Since "every thing that meets the eye is an effect of something interior to it and invisible," declared T. S. Arthur a decade later, the disruptions we face must have their roots in hidden, "spiritual" causes.[43] The unscrupulous were best equipped to profit from this confusion of realms. To the fictitious Ferret Snapp Newcraft, the art of speculation was simply a matter of concealment and penetration, of knowing how to advance with the market and when to see through its illusions. "In short," he concludes, "I could see my way clear in the darkest transaction, and split a hair with my eyes shut."[44] A devious "Bank Director" in the *United States Magazine and Democratic Review* provided the scholarly basis for Newcraft's assurance. " 'Species,' and consequently 'specie,' " he asserted, "has its root in a Latin word which . . . signifies to see, and therefore *species, specie,* and *specious,* correspond very nearly, in their primitive acceptation, with *idea* and *ideal.*"[45] To speculate was to see the wealth of deceptions concealed from normal sight.

By contrast, those who resist the market's corruption have hidden reserves accessible only to the true scrutiny of the sincere. Such a one is the London merchant Mr. Contract, of "London Fashionable Chit-Chat," who nobly suffers ruin and is sustained by a mind flowing "at a considerable depth below the surface." Normally he wears the gloss of conventional success, but "view him in seasons of difficulty" and he is suddenly transformed.[46] So, too, an enlightened reader will be able to perceive the calm security that resists market storms. Although the Ellsworth family in C. H. Butler's "The Bankrupt's Daughters" is forced to quit its fashionable dwelling, a *"mesmeric"* scrutiny into their humble apartment "would have seen as happy and cheerfull [*sic*] a group" as in the past.[47] Here, penetrating sympathy discloses the true depths of a family's inner worth, as that family enjoys a quiet life sheltered from the world. Such fictions tend to reinforce the sharp distinction between private and public spheres, between the preserve of value and the theater of commerce, with true vision reserved for the privileged interior. They answer the era's cry to see through the veil of the panic.

Interestingly, though, the fictional accounts often associate that domestic preserve with a peculiar kind of affective impotence. As in the death of the bank officer John Fleming, the merchant victim is often depicted as overwhelmed by feeling, as if the frenzied marketplace has penetrated his soul. A common scenario follows the bankrupt from the counting house to the sofa or sickbed. In Marcus Byron's *Herbert Tracy* (1851), for example, the title character fairly swoons in sentimental vulnerability, overwhelmed by a "bewilderment" that sent him "home [to] . . . his bed, with a burning fever, and left it not for two weeks."[48] Similarly, the prospect of penury in Frederick Jackson's *The Victim of Chancery* (1841) reduces the virtuous

Mr. Adams to "depression" and "anxious solicitude,"[49] and Mr. Townsend of T. S. Arthur's *Riches Have Wings* (1847) succumbs to such "a complete state of despondency"[50] that he buys laudanum and comes close to taking his life. The most thorough despair was reserved for imprisoned debtors. Charles Howard of "The Victim" is so prostrated that "his whole frame shook convulsively with his emotions." "It was a fearful sight," the narrator adds, "to see a strong man thus bowed in agony."[51] So low are such victims reduced that not even sympathy can save them.

The man's failure in these fictions is often tear-stained as well. When Charles Falconer, the bankrupt merchant of S. A. Hunt's "The Wife," comes face to face with his failure, he "pushed his chair back from the table, and leaning forward on his hands, yielded to his emotion."[52] Sad dreams disturb the suffering merchant of John Howard Payne's "The Uses of Adversity," as Mrs. Huntley finds her husband "bathed with tears" in his bed.[53] Even rogues cry like babies, as does the defeated shinplasterer in "Passages in the Life of Timothy Jenkins," who "burst[s] into tears" when his money runs out.[54] And although the tears men shed in this fiction are not often as idle as Jenkins's, all express a critical cultural problem that overt sentiment was intended to confront and resolve: the loss of autonomy. In shedding tears, these men were both rejecting the bankruptcy of a heartless market and mourning their own inability to control it. Their retreat to the home represented the desire for a vague alternative to the marketplace, but their weakness suggested that none existed on their own terms. The kind of independence they craved could not be recouped in the sentimental home, if it could be located anywhere at all.

Dramatic evidence of that problem can be seen by comparing two tales depicting emotional responses to the panic. In the first, one of the most extreme of all sentimental treatments, the Whig writer of "The Broken Merchants" gives an increasingly frenzied list of casualties. The young Marsden, married only a month, is "torn with contending emotions" as he contemplates his failure and comes close to suicide.[55] When his wife comforts him and exhorts him to persevere, "Tears burst from [his] eyes," and the despair that had "crushed" him dissolves in an access of joy (61). A German associate, a man of "ardent sensibility" (61), however, has a different reaction. "I am a bankrupt!" he writes in his suicide note, imitating Young Werther, "a dishonored thing to be scorned and pointed at by all who look upon me! *I will not survive it!* Ah, Matilda, I have truly loved you. . . . I seek forgetfulness in the grave" (62). The affectation and extremity of the scene, exploiting as it does one of sentimental literature's most powerful symbols of excess, points to an unresolved tension in the imagery associated with the panic. On the one hand, such imagery allows the reader to feel sympathy with fellow sufferers of ruin—to humanize and moralize a set of conditions that must have been frightening in the extreme. On the other hand, that same instrument of solidarity and moral power is also associated with capitulation and defeat, as if the sympathy is no sooner expressed than it subverts itself. For the panic raised the disturbing possibility that even responsible, self-controlled agents like young Marsden would find their best efforts sabotaged. Their failure exposed the fatal weakness of a paradigm stressing rigid self-control, oddly reflected in the figure of the suicide, whose stubborn insistence on honor also proves his undoing.

In contrast to these sentimental casualties, the fortunes of Harry Maverick in Epes Sargent's *Wealth and Worth; or, Which Makes the Man?* (1842) demonstrate the increasing difficulties of self-reliance in a postpanic America. Maverick, the volatile young heir to a mercantile fortune, must confront the conflicting imperatives of pragmatism and self-control. Exhorted by an adviser that he is "too malleable . . . and too easily take[s] impressions" from others,[56] Harry is soon confronted with the market's fatal exactions in the death of his father: "Last Friday night, he sat up writing and examining a variety of complicate [*sic*] accounts. . . . His protracted mental exertion, combined with anxiety and depression of spirits, produced a determination of blood to the head, which was fatal. He was found in the morning lifeless in his chair, a sheet of paper half covered with figures before him, and his fingers grasping the pen, as if about to write" (77). The elder Maverick's death is unfortunate but morally intelligible, since his crisis was brought on by rampant speculation. In his instance, the market seems to have fatally harmonized with the native Maverick impulsiveness. Indeed, it is from this calamity that Harry draws his most poignant life lesson: "It is th[e] 'power of not being acted upon' by others," he realizes, " . . . if accompanied by virtue and intelligence," that wins success. Conversely, failure means "The susceptibility of being acted upon" (102)—whether by unscrupulous competitors or by the market forces that felled his father. Autonomy, Harry concludes, is the chief attribute of virtue.

But although Harry rigorously adheres to this maxim, the times do not accord it a ringing endorsement. Offered a job as a teacher at a private academy, he rejects the position for the chance to study law. That principled stand makes a bitter enemy of his would-be benefactor, an enmity that causes one lawyer who had enlisted Harry's services to drop him and lands the young aspirant in a dead-end job. Three years later, Harry is staring down poverty, and only the timely charity of a faithful friend can save his shivering family from starvation. Inevitably, Harry goes on to make a name for himself. His delivering a stirring populist speech supporting the building of a water purification system despite the hard times "in all branches of business" (146) earns him city-wide acclaim and new clients. But his populism soon yields to expediency as his firm wins the contract of "a great rail-road company" that promises liberal fees (165). The novel thus concludes ambiguously. Given "the unexampled state of prostration" (146), mere resolve to maintain one's autonomy seems insufficient. To succeed, it takes a combination of principle, charitable friends, and the ability to adjust one's moral sentiments to the occasion. The novel's formula for success involves equal measures of avidity and virtue.

In some ways, Harry's checkered self-reliance points up an important shift occurring in many American households at midcentury. While rugged individualism was still celebrated, the activities of the son were often shaped and underwritten by intense pressures from home. Indeed, in her study of antebellum Utica, New York, Mary Ryan has argued that the impulse to sanctify a woman's sphere was a response to the same crisis that challenged the autonomy of the self-made man. As the sons of old-line artisans and farmers confronted a world that did not allow them to pursue their fathers' occupations, they were increasingly forced to develop new behaviors and "aptitude[s]" that the nurturing home was designed to foster. Affectionate mothers carefully trained and disciplined their sons for a harsher, more competitive business world, one that demanded resourcefulness and sympathy, moral independence and the need for love.[57] Certainly, Harry Maverick's tale, with its admixture of vulnerability, sentiment, and determination, captures that new sensibility. But that very sense of exposure to new forces allowed other writers, particularly women, to substitute heroines for wayfaring sons. If the requisite traits were affection, devotion, and singleness of purpose, why couldn't daughters and wives bear the burdens of breadwinning as easily as men, especially since it was mothers who were molding the breadwinners? In a number of responses to the panic, such heroines suggest a possible solution to the problem of the market's excesses by turning sentiment and sincerity into strategies for survival.[58]

As in the sentimental fiction of an earlier era, in which wayfaring women figured market stresses, the metaphor many writers seized on to confront new pressures was the mother or daughter who either leaves the house in search of support or invites the market into it. Significantly, in almost all cases, such assertiveness accompanies the feminization of the husband or father, who has retired to the home to escape market pressures. Thus, in Frederick Jackson's *The Victim of Chancery*, it is the bankrupt's wife, Mrs. Adams, who journeys seven hundred miles to seek the aid of her brother as the unfortunate Adams pines away in jail. Similarly, Eliza Follen's *Sketches of Married Life* displays the virtuous independence of Amy Weston, twice reduced by the bankruptcy of her fiancé and her father. When the fiancé, Edward Selmar, returns, reduced by cholera from his China voyage, Amy defies all custom by attending him in the quarantine hospital, to the risk of her reputation and health. Her exemplary status is heightened by her ability to exchange roles with defeated men, dispensing charity as she manages lives. Another sentimental treatment of the panic, T. S. Arthur's *Riches Have Wings*, allows a failed merchant's daughters to wander the city in search of pawnbrokers. When their mother laments that their sacrifice of jewelry and a piano will prove useless, they respond with words that could have been uttered by Harry Maverick himself: "There is no telling what . . . perseverance may accomplish. Is it not said, that where there is a will there is a way?"[59] Such figures literally redeem the market by adapting to its various demands.

Capitalizing on the ambivalence surrounding the panic, several fictions sought as well to domesticate the forces of exchange. The most common women's response to bankruptcy was to start a school. In doing intellectual work within the protected home, cultured daughters could reassert the moral autonomy lost by their fathers. In C. H. Butler's "The Bankrupt's Daughters," for example, the Ellsworths' new parlor is far humbler than that of their old establishment but still manages to retain the emblems of culture: a harp, a piano, and an ineffable charm. "[S]uch an air of comfort, and even elegance, was thrown over all by the presiding genius of taste, that even an eye accustomed only to the refined luxuries of the wealthy-great would have been arrested." The sensitive eye of the observer, so challenged by the hurly-burly of the panic, finds a safe haven in the Ellsworth home, a calm that remains undisturbed when the parlor doubles as a schoolroom. The daughters' "large number of pupils" allows for the exchange of money in an atmosphere where the quiet rule of taste prevents all market disruptions.[60]

Two tales by T. S. Arthur emphasize the redeeming function of women's work. In *The Debtor's Daughter* (1850), young Grace Wilkins not only saves her failed husband but also supports her father-in-law, a merchant who had formerly persecuted her own bankrupt father. When the bankrupt husband comes home complaining, "My strength is gone. . . . I have no power even to hold myself up," it is Grace who must sustain them. "If you are weak," she declares, "then will I be strong."[61] Proving as good as her word, she establishes a school and becomes the head of a little commonwealth. Moving effortlessly between the realms of commerce and family, she presides over the faculty, expands the school, and heads her household, earning a profit of well over two thousand dollars a year. The superiority of her sentimental pragmatism is seen when her crabbed father-in-law, Herman Links, also fails. Not only does she secretly support him, but she also takes him in and finds him work. "As the day is, so shall the strength be," is Grace's new motto (85). She sustains both work and spirit "as tenderly, carefully, and wisely, as if she were a mother protecting and caring for a helpless infant" (75). Once again, the rigorous autonomy that would master the marketplace or starve seems to be yielding to a more sensitive resolve.

Similarly, in *The Two Merchants* (1843), Arthur details the efforts of Miriam Newberry to rescue her threatened family. When the father returns home "depressed and disheartened,"[62] Miriam rallies, and "with a heart that fluttered in her bosom" (24), begins her assault on the world. Circulating in lower Manhattan, where she calls on former friends now grown cold, she finally locates a backer for her school, acting precisely like a drummer scaring up business. Her school so flourishes that she can eventually afford to hire one of her former persecutors, demonstrating that a fluttering heart is no indifferent preparation for success. In both cases, it is the daughter's pliability, her marriage of sympathy for ruined men and sensitivity to the market's demands, that saves her fortune. Mr. Newberry gives the best description of this attitude by calling it "true, self-devoted affection" (26). A sympathetic self-interest proves the most reliable formula for success.

Perhaps the most self-conscious rendition of the characterless woman appears in Follen's *Sketches of Married Life*. The didactic novel contrasts the fortunes of Amy Weston with those of her cousin, Fanny Herbert. While Amy marries the virtuous but failed Edward Selmar and sustains her father through his own bankruptcy, Fanny marries William Roberts, a reserved and dignified Bostonian who introduces her to the high life. Fanny's mordant irony cannot hide her increasing unhappiness, heightened by her husband's refusal to confront their problems. After his father dies, Fanny lapses into bitter selfishness and then into delirium when William decides to leave her. The root of her problem, as Amy sees it, is her refusal to be sincere. "You must tell him all that is in your heart," Amy advises before Fanny's breakdown. "You must confess to your husband every

weakness and sin of your own, as well as tell him every fault you find in him."[63]
That strategy, the novel demonstrates, is the source of Amy's happiness, as she
defies convention to save the men in her life from both illness and bankruptcy. Her
wandering alone into the dangerous male territory of a cholera hospital, braving
the scorn of family and doctors alike, is only the most vivid sign of her moral
independence. But it is an independence tied to a peculiar form of selflessness, as
if the highest kind of autonomy is to have no resistance at all. For what motivates
Amy is the maxim that husband and wife, with "their whole souls, should stand
all undisguised before the other, in the simplicity of truth" (98). Sincerity would
seem to assure autonomy in the very act of yielding it. Self-reliance comes about
by denying privacy, by exposing oneself to the scrutiny of others.

Despite Amy's stance against duplicity, however, Follen does not adopt the typical moralist's critique of the duplicitous marketplace or the evils of speculation.
Indeed, *Sketches* is noteworthy among sentimental novels of the period for the
degree to which it embraces the mores of the market. In her marital laments, for
example, Fanny Roberts often evokes the language of panic. "Now, my husband
has terrible arrears against me," she complains; "if he ever calls upon me for a just
settlement, what a poor bankrupt I shall be!" (158). Later, she condemns secrecy in
similar terms. Her New York friends who think her happy "know not . . . to what
bankrupt hearts they go asking for help, nor upon what fictitious foundations the
drafts are made that they receive so eagerly" (167). But despite such association of
sorrow with the ways of trade, it becomes clear that the moral center of the novel
endorses trade even as it craves sincerity. To Amy, trade is admirable because it
fosters "wide and various connexions with the human race" (199)—connections
that are sanctified through sentimental commerce. Thus, when years after his
bankruptcy, Edward is haunted by his failure to reimburse his creditors in full,
his confession to Amy produces an immediate resolve to pay off the remainder
of his debt. The same commitment to sincerity he made in his marriage Amy
convinces him to transfer to the marketplace. In this fashion will both husband
and wife become completely "transparent" (220) as they provide a model for
humane liberal behavior. Because all their conduct can be seen into, they will
greet the market with clear heads and hearts—an attitude, as Follen implies, that
the market will readily reward.

In his study of the modern prison, Michel Foucault argued that transparency
provided the nineteenth century with a disciplinary as well as an emotional ideal.

Transparent characters could be the more readily penetrated and controlled, and there seems to be a clear relation between the demand for sincerity in the nineteenth century and the needs of an emerging market culture. Where external constraints on free enterprise were being abandoned, the individual had to police himself all the more rigorously.[64] Follen's ideal of transparency thus bears closely on the characteristic demand of the Jacksonian era, for a medium of exchange that was both flexible and stable, one whose intrinsic value would be immediately identifiable but that would nevertheless allow for the full expression of Americans' expansionist energies. A sincere entrepreneur could be most successful by resolving to hold nothing back, allowing his feelings to be the true register and exchange of value. Obscure economic practices would then be banished, and the generous, open, self-sustaining market relations that Adam Smith and others imagined would be realized. Indeed, if the entire country were to adopt that attitude, speculative pressures and disastrous panics would immediately cease. For the first time, American business would nurture a truly familiar commerce.

## Spiritual Enterprise

As she emerged from postpanic fiction, the characterless heroine represented an ideal economic compromise. More successful than her failed male counterparts, she demonstrated that balance of enterprise and moral sensitivity sorely lacking in contemporary affairs. It was the characterless heroine's ability to yield to the economic currents around her that demonstrated her true value. She was in the world, fully equal to its demands, but not of it. One of the era's most widely read novelists approached this problem from an explicitly Christian perspective. In *Queechy*,[65] Susan Warner relates how the young Elfleda Ringgan manages to stave off ruin, save the family farm, and marry a baronial Christian, all while retaining a childlike innocence. Warner's novel takes the moral discourse of panic and reworks it into a vision of Christian economy.

*Queechy* is intimately related to its author's own experience in the panic. A member of the Manhattan elite, whose youthful friends included the Astors, Warner was forced to flee with her family to a country property near West Point after the panic wiped out her father's real estate holdings. Throughout the 1840s the family remained deeply in debt, returning to solvency only as Susan and her sister, Anna, took up writing. Like Warner herself, the novel's protagonist, Fleda

Ringgan, saves fortunes as well as souls, and does so by demonstrating both responsiveness and autonomy, sincerity and shrewd practicality. Her unfailing tact and inner determination, offset by her frailty and her susceptibility to illness, make her an effective register of the era's economic stresses and a model for how to meet them. To be successful, Warner argues, is to adapt to the world's excesses without sacrificing one's inner resolve. It is to temper the moral rigidities of the republican ethos with a more pliable opportunism in which sentiment and Christianity help to anchor the individual in an ever-shifting environment.

Like the aspirations of its Christian heroine, Warner's novel proceeds on two levels at once. Its conventional plot revolves around a Cinderella story in which Fleda rises from poverty to aristocracy. An orphan cared for by her paternal grandfather, she is summoned to Paris at age eleven after his death. There she enjoys a warm, wealthy, and cultured family life with her cousins, the Rossiturs, until the family is forced to return to New York and confront the collapse of its fortunes. By chance, the Ringgan farm in upstate New York becomes available, and the family returns to Fleda's birthplace. But their prospects are not brightened by her Uncle Rolf's resolve to mix no more with the world. Rather, European culture has unfitted them for the farm, and the Rossiturs are soon facing starvation. It falls upon the sixteen-year-old Fleda to rescue them by becoming a maid-of-all-trades, managing not only the household but a gang of farmworkers as well, mending spirits and minding accounts.

But she is not immured on the farm. Fusing the novel of manners with the novel of Christian sentiment, Warner periodically transports Fleda to a wealthy cousin in New York City, where she surveys and criticizes the opinions of fashionable life. It is in New York, too, that she once again encounters Guy Carleton, an English aristocrat who had been her protector after her grandfather's death. Although more than ten years her senior, he has returned after an eight-year absence to seek her out and propose—but not until the Rossitur fortunes are once more imperiled. Now the crisis involves the threat by an unscrupulous suitor of Fleda's to expose a forgery that Rolf Rossitur had committed years earlier. It takes the combined efforts of Fleda and Carleton to save the family, after which the way is cleared for Fleda's marriage and her retirement to England. There, presumably, she will enjoy a wider sphere of influence as the benevolent genius of the Carleton estate, surrounded by his Christian dependents.

But as the novel rewards Fleda with wealth, it is also a repudiation of the high life for the far more secure benefits of the afterlife. Here the struggle is to remain unspoiled, and Fleda's rise is measured not by money but by spirit. Warner's evangelicalism allows her to lard her examination of manners with Christian introspection, forcing the reader, like Fleda herself, to take a double view of the novel's events. In a passage singled out by Ann Douglas, for example, Warner interrupts Fleda's desperate struggle to save her Uncle Rossitur from arrest as a forger, in order to stage an accidental encounter with Carleton. The conversation is entirely ethereal:

> "How pretty the curl of blue smoke is from that chimney," he said.
>
> It was said with a tone so carelessly easy that Fleda's heart jumped for one instant in the persuasion that he had seen and noticed nothing peculiar about her.
>
> "I know it," she said eagerly,—"I have often thought of it—especially here in the city—"
>
> "Why is it? what is it?—"
>
> Fleda's eye gave one of its exploratory looks at his, such as he remembered from years ago, before she spoke.
>
> "Isn't it contrast?—or at least I think that helps the effect here."
>
> "What do you make the contrast?" he said quietly.
>
> "Isn't it," said Fleda with another glance, "the contrast of something pure and free and upward-tending with what is below it. I did not mean the mere painter's contrast. In the country smoke is more picturesque, but in the city I think it has more character."
>
> "To how many people do you suppose it ever occurred that smoke had a character?" said he smiling. (2:213)

According to Douglas, such passages demonstrate the utter self-absorption of a genre that sought to turn Protestant faith into feckless self-gratulation, and pious women into useless drones.[66] But, in the context of postpanic fiction, the passage actually bears more centrally on the chief moral and economic problem of the era: how to perceive or maintain character in a shifting and evanescent medium that challenged perception itself. How could one see and measure worth in an environment that seemed to negate or compromise all value?

Although Warner's Christian aestheticism may appear to answer those questions through the bland assertion that all's right with the world, it may be better seen as an attempt to make exchange value and intrinsic value coincide. As the smoke ascends, becoming increasingly transparent, its very transparency gives it a kind of character unattainable by other means. Pliable and tensile, it allows itself to be shaped by the atmosphere even as it points to a higher sphere. It discloses its worth through a clarity that observers share and cultivate, conscious that their own transparency will yield a like enduring value. Christian sensibility makes that intervention possible and suggests that vanishing smoke is itself a not inapt emblem for one's operations in the world. To remain active and sensitive, legible yet given shape by the elements is to assert the highest form of consciousness, and therefore the greatest autonomy. Christians, republicans, and entrepreneurs were thus linked to the same medium of exchange.

Fleda, of course, is the medium of this medium, the characterless woman who demonstrates intrinsic worth. As in other fictions of the period, she is repeatedly forced to compensate for impotent men whose failures dissolve them in sentimental weakness. Her grandfather, Elzevir Ringgan, was at one time a hale Revolutionary militiaman and stout farmer, but illness has gradually forced him into bankruptcy. "Every thing goes," he laments as the novel opens, "—I can't help it" (1:14). When his principal creditor becomes importunate and his income dries up, Ringgan betrays the symptoms of the era's other broken men in his "watering eye and unnerved lip" (1:32). But whereas Fleda's grandfather owes his ruin, at least in part, to questionable decisions regarding the management of his farm, her uncle is initially less responsible for his fall. "There was cloudy weather in the financial world of New York," Rossitur determines (1:213), and soon discovers that "people could fail that were not in business" (1:230). As a silent partner in a bankrupt enterprise, he must settle with his creditors for seventy cents on the dollar (1:234) and retire in disgrace to the country. The forgery, too, is connected to the panic: in the difficult "winter of '43" (2:247), pressed for funds to give his daughter a lavish wedding, he appropriates money and finds he has no means to pay. Like Elzevir Ringgan, Rolf Rossitur seems to wither away once his accustomed life is taken from him. Weary, despondent, and ineffectual, he abandons the family and takes most of its funds before Fleda tracks him down in New York and persuades him to return, during an interview bathed in tears. As in other panic fictions, too, the patriarch's impotence is captured through expressions of imprisonment. Ringgan can't go hunting with Carleton because he is lame and is increasingly confined to his bed, while Rossitur sits despondently all day in the farmhouse, rarely stirring unless he is forced into action. Under such circumstances, Fleda must act or face the destruction of her family.

To this end, the novel allows its protagonist an unusual mobility—not only to set right the paternal estate but also to circulate, observe, and criticize. When the Rossiturs return to Queechy from New York, Fleda engages in a whirl of activity. She enlists the aid of a reliable overseer to run the farm for her uncle, and artfully suggests to him the most productive methods by insinuating that they are the overseer's ideas. When two servants abruptly quit and demand wages that the Rossiturs don't have, Fleda finds the money and scours the region for a replacement. Later, still more strapped for funds, she sells vegetables and flowers from her garden, all the while managing the field hands and the household. And when Rossitur runs off to New York seeking passage to France to escape the forgery charge, it is Fleda who finds him, trudging through the anonymous streets as she circulates a newspaper advertisement. Ironically, the pressure of being "in three or four places at the same time" (2:16) enhances her intrinsic worth. "She has at least fifty times as much character as I have," declares her aunt. "And energy. She is admirable at managing people—she knows how to influence them somehow so that everybody does what she wants." And when asked "Who influences her," Mrs. Rossitur has a quick response: "Everybody that she loves" (1:348). Fleda's is the influence often found in the woman's sphere, but it is a mark of energy, not impotence. Strong natures like Fleda's submit to others in order to command themselves.

Fleda's mediatory role extends to the novel's politics as well. On the one hand, she is the vehicle for a full-throated endorsement of republicanism against the European prejudices of visitors. When her fashionable friends assert that farmers are boors, Fleda retorts by describing a carpenter she knew who amused himself by reading Macaulay and a farmer's daughter who studied Latin and Greek (2:70). To an English visitor who deplores American slavery, Fleda not only brings up the common rejoinders attacking the impressment of sailors and the enslavement of the English working class but also resurrects her grandfather's patriotism. If America was the natural birthplace of "prejudic[e]," as her critic maintains, it became so only through "maintaining the rights against the swords of Englishmen" (2:87). Even Carleton is not proof against such speeches. Americans honor worth, not pretense, she asserts. "And I confess I would rather see them a little rude in their independence than cringing before mere advantages of external position" (2:305). Christianity itself, she concludes, "tends directly to republicanism" (2:306). She also rejects inherited wealth for the uncertainties of achieved status, and she remains the best guarantee that want of fortune does not mean want of taste.

On the other hand, Fleda is often reminded that republican ways are themselves an acquired taste. When she goes visiting one farm family in search of kitchen help, she is repulsed by the casual hygiene of her hostess, who refuses to provide serving spoons at tea and uses molasses left from the children's dinner to make the next day's gingerbread. After finding a new cook, she must remind the Rossiturs that they are far from Paris, admitting that "these people don't know any manners" (1:299). And she herself is often disoriented by the stern demands of the marketplace—no more so than in her search for her uncle in New York. There she finds the press of business "bewildering" and is mortified to have to make her way through the public sphere, "edging by loitering groups that filled the whole sidewalk, or perhaps edging through them, groups whose general type of character was sufficiently plain and *un*mixed . . . venturing hardly her eyes beyond her thick veil" (2:207–8). The nearer her approach to the rough and tumble of the wide world, the more retiring Fleda becomes.

It is not surprising, then, that the novel's politics are ultimately paternalistic. Once she has severed her ties with Queechy and married her prince, Fleda is primed to assume the role of a dutiful wife whose influence will reinforce Carleton's stately Christian authority. Having himself been transformed from a world-weary cynic to a Christian benevolist, he discovers his life's work in "ameliorating the condition of the poorer classes on his estates" (2:380) by instituting adult schools and agricultural training. But improvement does not mean independence. When his tenants snuff the air of republicanism and engage in "[p]olitical disturbances" (2:348), he is quick to break off his courtship of Fleda and cross the Atlantic to put them down. As Carleton's stuffy mother avers, few other aristocrats have his ability "to deal successfully with the mind of the masses" (2:380). That paternalism, presumably, extends to his marriage. Although Carleton liberally acknowledges that "a woman's mind . . . should be nicely brought out and fashioned for its various ends" (2:73), those ends lie not in the characterless marketplace but in the stable preserve of the home. Hence, as she prepares herself for life as Lady Carleton, Fleda gratefully resigns not only her many-sidedness but even her adulthood. No sooner has Carleton proposed than she returns to being an eleven-year-old girl, luxuriating in "the old childish feeling . . . that she was in somebody's hands who had a marvellous happy way of managing things about her, and even of managing herself" (2:317). As Mrs. Carleton quickly realizes in conversing with her demure daughter-in-law, Guy Carleton "will be well suited in a wife" (2:370).

And yet so great is Fleda's integrity, so hard won her independence, that the reader can never quite forget that her marriage remains the consummation of a process incorporating widely divergent moments. Fleda is never simply child or manager, suppliant or entrepreneur. She is rather an amalgam of all of these, a character whose partial or simple responses would never be equal to the challenges she must master. Interestingly, a prime indication of her multifaceted responsiveness is also one of the chief markers of her sentimental vulnerability: her migraine headaches. Typically these appear after periods of intense mental or physical exertion when, forced to sit bolt upright on the edge of a sofa, her feet and hands rigidly extended to a chair back, she becomes a clenched knot of pain. After she learns of her uncle's forgery, for example, Fleda must endure not only the torments of illness and uncertainty but also the attentions of an unwanted suitor who has secretly brought the charges in order to force her into marriage. "I am not surprised . . . to find you suffering," he admits in his opening line. "I knew how your sensibilities must feel the shock" (2:193). Later, after she places the newspaper ads in New York, that sensibility is redoubled, as "[h]er nerves were alive to every stir," and every slight sound "made her tremble" (2:209–10). But such acute sensitivity finds its compensation in Fleda's enormous energy and is, indeed, the ground and motive of her resourcefulness. The sympathy that prostrates her in morbid impotence is identical to the force that drives her and makes her such an adept manager of others—a link reinforced by her rigid posture when sick, as if she is all iron nerve. She is like the smoke that registers the impression of every stray current but always manages to rise, a stance that, according to the novel's Christian politics, constitutes true autonomy.

Warner's heroine represents the furthest development of the characterless woman. Answering economic anxieties, Fleda endows work with a saintly pragmatism that redeems all around her. But her retirement from activity at the novel's end is not a sign that her cultural work had concluded. For by 1850, a new round of economic unrest would return her brand of sympathetic industry to the national stage. In the hands of a working-class poet from Brooklyn, characterlessness would become an American anthem.

# CHAPTER 5

# The Discipline of Whitman's Art

Perhaps the most famous photograph in American literature depicts Walt Whitman, in his first volume of poetry, as "one of the roughs." His open-throated coarse shirt, loose trousers, and broad-brimmed, angled hat suggest the unconventional, slightly menacing attitude of the common laborers with whom he liked to consort. This inaugural act of class assertion, though, was quite typical of an era that witnessed widening differences among social classes, both rough and polished. The decade of Whitman's emergence began with a sudden wave of working-class activism that spawned strikes and numerous unions before it broke in the panic of 1854. Concurrently, increasing numbers of tradesmen, clerks, and entrepreneurs had established their own distinctive attitudes in many northern cities, drawing on a common experience in church, leisure, and work to promote what Stuart Blumin calls "the emergence of the middle class."[1] The very use of the term "emergence" suggests the slow and steady accumulation of cultural materials—the accruing means by which "some men, as a result of common experiences (inherited or shared), feel and articulate . . . their interests as between themselves, and as against other men whose interests are different from (and usually opposed to) theirs."[2] E. P. Thompson's famous definition of (male) class consciousness seems to capture this pregnant period in American culture, when the nation's heightened tensions underscored social differences that would prove decisive after the Civil War.

Indeed, Whitman has in some ways come down to us as the embodiment of class affiliation. The poet seems a projection of that photograph: turbulent, fleshy, extravagantly populist, "resembling . . . some great mechanic or stevedore, or seaman, or grand laborer," in Richard Maurice Bucke's words—in Betsy Erkkila's words, a "revolutionary" democrat. Henry David Thoreau, with mild irony, called him "the greatest democrat the world has seen." To his most recent biographer, Jerome Loving, Whitman's power arose from his sympathy with the "humble and hard-working," a sympathy Whitman retained even in old age. "The great country . . . is not that which has the most capitalists, monopolists, immense grabbings, vast fortunes," Whitman remarked to Horace Traubel, " . . . but the land in which there are the most homesteads, freeholds. . . . The great country, in fact is the country of free labor." Such laborers, he insisted, were the audience and inspiration for his greatest poems.[3]

But the emphasis on distinctive class attributes, common both to these assessments of Whitman and to the new labor history from which more recent treatments arise, may also distort the immediate experience of class felt by the poet's contemporaries. By emphasizing shared articulations and feelings, many cultural critics and historians have simplified a complex process in which individuals displayed a variable sense of themselves and their class positions—now aggressively insisting on their distinctness, now desiring to merge with the multitude. This "bundle of contradictory experiences and perceptions," R. J. Morris observes of nineteenth-century Leeds, was "the raw material" of class distinctions—distinctions, however, rooted "in languages which still had many common features."[4] Sympathy, among all other common languages, best promoted this variable relation between class consciousness and what Anthony Giddens calls class awareness—the horizontal affiliations that might well cross class lines. As I will argue in this and the next chapter, the language of sentiment, in the years straddling the Civil War, became a crucial means of assessing, confronting, and often denying the strains associated with social class. Sympathy allowed writers like Whitman to experiment with bold forms of class solidarity. But because the language of feeling embraced multitudes, it could also be used to imagine wider sympathies that elided class. And in moments of economic or social crisis, sentimental imagery could help to redefine the nature of that wider mass in a way that ironically excluded many of its principals. In this manner, sympathy served a dialectical function: by insisting on the boundless affiliations of American life, writers often reinforced what was most distinctive about their own limited experience. Class consciousness, that is, arose in part through the sentimental denial of class boundaries—an effect that Whitman's muscular democrat both resisted and conveyed.

As a purveyor of democratic sympathy, Whitman was ideally positioned to capture these varied effects. Heir to a rich tradition of sentimental circulation, he could whirl through the nation, afoot with his vision, binding all readers in common experience. But that pragmatic sympathy had particular resonance during the turbulent first half of the 1850s, when labor activists invoked the same fund of sentiment for narrower purposes. Well before the panic of 1854, spokesmen appealed to the united sympathies of laborers to establish a distinctive republican culture that would reject predatory market practices. When those appeals collapsed in the panic, they were replaced by calls for labor discipline, more effective economic arrangements that would restore a shattered autonomy even as they echoed bourgeois norms. Whitman was uniquely positioned to articulate both appeals. Acting the role of what Antonio Gramsci called the "organic intellectual," he incorporated working-class sensibility into a vision of liberal order, a structure of feeling in which radical labor sympathies became the basis of market discipline. More than any other writer of his day, Whitman promoted the higher unities joining the republican idealism of working-class politics to the stringencies of a volatile market. His democratic, often feminized, sympathy turned the pragmatism of antebellum heroines into what Bruce Laurie calls "a force for integration."[5] In doing so, Whitman gave cultural sanction to the sentimental portrait of the market.

This view of Whitman as market pragmatist differs from many recent discussions of the poet's early career. While the past decade has seen valuable work on the social content of Whitman's poetry, he has often been depicted as both more radical and more conservative than a full consideration of his class background might suggest. To David Reynolds, for example, the antebellum decade marked the high point of Whitman's political activism, a vigorously republican attitude that would lapse into a tamer boosterism after the Civil War.[6] Readers have often traced this political anger to a deeper anxiety over the betrayal of the republic, sapped by what Betsy Erkkila calls "the dependence, dispossession, commodification, and merchandizing of the self fostered by market capitalism."[7] Artisan families like Whitman's, it is argued, lost their stature and their solvency as the factory system and sweated labor extinguished a way of life. Whitman alone was left to celebrate the fading dream. Seldom, though, have critics situated Whitman's class anxieties in the 1850s. For both Erkkila and Reynolds, Whitman's political critiques are rooted in the Age of Jackson, a mentality far removed from the more urgent labor politics in the Age of Millard Fillmore. Even M. Wynn Thomas, whose sense of Whitman's class affiliations is most acute, misses the poet's attachments to the labor discourse of the 1850s, and thus to the need for labor discipline. By grounding his discussion, too, in Jacksonian radicalism, Thomas sees Whitman as a contradictory figure unable to reconcile class sympathies with the "unattractive realities" of the market revolution from which he sought to escape.[8] But Whitman was not merely the poet of embattled artisans outraged at the course of democracy. He was also the prudent manager who, reflecting the arguments of labor radicals themselves, turned outrage into accommodation. His populism encouraged readers to adjust to dependence, commodification, and dispossession.

That ambiguous message is tied to Whitman's ambiguous class position. As a sometime editor, speculative building contractor, journeyman printer, publisher, and writer, Whitman had affinities to a group of antebellum workers that Bruce Laurie calls "men in the middle"—individuals with the means and energy, but not the authority or desire, to achieve bourgeois respectability. Such men, Laurie argues, crossed class lines. They clung to the artisan values of their fathers and grandfathers, even as they sought to leave those values behind. They felt threatened by the slave power and the wave of immigrants, yet struggled to find the means to distance themselves from those groups. Yet while Whitman sympathized with mechanics and the middling sort, his poetry melded an even greater range of attitudes. As a writer observing a resurgence in union activity during the early 1850s, he echoed the language of radicals and reformers. When the unions collapsed during the hard times of 1854, he refashioned that language into a vision of social renaissance—a vision based in labor's widespread appeal to sympathies shared by an emergent middle class. *Leaves of Grass* is the song of a social surveyor who transformed the class anxieties of antebellum republicans into the reassurances of American order.[9]

One of Bucke's anecdotes about Whitman captures that subtle mediation. On a packed horsecar during the Washington summer, so the story goes, Whitman observed "a young Englishwoman, of the working class" with her hands full. A toddler, cranky in the heat, was making such a "howling nuisance" that his perspiring mother was herself ready to cry "with weariness and vexation." Sensing the emergency, the man in the broad-brimmed hat gently disengaged the infant, removed to an open part of the car, and calmed the child, who, giving "a good long look squarely in his face . . . snuggles down with its head on his neck, and in less than a minute, is sound and peacefully asleep," to universal relief. But Whitman's tact does not stop there. As the conductor goes on a break, and with the baby still at his breast, the poet operates the car, "keeping his eye on the passengers inside, who have by this time thinned out greatly. He makes a very good conductor, too, pulling the bell to stop and go on as needed." Whitman's more than maternal solicitude has calmed a family storm as it has ensured efficient service. He is both the savior of the working class and the guarantor of smooth traffic. It was a role he would define in response to economic panic and the protests of the unemployed. As he shaped and reshaped *Leaves of Grass,* Whitman perfected the art of calming the nation's class anxieties with his maternal and muscular sympathy. That sympathy, in turn, was rooted in a working class that had itself become a howling nuisance in the early 1850s. To understand Whitman's early poetry is to take up the full range of their complaints. [10]

## *The Ends of Autonomy*

New York's midcentury prosperity stimulated a wave of labor activism that cast a long shadow on Whitman's work. Dormant since the collapse of the General Trades Union after the panic of 1837, workers' associations reconstituted themselves by the late 1840s, when California gold and exported grain created a trade boom in the metropolis. Workers' benefit groups like the cordwainers and jewelers' societies formed to provide mutual aid to distressed members, while more militant protective associations sought to control wage rates and limit the workday through strikes and collective bargaining. Cooperative associations attempted to bypass the bosses altogether by ordering their own affairs. "The idea seems to be," wrote the *Providence Post* approvingly, "that each association . . . shall . . . regulate its own prices, avoid competition with each other, and dispense with the use of capital which the laborer is not interested in and does not control." The *Springfield Republican and Gazette* echoed these views, in terms at once more radical and more cautious. Noting that New York led the nation in labor activism, it hailed cooperation in almost Constitutional terms: "Capital has power which is liable to abuse," and the associations will provide a much-needed "check" on that abuse. But labor, too, might become too powerful, necessitating, in turn, the "salutary checks" imposed by capital. The writer's penchant to see labor conflict in terms of grand balances speaks to labor's impulse, during the period, to inscribe ever larger circles of influence and control. [11]

That impulse was felt through a flood of ambitious new unions. Since the late 1840s, workers' representatives throughout the Northeast and West had met in annual industrial congresses to promote land reform and other labor issues. Now, as the nation's largest labor pool began to organize, the associations became ever more comprehensive. On 5 June 1850, New York workers formed an industrial congress of their own, and the body soon received official sanction by being permitted to hold its meetings in the new City Hall. By the end of the year, a larger Cooperative Labor League was proposed, as well as Industrial Reform Associations "in every Ward, Township, City and County in the United States." Journeymen printers issued their own call for an "extensive Organization, embracing the whole country," while New York mechanics were urged to form "an auxiliary Labor League in every Ward in the City" to regulate wages and prices. By December 1850, there was even an appeal "To the Workingmen of the World" for an international congress to be held in London in order to elaborate the *"general principle"* for universal cooperation. As Iver Bernstein has argued, these movements were not merely an expression of labor muscle. They betrayed the widely shared desire to "impos[e] coherence" on an increasingly fractious society. [12]

But despite this longing for order, the political strains that would test the nation in the 1850s were already apparent in the sharpened rhetoric many workers employed. The New York Window Shade Painters' Protective Association, for example, used its inaugural meeting to denounce "the trickish system of speculators—that makes use of us as machines" and "starv[es] us into low wages." The sentiment was echoed by Benjamin Price, who in August 1850 grimly noted that the laborer is expected "to wear himself out in the public service," the reward of which is a "premature old age and decay" while his exploiters riot in "luxury." Such language suggested a new, more militant national mood. "Capital has no right to prey upon labor by the extortion of interest and profits," declared delegates to the industrial congress in Cincinnati in March 1850. The "sword and the purse" have hitherto reduced workers to "unconditional chattel bondage," wrote the Mechanics and Workingmen of Philadelphia. "Henceforth the conflict on the world's arena will be between labor and capital." [13]

Worker militancy crested in the summer of 1850, when striking New York tailors became the first casualties of industrial warfare. Faced with a brutally segmented and sweated industry, the tailors, the city's most populous trade, joined to enforce wage rates and prevent underselling to the southern market. By July, they were striking recalcitrant establishments and meeting the organized resistance of the city's police. When, on 4 August, a large crowd attacked the home of a holdout journeyman, they were beaten back and two of their number killed. The incident merely dramatized the acute need for *"union,"* as the *New York Irish American* put it, to oppose the injustices of "the monopolist money-grubber." The oppressor had finally signified his resolve in blood. [14]

In response to these heightened threats and opportunities, labor spokesmen made three principal appeals to republican feeling that left their traces on Whitman's poetry. Faced with repression by hostile employers, many leaders recurred to a Jacksonian rhetoric that stressed the communal sympathies of righteous democrats. The language of democratic protest, however, was fundamentally ambiguous. To militants, it permitted a searching critique of capitalist discipline. Punitive employers threatened to destroy the most distinctive attribute of working-class culture—its spontaneous attachments that repudiated market exploitation. Only a rededication to republican feeling could defeat their evil designs. But these appeals to labor sympathy could also be tinged by a second appeal, a traditionalist nostalgia seeking to restore an agrarian simplicity to urban life. Inspired by what John Ashworth calls a "pastoral idyll" of undifferentiated equality, many labor activists sought through land reform those republican sympathies immune to corrosive social change. [15]

These impulses, in turn, existed in tension with a third one, born of the need to control the disruptions that workers faced. Accordingly, an array of voices during the period urged a different sympathy, one that counseled harmony between the activities of labor and the demands of the larger world. This doctrine of correspondence, though in some ways similar to Whig appeals for social harmony, was rooted in a shrewd desire to bend economic uncertainties to the ends of practical politics. The men who advocated these measures, many of them land reformers or cooperationists, attempted to incorporate elements of radical republican or pastoral sympathy into a new rhetoric responsive to more severe market conditions. Though temperamentally opposed to many of their prescriptions, Whitman would contribute to the same project. To appreciate how he incorporated these appeals, it will be necessary to examine each in turn.

Radical labor advocates were often the loudest proponents for labor sympathy. When the tailors' agitation was at its peak, for example, "A JOURNEYMAN TAILOR, WHO IN FOURTEEN YEARS HAS NEVER SEEN THE TRADE IN SUCH A BAD CONDITION," wrote to the *Tribune* that although "Organization and Cultivation of feeling" was the union's motto, now he was compelled to look on as the "cheap clothes economy" afforded workers little more than a trip to Greenwood cemetery. The riot was thus a call to the entire city to recapture the original communal concern lost in the latest demonstration of capitalist avarice. The German Central Committee of the United Trades agreed, worrying that repression of the tailors threatened "to destroy that sympathy of feeling on the part of the public" crucial to the rights of labor. The committee's declaration of support was an attempt to restore a shattered unity. "[W]ith all the power of a revolted feeling," they protested the conduct of strikebreaking police and resolved "That we sympathize with the Tailors now struggling for the maintenance" of a living wage. By displaying feeling, these documents sought to reassert the threatened principles of an ideal republic of labor. A similar sense of the community of feeling lies behind the discussion of a boilermakers' strike in 1851. The strikers complained of collusion by owners to lock out those "who sympathized in th[e] movement" for shorter hours, higher wages, and the "independence of labor." Those bosses who "tyrannize[d] over freemen" were thus not merely punishing workers; they were playing the role of a latter-day George III attacking a virtuous republican community—a community defined by its capacity for feeling. [16]

One of the most overt appeals to this sense of republican sympathy came from the bakers' union, which complained of long hours at low pay. The baker's life, declared John Z. Rennie and his associates, is subject to a double tyranny—that of his employer, who exacts twenty-four-hour shifts for little pay, and that of the public, which demands nothing less for fresh bread. But the most profound toll of this oppression is an emotional poverty, a stunting of the capacity to feel. Released from his drudgery, the baker "has little heart" to enjoy his leisure. "The domestic comforts do not cheer him; the love of a wife or the tenderness of a family fail to arouse him; his spirit is crushed; . . . his affections are deadened." The workers' regimen is thus doubly pernicious: not only are they too listless to resist tyranny, but the source of republican virtue, the family, is also denied them. They represent a genuine political crisis for which the "sympathy and support of the public" is the sole solution. Only if consumers were convinced that fresh bread was less important than a baker's soul would "the wrongs we are suffering" be eliminated. The bakers thus presented themselves as the moral register of a wider problem: capital's erosion of the nation's most precious resource, its republican feeling. Class solidarity would point the way to a restored national family. [17]

But in the treacherous currents of the 1850s, no successful workers' protest could afford to be entirely sentimental. The same sweeping forces of consolidation that were disrupting workers' lives, the shrewdest activists understood, had to be bent to their favor. One of the most rigorous efforts, that by the Journeymen Printers of the United States, used the language of sympathy in a different key. Declaring that there existed "a perpetual antagonism between Labor and Capital," the printers proposed a vast protective society that would fix wages, limit the number of apprentices, and even issue traveling certificates to keep tabs on workers. But such surveillance was not a sign of coercion. Rather, it was the very thing needed "to produce a warmer attachment on the part of superior men" who will be bound "in the ties of gratitude and in the luxurious fellowship of good deeds." The vision of masses of men regulated by mutual gratitude lent itself naturally to a language stressing "a sort of equilibrium in the power of the conflicting parties"— a language ironically close to the more sanguine pronouncements of capitalists themselves. [18]

The irony highlights the delicate position of radicals at midcentury. On the one hand, the printers rejected capitalist labor relations, vowing "to sell [themselves] no longer to speculators; but to become [their] own employer." They envisioned a truly new form of cooperative labor freed from "the shackles of a disastrous Conventionalism" that condemned them to a life without dignity or honor. Yet, on the other hand, when they imagined a social system fulfilling that vow, they recurred to an older imagery of balanced sympathies that tended to reflect an ideal version of the dominant order. That is, when the solidarity of republican feeling was filtered through the shifting demands of the marketplace, it often gave rise to disciplinary schemes converting spontaneous sympathy into social control—a response that could resist innovation as easily as it could promote it. A long and approving article in the *Tribune* on the workers' associations of Paris demonstrated a similar impulse. The Paris communes restored "fellowship between the members" of a trade by regulating their activities—setting wage rates and prices, rewarding innovation, and disciplining those who "calumniated others, or . . . used blameable means to influence them." As social relations decayed throughout the decade, these sympathies expressed more than republican enthusiasm. They figured an urgent appeal for social order. [19]

It was in rejecting this disciplined sympathy that land reformers, the second labor response noted above, made their most powerful appeal. Throughout the early 1850s, and particularly as New York's economy sagged in 1854, few utopian proposals omitted a version of agrarian order. Thomas Devyr, the English land reformer, had been preaching that gospel for more than a decade. To the New York tailors Devyr urged "True Freedom," provided through "a free farm of excellent land" whose return would be guaranteed by "the Being who created man and the earth and placed them in their present relation to each other." Such "beautiful harmony" was the true end of the working class. But the land reform option, with its aura of republican traditionalism, also represented a dramatic concession to the forces of economic change. In an appeal to the wounded autonomy of his readers, Devyr urged that workers' prosperity did not depend on the "organization" of laborers at all. To argue anything less was to accept that a man's quest for independence ought to be compromised through "the worthlessness and inefficiency of certain other men." By professing his faith in the orderly operations of an unfettered exchange, Devyr was exposing workers to the very atomizing forces that were threatening their security. Wholesale removal to the West could only weaken those whose prosperity demanded ready access to large markets at close quarters; fleeing the scene did not change the economic equations. In this manner, the transcendent claims of agrarian independence were made, insensibly, to support the market imperatives they resisted. Change ratified tradition.[20]

A similar drift to market discipline marked the third variety of labor sympathy, one that rejected unruly passions for the more orderly exchanges of feeling envisioned by Adam Smith. "Before an excited and sympathising [*sic*] crowd," wrote Horace Greeley after the tailors' riot, "we believe a man might make a pretty acceptable speech out of a few popular sentences, such as 'aristocrats,' 'rag barons,' 'grinding the face of the poor,' 'sweat and blood of the workingman' . . . without having developed a single fruitful or practical idea." Much more beneficial would be a labor program that could "so adjust and perfect . . . relations" among various workers' groups that there could be no occasion for idleness. Passions needed to be regulated and channeled into cooperative behavior that would bring prosperity and "[a] more republican relationship" to all. In an address to the Industrial Congress, R. J. Pond made the point more forcefully. While the Jeweler's Trade Society he represented felt "the deepest sympathy for the distress of others," it could not simply accede to the radical demands of tailors or any other group. Rather, workers needed to adopt a more gradualist, global approach that would make them more efficient. The most sympathetic response involved the regulation of trade—a scheme that would strictly limit sales and production, license cooperative stores, and balance wages against cheap goods. The Industrial Congress would thus become the arbiter of its own economy.[21]

Cooperationist schemes like those advanced by Pond and Greeley marked a crucial and fateful adjustment. For beneath the calls for economic autonomy, these more moderate spokesmen expressed the need to enlist and accommodate economic change. Indeed, on occasion, their schemes to harmonize workers' activities could seem as threatening as the discipline of the bosses. Pond, for example, saw free land as the salve to all labor ills. Only delegate the Industrial Congress to identify "surplus labor," and means could easily be devised to remove workers to the West. In this manner, even the antimarket appeals of the agrarians could be turned into visions of market discipline. In an era of consolidation, sympathy, too, could be an instrument of control. [22]

The relation between these versions of labor sympathy and Whitman's developing poetic role is suggested in a letter that the land reformer Dr. William J. Young wrote to the *Tribune* at the height of the labor agitation. Claiming that the wealthy were guilty of exploiting the nation's poor, Young declared himself a partisan of all reform schemes, for the more fully workers "can be induced to agitate and balance against each other reformatory measures and ideas," the sooner the entire society would improve. But even though the ills of laborers can be traced to the "want of fellow sympathy" from bosses, the most comprehensive solution would involve not organized resistance but a kind of higher assimilation:

> the day has dawned, it is hoped, when, through the art of printing, an electrifying intelligence will diffuse sympathy, faith and forethought among the masses and raise up prophets and preachers of duty and kindness, of social equality, of merit and of rights among them, equivalent to the attainment of the greatest good to the greatest number within the verge of possibilities, without in the least infringing upon any equitable right of the more sordid, luxurious and grasping of the conservativerace [*sic*], to whom all change is obnoxious because to them nothing is desirable or sacred but that which serves to sate their own sordid ambitions and appetites, and whose only happiness often consists in the consciousness of abundance while below them the multitude are struggling by every possible shift of mercenary contrivances to lift themselves above the waves, or save themselves from sinking as each fresh blast adds to the horror of their condition. [23]

The overblown sentence, straining in its very eagerness to embrace all possibilities, is at its core pragmatic and utilitarian. Although it expresses fine scorn for wealthy parasites, it does not eliminate them from the social system. Rather, it wants to incorporate them within a larger orbit governed by the gravity of sympathy. Guided by an electrifying intelligence, the masses of workers would arrange their own affairs in concert with the greater good of an abundant society. There was room for oppressors and laborers alike; indeed, the opponents would strike a balance for the good of all. Young's vision, the very image of liberal order, would not wait long for meters. As the labor movement collapsed in the panic of 1854, Whitman emerged to sing its fractured harmonies.

## *Revulsion*

Both Iver Bernstein and Sean Wilentz have noted the grim fate of this labor activism. Although the New York Industrial Congress had the same quasi-official status as its sister workers' cooperatives in radical Luxembourg, Germany, and France, the Americans made fateful errors by throwing in their lot with more mainstream politicians. The very structure of the congress as a forum for all views worked against its militancy, particularly after the tailors' riot, when it became absorbed with the plodding minutiae of investigating abusive employers or concocting grand schemes of union. In 1851, the congress veered toward coalition politics, responding to the call "to combine all true Democrats" to make land reform a "cardinal principl[e]" of the party, and frankly embraced Tammany Hall. And it was in this more moderate atmosphere that the jobless converged on City Hall Park in the winter of 1854, when yet another economic wave engulfed New York. The workers' demonstrations preceding the publication of *Leaves of Grass* were an act of radical defiance in which the last vestiges of Jacksonian radicalism were finally laid to rest. [24]

The latest business downturn began with a wave of bank failures in the Midwest. As ripple effects spread to the South and Northeast, railroads and other large companies suddenly had difficulty borrowing, and their retrenchment caused a crisis of business confidence. In New York, where short-term interest rates quickly shot up to 2 percent monthly, businesses of all sizes began layoffs. By the end of the year, large numbers of tradesmen were facing starvation. The *New York Herald* reported that more than half of all New York tailors and two-thirds of its masons were unemployed. Half of the city's plumbers were jobless, a third of its bookbinders, nearly three-quarters of its hatters. The printers had "not known so great a depression . . . for many years," and in the building trades, house carpenters like Whitman were "among the principal sufferers." As the weather turned severely cold, the unemployed took to the streets. In a vivid display of working-class outrage, the roughs sought refuge from the economic storm. [25]

The crowds that congregated in City Hall Park and elsewhere throughout the winter shared, in many respects, the mood of the union activists four years earlier.

They quickly organized themselves into deliberative bodies, elected officers and spokesmen, and drafted memorials, dreaming of grander pressure groups of all "the working classes." But while they thought big, they felt a greater urgency than did their predecessors in the Industrial Congress or Cooperative Labor League. Now their spokesmen often threatened "general outbreak" if they could not find work. Not only were the extravagant rich responsible for the workers' suffering, speakers argued, but the government itself was to blame. "When speculators and capitalists desired to have any measure passed," declared Ira B. Davis, they were instantly accommodated, whereas workers were routinely scorned. Now, many were willing to entertain the appeal of one demonstrator to "go down to South-street" and seize bread. "What it may lead to we know not," Daniel Walford warned a crowd in late December, "but unless relief is afforded, we may, perhaps, have civil war."[26]

But the very need for relief imposed a logic of its own, one that converted the demonstrators' genuine outrage into more passive accommodation. The hinge, once again, was the workers' threatened autonomy. Since outright handouts only underscored the "derangement and wrong" that workers were forced to endure from those speculators who scorned "republican blood," the unemployed had to "depend on [them]selves." That mood was made abundantly clear in an angry meeting at Hope Chapel in late December, when workers decisively rejected a proposal for a "Workingmen's Aid Society" that would have used Tract Society missionaries to collect and distribute aid to the deserving unemployed. Instead, the workers insisted on a program that "would strike at the root of the evil" by allowing them to provide for themselves. In almost every meeting and memorial during the panic, the program was the same: the ownership of private property. The resolutions adopted at a mass meeting held on 15 January 1855 are typical. The workers' committee urged the authorities to amend eviction laws to protect tenants, to distribute unoccupied state lands "free of charge" to the unemployed, and to pass a national Homestead Bill that would provide 160 acres to all applicants. "[L]and monopoly," both urban and rural, was the real source of the problem, and the only solution was an immediate and universal return of property to the people. Allow a poor man a "foodhold [sic] in the soil," and economic order could be restored.[27]

If land reform was the panacea, however, it did not function in quite the way its advocates intended. One problem involved the unacknowledged paradox of requiring government to restore independence. Although the demand harked back to the antimonopoly rhetoric of the Jacksonian era, the enemy was now more diffuse, the problem more pervasive. To the appeals for enforced autonomy, local, state, and national governments simply pleaded poverty or legal restrictions (as did New York's Fernando Wood) or professed their unwillingness to interfere in the very relations of private property that so distressed protesters. A wider problem involved the mentality of those making the demands, who were often willing to trade their outrage for security in a more stable order. "[M]ake the working classes more comfortable" by affording them land, Daniel Walford urged, and the workers will respond by being more "sober and industrious." Similarly, Ira B. Davis argued that employed mechanics would be better consumers, giving "a general stimulus to business, so that every class of citizens, laborers and traders, would . . . benefit." An acute illustration of this willingness surfaced during a meeting of the German workingmen, once among the most powerful New York unions. After a speech by Davis, the group, amid "[g]reat enthusiasm," endorsed a petition titled "RIGHT OF THE PEOPLE OF THE UNITED STATES TO THE FREE USE OF THE PUBLIC LANDS—SAYINGS OF THE GREAT AND GOOD." Among the great was Andrew Jackson, who declared that "every American citizen of enterprize [*sic*]" should enjoy an "independent freehold." Among the good was the prophet Nehemiah, who lamented that "we bring into bondage our sons and daughters" and cannot redeem them; "for other men have our lands." The petition's final thought belonged to Jesus: "Blessed are the meek, for they shall inherit the earth."[28]

This is not to suggest that formerly militant workers had abandoned their arms like troops in a panicky retreat. In the tumultuous meeting at Hope Chapel noted above, for example, the assembled workers vehemently rejected the land reform package of their committee, forced them to resign, and adopted a more stringent resolution advocating liberal currency, "free farms for the people," and "a Government of the American heart." But even these statements may indicate that land reform, with its rhetoric of balance and pragmatic sympathy, was helping to convert republican outrage into compromises with what one essayist called "the high-pressure atmosphere of industry." The pastoral idyll of Jacksonian autonomy was being radically transformed by the demands of the urban marketplace.[29]

But if the panic demonstrations marked the fateful collapse of antebellum radicalism, not all observers succumbed to hard times. Jacksonians had wanted to fuse republicanism and laissez-faire while resisting the non-egalitarian forces of the market. During the labor unrest of the early 1850s, that consensus split into its contradictory parts—a labor republicanism that clung to traditional notions of sympathy and unity, a radicalism that strove for new forms of association, and a liberal wing that embraced, but attempted to control, the market. In the first edition of *Leaves of Grass,* Whitman reasserted the possibility of fusion by stressing themes of republican sympathy and association yet incorporating civic feeling in wider circles of prudence, free labor, and possessive individualism. Through these means, he transformed the labor rhetoric of the 1850s into an enduring argument for the harmonies of the market revolution.

## *The Making of a Mediator*

Although Whitman was never directly involved in these labor struggles, there was much to make him sympathetic. The son of a farmer-turned-carpenter, weaned on the writings of Thomas Paine and Frances Wright, Whitman hewed to the rhythms and sentiments of working-class life. Like many mechanics in a period when the trades were being radically transformed, Whitman changed jobs frequently and often scrambled to find work. Between the ages of fifteen and twenty-one, he held at least ten teaching positions, most for brief, three-month terms. When he turned to journalism, he worked at seven different newspapers, established two newspapers of his own (both soon abandoned), and edited five more. He briefly owned a bookstore, was a journeyman carpenter, and acted as a petty entrepreneur, building and selling houses—all this in addition to freelance writing. Throughout this restless activity, as his brother George remarked, Whitman "had chances to make money," but he did not seem to be fashioning the kind of sturdy, middle-class career that Emerson admired in the Vermont lad who left the farm for newspaper work and a seat in Congress. Rather, Whitman's résumé resembles those of contemporary workers who, during the boom times of the late 1840s and early 1850s, changed jobs with startling rapidity. "[A] man may know his shopmates to-day," wrote one antebellum mechanic with only modest exaggeration, "while on the morrow he may find himself among strangers." In the printing trades, among the most highly paid in New York, the pace was similarly brisk, as is indicated by the career of Thomas Chamberlain, who in late 1845 averaged slightly more than two weeks at each of ten different jobs. In boom times, workers angled for advantage; in bad, they struggled for survival. Like Whitman, they pursued work tirelessly, if only to stay in place.[30]

Whitman's living arrangements were equally peripatetic. His family, which during the 1820s and 1840s shuttled between Long Island and Brooklyn, moved at least ten times, often changing residence annually. Between 1834, when Whitman was an apprentice, and 1863, when he left for Washington, D.C., he moved twenty-seven times, or about once a year. As his notebooks indicate, many of the moves, particularly during the 1850s, when he was house building, were effected on 1 May, the citywide day for vacating rented premises and signing new leases. Like the occupational mobility, this residential mobility was a condition of working-class life. It may have been an exaggeration, as one writer to the *New York Times* claimed in 1855, that the city's propertyless "change[d] their residence monthly," but the annual chaos of mass migration was one of the fixed rituals of the working class. Seeking better terms or facing hard times, workers routinely picked up stakes, making the mass movement, in Elizabeth Blackmar's words, a testament to the pervasiveness of the "market economy." In effect, the rapidity with which Whitman, like his contemporaries, changed homes and jobs vividly demonstrates how both people and commodities had become caught up in the accelerating pace of exchange, the "world of moving objects" engineered by the market revolution.[31]

But while Whitman sang and celebrated the rhythms of working-class life, he was not entirely bound by them. One distinction involves the way he made his living. As Anthony Giddens has observed, a prime difference between manual work and the kind of nonmanual labor that Whitman frequently performed involves the "manipulation of symbolic materials"—managing information instead of driving nails. Whitman was sensitive to this difference and, during his most earnest newspaper days, sought to elide it. If he reveled in editorials describing New York saunters, the hour spent in the window chair at the American Museum overlooking the crowds, or even his listless inability to find a suitable topic to write about, he also reminded his readers that editorship approached slavery. "That the labors of an editor are hard enough, is an undoubted fact," he declared in 1847. "The worst of it is, not that the work is hard, but that, in this country, one man has to do *so many things* in the paper." In his first editorial job with the *Aurora* in 1842, he confessed to how "[h]eavy" was the responsibility to provide "several thousand people" with a daily "repast—something *piquant,* and something solid, and something sentimental, and something humorous." The fact that his handiwork would be so rapidly consumed and required anew each morning must have reinforced in his own mind the links to a proletarianized working class that by the 1850s labored at a "railroad pace." But if brain work often felt like hard labor, there was no denying the more abstract nature of Whitman's vocation. While pressmen labored below, he had the option of soaring above the crowd, rendering panoramic portraits of New York. Like other intellectuals, he was not bound by the material conditions of his work. [32]

Equally suggestive is Whitman's work as a petty entrepreneur. At least three times before the first edition of *Leaves of Grass,* he worked for himself—and although none of the efforts could be described as lucrative, they do suggest how he crossed the psychological boundary between dependent laborer and autonomous agent. His early short-lived effort to found the *Long Islander* in 1838 was succeeded by a period of more intense activity in the 1850s. In 1851 he ran a modest bookstore and printing shop in which he published commercial notices for salesmen. The shop was also a testament to a somewhat more ambitious venture. In 1848 Whitman bought a lot on Myrtle Avenue, erecting the three-story building that would house his family and shop until he sold it in 1852. For the next two years, he continued the pattern of speculative buying, building, and selling, participating in the building boom that was transforming Brooklyn. To be sure, Whitman's speculations were modest in comparison to the wholesale construction of tenements that investors had been pursuing for years in Manhattan. It should also be noted that many carpenters and other workers of the period owned and often built their own homes. But what seems most striking about Whitman's speculative building is the way in which he yoked tradition and competition, the stem family and the mobile marketplace. By using the home, that durable symbol of working-class substance, as a temporary conveyance for his family and for profit, Whitman was breaching boundaries as surely as he did in the poetry he was writing during the same period. Unlike most property-owning laborers, he made use-value and exchange-value coincide. [33]

Publishing at a time of economic and political crisis, Whitman may have performed his most important cultural function as a mediatory intellectual. In his *Prison Notebooks* and elsewhere, Antonio Gramsci surveys several kinds of intellectual activity, and though his analysis is closely tied to Italian affairs between the wars, it is also suggestive for antebellum America. [34] Gramsci distinguishes between traditional intellectuals, who, through an *"esprit de corps,"* or shared discourse, experience themselves "as autonomous and independent of the dominant social group," and organic intellectuals, who are tied to the dominant order (303). Gramsci's chief example of traditional intellectuals is the clergy. Rooted in the feudal past, they are linked to a waning mode of production and to classes either disappearing or in danger of extinction. They cloak or obscure their class interests in the universal claims of a transcendent ideology, claims that often espouse powerful residual values. As Gramsci's disciples have demonstrated, the ascendance of bourgeois liberalism has meant absorbing, defeating, or transforming the residual appeal of these traditional figures.

Organic intellectuals present a more complex picture. All emerging social orders, Gramsci argues, recruit their own legitimators. In early-twentieth-century Italy these included writers, journalists, and philosophers, but also more practical business leaders, politicians, and educators. Drawn in part from "the petty and middle urban bourgeoisie" (306), these individuals acted very much like entrepreneurs, giving the dominant class a "homogeneity and awareness" of its social function. Like contemporary businessmen who thrived by stimulating confidence, organic intellectuals had to organize "masses of men" (301) so as to generate "intellectual wealth" (307). Such wealth constitutes the crucial human capital of industrial society—a society that survives through regulation and repression. Hence, Gramsci's descriptions of the organic intellectual in a liberal state often seem unduly rigid and mechanistic. Organic intellectuals, he frequently claims, are like "subaltern officers" in a huge military hierarchy, his choice metaphor for capitalist society. Urban intellectuals are particularly good examples of these subalterns, who "carry out the immediate execution of the production plan decided by the industrial general staff" (308). But this almost robotic view of liberal intellectual activity is considerably modified by other layers of meaning.

One layer involves Gramsci's parallel assertion that intellectuals may be found in all ranks of society. Although all people do not participate in organizing the social machine, all engage in the spontaneous mental activity that, on occasion, achieves a power of its own. Language confers one kind of power. Since all language implies an ideology or conception of the world, all speakers are practical philosophers, acting on and through language to alter their circumstances. Workers may also produce their own organic intellectuals capable of opposing exploitation.[35] The very dynamism of the capitalist system, finally, fosters new critical intellectuals capable of understanding their place in "a system of relations" and of spurring social revolution. In Gramsci's day, these favored few wrote for his political journal, *Ordine Nuovo,* which he saw as the meeting ground for liberals and communists. But his sense that the cultural moment held larger possibilities for the intellectual has important parallels in America during the 1850s, where contending intellectual voices struggled to redefine public policy and class conflict amid the breakdown of political alliances. Whitman would draw on this discourse as he sought, characteristically, to unify it. To appropriate the language of one Gramsci scholar, his response involved being "organic, traditional and new at once."[36]

To be sure, the Gramscian categories must be modified for an American context in which the language of radical critique itself combined the traditional and the progressive. Jacksonian attacks on monopolies and aggressive capitalists were often tinged with the desire to preserve precommercial values, and the ideals of republicanism could be pressed into service to support both the autonomy of artisans and the prosperity of middling entrepreneurs—the very dialectic that emerged in the New York labor activism of the 1850s. The rapid swings in New York's prosperity in the early 1850s, when Whitman was shaping *Leaves of Grass,* intensified the search for what John Higham has called "consolidation"—the widespread desire to discipline and organize the unruly forces of a modernizing society.[37] It was this deeply felt need that turned antebellum Americans into practical intellectuals, striving, in Gramsci's terms, to create the institutions of organic liberal order. Whitman turned their efforts into meter-making argument. His democratic sympathy provided a model for a more prudent, but no less heroic, republicanism.

## Ambivalent Designs

That Whitman the poet responded to the market crisis may be seen in a little-noticed passage near the beginning of the 1855 preface.[38] In contemplating America, he writes, one "must indeed own the riches of the summer and winter, and need never be bankrupt while corn grows from the ground or the orchards drop apples or the bays contain fish" (iii). The remark, echoing the balanced republicanism of spokesmen from Richard Price to Henry Clay, offers traditional reassurance in the face of rapid change. American abundance will enforce its own symmetries, linking the acts of scattered individuals into a grand, benevolent design. Inspiring that vision were the artisan republican values undermined in the latest panic—"the noble character of the young mechanics and of all free American workmen and workwomen" (iv). In espousing liberty, Whitman reaffirms the laborer's autonomy so often proclaimed by labor activists. "Liberty relies upon itself, invites no one, promises nothing, . . . and knows no discouragement," he asserts (viii). Even in the face of labor strife and market disruption, Whitman persisted in singing the old song of republican order.

Associated with that republican impulse is a literary and psychological attitude that might be called "identification." Anchored by the "wonderful sympathy" of America's workers (iii), the poet must express the common mind through images "commensurate with [the] people" (iv). Just as the republic is a harmonious balance of expanding forces, so the poet must faithfully mirror or embody the diverse national soul. "[T]he greatest poet," Whitman claims, "brings the spirit of any or all events and passions and scenes and persons . . . to bear on your individual character as you hear or read" (vi). Such inclusiveness captures the republican spirit through a kind of infinite sympathy in which the American character reiterates, unchanged, through time and space. Republican unity is a community of spirit, and the great poet merely identifies its ageless themes. In a significant phrase that signals his mediatory function, Whitman calls this attitude one of "prudence"—the impulse that "puts off nothing, permits no let-up for its own case or any case" (xi). This expansive identification is prudent only if the nation, with all its cleavages, is presumed to function according to republican principles. If all individuals are essentially equal, they will be evenly and harmoniously distributed across a society governed by natural law. Republican America, in short, was nature's nation.

That radical symmetry, however, is offset, in the preface, by other motives. Just as workers' producer associations sought to discipline themselves as a means of accommodating economic change, so Whitman projected a disciplinary impulse in his poetry. As an "individual," Whitman claims, the true poet is "the president of regulation" (v). If "precision and balance" (vi) can be discerned in human affairs, they exist because the poet insists on them. It is the poet who is "the arbiter of the diverse" and the "equalizer of his age" (iv). While the master trope remains one of balance, Whitman's tone here is more authoritarian than benign—closer to the labor discipline of Greeley and Pond than to the expansive sympathies of the workers' protective societies. This darker authoritarianism Whitman also labeled prudence; and in some sense the preface is an attempt to retain the regulatory vision without sacrificing an autonomous and perfect order. If America was essentially sound, why was there need for a disciplinary voice at all? If it were not sound, what combination of instinct and attitude could restore its lost harmony?[39]

Whitman pursues this issue through a long meditation on prudence, later incorporated, as "Poem of the Last Explanation of Prudence," into the second edition of *Leaves of Grass*. In its most severe sense, prudence stands for narrow materialism and selfishness. The true poet has "higher notions of prudence" and is not seduced by false "economies"—gluttony, "peculation," the "infinitessimals [*sic*] of parlors, or shameless stuffing while others starve" (ix–x). Such "melancholy prudence" abandons one "to the toss and pallor of years of moneymaking with all their scorching days and icy nights and all their stifling deceits and underhanded dodgings" (x). Authentic prudence, by contrast, discerns infinitude in the commonplace and recognizes that "all that has at any time been well suggested" or experienced contributes to "the prudence suitable for immortality" (x). Any lesser notion, as M. Wynn Thomas observes, merely strengthened the "debased philosophy" of the age. [40]

But in the context of the labor problems preceding Whitman's poetry, the difficulties surrounding prudence are not so easily resolved. For the sympathetic harmonies that seemed to guarantee labor's place in a benign order were undermined by the business cycle, and in their place spokesmen urged the very kinds of "prudent" interventions that Whitman denounced. To sustain republicanism, they claimed, it was imperative that workers manage their own economic affairs and cooperate with capitalists or become capitalists themselves. They had to be prudent in the organic sense that Gramsci describes and that Whitman seems to scorn in this passage. In the economic emergency, prudent behavior seemed to be the only way to restore traditional relations. Only then could prudence, as Whitman wrote in his notebook, remain "the right arm of independence." [41]

Whitman, too, confronted this split between traditional and organic attitudes. But while he was far from embracing the Whig pragmatism of a Horace Greeley, his unique background as an intellectual and working-class entrepreneur allowed him to fashion a hybrid stance. Retaining his passionate allegiance to the harmonious egalitarianism of his republican roots, he nevertheless modified that attitude through a shrewd sense of regulation and discipline—a higher prudence that did not lose touch with the need to earn, to exploit, to advertise. He was never so abstract and ethereal as his most cosmic passages; or, rather, his most cosmic passages were rooted in a sound pragmatic sense. The hybrid response was not original with Whitman, however; its roots may be traced back to Adam Smith's *The Theory of Moral Sentiments*—a social blueprint grounded in the operations of prudence. To be sure, there is no evidence of direct influence: Whitman was not composing *Leaves of Grass* with Smith at his elbow. And the differences between Smith's Enlightenment rationalism and Whitman's Romanticism remain considerable. But the adaptations of sympathy that Smith had established in 1759 and that were explored and transmitted in popular fiction remained an important imaginative basis for the pragmatic republicanism that many organic intellectuals were exploring one hundred years later. To understand Whitman's social positioning in *Leaves of Grass,* then, it is necessary to make a brief return to Smith's seminal work. [42]

Like Whitman's, Smith's social vision involved a fusion of egalitarianism and sentiment. While he recognized Augustan class distinctions, the champion of free enterprise nevertheless heaped scorn on the idle rich. Why should the well born, Smith asks, "regard it as worse than death" to live like a common laborer? "Do they imagine that their stomach is better, or their sleep sounder in a palace than in a cottage?" (I.iii.2.1, p. 50). So contemptible is the lust for the "general sympathy and attention" lavished on the wealthy that it has engendered all the "tumult and bustle . . . the rapine and injustice" in the world (I.iii.2.8, p. 57). Opposed to these false shows was the honest merit achieved through hard work, "superior knowledge, . . . and superior industry" (I.iii.2.5, p. 55). It was the great comfort of liberal ideology that the world favored such scrupulous behavior, that "[i]n the race for wealth, and honours," one might "strain every nerve and every muscle" to achieve just rewards (II.ii.2.1, p. 83). But there were limits to liberal ambition— limits that Smith termed prudence. Prudent behavior prompted competitors to restrain their passions to satisfy a deeper need: the approval and sympathy of others. Mutual recognition and esteem, the moral basis of an open society, ensured that individuals would ground their conduct in benevolence rather than avarice. The "sentiment or affection of the heart, from which any action proceeds, and upon which its whole virtue or vice depends" (II.i.2, p. 67) naturally impels individuals to moderation. Sentiment was thus a flywheel on the social machine, allowing for the widest and most efficient expression of individual energies and needs. [43]

The attractiveness of this vision for sentimental literature in general and for Whitman in particular lay in its intimacy. Smith's moral economy involved an infinitude of close encounters, face-to-face exchanges that generated a code of conduct through a Lockean association of responses. His prime metaphor for this process is the mirror. An isolated individual, Smith argues, would never have occasion to develop a social conscience. The "beauty or deformity of his own mind" is no more visible to him than is his own face. Introduce him into society, however, "and he is immediately provided with the mirror which he wanted before. It is placed in the countenance and behaviour of those he lives with, . . . and it is here that he first views the propriety and impropriety of his own passions, the beauty and deformity of his own mind" (III.i.3, p. 110). The mutual anxiety that censure creates turns us all into self-censors, the "spectators of our own behaviour" (III.i.5, p. 112). This imaginative leap through "the only looking-glass by which we can . . . with the eyes of other people, scrutinize . . . our own conduct" (III.i.5, p. 112) in turn creates that impartial spectator that regulates conscience. But if the desire to see and be seen ensures social harmony, it also suggests Smith's attachment to a milieu of local exchange and immediate response much closer to the rural village than to the commercial marketplace. The mirror, in short, had two faces. While it came to characterize the artificial world of exchange values endlessly reflected through trade, Smith's mirror retained a sympathetic immediacy. To see oneself in others was to grasp a moment before the bargaining began, when intrinsic value lit up the frame.[44]

The genius of Smith's moral system lies in this mixture of motives. At its core, it provides for a balance of sentiment and restraint, a way to indulge feeling without yielding to its excesses. For individuals, proper or prudent behavior involves an adjustment of impulses. As all individuals seek approval, they must learn to restrain their most violent emotions in order to secure the full sympathies of others. This mutual adjustment, Smith argues, is the basis of social order. From it flow the virtues of benevolence and the power of self-government—both the bonds and boundaries of society. The same principle, associated with feelings of gratitude and resentment, underlies justice, "the main pillar that upholds the whole edifice" (II.ii.3.4, p. 86) of society. Indeed, the balance of sympathies arising from the exchange of feelings unlocks the deepest secrets of the world. Smith's sympathetic actor "does not look upon himself, according to what self-love would suggest, as a whole, separated and detached from every other part of nature, to be taken care of by itself, and for itself. He regards himself in the light in which he imagines the great Genius of human nature, and of the world regards him. He enters, if I may say so, into the sentiments of that Divine Being, and considers himself as an atom, a particle, of an immense and infinite system, which must, and ought to be disposed of, according to the conveniency of the whole" (I.iii.2.9, p. 59). Reflected through the light of God's eyes, we are all involved in the same cosmic exchange. We are atoms belonging to ourselves, to others, and to the universe. For Smith, this Stoicism offered a rare glimpse of the metaphysics behind his social machine. It would take a poet to turn that glimpse into a vision of sympathetic order.[45]

The mixture of rational calculation and imaginative concession that characterized this moral universe suggests how Whitman would construct a solution to the labor crisis of the 1850s. Like Smith, he imagined a social system rooted in sympathetic exchange. Like Smith, too, he saw in those mutual concessions the most promising basis for the freewheeling autonomy of the dauntless actor who proclaimed himself with original energy. And like Smith, Whitman fashioned a complex prudence that permitted both discipline and intimacy, aggressive self-assertion and sentimental response. Whitman's poetic self was the moral agent of a truly republican market order, the mirror through which his readers encountered their own deepest needs. Through that mirror, Whitman would reflect the harmonies of a balanced society in which even antagonisms could be made to reveal democratic truths. The poet proclaiming sympathy was the regulator of the social order.

A particularly clear example of this intricate balance is evident in "The Sleepers." Schematically, the poem is a radiating demonstration of the harmony at its conclusion. Whitman begins "ill-assorted" and "contradictory" (70; 4) and ends by affirming the unity of all. At the center of the poem is a personal and national assertion of sympathy in the figure of George Washington. On either side of that center are complementary positions: figures of loss and return, instances of transformed individuals complemented by the large-scale "merg[ing]" (75; 142) of groups, confusion yielding to harmony. The concentric structure allows Whitman not only to demonstrate the sympathetic order he describes, but also to offer a metaphor for the prudential adjustments that might restore sentimental democracy to the embattled 1850s.

At the heart of "The Sleepers" lies an exchange of feeling. Recurring to the Battle of Brooklyn, familiar to him since childhood, Whitman imagines Washington's defeat as a tear-stained agony: "His face is cold and damp . . . . he cannot repress the weeping drops . . . the color is blanched from his cheeks" (73; 103). The bitter failure, one of the first of the Revolutionary War, forced the Americans to retreat before an overwhelming British force, thereby ceding control of Long Island. In this poem, though, the battle serves as a prelude to its heroic reversal in Washington's victorious farewell. The sentimental leave-taking depicts the general as an embryonic Whitman: he "encircles" his soldiers' necks "with his arm and kisses them on the cheek, / He kisses lightly the wet cheeks one after another" (74; 108–9). A "president of regulation," Washington nevertheless yields to emotion and erases all rank in his simple and human exchanges. Whitman, of course, had not originated these scenarios. As we have seen, they were already current during Washington's administration, when Pelatiah Webster used the sentimental general to argue for more military pay. And David Waldstreicher has shown how the sentimentalization of our first national hero helped to mold American character. In "The Sleepers," these complementary images of Washington suggest how sentiment literally saves the republic. The real strength of the war effort was not so much Washington's tactical genius as his ability to identify with his troops, suffer their losses, and thus inspire them with martial resolve. His embrace of common experience made the nation possible.[46]

For Whitman, Washington's heroic prudence is a proof text in national rededication. Encircling this episode, the poem provides radiating instances of loss and salvation, all anchored by the concessions of feeling. The first, interior ring, for example, echoes the Washington section by providing complementary images of death and recovery. A "beautiful gigantic swimmer" (73; 81) courageously breasting the sea is lost in "the circling eddies" (73; 90) until only his brave white corpse remains. A ship is dashed "helplessly" (73; 96) against the beach as the speaker hears the passengers' screams. A beautiful Indian visits a homestead, never to be seen again. A slave bitterly curses his oppressors for destroying his family. But, much like the Washington vignette, these searing images of loss prepare the prudent reader for reconciliation and return. "Elements merge in the night" (75; 142), Whitman writes, introducing a long catalogue of homeward voyages. "The homeward bound and the outward bound" (75; 150) anchor a wider reunion involving the broken swimmer and the Indian, the criminal and judge, "The antipodes, and every one between this and them" (75; 159). Prudence here, as in the preface, extends to all phenomena through a universal expansion of soul.

The acute need for that expansion is conveyed through the drama of the poem's initial disorientation. Framing the placid encounters of the circulating poet and the sleeping subjects of his poem is an almost Blakean rhetoric of despair:

> I wander all night in my vision,
> Stepping with light feet . . . . swiftly and noiselessly stepping and stopping,
> Bending with open eyes over the shut eyes of sleepers;
> Wandering and confused . . . . lost to myself . . . . ill-assorted . . . . contradictory.
>     (70; 1–4)

Like the aimless wanderer in Blake's "London," Whitman's speaker seems to be overborne by the sheer diversity of forms, many of them marked by woe:

The wretched features of enuyees, the white features of corpses, the livid faces of
   drunkards, the sick-gray faces of onanists,
The gashed bodies on battlefields, the insane in their strong-doored rooms, the sacred
   idiots. (70; 8–9)

Yet the sense of fragmentation arises not merely from these images of suffering,
counterbalanced in the opening sequence by scenes of loving couples. Rather,
the initial confusion is caused by the speaker's answering passivity, his inability,
like Blake's poet, to do more than dream or observe. If he is to be more than a
mere surveyor of the human drama, the poet, like Washington, will need to seek
sympathetic communion.

   The opening lines of the poem stage the awakening of the speaker's prudence
through a play of participles. This characteristically Whitmanesque device op-
poses the idling, distant observer to the poet afoot with his vision, capable of
merging with his subjects as the elements in the night will later merge. Thus,
as the poet wanders, his "confused" movements are expressed through a chain
of participles—"Pausing and gazing and bending and stopping" (70; 4, 5)—
all suggesting suspended motion. After enumerating these wretched and loving
sleepers, the poet again pauses, "stand[s]," and gestures—but does not yet make
contact: "I pass my hands soothingly to and fro a few inches from them; / The
restless sink in their beds . . . . they fitfully sleep" (71; 24–26). It is not until
he enters their beds and their dreams—"become[s] the other dreamers" (71;
31)—that the speaker masters contradiction. What had been experienced as a
fragmented panorama can thus be felt from the inside, as complementary design.
Paradoxically, this voluntary quiescence also liberates him, turns his abstraction
fit into permanent activity. "I am a dance," he proclaims, " . . . the fit is whirling
me fast" (71; 32). And with that renewed energy, the empathetic poet becomes
an omniscient regulator: "Well do they do their jobs, those journeymen divine, /
Only from me can they hide nothing and would not if they could; / I reckon I am
their boss, and they make me a pet besides" (71; 36–38). Using the language of the
working class, the speaker, like Washington, becomes a regulator. Sympathetic
identification has yielded prudent command.

   Significantly, one early sign of that transformation is the poet's gender crossing.
As he slips into dreams and beds, he becomes a female lover who "resign[s]"
herself to the dusk and her mate (72; 50). "I am she who adorned herself and

folded her hair expectantly," (s)he writes of the assignation; "I feel the hot moisture yet that he left me" (71; 46. 72; 54). As the man departs, the guilty and fantasizing lover becomes a naked, almost transparent presence, "thrust forth" into the street after her "clothes were stolen" (72; 62, 61). Taking her stand on a "Pier that I saw dimly . . . when I looked from the windows" (72; 63), (s)he is both subject to public scrutiny and herself a kind of "piering" gaze, whose very nakedness allows her to breach boundaries and survey experience: "I feel ashamed to go naked about the world, / And am curious to know where my feet stand . . . . and what is this flooding me, childhood or manhood . . . . and the hunger that crosses the bridge between" (72; 65–66). Several lines later the poet takes up residence in other women's bodies, this time those of a "yellow and wrinkled" grandmother and a sleepless widow (72; 73, 75). Such images dramatically extend the figure of the weeping Washington by fusing his heroic sympathy with a truly global humanity. With the capacity of the characterless woman, Whitman allows his visionary persona to bridge all experience.

Incited by the inspiring example of Washington, that personal transformation, by the end of the poem, unfolds in a vision of national reconciliation:

> The scholar kisses the teacher and the teacher kisses the scholar . . . . the wronged is
>     made right,
> The call of the slave is one with the master's call . . and the master salutes the slave,
> The felon steps forth from the prison . . . . the insane becomes sane . . . . the suffering
>     of sick persons is relieved. (76; 187–89)

This peace that passes understanding, Whitman suggests, is not merely phantasmal, the fleeting ecstasies of a poet's dream. Rather, "The Sleepers" argues that the deathlike and recurrent state to which all the living are reduced binds us in eternal ties, a universal medium that eliminates all difference. And if the ecstasy in "The Sleepers" is almost too easy, a fragmentation too readily overcome, it also exposes the depth of Whitman's desire for the kind of sentimental republican union that the figure of Washington embodied. The radiating harmonies of the poem literally incorporate—flesh out—that central abiding spirit.

The incarnation of republican sympathy is also the theme of another key poem in the first edition, "I Sing the Body Electric." The poem has rightly attracted attention for its righteous scorn of slavery. After a grand survey of the nation's bodies, Whitman ascends to "forms" of women and men, and from that divine vantage, surveys the pitiable enumerations of a slave auction. "Exquisite senses, lifelit eyes, pluck, volition" make up the advertisement for Whitman's slave, "And wonders within there yet" (81; 93, 95). "Whatever the bids of the bidders," he proclaims, "they cannot be high enough for him" (81; 86). Betsy Erkkila cites this caustic survey as evidence of Whitman's "attack on race and class attitudes in America"—both the racism of Hunkers and Doughfaces and the class-bound nativism of Old Whigs. To Erkkila, the author of "I Sing the Body Electric" was the renegade Free Soiler who sacrificed his editorship of the *Brooklyn Daily Eagle* to political principle and expressed his outrage through the radically democratic poetry of the 1850s. [47] While not rejecting this reading, I would like to broaden it by recalling the ambivalence of Whitman's poetic stance. As an avid democrat who witnessed the collapse of Jacksonian orthodoxy, Whitman sought to re-create the imaginative conditions for republican union through a regulated sympathy. In "I Sing the Body Electric," as elsewhere in the first edition, that sympathy is trained on the working class, the idled and doubting victims of the latest economic crisis. To that end, Whitman's poem is intended to protect the integrity not only of African Americans but also of beleaguered workers, and he does so by appropriating the language of slavery to dramatize the plight of laborers. Echoing worker-advocates of the early 1850s, he uses the abused bodies of slaves to defend the sanctity of threatened white labor.

Like "The Sleepers," which seeks to build a concentric structure around a central sympathetic image, "I Sing the Body Electric" uses the slave's body as a vehicle in an expanding metaphor. Whitman announces that structure in the poem's opening line: "The bodies of men and women engirth me, and I engirth them" (77; 1). The verb "to engirth" is a particularly resonant one. In addition to its sense of enclosing with weight or flesh—investing or incarnating— the word also implies "engirding"—encircling, but also girding, as with armor, and girdering, as in providing a basis or interior structure. The process, then, is one of reciprocal trying on and being tried on. Engirthing is both internal and external, the encircling of other bodies and being encircled in turn, in a mutually reflective activity that expands to include all humanity. Another version of Smith's prudence, engirthing extends the most intimate exchange into a vision of a balanced and stable order.

To that end, the poem unfolds like a logical proof. "Was it dreamed whether those who corrupted their own live bodies could conceal themselves," asks the poet in the opening passage, "And whether those who defiled the living were as bad as they who defiled the dead?" (77; 3–4). One hundred lines later the poem concludes, "Who degrades or defiles the living human body is cursed" (82; 118)—as corrupt as the desecrator of corpses. Between those points Whitman expands and contracts his focus, unfolding catalogues of bodies but homing in on republicans or members of the working class. After a survey of swimmers, "babes," and laborers, he focuses on two extended vignettes, wrestling apprentice-boys and firemen marching or returning from a fire (78; 21–26). There follows an extended meditation on an old "common farmer," hale and wise, distinguished not only for his "wonderful vigor" but also for his "calmness and beauty of person" (78; 29, 30). These figures are nature's noblemen, displaying a rude, untutored health through their "natural perfect and varied attitudes" (78; 26). Indeed, as the emotional center of a large progeny, the farmer functions as a latter-day Washington, universally "loved . . . with personal love" (79; 34). He inspires the sympathetic prudence shared by all seminal characters. Had you seen him, Whitman avers, "you would wish . . . that you and he might touch each other" (79; 38).

That prudential impulse soon leads Whitman to expand his axis of vision. In a cosmic inventory that anticipates the slave auction, he describes the "form[s]" (79; 46) of women and men. "A divine nimbus exhales from it" (79; 47), Whitman writes of the woman's body, whose erotic power undergirds the still greater potency of childbirth. "This is the nucleus," the "privilege" that "encloses the rest" (79; 58. 80; 60). The figure of the nucleus that both contains and expels is echoed in the description of the archetypal male who, more active than woman, nevertheless manages to contain and be contained. "[T]he flush of the known universe is in him"; yet he, too, "has his . . . place in the procession" (80; 67, 77). As these seminal figures "engirth" the many bodies in the poem, they point with even greater force to the slave, who enters on the heels of the heroic man. If "The man's body is sacred and the woman's body is sacred," Whitman plausibly asks, why not "a slave?" (80; 74–75). But his claim is even more radical, for the logic of the poem suggests that it is not the archetypal body that engirths the slave. Rather, the slave's body is the nucleus of all other forms.

Whitman makes that claim through republican genealogies. In the passages preceding the slave auction, almost all of the heroic bodies are progenitors. The farmer is surrounded by his sons and daughters. The woman, "both passive and active," conceives "daughters as well as sons and sons as well as daughters" (80; 63). The procession in which firemen or the sacred male marches looks forward to the future from the present, full-fleshed moment. When Whitman turns to the slave, however, his perspective notably broadens, for the slave's body is literally at the center of history. "For him the globe lay preparing quintillions of years," he writes; "For him the revolving cycles truly and steadily rolled" (81; 87–88). And as Whitman anatomizes the man, burrowing into his brain and blood, he cycles outward and forward to the slave's descendants, the "countless immortal lives with countless embodiments" of which the slave is the origin (81; 101). "In him the start of populous states and rich republics," Whitman proclaims (81; 100), as if the slave were a transfigured Washington.

But the slave anchors the republic in other ways as well. For his position at the center of the poem, engirthing the nation, allows him to gird or underlie the American commoners that precede him. Whitman excavates the slave to provide the foundation for this catalogue of republican figures. They depend on the slave—not in any cynical or exploitative sense, but logically, as a conclusion is derived from its premise. In other words, the beautiful republican forms that Whitman celebrates earlier in the poem can best be understood through their similarities with and differences from slaves.

Such racial measuring was particularly vibrant in the 1850s, when workers feared being reduced to chattel. New York bakers, declared Bartholomew Derham in 1850, must demand immediate relief, since they have "had to endure more suffering than the most ill-treated Slaves of the South." A year later, the bakers were still appealing to the "Humanity" of their fellows to help deliver them from "bondage and thraldom," and the Journeymen Printers looked forward to the day when "The shackles of a disastrous Conventionalism will have fallen from [their] limbs." But if enslavement provided a dramatic basis for workers' rights, the concept was also bound up with larger concerns about the erosion of labor power—an erosion that was often imagined through the body. New York bakers complained that their sweated labor in noxious conditions left them little time for "refreshing the body." And Dr. William Young lamented that machinery was drawing into emasculating competition "blood, brain and muscle against dead matter, sembling vitality." Like racial oppression, class conflict left its traces on the bodies of laborers. Whitman's imagery sought to engirth workers by making their condition immediate and universal. Their bodies, the source of all productive value, became the basis of national experience and the measure of material well-being. To abuse or neglect the bodies of laborers was to reduce them to slaves and to make slaves of their descendants, a prospect that could be reversed only through the reassertion of republican autonomy. Once those rights were secured, the shackles would disappear. A healthy body politic would reclaim the use of its faculties.[48]

In making this appeal for republican labor, it is important to recall, Whitman was not merely exploiting slavery. His protest through the body was a genuine extension of his republican principles. Just as the abuse of slaves inverts or threatens the chain of life, so, too, the presence of slavery in society threatens the social order. But the poem's interest in that order "engirths" its concern for slavery. Although Whitman may be savagely mocking the institution of slavery, his greater concern is for the preservation of free labor. Accordingly, "I Sing the Body Electric" is profoundly economic: it engages in system building, making the body the measure of all value. If all bodies could circulate and expand as freely as Whitman's poetic corpus, the republic was certain to thrive.

A similar desire for security emerges from "A Song for Occupations." Once again, Whitman seeks out transcendent principles of order. But while the poem appears to mount a plea for an intrinsic and immediate value more powerful than the taint of trade, it actually strengthens the assumptions of possessive individualism at the root of market culture. "What is it that you made money?" Whitman asks parenthetically, "what is it that you got what you wanted?" (61; 109). The essential self, it seems, standing apart from all pulling and hauling, should alone measure worth. And yet, in putting the autonomous and expressive self at the center of phenomena, Whitman does not succeed in providing a new or better register of value. Rather, he demonstrates the impossibility of insulating free labor from the inequities that threaten it. The higher laws Whitman glimpses in the poem turn out to be the founding principles of the market.

As M. Wynn Thomas has noted, "A Song for Occupations" begins with an apparent rejection of its own origins. "Push close my lovers and take the best I possess," the poet urges. "I was chilled with the cold types and cylinder and wet paper between us. / I pass so poorly with paper and types . . . . I must pass with the contact of bodies and souls" (57; 2, 5–6). The longing for union here is both somatic and spiritual, as if the poet were rejecting the material basis of labor. If the activities of most occupations are alienating, robbing the world of its spiritual essence, Whitman will work to recapture a primal unity. Thus the poet constantly seeks out the origin of all exchange. "I bring not money . . . ," he proclaims, "And send no agent or medium . . . . and offer no representative of value—but offer the value itself" (59; 46–7). That value is not limited by commerce or farmwork, by the demands of manufacturers or the ease of the leisure class. But all such values are elements in a larger transaction between free souls. "I take no sooner a large price than a small price," the poet declares; "I will be even with you, and you shall be even with me" (57; 14–15). This desire for an equivalence beyond the petty advantages of trade harks back to the sentimental commerce of Adam Smith, the sense that concession and imaginative sympathy ground all prudential motives. "I own publicly who you are," Whitman assures us, " . . . and see and hear you, and what you give and take" (58; 30).[49]

Once again, Whitman establishes his claim to immediacy through a survey of goods and services. All the objects and activities of the world, from surgical instruments and ships' rigging to "the building of cities" (61; 117) and the "cotton-picking" of the South (63; 145), suggest the absolute equivalence of all phenomena. Moreover, the endless catalogue of "Everyday objects" (62; 124) creates a kind of divine poetic economy in which articles circulate ideally and continuously, immune to the disruptions that marked most laborers' lives. Here was truly the basis of absolute value, an unreserved economy of spirit free of the dead weight of money. Reaching back to an imagined harmony, Whitman succeeds in smashing the iron grip of capital as if he were smashing an atom, liberating the dazzling energies of the material world—"The wonder every one sees in every one else he sees . . . . and the wonders that fill each minute of time forever and each acre of surface and space forever" (59; 63). Like the idyllic visions of republican society on which it is based, this transcendent economy reckons value not according to the most recent transaction, but according to all transactions, the sum total of well-being inherent in each individual exchange. Each element in such a system must be reckoned in relation to the universal good and to the community that sustains it. "The sum of all known value and respect" is thus latent in each individual and each act; "All doctrines, all politics and civilization exurge" from the private soul (60; 82, 87). Here was a thoroughly sympathetic order that preserved its serenity through an unrestrained yet benign operation.

As observer of this cosmic harmony, Whitman was both chief witness and practitioner. Asserting universal value, he sought it wherever he turned, recorded it in his poetry, and thus stimulated a reciprocal recognition in his audience. The hinge was his writing, which he strove to eliminate in an epiphany that would make words superfluous. But Whitman's attempt to erase all media of exchange could not excise the most intimate register of value, and in that necessary failure, the poem undoes its own work. At the root of the problem is the noble doubt

that Emerson expressed in the "Idealism" section of "Nature." "All architecture,"
Whitman avers in a sweeping assessment of the world's structure, "is what you do
to it when you look upon it" (61; 91). The forthright assertion of power that the
line implies soon yields a haunting series of questions: "Will the whole come back
then? / Can each see the signs of the best by a look in the lookingglass? Is there
nothing greater or more? / Does all sit there with you and here with me?" (61;
97-99). The answer is maybe. Up to this point, the poem has provided general
reflection and exhortation, almost too rarified to be convincing. The "Utahan,
Kansian, . . . Arkansian" pass before our eyes (58; 33), the sun, the stars, and the
"appleshaped earth" (59; 56). The survey is as massive and blurry as the world
to a newborn's eyes. But now Whitman unleashes his most sustained catalogue,
running on for sixty lines and including everything from mangers to bear hunts,
anvils to milliner's ribbons. The effect is to re-create the benign world but also
to ground it in the sharp material objects that the sympathetic mind generates.
There can be no question regarding the mind's unmediated power after such a
torrent. Anyone who can come up with such a survey—and Whitman contends
that anyone can—will be in little danger of losing touch with the world.

Nevertheless, this marriage of contemplation and practical action hits a snag
over the element that Whitman initially addressed but could not control—the cold
type conveying thought. Among the harmonies he seeks to embrace are "The
paper I write on or you write on . . and every word we write . . and every cross and
twirl of the pen . . and the curious way we write what we think . . . . yet very faintly"
(62; 129). Thus far, the description seems comprehensive, incorporating the act
of writing into the same pageant as glassblowing and "Shipcarpentering" (62;
134)—productive exchange. But the following line sets this activity apart: "The
directory, the detector, the ledger . . . . the books in ranks or the bookshelves
. . . . the clock attached to the wall" (62; 130). If there is any difference between
the two lines, it must reside in finished products: the twirl of the pen produces
manuscripts, perhaps more intimate than shelves of commercial registers. But the
collocation of banks, books, and "detector" is significant. All bankers since the
wildcat days of Jacksonian finance lived by the comparative assessment of paper
money issued by a bewildering number of banks (a list as lengthy as Whitman's
mammoth catalogue). Indeed, the bank detectors were the precise analogue of
Whitman's world of liberated commodities, stabilized by little more than the
shrewd eye of the beholder. Without a central standard of paper value, all such
measures of worth were unstable, if not worse, counterfeit. Here, once again,

was the dilemma of unrestrained operation, of an economy ever threatening to destroy its own reserves of sympathy. Only the comprehensive vision of a master poet could keep the world in perspective, Whitman seems to be implying—could eliminate counterfeit operations.

But if the line between genuineness and counterfeits was often uncertain in a market order where books recorded the fluctuating value of paper, the source of that uncertainty may have been far more elusive. Bank detectors sniffed out implausible notes, but what of distortions in the language of the books themselves? Whitman seems to play with that notion by concluding the poem with a string of arresting metaphors. "When the script preaches instead of the preacher" (64; 172), Whitman prophesies,

> When the minted gold in the vault smiles like the nightwatchman's daughter,
> When warantee deeds loafe in chairs opposite and are my friendly companions,
> I intend to reach them my hand and make as much of them as I do of men and women.
> (64; 176-78)

Thomas has plausibly argued that these images attack alienation by reducing it to absurdity. Of course, feeling is more important than cash, the reader perceives, and human values ought to eclipse the worship of commodities. Until pigs fly, Whitman will continue to insist on the spiritual relations advanced in the poem. But the images also remind us that poetry, if not all perception, is metaphoric. If the pulpit descends, if sacred vessels procreate, or warantee deeds loafe, they have simply recovered that mysterious energy that one finds throughout Whitman's poetry. The moving objects at the end of "A Song for Occupations" seem to fuse the spiritual and secular inventories that Whitman introduced earlier on. They circulate with their own, rather than the poet's, power. And if the animated objects seem implausible or counterfeit, they may simply expose the most subtle element in Whitman's argument: that the very process of creating value is metaphoric, and therefore arbitrary. Value does not lie in the other or the object, but in the eye of the beholder. For to perceive is to possess or occupy—to appropriate the common objects of the world. In effect, the poem is about occupation—about putting one's stamp on experience.[50]

Indeed, the eventual title of the poem itself seems eccentric, a distortion of language. In a song about occupations, it is remarkable how little work gets done. Of the 178 lines of the poem, only 17 directly discuss actual labor, with another 35 referring to the implements of work. For a catalogue of economic activities, one would be better served by reading "Song of the Broad-Axe," or what became section 15 of "Song of Myself." But if "occupation" is understood more broadly, Whitman's "A Song for Occupations" can be seen to demonstrate not only the practice but also the premises of labor. Occupation stakes a claim, establishes private property; and the poem that surveys the mind surveying the world does nothing if it does not demonstrate the poet appropriating that world. But this aggressive labeling of reality jars uncomfortably with Whitman's inaugural image of unmediated contact. He may wish to dissolve the barriers of print, but he must do so through the radical privacy of figurative language and the counterfeit agency of books. It is at this point, as the operations of sympathy clash with those of appropriation, that the implicit harmony of Whitman's vision falters. There is an instability in the conduct of market relations, he seems to be saying, an impulse to privacy that might resist the poet's most heroic exhortations. Counterfeits, misappropriations, the possessiveness of capitalists or slave owners were essentially similar to the "occupations" of farmers or laborers. All had to possess or regulate the world before they could claim higher truths. This was more than a mere truism. Republican autonomy sought a magical link between unlimited appropriation and perfect order, yet the years of Whitman's young manhood saw anything but the serene application of those principles. Once again, it seemed, the poet found himself caught between communal and private motives, between the traditional values of republicanism and the organic effects of the market. How was it possible to reconcile the two domains on the only level that theory allowed, the level of sympathetic feeling?

The most comprehensive response to that problem appears in the second edition of *Leaves of Grass*, in "Sun-Down Poem" ("Crossing Brooklyn Ferry"). A haunting meditation on mortality startling from a poet barely at middle age, the poem refigures Whitman as the spirit of history, reaching forward and back like a fluid form embracing the earth. His "network of sympathetic relationships," writes Denis Donoghue, not only frees the democratic reader from "time and transience," but also demonstrates "the essential unity of a world rampant with multiplicity." What has been less often noticed about the poem, however, is how it encloses a narrative of commerce within this narrative of time. Or rather, in providing a vision of time's circularity, Whitman allows us to glimpse a metaphysics of commerce. Like Joseph Conrad's Thames River, "crowded with memories of men and ships," Whitman's East River crowds its figures against an immense canvas of trade. And as he considers the cycles of river travel and his own life in relation to those cycles, he develops a model of spiritual conduct defined by material objects and the values we assign to them. His vision, that is to say, is profoundly economic: it offers a scheme for preserving the human face in a world of fleeting goods.[51]

From the opening lines disclosing "the shipping of Manhattan north and west" (15; 15), Whitman seldom lets us forget that the rhythm of this tableau is as much commercial as temporal. "[M]ast-hemm'd Manhatta" (98; 92) is awash in the teeming life rapidly making it a metropolis. On the far shore Whitman notices "the fires from the foundry chimneys," casting wide shadows over their neighborhoods (48; 47). He watches the freighters distribute their "shows" (130; 123); he looks on at "the big steam-tug" hauling the barges and hayboats (47; 46). For the poet, these familiar sights are spiritual capital: he has "laid in [his] stores in advance" (88; 87), invested these quotidian scenes with a typical power that will allow them to serve as media of exchange. For the tides of trade governed by the flow of the river are but reflections of the larger, temporal patterns governing all life. By making this symbolic leap, Whitman is able to explore the intimate links between himself and his readers, much as the hale republican farmer in "I Sing the Body Electric" transmitted his spirit to his progeny. We all become members of Whitman's transcendental family. Yet the temporal parallels do not submerge the relations of trade. Rather, the voyage outward in time grounds the commercial returns and gives a spiritual grammar to the language of the marketplace.

The rules of Whitman's spiritual grammar involve two complementary processes. By insisting that his experience precisely accords with that of his readers, he imagines history as typological, the events of the present mirroring those of the future. And because of that parallelism, it is possible for the poet to merge with his audience, as if their widely separated lives entirely coincided. The mirroring effects work on several levels. As Whitman gazes at the river he sees "the reflection of the summer-sky in the water" (32; 31), a serene symmetry that seems to mark his passage in time. Similarly, his fellow travelers on the ferry remind him of other travelers "who look back on me, because I looked forward to them" (55; 52), just as he glimpses the passengers in the water. His contemplation leads him further afield, to "The similitudes of the past and those of the future" (8; 8), and to that essential sympathy that binds the republic of spirit. "Just as you feel when you look on the river and sky," he concludes, "so I felt" (23; 22). Time, the ultimate democrat, levels all distinctions in an infinity of identical forms.

That mirroring is reflected in the text's structure, as well as in its meaning. Whitman writes large sections of the poem as if they were ripples bearing the same image, or carrying the same message. "Flood-tide of the river, flow on! I watch you, face to face!" the poem begins. "Clouds of the west! . . . I see you also face to face" (1–2). The symmetries he perceives comprise the rhythms of his passage through time:

> Just as any of you is one of a living crowd, I was one of a crowd,
> Just as you are refreshed by the gladness of the river, and the bright flow, I was refreshed,
> Just as you stand and lean on the rail, yet hurry with the swift current, I stood, yet was hurried,
> Just as you look on the numberless masts of ships, and the thick-stemmed pipes of steamboats, I looked (24–27; 22–26)

The repetitive structures that, in a catalogue like section 33 of "Song of Myself," may sometimes seem bombastic or bloated, here serve thematic and mimetic ends by creating the rhythms that link all the figures in Whitman's tableau. Those repetitions, borne by "the fine centrifugal spokes of light" (34; 33) emanating from the poet, express his spiritual exchanges through a single faculty and medium. His gaze trained at the passing scene merges with the reader's gaze at the images on the page and the structure of the passages beneath the reader's eyes. All "Looked on the haze on the hills southward and southwestward, / Looked on the vapor as it flew in fleeces tinged with violet, / Looked toward the lower bay to notice the arriving ships" (35–37; 34–36). As we read, we see the harmonies through Whitman's syntax itself. "You have waited, you always wait," Whitman tells us, "insatiate" witnesses to the symmetries he discloses (137, 138; 126, 127).

In his emphasis on the eternal gaze, Whitman does not lose sight of the commercial tide driving his reflections. As Jean-Joseph Goux notes, the values we assign to commodities arise through "*equation*[s]" established by the eye. Explicating Marx, Goux argues that the origins of capital lie in the drama of individual encounters. The ontology of value derives from the mutual regard of commodities, which, "[i]n each other's presence, . . . recognize each other as *similar*." That is to say, commodities have their own semiotic relations that have psychological, as well as material, consequences: "In fact, the relation between these two forms of the same value is none other than a specular relation, a mirroring. One of the commodities expresses its value in the *body* of the other, which serves as *matter* (mother, material, matrix) for this expression." Marx himself, as Goux notes, grounds the commodity relation in human psychology. In *Capital* Marx asserts that "it is with the human being as with the commodity": "Since the human being does not come into the world bringing a mirror with him, nor yet as a Fichtean philosopher able to say 'I am myself,' he recognises himself as reflected in other men. The man Peter grasps his relation to himself as a human being through becoming aware of his relation to the man Paul as a being of like kind with himself. Thereupon Paul, with flesh and bone, with all his Pauline corporeality, becomes for Peter the phenomenal form of the human kind." This translation of Smith's metaphor of the mirror points in two directions—to the spectral, alienating character of market relations and to their irreducible humanity. In "Sun-Down Poem," Whitman reclaimed the human element by universalizing it. Time becomes his medium of exchange, and the common objects of the harbor become the mirrors that allow one to say, "I am myself." At sundown, he glimpses an incorruptible economy.[52]

It is appropriate, then, that Whitman conveys his temporal connections through a kind of sublime accounting. As the "hundreds and hundreds" of ferry boats cross the river, so, too, Whitman tallies the human transaction he has established with his readers:

> What is it, then, between us? What is the count of the scores or hundreds of years
>      between us?
> Whatever it is, it avails not—distance avails not, and place avails not. (57–58; 54–56)

The poetry itself, that "simple, compact, well-joined scheme" (7; 7), acts like the river, as a medium for the effortless and endless flow of sympathies. For Whitman, this commerce, which "fuses me into you now" (101; 97), effortlessly regulates and reassures all those borne on by the tide. All anxieties, all the press and hazard of daily experience, are smoothed over by the equivalence between the humble materials of human life and eternal truth. This spiritual reassurance must have resonated particularly well with Whitman's ideal readers of the working class, who longed, in the mid-1850s, for the massive stability that the poem's measured cadences implied. Whitman was evoking the balanced republican world that still emerged whenever spokesmen denounced speculators or urged the latest market reform. As Oliver Wendell Holmes observed, "He carries the principle of republicanism through the whole world of created objects."[53] But the poem actually allowed him to play a dual role. While evoking a republican utopia, Whitman also demonstrated the true insight of the seasoned entrepreneur.

"Sun-Down Poem" summarizes the complex relations between protest and discipline that workers experienced in the early 1850s. Like the cooperationists and land reformers, Whitman, too, sought to rise above the distortions of trade to secure the simple, mirrorlike relations between producers, their goods, and their world. But in imagining this universal sympathy, Whitman was also assuming the role of the prudent entrepreneur whose keen powers allow him to perceive all value. "He is to look at his books," wrote John Sergeant of the heroic trader, "not to see the figures there set down, but whether the value is what they represent." To a merchant's eyes, contemporaries claimed, the whole world of objects is alive with meaning. The graceful muff lying in the parlor has a history of risk and peril and the echoes of the weary hunter "fling[ing] down his pack before the evening fire." The commonest table was loaded with the goods of every climate, a world of objects saturated with movement and meaning.[54] Like the trader capable of reading these signs, Whitman sees in the common sights of the harbor the histories of a larger field, one in which objects mirror lives. Adam Smith's prudential world reclaims the ground that panic and labor conflict had eroded. In his poetry, if nowhere else, the market's native generosity would continue to thrive.

It is through this vision of heroic sympathy that Whitman attempts to respond to the crisis of antebellum republicanism. By identifying with the bewildering range of American phenomena, he demonstrates the continued vigor of an old ideal. Republican sympathy was still capable of leveling all distinctions, conveying the essential harmony of democratic life. Yet the restless spokesman for that principle was also an agent of constant change, ever adjusting to and regulating his environment. Dynamic, stable, and infinitely aroused, Whitman's "self" was the ideal exponent of that threshold psychology that Jean-Christophe Agnew associates with market behavior. Every encounter promised infinite reward; every reward fueled the need for new encounters. And yet Whitman was no aggressive entrepreneur, no mere soldier in the army of organic intellectuals. Rather, he imagined himself as an inspiring force who transformed latent feeling into revolutionary power. In and out of the game, restless yet satisfied, the poet used sympathy to define a new, liberal autonomy.

### The Fate of Sympathy

A year after the second edition of *Leaves of Grass* appeared, a French actress marked the outer verge of Whitman's characterless appeal. In November 1857,

Térèsina Rank mounted a chair to address a crowd of hungry workmen who had gathered daily in New York's Tompkins Square Park after yet another panic had thrown them out of work. She talked of her scheme for a Temple of Harmony, a colossal exhibition space that would pay for an enormous residence for the poor and an equally enormous church, and incidentally pay off her own debts as well. Overshadowing any modest benefits she might procure from the scheme, however, was her Christ-like devotion to the masses. "I would cut myself in twenty pieces and give my life in the bargain, and shed all the blood that runs in my veins if I could serve and help you," she melodramatically proclaimed. "Do not accuse me of being bold," Rank urged in her thick French accent. "No; you know better. My heart is good. I come to you with good feelings, like Miss Nightingale going to the Crimea with the same feeling as I do." A mediatory figure counseling restraint, she offered to embrace both rich and poor. "I am like you, poor," she claimed. "We must all take what we can get and not murmur." And when the crowd challenged her philanthropic credentials, she responded, "I'll tell you who I am. In the parlor, I am a lady; in business, I am a man. In my professions, I am a hero; and in avenging an insult, I am a warrior." In the role of nursing mother, she portrayed herself as Everyman. [55]

Rank's expansive appeal, however, failed to have the magic effect envisioned by the likes of Whitman. The workmen were too desperate to listen long, and they soon sent angry committees to City Hall demanding immediate aid that was not forthcoming. Newspapers ridiculed Rank as a "socialis[t]" and attacked the demonstrators, "the lowest of the lower classes," as dangerous revolutionaries who had to be vigorously suppressed. Even members of her audience rebelled. "Men, all of you, is it a woman that we want to tell us what to do?" demanded one demonstrator. "To hell with her. . . . We won't be led by a woman; we are men and can transact our own affairs." Rank soon retired into obscurity, her grandiose Temple of Harmony reduced to a flimsy pamphlet. The unemployed workmen shivered until the spring, and some of them starved much longer. [56]

But to the clerks, lawyers, and other middling readers who followed the demonstrations in the local newspapers, Rank's characterless appeal, the dream of sympathetic regulation advanced by Whitman, had become something quite different. Within the Temple of Harmony, it turned out, was the holy site of class exclusion. To these readers, the threat of labor violence imposed harsh limits on sympathy. Nowhere is this shift more clear than in the speech of Edward Livingstone, protagonist of Dion Boucicault's play *The Poor of New York,* which premiered in New York's Wallack's Theater shortly after the demonstrations.

Himself a victim of the panic, Livingstone gives voice to a more restrictive sentimentalism:

> The poor!—whom do you call the poor? Do you know them? do you see them? they
> are more frequently found under a black coat than under a red shirt. The poor man
> is the clerk with a family, forced to maintain a decent suit of clothes, paid for out of
> the hunger of his children. The poor man is the artist who is obliged to pledge the
> tools of his trade to buy medicines for his sick wife. The lawyer who, craving for
> employment, buttons up his thin paletot to hide his shirtless breast. These needy
> wretches are poorer than the poor, for they are obliged to conceal their poverty with
> the false mask of content—smoking a cigar to disguise their hunger—they drag from
> their pockets their last quarter, to cast it with studied carelessness, to the begger
> [sic], whose mattress at home is lined with gold. These are the most miserable of
> the Poor of New York.[57]

According to this new creed, panic had created a new class, more needy than the
abject poor because more sensitive to the stings of depression. In stringent times,
sentiment could not be wasted on the lowly. Even as Whitman expanded *Leaves
of Grass,* an increasing number of popular fictions sought to erect a new structure
of feeling, the exclusive property of the middle class. Ironically, the poet's attempt
to forge a language of commercial sympathy was shadowed by the efforts of the
masters of commerce to retreat from the discourse they had spawned.

# CHAPTER 6

# Class Acts

&.

Until fairly recently, American historiography has treated the middle class like a poor relative at the banquet: often observed, seldom distinguished. In contrast to their depiction of the stormy lives of the working class, scholars of middling Americans evince an almost geological deliberativeness. Workers came into the world gnashing their teeth at injustice, but the middling sort seem always to have been with us. Even recent studies that stress the urgency of bourgeois life—its search for order through moral and social reform—often measure that life through long-standing social institutions: evangelical Christianity, consumption, the home. Although most scholars have abandoned the consensus view of American culture once advanced by Richard Hofstadter and Louis Hartz and cogently revised by Sacvan Bercovitch, there is less agreement over where and how (if ever) nineteenth-century middling Americans understood themselves as distinctive. At what point did their sense of shared values seem sufficiently threatened to generate a sustained sense of embattled virtue, a consciousness of their own insularity? When and how, to use Stuart Blumin's influential formulation, did the middle class truly emerge?[1]

The most convincing historical evidence points to an accretion of factors that reached a critical mass sometime after the Civil War. As Blumin and Elizabeth Blackmar have demonstrated, cities had been gradually segregating into class-based neighborhoods since the turn of the nineteenth century, a process accelerated by the tide of immigrants after 1840. The close urban quarters also stimulated a disciplinary response—a desire not only to reform the poor but also to preserve a native gentility behind an armor of polite culture. And for years the most concerted defense involved evangelicalism, with its perfectionist distinction between the regenerate and the unredeemed. What Charles Sellers calls "the bourgeois republic" involved a massive effort to claim the American middle for like-minded believers in benevolence, God, and rigorous self-control.

These attitudes in postbellum America shaped true believers into a disciplined workforce, the growing army of clerks and office functionaries who, like Whitman himself, found safe berths from unsettled times. Indeed, as Cindy Sondik Aron has observed, many of these middling workers were taking refuge not only from the uncertainties of civil war, but also from economic perils that had brought them to the brink of ruin. Virtuous consumption was their sign and seal of deliverance. [2]

Before the Civil War, however, the relation between these responses and middle-class consciousness remained diffuse and variable. Middling evangelicals often chastened the poor with one hand and embraced them with the other, as subjects of God's universal love. Both groups, writes Paul Boyer, shared "a nexus of . . . social assumptions and aspirations linking the 'controllers' and the 'controlled.' " Among those assumptions were a core belief in self-reliance and the dignity of labor, as well as a basic faith in democratic norms. Even fears of the "dissolute" masses could not entirely shake this bond, as Children's Aid Society head Charles Loring Brace revealed in praising the "bright, sharp, bold, racy . . . crowd" of New York street urchins for "steer[ing] their own canoe." "Class formation," as R. J. Morris observes of the period, remained "immature, continuous and contested by other loyalties."[3] But one often overlooked spur to middle-class consciousness—market panic—might well have been crucial to its maturity. The frequent, apparently unavoidable economic shocks that marked the lives of middling antebellum Americans challenged the core belief in self-reliance, in autonomous free labor, and sparked a sustained search for a pragmatic alternative to insecurity. In the 1840s, popular literature had reflected that search by imagining "characterless" heroines capable of sustaining severe loss. These microhistories, however, were largely time specific. They responded to the immediate strains of the most severe economic depression Americans had yet witnessed. By the late 1850s, after two more downturns accentuated by vast new numbers of immigrant poor, many of these same writers were concluding that panic was not accidental, that insecurity was permanent. At midcentury, the market had come to seem much more volatile than even its most ardent players could have imagined. Their response to insecurity was to intensify the sentimental attributes of class.

Once again, popular fiction treated market volatility by feminizing it. But the response to structural uncertainty differed in two ways from earlier treatments. First, *men* increasingly figured as the representatives of characterlessness, the resourceful but pliant individuals who turned weakness into a kind of strength. Often likened to women, the young merchants in this new fiction converted dependence and insecurity into virtuous pragmatism. If to be ruined by the market was once a sign of disgrace, these figures erased the stain of frailty and found virtue in accommodation.

Such pliancy was a crucial extension of middle-class awareness. As Edward Balleisen has argued, the widespread experience of bankruptcy in the 1840s permanently shaped the sentiments of chastened entrepreneurs, who began to see virtue in wage earning rather than in risk taking. Accepting a salary, once anathema to self-reliant character, became increasingly acceptable to these fathers of the middle class. [4] But class consciousness involves more than a shared sense of frailty or desire; it also involves an urgent antagonism, a righteous determination to oppose other groups. That consciousness, also reflected in popular fiction, developed gradually throughout the 1850s. Early in the period, panic fictions tended to depict the poor as tainted by the same vices that afflicted their social betters. All had succumbed to urban sin, but might be restored through Christian love. By the late 1850s, however, urban writers began to imagine a new scenario in which the pestilent poor were impervious to sentimental appeals. Market fictions came to insist that feeling was the preserve of an embattled middle class whose insecurity was both a distinction and a threat. Within the bounds of increasingly sharp class lines, readers of sentimental fictions could celebrate their resourceful, feminized yielding to mighty economic forces. They found virtue in dependency by reinterpreting their behavior as economic law. Without doors, beyond their neighborhoods and class affiliations, they saw only the vicious weaknesses of the working class and the poor—dependencies they desired not only to control but to exterminate. In this manner, midcentury market fictions helped to sharpen the consciousness of a middle class for which vulnerability had become the poignant but indispensable sign of maturity. Sympathetic readers admitted in themselves what they vigorously repressed in others. In so doing, they laid the basis for a vision of the market that was both intimate and punitive, the cruel but permissive sovereign of a distinctive middle-class consciousness.

### Desperate Measures

By the mid-1850s, as Whitman was polishing his catalogues, the market revolution had firmly taken hold. Extensive construction of railroads had cemented a national market, stimulated by increases in factory production, business organization, and finance. By 1859, manufacturing accounted for nearly a third of national income. The goods were distributed through a widespread rail network that had reduced shipping costs by more than half since 1840. Integrating that network stimulated business efficiency, leading to management innovations that would be widely adopted as companies increased in size and scale. Financial efficiencies had also evolved, with large cities like New York adopting clearinghouses to rationalize currency exchange. And the cities' explosive growth spiked production of all kinds, from clothing and furniture to housing and ironworks.[5] Yet the buoyant energy of this expansive period, an energy conveyed in Whitman's poetry, was often tempered in the era's popular novels. Even had sectionalism never existed to stir up national anxiety, writers would still have found plenty to brood about in the capriciousness of their economic system. "In this republican country, amid the fluctuating waves of our social life," wrote Nathaniel Hawthorne in 1851, "somebody is always at the drowning-point."[6] Fully fifty novels in the two decades surrounding the Civil War suggest that all too many republicans did not know how to swim.

Those fears were reignited in 1857 by the continuing vagaries of the banking system. The failure of the Ohio Life Insurance and Trust Company on 24 August upset credit relations throughout the North, causing hundreds of businesses to suspend or scramble for loans. By late September, the strain had proved too great. A run on the Bank of Philadelphia forced it to suspend specie payments, and the ripple effects caused dozens of other banks to close. With credit suspended, business ground to a halt and workers were soon clamoring for relief. In Providence, Rhode Island, three-quarters of the city's jewelry workers were laid off; in New York, a similar proportion of shipbuilders, coopers, and garment workers lost their jobs. Cities as far west as Chicago, Louisville, and Saint Louis were affected, as the unemployed went out of doors and petitions for relief flooded local newspapers. In New York, for example, thousands of demonstrators heard the fiery John Martell demand that the city provide jobs and a guaranteed income of one thousand dollars a year. Declaring that "the voice of the workingmen . . . is the voice of God," he was silenced only when a fire hose was turned on him. The following afternoon, the labor activist Ira B. Davis told a crowd of three thousand that they were little better than slaves. Others branded capitalists the enemies of workingmen. "If we cannot get work peacefully," shouted George Campbell to loud applause, "we must get bread by violence."[7]

Although such militancy soon subsided before a bitterly cold winter and modest relief efforts, its effects lingered in a new wave of market fictions. These narratives, amounting to a literary subgenre that had a wide audience throughout the decade, echoed their predecessors of the 1840s in seeking to master market disruptions through moral reform. But they also expressed a new and haunting malaise. Among middling readers, the panic of 1857 caused considerable worry and many bankruptcies, but the real suffering centered on the lower orders. Their social betters claimed to be largely spared the shock they had felt twenty years earlier. By January 1858, *Hunt's Merchant's Magazine, The Banker's Magazine,* and other publications were confidently predicting an end to the disruption and discussing how fine-tuning the currency would eliminate such episodes. Popular novelists, however, were often unmoved by such optimism. What Raymond Williams writes of English novels in the 1840s applies equally to American fiction a decade later: "What comes through with great force is a pervasive atmosphere of instability and debt. . . . Debt and ruin haunt this apparently confident world, and in a majority of cases simply happen to the characters, as a result of a process outside them." The moral victory these fictions propose involves the protagonist's struggle to lower expectations, accept defeat, or adjust to the harsh conditions of a risky economy.[8]

One reason for the continuing malaise was the grim fact that many perfectly respectable men in America failed—some many times over. Although risk is inherent in free enterprise, the combination of a wide-open market and relatively few restrictions on business organization and conduct heightened uncertainty. As credit reports of the Mercantile Agency reveal, businessmen often experienced tumultuous careers. The agency, begun by Lewis Tappan in 1841, provides an indispensable picture of enterprise during the period. James French, a New York City shoe merchant, for example, had already failed in 1851 when he took a new partner to provide much-needed capital. But the partner "proved to be wild & speculative," and they failed again in 1852. Back in business by the late '50s, French was "embarrass[ed]" during the panic of 1857, when some of his notes were protested. Another New York broker in coffee and spices, Michael Casse, was deemed honest but "unfortunate" after he had failed "3 or 4 times" during the 1850s, including a bankruptcy after the panic of 1857 from which he emerged by compromising with his creditors at thirty to forty cents on the dollar. By 1866 he had repaid all his old liabilities and had gone into business with his sons, but an accusation of fraud committed against new creditors later hurt the firm again. Failure occasionally ran in families. In 1858 Meyer Hecht, a New York fancy goods merchant, bought out the firm of Mrs. Asher Hecht, whose husband had failed in Baltimore. Meyer's brother Reinhard, who had failed in Chicago, helped to underwrite the venture.[9]

Even successful merchants often had a background of failure. When Cyrus Schoonmaker went into business with George Parsons, a New York toy and fancy goods merchant, in 1866, the firm had a combined history of three failures—one for Parsons and two for Schoonmaker. "We find this conc[ern] in a v[er]y bad odor," wrote the credit reporter. Yet Schoonmaker managed to repay all his creditors in full and was soon said to be a director of the Oriental Bank.[10] Although the antebellum failure rate has been estimated at about 40 percent, to many nervous observers it seemed far higher. "[M]ercantile life is the very worst," complains one character in Alonzo Tripp's *The Fisher Boy* (1857); "not one in ten succeeds"—a sentiment echoed in other publications of the period. For all too many Americans, prominent and obscure, the market revolution had made failure a way of life.[11]

Many writers and publishers of the period keenly felt this heightened vulnerability. Entrepreneurs in a volatile marketplace, they were linked by the uncertainties of their profession. Antebellum book publishing, to quote one scholar, was like a "giant gambling game" conducted in a risky market that was "primitive and uncontrolled." The panic of 1857 was only the most visible sign of the dangers. Among the houses forced to suspend or curtail publication were New York's G. P. Putnam (*Putnam's Monthly* folded) and Miller, Orton, and Co. An item in *New York Life Illustrated* in late October 1857 listed fifteen prominent casualties. In Boston, the firms of Phillips Sampson and Co., which published Emerson's *English Traits,* and John P. Jewett, whose successes included *Uncle Tom's Cabin* and Maria Cummins's *The Lamplighter,* did not survive.[12]

Lesser publishers also withered throughout the 1850s. A credit reporter for the Mercantile Agency followed the efforts of Charles B. Norton to establish a bookshop and literary journal in New York City early in the decade. Arriving from Boston he clerked at the house of D. Appleton, and then, with capital provided by his father, commenced business alone. In 1852 he was considered "worthy of confidence," and two years later was deemed to have "a good safe" house. Thereafter, his fortunes began to decline as he had trouble making payments, and by 1855 he had failed, along with his fledgling *Literary Gazette.* Another small New York publisher found even less success. C. W. Hewett was ambitious but seemed to have "no capac[ity] whatever for merc[antile] pursuits." By 1852 he had failed to bring to market a "splendid illustrated edition of Shakespeare," had sold out to the Harpers, "was burned out," then failed with several other illustrated editions. Even seasoned entrepreneurs found the literary trade a cruel business. Pliny Smith turned to publishing after a successful career in merchandising fizzled. When, in 1867, he lost his capital to "fluctuations in gold" he closed his well-reputed sock and tie shop, tried to reopen it, and failed again. By the early 1870s he had turned to publishing—first putting out a journal called the *Christian Year* and later one called *Smith's Dollar Magazine,* "every alternate page of which will be devoted to advertisements." Both failed within several months. As publishing expanded at midcentury, the market severely penalized those who could not meet its heightened demands for prudence, capital, or sheer luck.[13]

Writers responded to these uncertainties in a variety of ways. As is well known, canonical figures like Melville, Hawthorne, and Thoreau developed an uneasy, defensive relationship with the literary marketplace, often facing difficulties similar to those of struggling publishers. Melville, for example, revisited in *Redburn* the family bankruptcy that drove him to whaling, and cynically predicted he would "fail" after the commercial disappointments of the 1850s. Lesser writers had equal difficulty. At the height of the panic the *New York Herald* worried that writers who churned out sensational fiction were failing "by hundreds in the city," a calamity brought on by cutbacks in the weekly press. In October 1857 the popular writer Maria McIntosh felt the pressure, wondering when she would see her next check from John Jewett. "If I were only not in debt," she wrote to Maria Cummins, "I should care for nothing—but that . . . I should be compelled to fail in my obligations troubles me a little." Jewett's failure must have tormented her much more. Other writers saw in the agitated times a melodramatic expression of their unsettled lives. Fanny Fern (Sara Parton) and E. D. E. N. Southworth both wrote best-selling novels about struggling outcasts, reflecting their own bouts with poverty. And Azel Roe, whose novels often trace the trials of vulnerable entrepreneurs, may have been revisiting his own bankruptcy, brought about when protested notes he had endorsed forced him to shut his wine-importing business. Roe's novels were typical of a widespread need during the period to confront the effects of economic uncertainty.[14]

This shared sense of vulnerability, in turn, contributed to a growing awareness of class. Most historians have argued that, by the 1850s, middling Americans had developed class awareness through a fund of common attitudes and practices arising from work, consumption, the household, and community life. Such experiences allowed individuals to recognize their bonds with others and, occasionally, to see themselves as socially distinctive, set off from other classes. These beliefs may well have been intensified, however, by the sense of fragility that shadowed them. As Margaret Hunt has argued for the "middling sort" of eighteenth-century England, "[a] central part of these people's individual and collective story" involved confronting an "inhospitable economic environment." Merchants depended on the uncertainties of debt collection and far-flung credit. They knew that the failure of a large debtor could ruin them and that their household goods might be seized in compensation. They experienced independence, that is to say, "not without a covert glance over their shoulders." Theodore Koditschek has noted the same attitudes in the nineteenth-century English city of Bradford, where bankruptcy left "deep scars" and a lifelong sense of "insecurity" in most entrepreneurs. Similar conditions existed in antebellum America. Edward Balleisen has argued that "bankruptcies touched the lives of most people," and Cindy Sondik Aron suggests that "frequent business failures" created a "considerable zone of insecurity within the nineteenth-century middle class." In a sense, there could have been no distinctive neighborhoods, consumption patterns, or habits of association without the prospect that all could be utterly wiped away.[15]

Doubtless, this sense of vulnerability sharpened the drive to succeed, but it also underscored the distinctive nature of the experience. Poised between wealth and sudden poverty, the middle class came to see itself as enacting a drama of avoidance. At one extreme were the corrupt speculations of the wealthy; at the other, the degradation of the poor. Between them perched the high-wire act of shrewd survivors struggling to adapt republican pieties to the demands of competition. Their plight would become the stuff of sentimental narratives, as anxious readers sought explanations for their insecurity.

Two files from the Mercantile Agency indicate how failure stimulated class awareness. The first suggests a traditional moral assessment in which speculative excess distinguishes wealthy bankrupts from deserving entrepreneurs. A. D. Y. Henriquez, a New York importer and hotel owner, hailed from Jamaica, where he failed three times. After his first failure, he converted his stock to cash, entrusting it to an associate who was supposed to act as his agent in America. But when Henriquez, who had in the meantime been imprisoned for debt, finally made it to the United States, the associate "refused to acknowledge him" and the money was lost. Two failures later, and Henriquez was ready to leave Jamaica for good, residing first in New Orleans and then in New York, where he became an importer and hotelier. One of his partners was another bankrupt, Alexander Isaacs, who had failed for thirty-six thousand pounds in Montego Bay. Although Henriquez was eventually worth up to thirty thousand dollars, he remained steeped in failure, and his firm seems the refuge of scoundrels. Isaacs "lived in great splendour for sev[eral] yrs" after his failure and even "came down so low [as?] to go into partnership with 'Edward Smith,' who is now in States Prison for 5 yrs, for perjury in the case of [George] 'Thompson' the 'confidence man.' " He could have joined forces with Henriquez for one purpose only: to establish credit in order to make "a heavy sweep hereafter." When the inevitable happened and the firm failed in January 1853, the reporter adds a fitting coda. Henriquez "has gone to England with his mistress—Left his fam[ily] unprovided for." Henriquez represented not only a credit risk but a moral menace. His career reinforces the commercial pieties of his credit evaluators.[16]

By its very nature, Tappan's agency sought to defend commercial probity against corrupt pretenders. But his credit reporters had more trouble assessing men in the middle—wily entrepreneurs, no better than they should be, who demonstrated a formidable resourcefulness. These figures represented a pragmatic middle class struggling to meet adverse conditions, and their efforts often forced evaluators to alter their moral criteria. Typical of this class was Dwight Bishop, a New York City furniture maker whose frequent scrapes caused him to be labeled the "failing man."[17] According to his credit history, compiled from 1851 to 1861, Bishop's initial foray, a partnership in a Broadway shop, ended in 1845 in an acrimonious failure that left him with substantial debts. After settling these accounts, he reopened a year later, relying on credit and selling for cash. His business plan appears to have involved underselling competitors and using the ready money to pay down debt. In 1850, seeking to shore up his credit, he took a partner, who "soon became dissipated" and absconded with sixteen hundred dollars (396). By 1851 Bishop seems to have recovered from the blow, but three years later he once again encountered heavy weather. With interest payments "eating him up" (396), he finally failed and settled with his creditors for twenty-five cents on the dollar.

But this was only the second act in his drama. By the fall of 1856, around two years after his second failure, he was back in business, having cleared off old liabilities and restocked his inventory. During the panic months of 1857 he had difficulty in meeting his payments but survived and appears to have thrived. "His retail trade has been better during the past season, than that of most of his neighbors," notes the credit reporter approvingly, "& his sales are mostly for cash" (400B). In the agitated credit market of the late 1850s, however, Bishop's reliance on marginal funding proved too risky, and he was finally forced to sell out in August 1861, his status as the "failing man" all too evidently confirmed.

But what made Bishop's case so noteworthy to the credit reporters, who followed his trials across two large ledger pages, were not his bankruptcies alone. Rather, Bishop's risk strategy seemed to defy the conventional categories of prudence and regularity by which credit judgments were often made. There was something remarkable about a two-time loser who tried to play by the rules. Should he be seen as rash, unfortunate, or foolish? The business community was not entirely sure. In 1851 he was reported "steady & atten.[tive] to bus.[iness]," and his difficulty with his former partner was not thought to "reflect injuriously on him" (396). By 1854, the signals were much more mixed. Now he was doing an "extens.[ive] bus.," but had trouble making payments, despite his attempts to retrench. Ordinarily, the fractional repayments Bishop made after his second bankruptcy in 1854 would have destroyed his credit, and a reporter groused that nearly a year later he had made only one installment. But somehow Bishop found the means to pay off the debt and his credit began "improving . . . slowly" (400B). Evidently, his ability to weather the panic enhanced his reputation, for in 1858 many thought him in "fair standing" and loaned him money "with confidence" (400B). Clearly, Bishop's main problem was that he was undercapitalized in an uncertain market. The fact that he relied on the tolerance of creditors, who evidently had no wish to cripple him, may have incited contradictory interpretations of his conduct. But his moral authority, to those who loaned him money, arose from his determination to survive despite the dissipation and chaos surrounding him. His career thus took shape as a contest with menaces not entirely assessed by the old categories of republican probity. Determined to avoid poverty, refusing to speculate, and unwilling to work for others, he seemed the embodiment of a tough, new pragmatism.

For novelists of the 1850s and 1860s, Bishop's wily but principled survival became a kind of touchstone. But these writers also probed the problems of vulnerability in unsettling new ways. Assaulted by the business cycle, they recurred to sentimental tropes to confront their weakness and dependence. They relied, as did earlier writers, on a rhetoric of purity to legitimate their market behavior. But they also sought new explanations for the moral impurities that survival forced on them. Threatened by both immorality and dependence, they responded with

fictions of exposure and exclusion. The former led them to embrace the sentimental trope of characterlessness. The latter caused them to turn their anguish
on the poor.

## Wastrels and Entrepreneurs

Market fictions, in the years surrounding the Civil War, performed a double
function. While reinforcing old commercial pieties, they sought to account for
chronic uncertainty. The most comforting explanation for the new round of
failures remained moral weakness, as is the case for the Roffs in Azel Roe's *Like
and Unlike* (1862).[18] Addicted, like A. D. Y. Henriquez, to luxury and display,
the elder Mr. Roff overextends himself, lives on credit, and dies a bankrupt.
Confronting this sudden loss of capital, Roff's equally avaricious son does what
any indolent social climber would do: he marries rich. But Junius Roff also marries
wrong, and within a year, his wife's paper wealth dissolves, throwing the young
man on his own resources (492–93). By contrast, when James Beaufort, a virtuous
clerk in the office of Roff's brother-in-law, is left without prospects after the
merchant's untimely death, he resolves to put off his dreams of "[i]ndependence"
and make "a strong effort to rise above . . . misfortune" (434). Selfishness, in
this almost animistic view, engenders its own punishment, as virtue secures its
own reward.

A didactic short story appearing at the height of the panic, Beulah Hirst's "Love
and Luxury," captures this moral tone.[19] Anna Ashurst is a frivolous debutante
obsessed with fine clothing even though her overworked father complains of
"hard times" (19) and urges her to retrench. Her taste for extravagance compels
her to put off marriage to a virtuous young doctor, who determines to seek his
fortune in the California gold fields to secure her the kind of life she craves.
"Father suffered reverses in the early years of his married life," she explains, and
so severe was her parents' ordeal that Anna "cannot be tempted to run the risk"
of such insecurity (18). But risk claims another victim when Mr. Ashurst returns
home, confesses he is bankrupt, and immediately dies. Anna, now assuming the
role of heroic daughter, moves with her mother to a small seaside cottage, where
she takes in boarders, mends her ways, and becomes renowned for her skill in
nursing. When a fierce storm hits the coast—analogue to the financial storm of
1857—she must put her skills to good use: a castaway turns out to be her fiancé,

returning with a fortune that she will now use wisely. She has learned to practice "self-denial" (29) and to make philanthropy her only extravagance.

Such moral materialism became a key expression of entrepreneurial desire. Readers of these tales imagined themselves in vanity fair surrounded by the tainted goods of sensual gratification that could be mastered only through rigorous self-sacrifice. Adversity was God's ledger, a function of the divine economy. "There is . . . an overruling Providence that has some reference to man's external condition in the world," remarks a chastened bankrupt in T. S. Arthur's "Don't Be Discouraged" (1851), [20] "—permitting one to grow rich and keep another poor" (208–9). "External things . . . are so governed as to lead us to think of interior things" (209). Wisdom, in these fictions, involves seeing the interior life from a providential perspective that limited private design. The need for a metaphysics of trade was sharpened, though, by the cruelty of the economy. "Don't Be Discouraged" presents the trials of a three-time loser, a young entrepreneur whose risky behavior ruins him. Only when he accepts a more modest role as a salaried clerk, dependent on someone else's decision making, does he begin to thrive. To succeed he must learn not to mimic the excesses of the economy, but to practice the same wise balance as the harmonious order he serves. Along with that truth comes a harsher recognition of the limitations on free enterprise, as the chastened clerk must accept his own diminished effectiveness. The path to the Heavenly City of prosperity lay through the narrow gate of financial embarrassment.

Another story in the same volume suggests more strongly the nagging underside of entrepreneurial resolve. Young Burton, the protagonist of "A Strange Story," is an entrepreneur in the "Poor Richard" mold—plating self-interest with benevolence. When he spies a well-dressed young woman stealing a pair of gloves from his store, he threatens to expose her unless she marries him. This devil's bargain the woman accepts, and brings to the marriage a considerable dowry. Surprisingly, the union turns out to be a happy one, until the old urge returns. Now wealthy, she cannot master her "strange propensity . . . like a kind of mania," to steal (172). Even her tear-stained Bible, ever opened to the eighth commandment, cannot change her ways, and Burton is forced to abscond, like a bankrupt fleeing his creditors, to escape blackmail. The story's manifest message seems clear enough: Burton's moral flaw had mysterious, magnified consequences. But to some readers the latent content of the story must have been more menacing, since Mrs. Burton's behavior lies outside moral economy. Conscious resolve has no effect on her affliction. [21]

Indeed, in many novels of the period, it is the capriciousness, rather than the rationality, of economic life that is most striking. "Every few years some derangement took place in monetary affairs," laments the narrator of A. S. Roe's *Looking Around* (1865).[22] To the eager protagonist of Roe's *To Love and to Be Loved* (1851),[23] the world itself seemed predatory, "for the great city was just then suffering under one of those terrible revulsions in trade which . . . throws a gloom over every mercantile interest; when merchants stand listlessly at their doors, or lounge in their office chairs, thinking over bad speculations, bad debts, doubtful notes and heavy payments ahead" (11). Under such conditions, Arthur's convenient equation between probity and profit seems increasingly strained. In *To Love and to Be Loved,* for example, the protagonist's father inherits a North Carolina estate so deeply mortgaged that he is forced to sell it to meet demands. Moving with his family to New York and establishing a small store, he soon finds that "[h]e could not . . . bind the fine feelings of his sensitive mind" to the demands of trade (19). His "soul-sickening" struggle and sincere love for his family do not prevent a steady slide into poverty, despair, and death (19). His son, James Edwards, proves much more energetic, but even he must endure bitter disappointment. Once again, "business seems to be at a stand" (52) as he seeks to support his family, and when he does finally land a job with a firm, he is framed for robbery by a peculating partner. "There always will be these reverses in business when things are all turned heels uppermost" (54), laments James's pious confidant, Mr. Upjohn. But Upjohn's counsel of stoic patience does not quite inspire that business confidence so crucial for success. "I wish I had a good trade, Mr. Upjohn," confesses James, expressing the clerk's nostalgia for a precapitalist security. "I would hardly care what it was, if it would only afford me an honest living" (53). For the young Edwards, gloom is almost a permanent attribute of the market. Although he is ultimately exonerated and restored to prosperity, the severity of Edwards's ordeal seems to put the market itself on trial. The melodramatic peripety, when the real villain, Rudolph Hunt, confesses his guilt after damaging testimony in court, only reinforces James's vulnerability and the almost accidental nature of his success. Even his promotion to partner in place of Hunt is overshadowed by Hunt's nearly successful attempt to assassinate him. For Roe, survival in such a treacherous market comes only at great psychic and physical cost.

A similar disjunction appears in the pages of Richard Kimball's *Undercurrents of Wall-Street* (1862).[24] Subtitled *A Romance of Business,* the novel set itself the formidable challenge of grafting a sentimental tale onto a business exposé. Charles E. Parkinson never quite recovers from the "universal ruin" (11) of the panic of 1837 and is forced into the moral netherworld of note shaving (discounting) to support his family: "Day by day, when wearied and worn out with incessant toil, and humiliated by . . . never-ending exhibitions of coarseness and arrogance, I would go to my home, resolving never again to expose myself to these [influences], the sight of . . . two motherless daughters—and a son . . . dying gradually of consumption, would send me back the next morning to the 'street,' meek, sorrowful, submissive" (10). The family's urgent dependence on his hustling is matched only by Parkinson's submission to a capricious marketplace that ruins him once every decade. Under these circumstances, Kimball argues, the integrity touted by market moralists is only half true. Time and again, inner resolve fails to lift Parkinson above his circumstances. An erroneous credit report damages his prospects. A partner touting mining schemes in the West runs up so many business expenses that Parkinson finds himself deeply in debt. Prudence and circumspection do not protect his firm from the misfortunes of southern trading houses, whose protested bills precipitate his failure. Significantly, one of the novel's heroes is a man wily in the ways of the street, yet resistant to its worst scams. Solomon Downer, like Parkinson, has been forced to become a financial scavenger, lurking about for the main chance while avoiding overnice questions about propriety. Yet Downer keeps a Christian family in modest comfort, aids Parkinson when he suffers losses, and sacrifices his health to seal a final transaction that will secure his family after his death. Like Parkinson, Downer "sees glimpses of green fields, and clear skies, and a pure moral atmosphere away yonder, but he has no time to visit them" (145). These operatives inhabit a murky middle region, somewhere between profit and loss.

Characters like Charles Parkinson are lineal descendants of the failed merchants of the Jacksonian era. What distinguishes Parkinson is that his insecurities are linked not to a crisis but to a condition. His uncertainty is a state of being. The moral ambiguities surrounding his attempts to provide a proper living through improper means reflect Kimball's attempt to find a vocabulary flexible enough to address the broader ambiguities of market fluctuations. One of his most interesting attempts involves transposing the old discourse of sympathy into a new key, that of class. Some writers, Kimball suggests, are preoccupied with "harrowing tales of pauper life." Yet "[i]f they could experience ten years in Wall-street they would dispose of their present stock in trade, and eagerly seize on this. There exist in that street those who suffer more than the pauper, and the men, women and children in the mines and collieries, and shops and factories, for they have sharper sensibilities, and keener appreciations, and a more vivid despair" (144). Here, the dependence and sensibility resulting from economic loss are not the attributes of isolated merchants. Sensibility now stands for a way of life both distinct from "the 'lower classes' " (340) and linked to the marketplace. If readers knew "the aching *hearts* concealed under a most respectable exterior," testaments of a "suffering" greater than "bodily want" he adds, echoing Boucicault's Edward Livingstone, they would extend relief to all the economically vulnerable—all those on the heartsick margins of respectability (340). Nowhere is Kimball's desire to broaden sympathy more evident than in his invocation of a bourgeois Christ. "Our SAVIOUR said: 'Ye have the poor always with you.' Doubtless, we shall have the miserable also. Still, we attempt to assist the poor; let us try to relieve the heavy-hearted" (340–41). Christian sympathy now was not confined to the poor. It was the distinct attribute of an economically squeezed middle class.

Along with the uncertainties surrounding self-denial, there appeared in several novels another ambiguity concerning the very meaning of independence. That most treasured of republican attributes took a battering with every jolt of the business cycle, leading some writers to seek alternatives. Again, Kimball took the lead in *Undercurrents*. While Charles Parkinson does not disown the ideal of self-reliance, he recognizes a competing, Darwinian impulse in market behavior: "Step by step we become accustomed to what happens. Gradually pushed from one stand-point to another, we learn to submit. Wonderful is the power of adaptation in man; . . . Give him sway, he is a very lord paramount. . . . Important and self-sufficient, he shows it in his look, his walk, his gesture, his surroundings. Let the hand be put forth against him, and does he fall, does he wither into insignificance? No; he adapts himself to his new state" (74–75). Each state commands its own rationale, its own version of inner resolve. Much the same realization strikes the young entrepreneurs of Azel Roe's *James Montjoy* (1850).[25] Rocked by a financial "earthquake" (209), they must learn the limits of private enterprise: "It is not, of necessity, the fault of those who wield [credit], that it should often press with such sickening, despairing force; so long as enterprise shall stimulate man to go a step beyond the means at his own disposal, must he in some measure depend upon the aid of others; and once dependent, he can never calculate with certainty upon enduring peace of mind" (261). Under such conditions, the old moral equation of enterprise with character must be modified, for "the high-minded, honorable

man is obliged to stand before the same tribunal with the mean and designing"
(261). Adapting to the market was like enduring the weather. Both were aimless,
erratic, amoral.

To be sure, most authors did not therefore renounce moral character, but they
began to recognize how sharply circumscribed were its claims. Whereas hard-line
Jacksonians had viewed bankruptcy as the scarlet badge of corruption, after 1850
even doctrinaire moralists often understood the complex relation between moral
and monetary affairs. T. S. Arthur's *Trial and Triumph* (1855),[26] for example,
contrasts the firmness of Mary Lynn with the unscrupulous scheming of her
mother. The vulnerable Lynns have been left on the edge of ruin by Mr. Lynn's
untimely death, and only a rich marriage can preserve their status. Because Mary
refuses to sacrifice herself to a wealthy but vicious suitor, Philip Emerson, the
Lynns must sell off their furniture and move. Mary finds work as a governess and
eventually exposes Emerson as a bankrupt embezzler—all true to sentimental
form. But Arthur comes close to revealing the irrationality shadowing prudence
in his account of the panic that nearly ruins the Lynns. The family legacy, fifty
thousand dollars in bank stock, is an investment so volatile that it quickly loses
most of its value. Resisting the urge to sell on the advice of her agent, Mrs. Lynn
is soon holding worthless paper. "What had I best to do?" she pleads. "I do not
like the responsibility of throwing away my children's property in this way" (17).
But the agent can offer little more than statistical consolation, claiming that if he
misjudged the market, "thousands have erred with me" (16). Mrs. Lynn's terrified
appeals to have him think for her—"If you were in my place, what would you do?"
(18)—evoke only the agent's bafflement. Here is a moral sickness, Arthur seems to
be saying: Mrs. Lynn's failure to take responsibility demonstrates the same want
of independence exhibited in her cupidity and in the speculative investments. But
her poignant plea that her family's security rests on these investments cannot be so
easily dismissed. As the market's need for credit expanded, countless "thousands"
were put in the position of the agent, who can only aver, "I am totally in the dark"
(18). All too many were benighted in precisely the same fashion.

Jacksonian novelists, when confronting the market's ambiguities, sought comfort
in the figure of the characterless woman whose sincerity ensured success. In
the period after the panic of 1857, however, the most urgent response to insecurity extended that trope in unsettling ways. In *Phemie's Temptation* (1869),[27]
Marion Harland (Mary Terhune) explores a hard-won independence that links

affectionate relations, radical critique, and the more dangerous pragmatism in which many entrepreneurs engaged. Like her Jacksonian predecessors, Euphemia Rowland is forced to support her family when males falter: her father dies intestate and her younger brother, Albert, is blinded in an accident. Working her way up from impoverished seamstress, to sales clerk, to bookkeeper, she uses odd hours to compose a chemistry textbook and to write literary sketches. Yet because Phemie is a worker rather than an owner, she is more sensitive to middle-class anxieties. Harland nicely captures the problem by relating writing, money, and marriage. Phemie's unremitting toil has made her wryly familiar with the weaknesses of men: "The cant of trade was familiar to her as her alphabet, and recalling her father's oft-reiterated prognostications of ruin and ceaseless desires for wealth during the latter months of his life, she believed that all men talked it" (62). At any rate, almost all men in the novel talk and think this way. But the passage also captures Phemie's naïveté. So demoralized is she by her own disappointments that she cannot imagine attitudes different from those surrounding her. The novel will seek to educate both Phemie and her audience.

Robert Hart, a publisher, seems to be an exception to the rule. It is he who contracts with her to write the chemistry text, and his cultured talk induces her to imagine that there is an alternative to boorish trade. Yet she resists marrying him, in part from the proud need to support her family alone. When her sisters marry and her motives for independence dissolve, she relents—only to discover that marriage is also subject to the cant of trade. Her troubles with Hart arise from a novel she publishes anonymously through his firm and reveals after the book has become a best-seller. Phemie's obvious brilliance and independent income shake Hart's prickly self-confidence precisely as would a failure in business, and his anger takes the form of a commercial tirade. Female scribblers, he claims,

> are the most arrant and obtrusive set of egotists under heaven. They write their own lives over and over, until the public taste revolts, and then they make capital of their friends. . . . Their loves, their hates, their griefs, are so much available capital to be served up . . . at whatever they can get per page. They are mercenary to a proverb—grasping and grinding, with all their talk of doing good, helping the weak and the like bosh. They write for money! money! and the only way to quench their genius is not to pay them. (185)

Robert's vicious sarcasm presents Phemie with an excruciating double bind. Morbidly conscious that he has married beneath his class, Hart has made Phemie into a trophy wife draped in silks and pearls. But her attempt to demonstrate her renunciation of enterprise by donating the profits of her book to others only underscores her independence. She cannot act with her native resolve without recalling for Hart those very traits of bourgeois self-reliance he is so eager to suppress. And she cannot submit to him without plunging once again into the language of ownership and loss—the threadbare cant of trade she detests. Faced with this cruel choice, Phemie opts for a proud but painful silence.

When Hart faces bankruptcy, Phemie sees one last opportunity to save her marriage. In the months following the publication of the novel Hart had been increasingly contemptuous, expressing his anger through absence and alcohol. But when word comes that his business has failed, Phemie is suddenly hopeful, sensing an entry for her entrepreneurial talents. "He would let her help him now," she imagines, if not through writing then through trade. "She could keep books, or copy deeds, or be his saleswoman behind the counter of some unpretending little shop" (226). Surely one remedy to their problems is renunciation of wealth for a modest competency, and if her writing, which could not in some measure escape the taint of commerce, were implicated in that wealth, she is willing to renounce it as well. But ironically, Phemie's fantasies of her bankrupt husband reveal how she is still influenced by the cant of trade. Surely now, she imagines, Robert would be abject:

> She pictured him to herself lagging homeward, his hat slouched over his brows, frenzied by defeat, and shrinking from communication with his associates. . . . Her heart bled until she sobbed outright at the thought of the suppressed agony. . . .
>
> She longed to kneel to him, and pray for forgiveness; to make of her affection a bulwark that should break the force of the assaults he must sustain from the rebuffs of fickle friends; . . . and her cheek glowed with bride-like roses at thought of the well of consolation of which she held the key. (226–27)

But Hart refuses to play this sentimental role and absconds instead, leaving behind a curt note in which he bestows her freedom along with his considerable debts. This final disappointment reveals not only Phemie's selflessness but also her crying need for a relationship uncorrupted by the cant of property. In short, the failure of her marriage is also the failure of an ideological construct that saw sentimental women as the saviors of abject, failed men. A different paradigm was in order.

Harland's surprising solution to Phemie's problem—a departure from her other, more conventional, novels—is to overturn almost all of the tropes of sentimental marriage.[28] With Phemie pregnant and penniless after creditors lay claim to the estate, she applies to her dearest friend, Ruth Darcy. Darcy is a radically "characterless" woman, an ardent feminist, editor, and educator who demanded "other avenues of honorable labor for women than the crowded lanes in which they were beaten down by competition" (72). Darcy takes her to her family farm and reveals her own history, a tale of love and betrayal similar to Phemie's with one significant addition: Darcy later finds her lover an insane pauper driven desperate by his failure in life. The madwoman in the attic has become the madman in the streets. The disclosure heightens an intimacy between the two that is rooted in, but does not revolve around, the necessities of trade or social position. Darcy finds bookkeeping work for Phemie until she has recovered from childbirth, whereupon they return to the city and establish what Harland calls a "family" (271) in a neat little cottage. Work dominates their relationship: Darcy labors among stacks of books in the parlor while Phemie turns out fiction in a front room and baby Ruth—named for Darcy—plays amid the manuscripts. Their relation is strong enough to survive the "dull" economic seasons that "recurred at the end of every three years" (274) and even a return visit from Hart, who steals and squanders Phemie's income and finally strikes the baby. That violence precipitates Phemie's declaration of independence. When Hart commands her to choose between him and Darcy, Phemie declares, "I promised to be a wife— not a slave. . . . My husband has not left me the means wherewith to pay for a night's lodgings for myself and child. The Lord judge between me and him. I have made my choice" (307). Harland thus seeks to turn Phemie into a latter-day Hester Prynne. Having succumbed to the temptation of marriage, she has at last overthrown the whole system of ancient prejudice binding women to men.

Neither Ruth Darcy, however, nor the fortunes of Euphemia Hart were ultimately comforting to anxious men worried about their own success. Men like Dwight Bishop knew the tough choices the marketplace exacted, and moralists needed to find a way to keep pragmatic businessmen from selling their souls. Ann Stephens's *Fashion and Famine* (1854) presents one solution in the figure of a sleeping boy.[29] Although nineteen years old, Robert Otis still seems a child—a feminine child. His "masses of chestnut curls, rich with a tinge of gold," the "rich rose tint" of his cheeks and his cherry-red, lustrous lips, the snowy hands and the limbs "rounded almost to a tone of feminine symmetry" (81–82) suggest an abiding innocence impervious to market corruptions. Even after the young clerk, mentored by the villainous Leicester, is lured into gambling and forgery, Otis remains the image of pristine virtue, a Dorian Gray without the telltale portrait. "You have abilities of a high order," Leicester assures him, "industry, talent, everything requisite for success" (85–86). Characters like Robert Otis assured readers that the compromises of the marketplace would not affect their probity and that the self-reliant entrepreneur could be as yielding as a little child. "Nothing could have been more beautiful" than the young clerk, writes Stephens (87). It would be a statement that numerous readers would take to heart.

## Spiritual Commerce

In their correspondence at the turn of the nineteenth century, Toby Ditz has argued, Philadelphia merchants used the tropes of sentimental fiction to reflect on their fortunes. Moral compromises, misjudgments of the market, severe losses— all were imagined through the language of sexual contest in which merchants played the threatened heroine. "Ruined" merchants, like fallen women, risked "reputation, social standing, and the moral stature on which they rest."[30] Such imagery, Ditz shows, allowed the letter writers to legitimate their compromising behavior without succumbing to it. When a merchant imagined himself as a heroine, he knew he was presenting a contrary-to-fact scenario, a theatrical role he could later disavow. But he was also allowing himself a precious moment of vulnerability, the confession of a weakness he could expose in no other way. By midcentury, after the market revolution had widened the middle classes, the role of the feminine merchant had moved to the main stage. The entrepreneurial daughters of popular fiction who once helped to save ruined families had prepared the way for a new breed of sentimental trader for whom commerce itself was a delicate exchange of feelings. Such androgynous heroes marked an important adjustment to an economy that could and often did turn owners into debtors, and masters into the overmastered. Crossing gender lines gave moral depth to the fluctuations of business and legitimated the pragmatic compromises of calculating businessmen. It made feminized behavior a sign of entrepreneurial resolve. And such behavior sharpened the identity of a middle class seeking a new rationale for its experience. The Dwight Bishops of the world could be redeemed by refiguring their actions as the all-embracing sympathies of feminized youths.

In many typical coming-of-age narratives of the 1850s and 1860s, the most promising candidates are often blushing beauties. In Charles Smith's *George Melville* (1858),[31] for example, the star clerk in a prominent New York importing house is William Hastings, fresh from rural Oneida County. At first sight, Hastings does not seem to have what it takes to survive in the rough and tumble of New York trade. Like Otis he is eighteen or nineteen, "small in stature, having black hair falling from his temples in graceful curls," with exquisitely white teeth and a "complexion clear and brilliant" (160). The features give the impression of "almost feminine beauty" (161). But the sensitive young man makes good use of his attributes. The typical trading house, he discovers, is poorly integrated, with an inefficient exchange of information between suppliers and sellers. Hastings seeks to change all that. Traveling throughout the Union, he makes market studies and sales projections and uses them to increase earnings. By the end of the season the firm has sold out its inventory, and its losses "by failure of jobbers to meet their payments, were not worthy an entry on the account of profit and loss" (165). Hastings, in short, has rationalized his company's operations so successfully that he becomes a junior partner by the age of twenty-one. His success is intimately tied to his effeminacy, for the sensibility that gives such a delicate cast to his features is the same trait that allows him to rove the country absorbing the subtleties of diverse regions. In effect, he has come to embody the Enlightenment dream of *le doux commerce,* a noble exchange of goods among generous, sensitive agents. Trade, he proves, could nurture as well as destroy.

Other novelists echoed these themes. In Azel Roe's *True to the Last* (1858),[32] the orphaned Henry Thornton mixes delicacy and drive. "He had a peculiar fondness for that which was beautiful," abandoning the rough play of boys for the more soothing company of girls. Their "tender influence had given a tone to his feelings and a gentleness to his character" that resembled "effeminacy" (66–67), yet such traits do not prevent him from forging his own way in the world. Rather, acute sensitivity makes him adaptable. Just as his features display "softness, and yet energy," so in his struggles for success there is "a kind of determination that would make him go ahead, although his feelings might shrink at the encounter" (81). Shrinking feelings turn adolescent enthusiasm into adult prudence. James Edwards, the rising young man of Roe's *To Love and to Be Loved,* is similarly described as having "a softness to his complexion, bordering upon effeminacy" (13), a trait most evident in his blushing when aroused by strong feeling (57). Adults, too, evince this behavior. Lawrence Newt, the wealthy merchant of George William Curtis's *Trumps* (1861), combines mercantile "skill and knowledge . . . with a womanly reserve and softness."[33] The prosperous William Wumble in John Jones's *The City Merchant* (1851)[34] sobs when he hears news that his best friend has failed (53), and Joe Bonney, Phemie Hart's mercantile brother-in-law in

*Phemie's Temptation,* bursts into abject tears when he learns of her abandonment (238). Such womanly behavior underscores the honor in vulnerability. For these sensitive merchants, softness and strength coincide.

The most pronounced expression of this theme appears in Mary Townsend's *The Brother Clerks* (1857).[35] A didactic novel, it traces the fortunes of Arthur and Gulian Pratt, forced to seek work in New Orleans when their father's death leaves the family penniless. The older Arthur is rough and impetuous and will soon succumb to the city's dark temptations. Guly's is a more spiritual disposition— but a spirituality that makes his fortune. A mere child, he has a figure "slender and delicate as a girl's" (10), with a white, transparent skin that seems, were it "held . . . towards the light," as if one could "look through it" (37). So pronounced is his effeminacy that at his first interview with his new employer, Mr. Delancey, he faints. Yet Guly's innocent faith anchors the novel, allowing him to remain untouched by urban vice as he works his way to head clerk and adoption by his once skeptical boss.

Guly's success as the commercial equivalent of Little Eva, however, has other wide-ranging and curious effects. While his calm Christianity helps to suppress dishonesty in the store and curbs his brother's drinking, he develops a different re-lationship with the head clerk, Bernard Wilkins. A subplot has Wilkins enamored of Delancey's daughter, who is forbidden from marrying beneath her class. All this Wilkins confesses to Guly, whose deep sympathy promotes a Whitmanesque bond: "Wilkins . . . drew the slight form closer in silent sympathy. The hours went on, and midnight still saw them sitting there together—the golden head upon the broad, kind breast" (161). It is a relationship that defies categories— hyperemotional but not quite erotic, filial but also alien. Guly seems to have the kind of magnetic spirituality that Little Eva displays, yet its moral effects are quite different. If Wilkins evinces a saintly sympathy in his chamber, out of doors he is also a bigamist, whose first, secret marriage is to Della Delancey's black slave, Minny. In a wildly improbable catastrophe, Wilkins kills Minny to secure his second marriage, receives her dying blessing, and resolves to go straight. The murder remains unpunished, and Wilkins finds happiness abroad. It is Guly's transparent presence that is supposed to save this episode from moral lunacy. His mediating spirituality, Townsend implies, can bind up all wounds.

Above all, Gulian Pratt represents a moral pragmatism closely suited to the demands of a fluid marketplace. Almost any outrage, Townsend suggests, may be redeemed through the right intentions. It is not surprising, then, to find his mediatory effects in other contemporary novels. Feminized merchants, like the resourceful daughters of earlier bankruptcy fiction, hold together the conflicting demands of a world made volatile by the market. Lawrence Newt, for example, the honorable merchant of George Curtis's *Trumps,* has adapted himself to the severities of trade without sacrificing Guly's sentimental sincerity. Newt is a figure of Dickensian eccentricity, fond of non sequiturs, quaint maxims, and mild irony. When asked for a job by yet another saintly novice, the young Gabriel Bennet, Newt responds with a paradoxical sanction of both ambition and restraint: "My young friend, you are of opinion that a half loaf is better than no bread. True—so am I. But never make the mistake of supposing a half to be the whole. Content is a good thing. When the man sent for cake, and said, 'John, if you can't get cake, get smelts,' he did wisely. But smelts are not cake for all that" (83). The queer moralizing is later revealed to be intimately connected with Newt's amatory affairs. Having lost his young lover to an arranged marriage, he spends the novel searching for the whole loaf in a new wife. In the meantime, he has made a fortune in a hostile market and learned how to bestow it upon others, acting as counselor and friend to a host of deserving petitioners. His "soft, manly earnestness," the peculiar mixture of "skill and knowledge, combined with a womanly reserve" (341), makes him an ideal go-between, a healer of social wounds. In light of Newt's agile benevolence, it is clear that his parable of the loaves and the fishes has allowed him to gain wealth without sacrificing his soul.

So, too, this feminized merchant retains the guileless sincerity that marked an earlier generation of characterless women. With young Bennet, Newt's eyes gaze "so keenly that they seemed to be mere windows through which his soul was looking" (83). Even when he is most inscrutable, his instincts urge transparency. During a benevolent visit to Jane Simcoe, attendant to his protégée Hope Wayne, for example, Simcoe reflects that his face "is not so clear as it used to be" (155). The remark draws this ironic, self-deprecating rejoinder: "My face is the lid of a chest full of the most precious secrets; would you have the lid transparent? I am a merchant. Suppose every body could look in through my face and see what I really think of the merchandise I am selling! What profit do you think I should make? No, no, we want no tell-tale faces in South Street" (156). But Newt's career has demonstrated just the opposite—that an individual who has "lived every where" and "seen every thing, and . . . known every body" (98) can retain the lover's untarnished idealism, even as he manipulates the market. His behavior precisely duplicates that of Mrs. Montjoy in Roe's *James Montjoy,* who comforts her sons as they face bankruptcy. "She had accustomed them to tell her all their thoughts, . . . and opening . . . the fountain of their soul, she watched each bubble that came sparkling up, cleared all the dross and specks away, with sweet maternal care" (211). The speculative bubbles of trade are transformed into tokens of affection beneath this clear maternal gaze.

Such professions of transparency lie at the midpoint between middle-class awareness and class consciousness. By proclaiming the clarity of sentiment, popular novelists of the 1850s resolved the doubts of their Jacksonian predecessors. Only sensitive, feminized merchants, these later fictions contended, had the capacity to measure a market that fashioned individuals with the mirrorlike facility that Marx saw in commodity relations. Sentimental merchants were also successful merchants because they felt an essential link with a market that was no longer obscure, but as limpid as a young girl's soul. By imagining this sentimental economy as the distinctive refinement of middling entrepreneurs, these fictions also advanced the long project of class awareness begun by early national writers. The fictions, that is to say, contributed to an ideology of class by presenting its premises as universal, as "the common interest of all the members of society," who would be saved by a merchant's benevolence. For the emergent middle class, transparency, benevolence, and sympathy were both moral and market indicators. Transparent, sympathetic individuals were mediators. Evacuated of all mean egotism, they became the means to imagine a harmonious world. They transformed dependency and weakness into selfless affinity, and their exchange of feeling redeemed the exchanges of the marketplace. Submission and dependence thus became the signs of seamless order.[36]

Azel Roe's *Like and Unlike* offers a nice illustration of the process. The Reverend Goodman is involved in a struggle with several officious members of his church who have campaigned to expel him because he is too liberal. The controversy takes a physical toll on the minister, but he is brought to the brink of despair by a further trouble. His brother's bankruptcy has left him, as endorser, responsible for a three-thousand-dollar debt. Never prosperous, Goodman is about to sink into poverty. It is then that he is visited by three merchants led by James Sterling, to whom Goodman, "pale, and . . . more than usually wan and weak" (165), discloses his problems. Only one of the three, however, Mr. Bustle, is a member of the church, and his attendance at the meeting, over the objections of his wife, is a bold step: "He knew well the [benevolent] feelings of one of the parties, and had no doubt the other sympathized in these feelings. . . . To meet such a storm as was now clearly brewing . . . was a little too much for Mr. Bustle's nerves, and his knees fairly trembled; he was glad to take a seat as soon as possible" (166). The emotional "business," as Sterling calls it, is soon transacted: Goodman is saved from ruin through the merchants' selfless gift, and faith as well as property is fortified. Bustle, "warmed . . . to a pitch beyond his power to control," dissolves into tears, and even his hardened companion is forced to confess that "there is good to be done with money, besides making a show or feeling independent" (170). Goodman's weakness thus becomes powerful, since the act has strengthened belief among these worldly donors, the magi of the middle class. The minister's parlor is the symbolic center of a more harmonious social order, grounded in equal measures of sentiment and cash.

But in its very claim to universality, this Christian economy provokes a further dialectical move that marks a shift from class awareness to class consciousness. For popular fictions also depicted another kind of market casualty—those characters incapable of reflecting the sympathies of exchange. Throughout the 1850s, urban novelists wrestled with this contradiction. Desiring a Christian republic, they depicted vicious cityscapes in desperate need of moral reform. In such a milieu, fraudulent clerks and conniving prostitutes were outgrowths of the same social cancer joining all citizens in moral frailty. As frailty became a badge of economic resilience, however, writers increasingly sought to preserve this imperative from the working class and the poor. Those who resisted the transparent sympathies of benevolent merchants or who lacked the capacity for sentimental responsiveness seemed to be opposed to the common interests of society. In times of panic, they did not react with the disarming candor of middling heroes and heroines. Instead, they rejected sympathy, became as opaque and menacing as the unpredictable market itself. Because they increased the vulnerability of what Leonore Davidoff and Catherine Hall term a still "fragile" middle class, they needed to be vigorously suppressed.[37] The cultivated frailties of entrepreneurs could neither incorporate nor yield to this hostile social mass. By excluding them, middle class readers came truly into their own.

## Owned and Disowned

Americans in the mid–nineteenth century were obsessed by self-control. As Charles Sellers argues, the Protestant regulation of impulses profoundly resonated with the stringent demands of a capitalist marketplace that rewarded disciplined economic behavior. The marriage between evangelical Christianity and capitalism, Sellers suggests, was one of the most important effects of the market revolution.[38] Viewed from a certain angle, the great majority of American novels during this period took up aspects of the capitalist agenda, whether through accounts of Christian fortitude, heroic self-sacrifice, or trial and triumph. The story Americans never tired of telling themselves involved the threatened hero or heroine whose character proved equal to all odds. As market pressures posed increasingly severe challenges to mere moral resolve, however, novelists began to seek another narrative to explain failure. The lower orders, clamoring for relief in each new panic, came to be associated with the disruptive force of panic itself, restricting and threatening the sentimental authority of the middle class. If all their adjustments still failed to eradicate panic, the problem lay not in themselves. The poor were the source of the social disease and the defining agents of middle-class consciousness.

One of the most hallucinatory examples of this new microhistory is an abolitionist novel by Van Buren Denslow, *Owned and Disowned* (1857).[39] So fragmented and improbable is the novel's plot—improbable even by Victorian standards— that it can be understood only as an allegory of self-control. The hero, Walter Defoe, a youth with a smooth, beardless face; "long, waving locks . . . over his shoulders" (25); and a disposition both energetic and mild (26), is traveling south in search of Julia Preston, who had once helped his sick mother. At the Preston plantation, he is mistaken for his brother Conrad, a notorious confederate of the pirate Jean Lafitte. Refraining from correcting the error, Walter learns that the planter, Butler Preston, has agreed to sell his octoroon slave-daughter Julia to avoid bankruptcy. When Julia learns of the agreement she escapes and flees to New Orleans, where she seeks refuge in a convent. Her half-sister, Ada, is abducted by pirates. From this point, the novel measures the sisters' ability to rise above imprisonment. Julia devises a way to escape the oppressive Roman Catholics, only to be betrayed and returned to slavery. Ada languishes aboard the pirate ship, is taken to a secret pirate resort, and lives in sin with Conrad. Redemption comes at a stiff price: the pirates turn patriotic and die for the cause in the War of 1812. Ada drowns herself after paying one last visit to the bankrupt Preston plantation. Julia is nearly sold at auction before she is rescued by Walter, whose final act is to free the Preston slaves and move north. One more southern nest of sin has thus been razed.

The ideological core of this novel involves free labor. Walter establishes his moral credentials as an orphan in a New England factory, where he first discovers the leisure class. Watching them at play through the wrought iron fences around their mansions, he thinks "what a fine place this world must be for them" (32) and upbraids them for not saving "little children everywhere from having such a hard life as he had, which made him feel often as if he could not help stealing something" (33). But his dying mother's plea that he remain "unspotted from the world" (33) inspires him, and he toils on all the way to Yale College. Remaining unspotted in the South is a greater challenge, however, for there distortions of property and power have tainted everyone. Piracy and bankruptcy, rape and abduction, tropical resort and city convent rest on a foundation of avarice too deep to dislodge. At the center of these circles of hell is the anti-Semitic figure of Iasaacks, a crazed miser who squats half-naked in a bare, filthy cellar beside an open coffin. It is Iasaacks who holds the Preston mortgage, and his "small, snake-like eyes emitting a wild maniac glare, by which they seemed to have looked themselves into blindness" (166) are an apt emblem of the single-minded pursuit of wealth. In this demonic parody of self-denial Iasaacks suggests the darkest contradictions of Walter's own work ethic. Without love to temper ambition, all of America would soon resemble this southern hovel.

But in using this repulsive figure to exorcise liberal demons, Denslow also avails himself of a more powerful prejudice. Iasaack's neighborhood is a bleak register of Calvinist depravity. As the benevolent nun and Julia's defender, Sister Clara, walks through it, she reflects on its hopelessness: "Here, out of one generation loathsome with inherited and acquired sins and diseases, is constantly issuing another, which, by the law of hereditary transmission, enters the world the involuntary heir of wicked hearts and diseased bodies, in which the soul of a saint could not live righteously" (172). "Oh . . . that I had a thousand lives, that I might give them all up to save these miserable wretches," Clara exclaims (173). But this echo of Thérèsina Rank's melodramatic appeal underscores the hopelessness of the fantasy. Like Rank's unemployed workers, whose threats of violence allow a middle-class audience to retract its universal sympathy, these urban poor permit northern readers to attenuate their feelings. The effect is accomplished in a fascinating and contradictory manner. On the one hand, the depraved poor permit Denslow to refute one of the South's most frequent charges, that there was little difference between the impoverished New England factory worker and the southern slave. The slum dwellers of New Orleans suggest that poverty was native to the South, whereas factory workers like Walter were virtuous. On the other hand, Denslow makes this claim not by rejecting the racist argument that supposed a group of people incapable of freedom, but merely by redirecting that argument toward the urban poor. And because the poor, as a class, are incapable of moral agency, Walter must be their guardian as surely as southerners must guard slaves. This fundamental identity is reflected in the novel's final scene, in which Walter acquires the Preston land and becomes responsible for its freed slaves. He has thus managed to perform the difficult moral feat of accepting the wealth of the plantation without being tainted by it. The stain on property has been washed away, and the owners of mansions can continue to recline behind their iron gates, which now keep out the hereditary slaves of poverty.

Denslow's attempt to sharpen class lines by adopting the language of slavery was symptomatic of a move by many writers to forge a national language of class. As Mary Ryan has argued, the impulse to distance a middle-class audience from the poor had its roots in changing perceptions of antebellum cities. Whereas social classes freely mingled in the cities of the early republic, an influx of single, poor, and foreign workers caused more established residents to view antebellum cities as dangerous places beset by vice often emanating from the poor. The waves of urban reformers, from temperance societies and tract visitors to female missionaries and Sunday school superintendents, have often been viewed as symptoms of an impulse to restrain these dangerous elements. [40] But the spectacular fiction that grew up around their efforts served the interests of class only obliquely. The urban exposés of George Foster, Ned Buntline (Edward Judson), George Lippard, and others depicted the city as a dangerous but undifferentiated terrain united by the moral blindness of rich and poor alike. This evangelical portrait would have to be sharpened for a middle-class consciousness fully to emerge.

Ned Buntline's *The Mysteries and Miseries of New York* (1848) [41] is a good example of the evangelical approach. Set in 1841, during the height of an economic depression, its chief lament is that all are "ruined." Charles Meadows, the young clerk lured into gambling, embezzlement, and murder, utters the claim to his tormentor, Henry Carlton (2.60), as does a succession of betrayed women. "I'm ruined for everything but this," moans one prostitute. "No one would give me work—I could not get a place anywhere, it is my only chance for a decent living" (3.104). But the wealthy rakes and commoners who patronize her or haunt gambling dens are ruined in much the same manner. In one vivid scene, Buntline follows some young swells to Almack's, the Five Points club that Charles Dickens immortalized. While "Pete Williams' Juba dancers" (2.79) perform out front, sailors gamble in back, and when the notorious white saloon keeper and self-described "gentleman" (80), Butcher Bill Poole, roars for a dance partner, his first response is from a "one-eyed, poc-marked [*sic*] ragged girl, who looked as if she had been . . . [a] scullion" (81). The same class relations prevail at a Greenwich Street boardinghouse kept by a widow "of that 'class which has seen better days.'" Around her threadbare tablecloth are ranged boarders of "nearly every class," from clerks and medical students to sewing girls and "rough looking mechanics . . . who paid their board" (1.105). "Class" here is more closely related to "category" than to "social rank," but the shabby democracy of the table, including the upwardly mobile and the most vulnerable, suggests that Buntline made no attempt to draw sharp economic distinctions. His intent was to arouse a moral anxiety that elided class differences. Hence in a description of the sneak thief Lize, modeled on the notorious six-foot-tall bandit Gallus Mag, Buntline claims, "We could not be so entirely *unfashionable* . . . as to insinuate that this depraved and fallen female could possess the same feelings which *others* feel, but they were *very* like" (3.40). Sentiment was a currency that knew no social barriers.

George Foster's *New York by Gas-Light* (1850)[42] provides a striking example of how class interests were both stimulated and muted by portraits of the vicious city. In Foster's sketches, as in others of the genre, all of the city's social groups, from the wealthy patrons of Delmonico's to the poorest bar crawlers of the Five Points, abandon themselves to their prodigious appetites. Moral probity, when it is found at all, rests on the capacity for temperance amid the excess. Hence, in a tour of ice cream parlors Foster contrasts the idle immorality of fashionable establishments, patronized by couples who seem to be "man and wife—though not *each other's!*" (66), to the family atmosphere of the Patent Steam Ice-Cream Saloon. Here can be seen "the wives and daughters of the substantial tradesmen, mechanics, and artizans [*sic*] of the city, the great middle class, whose aspirations, reaching the full standard of well-to-do content, wisely fall short of . . . snobbish longing after social notoriety" (69). Such individuals work well, eat heartily, and "have minds and hearts keen to appreciate and quick to feel" (69). In Foster's shadowy city, where so many relations are ambiguous, class is registered through conduct and "human physiology" (69). Moderation keeps feeling authentic, and feeling, in turn, confirms social rank. Sincerity remains the true register of social order, allowing for all true republicans to enter the ranks of the middle class.

But the republican vigor of the term "middle class" faltered when Foster tried to apply it to those with less leisure. In his most famous sketch in the volume, he depicted the Bowery b'hoy as the American representative of "the great middle classes in all countries" (101), a status that includes American trappers, farmers, and gold diggers as well as European peasants. What distinguishes the New Yorker is a defiance born, as historians have demonstrated, of economic frustration.[43] The b'hoy was often a member of a marginalized trade, caught in the capitalist transformation of New York's artisan culture. Unable, as in a former era, to own the means of production and finding his wages squeezed by fierce competition, he sought out the camaraderie of the bar and the fire company to compensate for his lapsed autonomy. Although Foster cannot be expected to have grasped all these developments, he does hint at his general awareness of them. In *New York in Slices* (1849), he remarks that the b'hoy "gladly embraces the career of vulgar rowdyism—simply because he must have *some* career, and there is no other within his reach."[44] Yet the moral terms of this social portrait cannot comfortably embrace both economic dependence and autonomy, and Foster is forced to adopt an ambiguous middle ground: "The governing sentiment, pride and passion of the b'hoy is independence. . . . He abhors dependence, obligation, and exaggerates the feeling of self-reliance so much as to appear, on the surface, rude and boorish. But the appeal of helplessness or the cry of suffering unlocks his heart at once, whence all manner of good and tender and magnanimous qualities leap out" (*Gas-Light,* 105). Once again, sentiment emerges as the mark of a threatened autonomy; but in this case, sentiment is an unsatisfactory register of class. It was the menacing b'hoys, after all, who so unnerved New York's respectable citizens by brawling in fire companies or battling at Astor Place. Anxious writers would have to find a more sensitive way to render these shades of social and cultural rank.

Many did so by turning on the dependent poor. In *The Tenant-House* (1857),[45] Augustine Duganne tells the story of Foley's Barracks, a tenement row housing the most desperate New Yorkers. Like Denslow's rendering of New Orleans poverty, this neighborhood is far removed from the residence of the wealthy (and Jewish) landlord, Mordecai Kolephat; indeed, the novel's plot reunites Mordecai with a daughter kidnapped from him years before and deprived of her rightful social place. Yet despite its sympathy for many of its poor sufferers, the novel does not seek to punish Kolephat, who may be guilty of avarice but is equally victimized by a niece and her rakish lover, who plot his murder. Instead, the novel blames the pestilential atmosphere of the slums for an irresistible depravity. Like the cholera emitted from its hovels, Foley's Barracks is the site of social disease, and although the sources of the pestilence are moral, the novel holds forth little hope of a cure. Imagine children reared amid "filth" and "disease" (220) early inured to beggary and "swarming out upon the wharves and streets" to become "river-thieves," brawlers, or gamblers. Their neglected sisters, meanwhile, learn "the worst lessons at the tenderest years" until their "ways of wickedness . . . lead to early death" (219–20). The swarming poor creep miasmically over the city, until their "pestilence" (15) unites all in suffering. Duganne does not abandon all evangelical optimism. He can still claim that "brotherhood is not in the body, but in the soul" and that liberty is a matter of a "pure . . . heart" (291, 292). And he urges the "philanthropist" to consider how dim are these impoverished souls (293). But his loathsome characters experience few moral victories, and the novel's overriding sense is one of irrevocable menace. The "civilization" whose "commerce" has created these massive ills is unlikely to sweep them away (220).

A more extreme version of this anxiety is presented in Azel Roe's *How Could He Help It?* (1860).[46] Here, humanitarian sensibility spars with menacing poverty, and sensibility quits the ring. The stew of urban vice is now named Hunker's Alley, one of those "leprous spots . . . in which were congregated persons of all colors and characters" (48). The pestilential lair, not far removed from Milton's hell, is a place "where fallen humanity, in its most hideous forms, will send the thrill of horror through your veins" (87), and where "blacks and whites" are herded together like so many sheep (275). The emphasis on promiscuity, both physical and sexual, reflects the growing need of a middle-class audience to distance itself from the swarming poor. Where a generation before, social classes still mingled in urban neighborhoods, now the democratic nature of poverty was its greatest menace. Such skepticism helped to consolidate a middle class made anxious by its own dependency on a market that showed little pity for its numerous losers.

One of those losers in *How Could He Help It?* is the Jones family, and the novel uses their struggles to isolate the undeserving poor. Jasper Jones was a poor merchant, lacking the aggressiveness to succeed in international trade and failing as a small urban grocer. When his business woes exhaust him and he dies, his family is saddled with debt, and rather than face destitution, seventeen-year-old Herbert—"very fair, somewhat pale, but easily flushed, for his feelings were extremely sensitive" (17)—determines to take over the store. Despite his tender age, he receives the backing of two of his father's creditors, the firm of Granite and Blagg, who continue to nurture the boy until he has a prosperous dry goods shop in Maiden Lane. Clearly Herbert deserves their benevolence, for he wants to work diligently to avoid both the bankruptcy of his father and a "dependence upon relations" (36). With his sensitive self-reliance, he represents the hope of the middle class.

The moral spokesman of the novel is not Herbert Jones, however, but Mr. Blagg. Like Lawrence Newt of *Trumps,* Blagg is a sharp entrepreneur with a heart of gold. At the office he is all business, permitting no disorder and little leisure in the great pursuit of wealth. "Business was business," he declared. "It was a serious matter—great interests were at stake, and the mind must be intent upon it" (25). But Blagg is also a sentimentalist, with "a very sensitive heart; easily wounded, and very, very easily wrought up—melted—'broken all to pieces' " (24). His goodness leads him to back a more ambitious work of benevolence advanced by a wealthy young nephew, who designs to buy up and renovate a tenement and to fund its largely Irish inhabitants. The results are disastrous. An Irish worker sponsored in a manner similar to Herbert Jones drinks up his loan; the renovated tenement soon returns to its former decrepitude; and when Blagg arrives to lecture the tenants on responsibility, he is deluged with scalding slops. The world is "crooked," he tells his benevolent nephew. "You and I can't straighten it; all we can do is to ease it up a little—do it softly, too" (278).

Blagg's motto of proceeding "softly" captures his desire to preserve his pose of sensitive mediator while severely restricting the objects of his love. Poverty and wretchedness, he now claims, using a statistic formerly applied to bankrupt merchants, "is, in nine cases out of ten, the result of . . . depraved habits and depraved tastes. It seems to me . . . almost a necessity that there should be these leprous spots about, where human nature . . . may show out the terrible defilement there is in the heart of man. . . . Here they have none to shame them by a better life, and all the evil that is within comes out, runs riot, and sends odious incense up to heaven!" (332). The moral faults of the poor are now distinctive and serve to insulate the middle class, whose sensitivity marks the bounds of a worthy dependency. Sinking into poverty, as did Jasper Jones, may still be praiseworthy, if it is accomplished with a fitting heart. Reveling in poverty is evil because it stunts the capacity for sympathetic response. Blagg's critique of the poor has thus closed the circle of feeling by making it a distinctive attribute of the middle class.

By restricting the range of middle-class benevolence, works like *How Could He Help It?* were making palatable the new and permanent dependencies of their readers. As the republican ideal of economic autonomy faded, novelist-ideologues first redefined autonomy as sensibility, then used the intimacy of feeling to exclude the poor, who were incapable of such refinement. Ironically, benevolence, divorced from its universalizing agency, became a barrier that only the most sensitive could cross. And because membership in a social class was conceived primarily in terms of feeling, market fluctuations became less decisive. One could endure any number of bankruptcies and still rank oneself as self-reliant, for the emphasis was on private response. In this manner class itself was mystified, rendered a kind of voluntary association despite the most pressing constraints. Middle-class consciousness was stimulated by this new, hostile sympathy.

Racism was another way to insulate the middle classes. In *The City Merchant*, John Jones combines Whig ideology, antiabolitionism, and a yearning for sincerity to produce a unique version of antebellum autonomy. Set in 1836, months before the economic downturn, the novel follows the business decisions of Edgar Saxon, who has a family history of failure. Both his father and grandfather had been merchants, and "both had died bankrupts" (21)—the grandfather swallowed up by bad loans attending the Revolutionary War, the father falling victim to the derangement in credit following the War of 1812. Determined to avoid their fate and supported by a business manual bequeathed by his father, Saxon reads the signs of the times and begins operating on a cash-only basis while his competitors continue to rely on credit. The action throws a panic into his Philadelphia customers, who flock to his store to settle accounts. Even Nicholas Biddle, the embattled but "majestic" (72) president of the Bank of the United States, notices, and summoning Saxon to his mansion, lectures him on his social duties: "the men engaged in commerce . . . are the men who wield the greatest amount of capital; and if they assert their rights with unanimity they must become in reality . . . 'Merchant Princes' " (76). Wealth creates a distinct social experience, he argues. The sons of merchants enjoy an elite education, merchants fund the finest cultural institutions, and the best and brightest farmers' sons aspire to be merchants themselves. Wealth thus gives them the crucial autonomy that others lack, and a common experience, with common enemies, defines them as a "class" (79). Whether the nation will be overrun by a Jacksonian rabble or controlled by a Whig elite, claims Biddle, "there will be distinctions and classes in society" (80). Why shouldn't the merchant class be dominant?

Saxon says much the same in his own office. His distrust of bankers and politicians magnifies his desire for a class of benevolent merchants to assume "the exalted rank in society to which their intelligence and wealth will entitle them"

(33). Once again, "class" here does not yet have the signification of socioeconomic group, but more properly refers to occupation. Yet the class rhetoric surrounding the Bank War had a heightened meaning in the early 1850s, when urban Whig elites tried to consolidate power by aligning themselves with the Know-Nothing Party. *The City Merchant* advances that project by turning Saxon's contempt for credit into a social vision.

The occasion for that sharpened vision is the attack on Pennsylvania Hall. In May 1838, as Philadelphia reeled under the effects of the panic, the city's abolitionists opened a large lecture hall for the use of reform associations. The event heightened long-standing tensions between abolitionists and Philadelphia's elite and working classes, tensions that erupted in violence on the night of 17 May. A crowd of three thousand sacked and burned the hall, abetted by fire companies who did nothing to save the structure. The following day the Shelter for Colored Orphans was attacked, although the building was ultimately saved.[47] Jones uses the riot to focus the class anxieties aroused by the panic. As abolitionists gather around the hall, a black delegate insults Saxon's daughter. It takes Saxon's faithful Irish employee only a few hours to round up avengers, and the "villainous" place is consumed (139). When some nights later, Alice Saxon is kidnapped and surrounded by a black mob bent on retaliation, Saxon himself leads the bloody charge. Now "[m]any thousands" (190) are involved in the pitched battles, the whites urged on by the cry, "[I]f you are true Americans, and love your country . . . suppress the ——— negroes" (191). The deep economic depression following these race riots only underscores the peril of the city's merchant princes.

But who are the true Americans? The riots, as frightening as they seem, represent a deeper social problem equally evident in the panic. For the desire for racial sincerity is but a variant of the desire for fiscal purity. Although Saxon, like George Curtis's Lawrence Newt, seems inscrutable to business associates intent on paper wealth, his withdrawal from commerce is really a stand for true feeling. On the day he decides to retrench, for instance, he gives a private office "celebration, in a quiet and genteel manner," Saxon urging his employees to be "gay" and assuring them of his interest and "protection" (63–64). So, too, his rejection of vicious abolitionists and blacks helps him stake out a purified realm of social relations immune to the "frenzy" of "ardent spirits" (129)—reformist spirits, that is. Class anxieties are projected outward upon alien, destructive forces, a move that allows Saxon to redefine his chastened merchants as morally pure. The mysterious merchant truly embodies the gold standard of a vulnerable middle class.

John Jones's work captures the transitional nature of middle-class conscious-ness at midcentury. Portraying a "whig" (119), in the waning days of the Whig party, Jones attempted to shore up Saxon's social status through a network of alliances and exclusions. Philadelphia's working classes, relatively militant until the panic crushed their spirit, unite with their employers to meet the common threat. Alternatively, Saxon also embraces the wealthy but measures his distance from them through a skepticism of the market. Unlike his political allies, however, Jones's merchant is well schooled in the ethics of failure, and his awareness hinges on a subtle balancing act. Like a photosensitive lens constantly adapting to changes in light, Saxon can be sentimental or vindictive, prudent or aggressive depending upon audience, occasion, or circumstance. In the midst of overwhelming social forces, he adjusts by adhering to the democratic openness of his forebears yet punishing the democratic excesses of his contemporaries. African Americans, like the wretchedly poor, mark the outer bounds of social failure and thus shore up his own sense of independence. To be a responsible member of the merchant class, Saxon shows, is to transform fragility into power. Like other chastened merchants of the 1850s and '60s, Saxon turned weakness into an incipient language of class.

# CHAPTER 7

# Infinite Systems

⁊&

With their acerbic attacks on the poor, sentimental fictions at midcentury completed their cultural task. Having arisen in response to doubts about individual autonomy during market crises, these texts reimagined independence as a subtle form of yielding in which the actor responded to his milieu. That capacity, originally the hallmark of feminine sensibility, was gradually transferred, through a massive cultural experiment, from the privacy of domestic life to the conflicts of international trade, and thence to a domestic market where men came to adopt the "feminine" characteristics of transparency and compromise. By midcentury, critical fictions had refigured republican probity as active accommodation and turned autonomy into a refined defense of social class.

But despite the considerable changes that critical fictions helped to bring about, their effect, by the Civil War, was also to return to origins. For the ideological work of market narratives, from Crèvecoeur forward, was larger than an immediate response to crisis. More effectively than political rhetoric or journalism, these texts attempted to imagine the invisible agencies that wrought such devastating changes. Critical fictions captured, through a process of sentimental embodiment, the host of abstract forces, the larger system of relations, that haunted Americans' claims to autonomy. As Gordon Wood has argued, it was the nation's psychological resistance to those influences that spawned and sustained its paranoid style, the steadfast refusal "to embrace fully and unequivocally any notion that stressed the impersonal and collective nature of the workings of society." In offering microhistories of sentimental accommodation, critical fictions contributed to a new mode of understanding. Sentiment came to figure collective nature and the individual's altered role within a dominant order. These narratives rendered Adam Smith's "immense and infinite system" in comforting human terms. Under their influence, Americans came slowly to accept the new world they had made.[1]

The new world was more mechanistic, more anonymous, than its predecessor. Individuals, now, were increasingly seen as effects, not causes, as expressions of what William Graham Sumner called "[t]he great stream of time and earthly things . . . [that] sweep on just the same in spite of us."[2] That drift toward naturalism and the eclipse of the individual can be grasped through a revealing contrast in responses to economic crisis. After the panic of 1857, as James Huston has shown, almost every commentator blamed the problem on a gross lapse of authority by the nation's managers, who distorted an otherwise equitable system of exchange. The rise of large corporations like railroads insidiously "released managers from personal responsibility." Investors became greedy speculators, destroying currency exchange. And bankers turned ruthless oppressors, exacting payment "every discount day and reduc[ing] the community to the extremity of desperation." These popular explanations, rooted in an antebellum ethic of moral autonomy, saw personal action as the source of public life. Even though the "economic system" was to blame for the crisis, that system still retained a moral soul.[3]

Far different were economic analyses after the Civil War. In its survey of congressional testimony on the panic of 1873, Carroll Wright's Labor Bureau compiled a list of 174 causes under sixty-nine headings, ranging from expansion of credit and commercial crises to high telegraph rates and bad sanitation. Moral causes like corruption, extravagance, and intemperance remain, but they are vastly overshadowed by the dense array of "contradictory" causes that defy reduction to a simple formula. The panic of 1882 had a similar profile. In the Labor Bureau's first annual report, titled *Industrial Depressions,* moral causes like "lack of integrity" pale before a complex network of political, commercial, financial, and "mechanical" influences. Like his antebellum predecessors, Wright blames the depression on a "chain of causes, or rather a combination of coacting causes." But he goes on to assert that "no human device or combination of devices can be instituted powerful enough to prevent the recurrence of financial and commercial crises and industrial depressions."[4] Causation had shifted from the malevolent agent to the passionless system, an arena where individual virtue played an insignificant role. The anonymous market, not the energetic individual, had become the locus of economic crisis.

What role did feeling play in this new ideological structure? How could sentiment, the most intimate expression of private value, survive in an environment that seemed to obliterate feeling and humanity itself in its faceless operation? More particularly, how adaptable was the ideology of sentiment in the alien milieu of the postwar market? A final set of literary reflections, by a theorist of market crisis, might provide one answer. Ralph Waldo Emerson's *The Conduct of Life* (1860)[5] hews a passage to that new world with the emotional tools of the old. His essays suggest an end and a beginning for the sentimental apprehension of the market.

## Wealth

In his last collection of essays before the Civil War, Ralph Waldo Emerson attempted to reiterate old themes in a new key. *The Conduct of Life,* as Thomas Carlyle enthusiastically wrote, revealed a thinker "grown older, more pungent, piercing . . . into the deeps of a philosophy, wh[ic]h the vulgar has not, wh[ic]h hardly 3 men living *have,* yet dreamt of!"[6] As Carlyle implies, Emerson's calls for spiritual probity were now contained in searching analyses of Wealth and Power, of Fate, Freedom, and Culture, as if defining the coordinates of a more commanding self-reliance. Viewed in the context of his career, the essays seem to ratify Emerson's extraordinary success. Addressing a national market, commanding as much as nine hundred dollars per lecture series, he seemed to embody the self-reliant entrepreneur of culture and conscience he had long been urging on his readers. It is significant, then, that in one of the most wide-ranging essays in the volume, Emerson returns to the reflections on panic made at the beginning of his career:

> Bad times have a scientific value. These are occasions a good learner would not miss. As we go gladly to Faneuil Hall to be played upon by the stormy winds and strong fingers of enraged patriotism, so is a fanatical persecution, civil war, national bankruptcy or revolution more rich in the central tones than languid years of prosperity. What had been, ever since our memory, solid continent, yawns apart and discloses its composition and genesis. We learn geology the morning after the earthquake, on ghastly diagrams of cloven mountains, upheaved plains, and the dry bed of the sea. ("Considerations by the Way," 248–49)

The passage, a version of a journal entry for 22 May 1837,[7] underscores the rhetorical strategy of most of the essays in the volume (if not in Emerson's oeuvre): the wisdom derived from the balancing of opposites. But the reference to national bankruptcy also captures the enduring effects of impotence in an intensified strategy of power. In revisiting the significance of life after two decades of financial embarrassment, Emerson would be forced to redefine individualism itself.

A primary purpose of Emerson's volume, and one that has often drawn the fire of scholars, is the celebration of the new industrial order. Northern prosperity appeared to endorse a success ethic that harnessed "all grand and subtile things, minerals, gases, ethers, passions" as if the world were an inexhaustible "tool-chest" ("Wealth," 89). Such imagery allowed Emerson to reinvigorate the language of republicanism he had been using throughout his career, with its emphasis on privacy, integrity, and character. If the effect of the market revolution was to render men "consumer[s]," their fundamental identity remained that of producers who not only pay their debts but "ad[d] something to the common wealth" ("Wealth," 85). Those who establish worth through independent activity are also reaffirming character, since independence breeds virtue. "The subject of economy mixes itself with morals," Emerson declares in "Wealth," "inasmuch as it is a peremptory point of virtue that a man's independence be secured. Poverty demoralizes" (90). Manliness means founding faith in the determined, honest efforts of the individual, efforts the world will inevitably reward. What Emerson calls Power is the gravitational attraction of circumstance to force of character, the orbiting of events around an imperturbable will. "Men of sense esteem wealth to be the assimilation of nature to themselves," he claims ("Wealth," 92). "He who sees through the design, presides over it, and must will that which must be" ("Fate," 31). In passages such as these, the entrepreneur becomes a kind of Whitmanesque seer, embracing multitudes in his single-minded command of nature. That command, Emerson implies, is the inevitable effect of republican probity.

But the expanding American marketplace had raised potent challenges to republican control. Not all materials proved as pliant to industrial demand as the minerals and gases of nature. For prosperity also attracted European immigrants, and when the market sagged, Americans were forced to support the immigrant poor. "Again," Emerson laments, "it turns out that the largest proportion of crimes are committed by foreigners. . . . We cannot get rid of these people, and we cannot get rid of their will to be supported" ("Wealth," 108). Indeed, the swarming poor have given rise to a new term absent from Emerson's early essays: the "masses." "Masses are rude, lame, unmade, pernicious in their demands and influence," and almost immune to change. "The worst of charity is that the lives you are asked to preserve are not worth preserving. Masses! the calamity is the masses" ("Considerations," 237). The evil dollar that Emerson once reluctantly gave to the poor now pales before this far greater menace to charity, captured in the "little fatty face, pig-eye, and squat form" ("Fate," 16) of the diminished laborer, or the "guano"-laden destinies of the "German and Irish millions" (21). Here self-reliance seems hemmed in by the multitude of other selves crowding America's cities and leeching into its hinterlands. Echoing the novelists of urban poverty, Emerson defends an American faith by assailing the un-American poor.

Like unruly markets, the unruly masses seem to present ideological challenges far greater than the loss of social control. Alien influences—in cities, across oceans, from far-flung economies—imposed checks on moral autonomy. How was it possible, Emerson asks in the essays, for a system devised by commanding individuals to produce the means of their undoing? Boundless drive and authority, it seemed, had inspired an equally boundless resistance. In *The Conduct of Life,* Emerson seeks to respond to these problems by insisting on the truisms of liberalism, softened and refined by the rhetoric of sympathy. He attempts both to illuminate a global system of influences and to depict the moral agent in its reflected light. In doing so, he absorbs the imagery of feminine submissiveness into a new language of power. [8]

One way to explain challenges to individual power was to apprehend them, like Wright's Labor Bureau, within a larger array of forces. If individual power has inherent limits, Emerson contended, those limits are imposed by higher law. "Wealth brings with it its own checks and balances," he asserts with constitutional precision. "The basis of political economy is non-interference. The only safe rule is found in the self-adjusting meter of demand and supply" ("Wealth," 104). But where these old liberal verities might once have comforted, they are often overshadowed in the essays by an incipient pessimism, a bowing before cosmic forces that impose more checks than balances. Emerson deliberately creates this impression by opening with the essay "Fate," whose dark assertions about the insignificance of human effort seem to mock his earlier idealism. "Once we thought positive power was all. Now we learn that negative power, or circumstance, is half. Nature is the tyrannous circumstance, the thick skull, the sheathed snake . . . ; necessitated activity; violent direction" (20). As he does in subsequent essays, Emerson seeks to confine these perils by counterbalancing fateful circumstance with an equally potent liberty. To be free, under these severe conditions, is to be able to comprehend life's limits and focus one's curtailed powers. "Success goes thus invariably with a certain *plus* or positive power: an ounce of power must balance an ounce of weight." By "concentrating our force on one or a few points" ("Power," 73–74), we can overcome nature's inertia and reassert personal authority.

But what specific elements of character take best advantage of these moral mechanics? In a telling convergence of metaphors, Emerson equates the behavior of currency with the aptitudes of great men. Money, he claims in "Wealth," "is representative, and follows the nature and fortunes of the owner. The coin is a delicate meter of civil, social and moral changes" (100). Thus the value of a dollar, its moral significance, changes with the occupation, zeal, and circumstances of the laborer, so that the dollar of a farmer has more "force" than the dollar of a speculator. Money, in short, is morally sensitive and impressionable. Not surprisingly, the laws of money also apply to social relations: "All power is of one kind, a sharing of the nature of the world. The mind that is parallel with the laws of nature will be in the current of events and strong with their strength. One man is made of the same stuff of which events are made; is in sympathy with the course of things; can predict it. Whatever befalls, befalls him first; so that he is equal to whatever shall happen" ("Power," 58). To be in sympathy with the great forces of the world is to have an inner knowledge of their effects—to feel those effects intimately—and thus to react to them most sensitively. Money and personal authority are mirror images of the most important attribute of market culture, the ability to respond sympathetically to the world.

Like money, sympathy functions as a medium between the energies of individuals and a daunting mass of conditions and determinations. Indeed, for Emerson, the ability to register and submit to larger forces becomes a new measure of social power. The greatest minds, he insists, become so by making themselves most "impressionable" ("Fate," 47) to these currents, swayed almost involuntarily by the forces of nature. Emerson illustrates this premise in several ways. Reasserting the force of ideas, he claims that scientists merely register again and again the convergence of similar insights. "No one can read the history of astronomy," he claims, without concluding that figures like Copernicus and Newton had been anticipated by the likes of Empedocles and Pythagoras. "[E]ach had the same tense geometrical brain, . . . a mind parallel to the movement of the world" ("Fate," 23). Political figures like Bonaparte exercise the same measured power, "the pure sympathy with universal ends [that] is an infinite force" ("Fate," 33). And captains of industry like the Boston Associates assert their greatest effect by so harmonizing with the natural conditions of the area as to direct them. Thus, the most influential men are, "in . . . brain and performance, an explanation of the tillage, production, factories, banks, churches, ways of living and society" of their regions—so much so that, "if they were transparent, [they] would seem . . . not so much men as walking cities" ("Fate," 45). Powerful men, like solvent banknotes, are infinitely convertible, now reflecting, now conferring value on objects with which they are associated. Exquisitely attuned to their environment, they become the measure of all wealth.

This yielding expression of power, the authentic register of forces beyond the self, is the enduring sign of Emerson's own transformation. The self-reliance of his early career has been tempered, made to respond to the determining economic and political forces that would soon irrevocably alter the nation. That new sensibility, in turn, demanded a new sexual pliancy, a means of expressing masculine dominance through a submission that his culture still associated with women. Emerson responds to the need by blurring genders, merging sensibilities in what he calls "sex of mind": "In every company there is not only the active and passive sex, but in both men and women a deeper and more important *sex of mind,* namely the inventive or creative class of both men and women, and the uninventive or accepting class" ("Power," 59). Just as he seeks to transcend vulnerability by yielding to higher law, so Emerson seeks to overcome passivity by identifying a genderless spirit. Such inner activity, too subtle to be detected by the normal physical markers, allows the individual to remain active without activity, and to subscribe to an intrinsic "class" immune to the dislocations of society. At this deep level, to be wholly sympathetic is to lose almost all outward distinctions, all resistance to historical and physical change. But the inventive, creative class is also the perfect corporate citizen, anticipating and embodying the shaping forces of the world. Such individuals are both active and passive, male and female, both in and out of the game. Cultural innovators, they are shaped by the world they refine. Like many of his contemporaries, Emerson had found the means to respond to an increasing range of ethical restraints. By the magic of cultural fiction, yielding had become a form of control.

CHAPTER 1. *Legends of the Fall*

1. *Annals of Congress,* 25th Cong., 1st sess., 151, 152.

2. On figuring the market as female, see Terry Mulcaire, "Public Credit; or, The Feminization of Virtue in the Marketplace," *PMLA* 114 (1999): esp. 1030, 1034.

3. Fredric Jameson, *The Political Unconscious: Narrative as a Socially Symbolic Act* (Ithaca: Cornell University Press, 1981), 82.

4. Ann Douglas, *The Feminization of American Culture* (New York: Knopf, 1977), esp. 57–60; Jane Tompkins, *Sensational Designs: The Cultural Work of American Fiction, 1790–1860* (New York: Oxford University Press, 1985), 132; Nina Baym, *Woman's Fiction: A Guide to Novels by and about Women in America, 1820–1870* (Ithaca: Cornell University Press, 1978), 40, 47–49; Julia Stern, *The Plight of Feeling: Sympathy and Dissent in the Early American Novel* (Chicago: University of Chicago Press, 1997), 73, 190–93; Cathy Davidson, *Revolution and the Word: The Rise of the Novel in America* (New York: Oxford University Press, 1986), 147, 143. See also Philip Fisher, *Hard Facts: Setting and Form in the American Novel* (New York: Oxford University Press, 1985), 100–101; and Elizabeth Barnes, *States of Sympathy: Seduction and Democracy in the American Novel* (New York: Columbia University Press, 1997), 8–13.

5. Stern, *Plight of Feeling,* 6; Terry Eagleton, *Ideology: An Introduction* (London: Verso, 1991), 116; Michael Gilmore, *American Romanticism and the Marketplace* (Chicago: University of Chicago Press, 1985), 112.

6. Charles Sellers, *The Market Revolution: Jacksonian America, 1815–1846* (New York: Oxford University Press, 1991), 364–94; Douglas, *Feminization of American Culture,* 60; Ann Fabian, *Card Sharps, Dream Books, and Bucket Shops: Gambling in Nineteenth-Century America* (Ithaca: Cornell University Press, 1990), 12–107; Richard Brodhead, *Cultures of Letters: Scenes of Reading and Writing in Nineteenth-Century America* (Chicago: University of Chicago Press, 1993), 13–47; Gillian Brown, *Domestic Individualism: Imagining Self in Nineteenth-Century America* (Berkeley: University of California Press, 1990), 39–53 (citations on pp. 41 and 47); Susan Coultrap-McQuin, *Doing Literary*

*Business: American Women Writers in the Nineteenth Century* (Chapel Hill: University of North Carolina Press, 1990), 23, 38–48; Michael Newbury, *Figuring Authorship in Antebellum America* (Stanford: Stanford University Press, 1997), 19–157; Colin Campbell, *The Romantic Ethic and the Spirit of Modern Consumerism* (Oxford: Blackwell, 1987), 95; T. J. Jackson Lears, *Fables of Abundance: A Cultural History of Advertising in America* (New York: Basic Books, 1994), 46–53.

7. C. B. Macpherson, *The Political Theory of Possessive Individualism: Hobbes to Locke* (Oxford: Oxford University Press, 1962), 3; Steven Watts, *The Romance of Real Life: Charles Brockden Brown and the Origins of American Culture* (Baltimore: Johns Hopkins University Press, 1994), 20; Mulcaire, "Public Credit," 1035; Walter Benjamin, cited in Patrick Brantlinger, *Fictions of State: Culture and Credit in Britain, 1694–1994* (Ithaca: Cornell University Press, 1996), 148; Watts, *Romance of Real Life,* 77, 96. See also Robert Levine, *Conspiracy and Romance: Studies in Brockden Brown, Cooper, Hawthorne, and Melville* (Cambridge: Cambridge University Press, 1989), 32–39, 47–53; Carroll Smith-Rosenberg, "Domesticating 'Virtue': Coquettes and Revolutionaries in Young America," in *Literature and the Body: Essays on Populations and Persons,* ed. Elaine Scarry (Baltimore: Johns Hopkins University Press, 1988), 160–84; Karen Halttunen, *Confidence Men and Painted Women: A Study of Middle-Class Culture in America, 1830–1870* (New Haven: Yale University Press, 1982), 157, 163–67; Halttunen, " 'Domestic Differences': Competing Narratives of Womanhood in the Murder Trial of Lucretia Chapman," in *The Culture of Sentiment: Race, Gender, and Sentimentality in Nineteenth Century America,* ed. Shirley Samuels (New York: Oxford University Press, 1992), 39–57; Andrea Henderson, " 'An Embarrassing Subject': Use Value and Exchange Value in Early Gothic Characterization," in *At the Limits of Romanticism: Essays in Cultural, Feminist, and Materialist Criticism,* ed. Mary Favret and Nicola Watson (Bloomington: Indiana University Press, 1994), 225–45; and Elizabeth Jane Wall Hinds, *Private Property: Charles Brockden Brown's Gendered Economics of Virtue* (Newark: University of Delaware Press, 1997), 23, 44–67.

8. Liah Greenfield, *Nationalism: Five Roads to Modernity* (Cambridge: Harvard University Press, 1992), 11, cited in Brantlinger, *Fictions of State,* 17; Markman Ellis, *The Politics of Sensibility: Race, Gender and Commerce in the Sentimental Novel* (Cambridge: Cambridge University Press, 1996), 153; David Waldstreicher, *In the Midst of Perpetual Fetes: The Making of American Nationalism, 1776–1820* (Chapel Hill: University of North Carolina Press, 1997), 142, 1–2, 90–107; Shirley Samuels, *Romances of the Republic: Women, the Family, and Violence in the Literature of the Early American Nation* (New York: Oxford University Press, 1996), 12–20, 23–29, 46–54; Teresa Goddu, *Gothic America: Narrative, History, and Nation* (New York: Columbia University Press, 1997), 13–26, 94–105, 119–20; James Madison, *The Federalist: A Collection of Essays Written in Favor of the Constitution,* 2 vols. (New York: J. and A. M'Lean, 1788), vol. 1, no. 14, p. 84;

Samuels, *Romances of the Republic,* 12. See also Jay Fliegelman, *Prodigals and Pilgrims: The American Revolution against Patriarchal Authority, 1750–1800* (Cambridge: Cambridge University Press, 1982), 230–40; and Christine Holbo, "Imagination, Commerce, and the Politics of Associationism in Crèvecoeur's *Letters from an American Farmer,*" *Early American Literature* 32 (1997): 20–65.

9. Slavoj Zizek, *The Sublime Object of Ideology* (London: Verso, 1989), esp. 43, 71.

10. Raymond Williams, *Marxism and Literature* (Oxford: Oxford University Press, 1977), 130, 128, 130, 133, 134, 111. Glenn Hendler discusses structures of feeling in relation to antebellum literature—without, however, examining the dialectical nature of Williams's formulation. See *Public Sentiments: Structures of Feeling in Nineteenth-Century American Literature* (Chapel Hill: University of North Carolina Press, 2001), 10–11.

11. Raymond Williams, *The Sociology of Culture* (New York: Schocken, 1982), 29.

12. Michael McKeon, *The Origins of the English Novel, 1600–1740* (Baltimore: Johns Hopkins University Press, 1987), 215, 174, 223.

13. Although historians have often noted class frictions in America well before the Civil War, I will argue that class identifications were variable during this period and lacked the permanency and vehemence of the English experience. See pages 161–63, 202–3. For some treatments of colonial and antebellum class friction, see Gary Nash, *The Urban Crucible: Social Change, Political Consciousness, and the Origins of the American Revolution* (Cambridge: Harvard University Press, 1979), 340–84; Waldstreicher, *In the Midst of Perpetual Fetes,* esp. 37–39, 93–96, 242–45; Sellers, *Market Revolution,* esp. 10–33; and Sean Wilentz, *Chants Democratic: New York City and the Rise of the American Working Class, 1788–1850* (New York: Oxford University Press, 1984), esp. 97–103, and chapters 3–6.

14. Adam Smith, *The Theory of Moral Sentiments,* ed. D. D. Raphael and A. L. Macfie (Indianapolis: Liberty Fund, 1984), I.i.4.7, p. 22; I.i.4.6, p. 21; I.i.4.7, p. 22.

15. A. J. Greimas, *Structural Semantics: An Attempt at a Method,* trans. Daniele McDowell, Ronald Schleifer, and Alan Velie (Lincoln: University of Nebraska Press, 1983), xxxi–xxxvi, 23–25; Greimas and F. Rastier, "The Interaction of Semiotic Constraints," *Yale French Studies* 41 (1968): 86–105; Jameson, *Political Unconscious,* 118–49; see also 87–88, 95–97, 110.

16. John Higham, *From Boundlessness to Consolidation: The Transformation of American Culture, 1848–1860* (Ann Arbor, Mich.: William J. Clements Library, 1969), 6–13.

17. Nancy Armstrong, *Desire and Domestic Fiction: A Political History of the Novel* (New York: Oxford University Press, 1987), 9.

18. Anthony Giddens, *The Class Structure of the Advanced Societies* (New York: Harper and Row, 1973), 111.

19. Jameson, *Political Unconscious,* 9.

20. Anthony Giddens, *Central Problems in Social Theory: Action, Structure and Contradiction in Social Analysis* (Berkeley: University of California Press, 1979), 127–28.

21. Ralph Waldo Emerson, *The Journals and Miscellaneous Notebooks of Ralph Waldo Emerson,* ed. William Gilman et al., 16 vols. (Cambridge: Harvard University Press, 1960–82), 5:332–33.

22. David Hackett Fischer, *The Great Wave: Price Revolutions and the Rhythm of History* (New York: Oxford University Press, 1996), 168.

23. Wesley Mitchell, *Business Cycles: The Problem and Its Setting* (New York: National Bureau of Economic Research, 1927), 444; Herman Krooss, *American Economic Development: The Progress of a Business Civilization,* 3rd ed. (Englewood Cliffs, N.J.: Prentice-Hall, 1974), 15. An account of the panic of 1791–92 appears in Stanley Elkins and Eric McKitrick, *The Age of Federalism: The Early American Republic, 1788–1800* (New York: Oxford University Press, 1993), 270, 272–76.

24. *Richmond Enquirer,* 25 May 1819.

25. *Niles' Weekly Register,* 29 April 1837, 130.

26. *Harper's Weekly,* 10 October 1857; quoted in George Van Vleck, *The Panic of 1857: An Analytical Study* (New York: Columbia University Press, 1943), 73.

27. Quoted in Samuel Rezneck, "The Influence of Depression upon American Opinion, 1857–1859," *The Journal of Economic History* 2, no. 1 (1942): 8.

28. Joel Silbey, *The American Political Nation, 1838–1893* (Stanford: Stanford University Press, 1991), 92.

29. Henry Ward Beecher, "The Benefits and Evils of Commerce," *Hunt's Merchants' Magazine and Commercial Review* 24 (February 1851): 149.

30. "The True Mercantile Character," *Hunt's Merchants' Magazine and Commercial Review* 34 (January 1856): 61.

31. Tony Freyer, *Producers versus Capitalists: Constitutional Conflict in Antebellum America* (Charlottesville: University Press of Virginia, 1994), 39.

32. Sellers, *Market Revolution,* 364–94; Sean Wilentz, "Society, Politics, and the Market Revolution, 1815–1848," in *The New American History,* ed. Eric Foner (Philadelphia: Temple University Press, 1990), 51–71. See also the essays in *The Market Revolution in America: Social, Political, and Religious Expressions, 1800–1880,* ed. Melvyn Stokes and Stephen Conway (Charlottesville: University Press of Virginia, 1996).

33. See, for example, "The Chances of Mercantile Life," *The Merchants' Magazine and Commercial Review* 15 (November 1846), 475–77; "Bankruptcy-Banking," *Merchants' Magazine* 21 (November 1849), 513; "Traits of Trade—Laudable and Iniquitous," *Merchants' Magazine* 29 (September 1853), 315; "Insolvency among Merchants," *De Bow's Review* 16 (March 1854), 311. See also Edward Balleisen, "Navigating Failure: Bankruptcy in Antebellum America" (Ph.D. diss., Yale University, 1995), 1:6–7.

34. Gordon Wood, "Conspiracy and the Paranoid Style: Causality and Deceit in the Eighteenth Century," *William and Mary Quarterly* 39 (1982): 401–41.

35. Colin Campbell, *The Romantic Ethic and the Spirit of Modern Consumerism,* esp. 36–57.

36. Ralph Waldo Emerson, "Nature," in *The Collected Works of Ralph Waldo Emerson,* ed. Alfred Ferguson et al. (Cambridge: Harvard University Press, 1971–), 1:24.

CHAPTER 2. *Captives of the Market*

1. Drew McCoy, *The Elusive Republic: Political Economy in Jeffersonian America* (Chapel Hill: University of North Carolina Press, 1980), 89.

2. See also Gordon Wood, *The Radicalism of the American Revolution* (New York: Knopf, 1992), 336–41; Joyce Appleby, *Capitalism and a New Social Order: The Republican Vision of the 1790s* (New York: New York University Press, 1984); Idem, *Liberalism and Republicanism in the Historical Imagination* (Cambridge: Harvard University Press, 1992), 268–73; Michael Zuckerman, "A Different Thermidor: The Revolution beyond the American Revolution," in *The Transformation of Early American History: Society, Authority, and Ideology,* ed. James Henretta, Michael Kammen, and Stanley Katz (New York: Knopf, 1991), 185, 190.

3. Appleby, *Liberalism and Republicanism,* 216.

4. Wood, *Radicalism of the American Revolution,* 248–51.

5. T. H. Breen is the most careful student of the consumer revolution in colonial America. See the following articles: " 'Baubles of Britain': The American and Consumer Revolutions of the Eighteenth Century," *Past and Present* 119 (May 1988): 73–104; "An Empire of Goods: The Anglicization of Colonial America, 1690–1776," *Journal of British Studies* 25 (1986): 467–99; "The Meaning of 'Likeness': Portrait Painting in an Eighteenth-Century Consumer Society," *Word and Image* 6 (1990): 325–50; "The Meanings of Things: Interpreting the Consumer Economy of the Eighteenth Century," in *Consumption and the World of Goods,* ed. John Brewer and Roy Porter (London: Routledge, 1993), 249–60; and "Narrative of Commercial Life: Consumption, Ideology, and Community on the Eve of the American Revolution," *William and Mary Quarterly* 50 (1993): 471–501. See also Carole Shammas, *The Pre-Industrial Consumer in England and America* (Oxford: Oxford University Press, 1990); Neil McKendrick et al., *The Birth of a Consumer Society: The Commercialization of Eighteenth-Century England* (Bloomington: Indiana University Press, 1982); and Wood, *Radicalism of the American Revolution,* 135–37.

6. Claude Robin, *New Travels through North-America: In a Series of Letters* (Philadelphia: Bell, 1783), 36, 82.

7. John F. D. Smyth, *A Tour in the United States of America*, 2 vols. (London: For G. Robinson, 1784), 1:145. Subsequent citations will be given parenthetically in the text.

8. Thomas Anburey, *Travels through the Interior Parts of America. In a Series of Letters*, 2 vols. (London: Printed for W. Lane, 1789), 2:43.

9. [Thomas Brockway?], *The European Traveller in America, Contained in Three Letters to His Friend in London* (Hartford: Hudson and Goodwin, 1785), 15. Subsequent citations will be given parenthetically in the text.

10. *Charleston Morning Post, and Daily Advertiser*, 21 January 1786.

11. *The Worcester Magazine*, no. 25 (third week in September 1786): 301. See also Stephen Patterson, "The Federalist Reaction to Shays's Rebellion," in *In Debt to Shays: The Bicentennial of an Agrarian Rebellion*, ed. Robert Gross (Charlottesville: University Press of Virginia, 1993), 106–8.

12. *Boston Independent Chronicle*, 21 September 1786.

13. "Humorous Description of a Busy Wife," *Continental Journal, and the Weekly Advertiser*, 29 December 1785.

14. *Independent Chronicle*, 1 September 1785.

15. "The Warner, No. 1," *Independent Chronicle*, 16 June 1785.

16. "On Contentment," *Continental Journal*, 9 February 1786.

17. "An Essay on Contentment—and Caution in Prosperity," *Continental Journal*, 16 February 1786.

18. Jean-Christophe Agnew, *Worlds Apart: The Market and the Theater in Anglo-American Thought, 1550–1750* (Cambridge: Cambridge University Press, 1986), 4.

19. "On Contentment," *Continental Journal*.

20. *Hartford American Mercury*, 26 December 1785.

21. "The Warner, No. 9," *Independent Chronicle*, 19 October 1786.

22. "Katoptes," "For the *Hampshire Gazette*, printed at Northampton, Dec. 13, 1786," *Independent Chronicle*, 28 December 1786.

23. "Political Paragraphs. Massachusetts," *Connecticut Courant*, 27 November 1786.

24. *Independent Chronicle*, 1 March 1787.

25. "Passion Triumphant over Reason. A Parable," *The Norwich Packet and the Country Journal*, 5 April 1787.

26. "Answer of the Town of Greenwich to the Circular Letter from Boston," *The Worcester Magazine* 2, no. 35 (last week in November 1786): 423.

27. Ibid., no. 25 (third week in September 1786): 301; No. 27 (first week in October 1786): 322.

28. *Continental Journal and the Weekly Advertiser*, 13 April 1786.

29. "Antispumatist," *Independent Chronicle*, 28 October 1784.

30. *Independent Chronicle*, 1 September 1785.

31.  Ibid., 1 March 1787.

32.  The *Norwich Packet,* 12 January 1786. The narrative also appeared in the follow-ing newspapers: *New York Daily Advertiser,* 19 December 1785; *Philadelphia Freeman's Journal,* 14 December 1785; *Middlesex Gazette* (Middletown, Conn.), 3 January 1786; *Hartford American Mercury,* 2 January 1786. It was reprinted as a pamphlet titled *A True and Wonderful Narrative of the Surprising Captivity and Remarkable Deliverance of Mrs. Francis Scott* (Boston: Russell, 1786), and embellished by "a Number of Passages of Sacred Writ . . . for the Benefit of the pious Reader." Citations, from the pamphlet, will be given parenthetically in the text.

33.  "A Contented Subject," *Independent Chronicle,* 28 September 1786.

34.  Norman Grabo, "Crèvecoeur's American: Beginning the World Anew," *William and Mary Quarterly* 48 (1991): 164; Myra Jehlen, "J. Hector St. John de Crèvecoeur: A Monarcho-Anarchist in Revolutionary America," *American Quarterly* 31 (1979): 221. See also Marcus Cunliffe, "Crèvecoeur Revisited," *American Studies* 9 (1975): 135, 139; Bernard Chevignard, "St. John de Crèvecoeur in the Looking Glass: *Letters from an American Farmer* and the Making of a Man of Letters," *Early American Literature* 19 (1984): 176–77; A. W. Plumstead, "Crèvecoeur: A 'Man of Sorrows' and the American Revolution," *Massachusetts Review* 17 (1976): 299; Mary Rucker, "Crèvecoeur's *Letters* and Enlightenment Doctrine," *Early American Literature* 13 (1978): 195–208.

35.  J. Hector St. John [de Crèvecoeur], *Letters from an American Farmer* (London: Printed for T. Davies: 1782), 50. Subsequent citations will be given parenthetically in the text.

36.  Richard Halpern, *The Poetics of Primitive Accumulation: English Renaissance Culture and the Genealogy of Capital* (Ithaca: Cornell University Press, 1991), 158.

37.  See Elayne Rapping, "Theory and Experience in Crèvecoeur's America," *American Quarterly* 19 (1967): 711–13; Robert Winston, " 'Strange Order of Things!': The Journey to Chaos in *Letters from an American Farmer,*" *Early American Literature* 19 (1984/85): 258–61; James Mohr, "Calculated Disillusionment: Crèvecoeur's *Letters* Reconsidered," *South Atlantic Quarterly* 69 (1970): 358–60.

38.  Mary Louise Pratt, *Imperial Eyes: Travel Writing and Transculturation* (London: Routledge, 1992), 29–30.

39.  Clifford Geertz, "Ritual and Social Change: A Javanese Example," in *The Interpretation of Cultures* (New York: Basic Books, 1973), 146–62. For an American context, see Richard White, *The Middle Ground: Indians, Empires, and Republics in the Great Lakes Region, 1650–1815* (Cambridge: Cambridge University Press, 1991), esp. ix–x, 50–93.

40.  Joyce Appleby, "New Cultural Heroes in the Early National Period," in *The Culture of the Market: Historical Essays,* ed. Thomas L. Haskell and Richard Teichgraeber III (Cambridge: Cambridge University Press, 1993), 165.

41. Colin Campbell, *The Romantic Ethic and the Spirit of Modern Consumerism* (Oxford: Blackwell, 1987), 69–71, 77–78.

42. Olaudah Equiano, *The Interesting Narrative of the Life of Olaudah Equiano, or Gustavus Vassa, the African. Written by Himself,* 2 vols. (New York: Durell, 1791), 1:161. Subsequent citations from this first American edition will be given parenthetically in the text.

43. John Milton, *Paradise Lost, Complete Poems and Major Prose,* ed. Merritt Hughes (Indianapolis: Odyssey, 1957), II.271.

44. Houston Baker, *Blues, Ideology, and Afro-American Literature: A Vernacular Theory* (Chicago: University of Chicago Press, 1984), 38. For modern critiques, see Frances Foster, *Witnessing Slavery: The Development of Ante-bellum Slave Narratives* (Westport, Conn.: Greenwood, 1979), 49; Keith Sandiford, *Measuring the Moment: Strategies of Protest in Eighteenth-Century Afro-English Writing* (Selinsgrove, Pa.: Susquehanna University Press, 1988), 147; Chinosole, "Tryin' to Get Over: Narrative Posture in Equiano's Autobiography," in *The Art of Slave Narrative,* ed. John Sekora and Darwin Turner (Macomb: Western Illinois University Press, 1982), 51; and Marion Rust, "The Subaltern As Imperialist: Speaking of Olaudah Equiano," in *Passing and the Fictions of Identity,* ed. Elaine Ginsberg (Durham, N.C.: Duke University Press, 1996), 21–36. For a more favorable response, see William Andrews, "The First Fifty Years of the Slave Narrative, 1760–1810," in *Art of Slave Narrative,* 21. On Anglo-African trade as a "commercial utopia," see Baker, *Blues, Ideology, and Afro-American Literature,* 38.

45. Charlotte Sussman, *Consuming Anxieties: Consumer Protest, Gender, and British Slavery, 1713–1833* (Stanford: Stanford University Press, 2000), 14, 43, 24.

46. Philip Curtin, *The Image of Africa: British Ideas and Action, 1780–1850* (Madison: University of Wisconsin Press, 1964), viii; Thomas Astley, *A New General Collection of Voyages and Travels,* 4 vols. (London: printed for T. Astley, 1745–47), 3:98, 2:265.

47. John Corry, *Observations upon the Windward Coast of Africa . . .* (London: G. and W. Nicol and James Asperne, 1807), 66.

48. Astley, *New General Collection,* 3:16.

49. Adiele Afigbo, *Ropes of Sand: Studies in Igbo History and Culture* (Ibadan: Oxford University Press, 1981), 147–48, 150. For the provocative argument that Equiano's childhood memories were fabricated by a well-read American, see Vincent Carretta, "Olaudah Equiano or Gustavas Vassa? New Light on an Eighteenth-Century Question of Identity," *Slavery and Abolition* 20, no. 3 (1999): 96–105.

50. Afigbo, *Ropes of Sand,* 152.

51. J. R. Ward, *British West Indian Slavery, 1750–1834: The Process of Amelioration* (Oxford: Clarendon Press, 1988), 125.

52. Breen, "Empire of Goods," 489.

53. Baker, *Blues, Ideology, and Afro-American Literature,* 35–36.

54. Karl Marx, *Capital: A Critical Analysis of Capitalist Production,* trans. Samuel Moore and Edward Aveling, ed. Friedrich Engels (New York: International, 1947), 1:55.

55. Marx, *Grundrisse: Foundations of the Critique of Political Economy,* trans. Martin Nicolaus (New York: Random House, 1973), 141, 133.

56. Henry Louis Gates Jr., *The Signifying Monkey: A Theory of African-American Literary Criticism* (New York: Oxford University Press, 1988), 155–57.

57. Akiyo Ito, "Olaudah Equiano and the New York Artisans: The First American Edition of *The Interesting Narrative . . . ,*" *Early American Literature* 32 (1997): 89.

58. Orlando Patterson, *Slavery and Social Death: A Comparative Study* (Cambridge: Harvard University Press, 1982), 294.

59. Robert Allison, "Introduction," in *The Interesting Narrative of the Life of Olaudah Equiano,* ed. Robert Allison (New York: Bedford, 1995), 7.

60. Thomas Haskell, "Capitalism and the Origins of the Humanitarian Sensibility, Part 2," in *The Antislavery Debate: Capitalism and Abolitionism As a Problem in Historical Interpretation,* ed. Thomas Bender (Berkeley: University of California Press, 1992), 136–60.

61. Cited in Allison, ed., *Interesting Narrative,* 194.


CHAPTER 3. *Lovers and Citizens*

1. "The Impressed Seaman," *Philadelphia Minerva,* 21 October 1797.

2. *Philadelphia Minerva,* 28 October 1797.

3. John Dwyer, *The Age of the Passions: An Interpretation of Adam Smith and Scottish Enlightenment Culture* (East Linton, Scotland: Tuckwell, 1998), 20.

4. Ibid., 21; Adam Smith, *The Theory of Moral Sentiments,* ed. D. D. Raphael and A. L. Macfie (Indianapolis: Liberty Fund, 1984), I.i.4.7, p. 22.

5. "Brutus, No. III," *New-York Journal, and Weekly Register,* 15 November 1787.

6. [Nicholas Collin,] "An Essay on the Means of Promoting Federal Sentiments in the United States, by a Foreign Spectator," The *Independent Gazeteer; or, the Chronicle of Freedom,* 4 September 1787.

7. Ibid., 6 September 1787.

8. Ibid., 4 September 1787.

9. James Madison, *The Federalist: A Collection of Essays Written in Favor of the Constitution,* 2 vols. (New York: J. and A. M'Lean, 1788), vol. 1, no. 35, p. 216. Subsequent citations from this edition will be given parenthetically in the text.

10. See Robert H. Wiebe, *The Opening of American Society: From the Adoption of the Constitution to the Eve of Disunion* (New York: Knopf, 1984), esp. 257–375.

11.  J. G. A. Pocock, "The Mobility of Property and the Rise of Eighteenth-Century Sociology," in *Theories of Property: Aristotle to the Present,* ed. Anthony Parel and Thomas Flanagan (Waterloo, Ontario: Wilfred Laurier University Press, 1979), 147; cited in Jean-Christophe Agnew, *Worlds Apart: The Market and the Theater in Anglo-American Thought, 1550–1750* (Cambridge: Cambridge University Press, 1986), 175.

12.  E. James Ferguson, *The Power of the Purse: A History of American Finance, 1776–1790* (Chapel Hill: University of North Carolina Press, 1961), 330.

13.  *Annals of Congress,* 1st Cong., 2nd sess., 1196–97. Citations from this debate will be given parenthetically in the text. The debate appears in volume 2 of *Debates and Proceedings in the Congress of the United States* (Washington: Gales and Seaton, 1834).

14.  Pelatiah Webster, "A Plea for the Poor Soldiers," in *Political Essays on the Nature and Operation of Money, Public Finances and Other Subjects* (1791; reprint, New York: Franklin, 1969), 325.

15.  Jay Fliegelman, *Prodigals and Pilgrims: The American Revolution against Patriarchal Authority, 1750–1800* (Cambridge: Cambridge University Press, 1982), 200.

16.  Pelatiah Webster, "A Seventh Essay on Free Trade and Finance," in *Political Essays,* 297.

17.  John Swanwick, "(Circular.)," (Philadelphia: n.p., 1797), 1. Subsequent citations will be given parenthetically in the text.

18.  "From the Weekly Oracle," *Norwich Packet,* 4 May 1797.

19.  *Annals of Congress,* 4th Cong., 2nd sess., 1621.

20.  "The Uniform Federalist, No. II," *National Gazette,* 8 December 1792.

21.  *The Literary Museum,* June 1797, 315.

22.  *Annals of Congress,* 9th Cong., 1st sess., 755. Subsequent citations from this debate will be given parenthetically in the text.

23.  "Memorial of the Merchants and Traders of the City of Philadelphia," *Annals of Congress,* Appendix to 9th Cong., 817.

24.  "The Memorial of the President and Directors of the South Carolina Insurance Company . . . ," Appendix to 9th Cong., 823.

25.  "Memorial of the Merchants of New York," Appendix to 9th Cong., 813.

26.  *Annals of Congress,* 9th Cong., 1st sess., 733, 808, 734.

27.  "Boston Memorial," Appendix to 9th Cong., 890; "Memorial of the Merchants of New York," 812.

28.  Toby Ditz, "Shipwrecked, or, Masculinity Imperiled: Mercantile Representations of Failure and the Gendered Self in Eighteenth-Century Philadelphia," *The Journal of American History* 81 (1994): 51–80.

29.  Ibid., 72.

30.  *Annals of Congress,* 9th Cong., 1st sess., 722.

31.  Ibid., 648.

32. "Memorial of the Merchants of New York," 817.

33. *Boston Patriot,* 29 November 1809.

34. "Maria; or, The Seduction," *The New-York Weekly Magazine,* 26 October 1796, 131.

35. "The History of Melidor and Clarinda; or, The Progress of Infidelity," *The Universal Asylum and Columbian Magazine,* November 1791, 323.

36. *Sincerity; A Novel in a Series of Original Letters, Boston Weekly Magazine; or, Ladies' and Gentlemen's Miscellany,* 5 November 1803, 8.

37. Ditz, "Shipwrecked," 68.

38. *Margaretta,* hitherto assumed to have an anonymous author, first appeared in Isaac Newton Ralston's New York *Lady's Monitor* on 12 September 1801 and ran for four issues (12 September, 19 September, 26 September, and 3 October), before Ralston handed over publication of the journal to P. Heard and the serialization ceased. In a show of literary force comparable to Charles Brockden Brown's domination of the Philadelphia *Weekly Magazine* in 1798, Read also serialized *Monima,* which Ralston subsequently saw into print, and an essay titled "A Second Vindication of the Rights of Women," of which two installments survive (22 August and 5 September 1801). Citations from "A Second Vindication" will be given parenthetically in the text.

39. Martha Meredith Read, *Margaretta; or, The Intricacies of the Heart* (Charleston: Morford, 1807). Citations will be given parenthetically in the text.

40. Michael McKeon, *The Origins of the English Novel, 1600–1740* (Baltimore: Johns Hopkins University Press, 1987), 131–33, 171, 212–13.

41. Colin Campbell, *The Romantic Ethic and the Spirit of Modern Consumerism* (Oxford: Blackwell, 1987), 151–52.

42. Anne Dalke, "Original Vice: The Political Implications of Incest in the Early American Novel," *Early American Literature* 23 (1988): 188–201; Glenn Hendler, "The Limits of Sympathy: Louisa May Alcott and the Sentimental Novel," *American Literary History* 3 (1991): 688–90; James Twitchell, *Forbidden Partners: The Incest Taboo in Modern Culture* (New York: Columbia University Press, 1987), 188; Elizabeth Hinds, *Private Property: Charles Brockden Brown's Gendered Economics of Virtue* (Newark: University of Delaware Press, 1997), 29, 104–6; Julia Stern, *The Plight of Feeling: Sympathy and Dissent in the Early American Novel* (Chicago: University of Chicago Press, 1997), 28.

43. "Memorial of the Merchants of New York," 807.

44. Cathy Davidson, *Revolution and the Word: The Rise of the Novel in America* (New York: Oxford University Press, 1986), 222, 226, 222.

45. Ibid., 230.

46. Mitchell published the original Alonzo and Melissa tale in his Poughkeepsie newspaper, *Political Barometer,* from 5 June to 30 October 1804. In the concluding installment he confessed that some of his scenes were "hurried over with too much

rapidity for the *contour* of a perfect novel," but promised, with greater space, both to enhance the details and include a European narrative (*Political Barometer,* 30 October 1804). At the end of August 1806 Mitchell sold the newspaper, moved to Albany, and began publishing *Republican Crisis,* selling it in November 1807. During the period of the embargo and trade crises he was without a newspaper and must have been rewriting *The Asylum,* a copyright for which was filed on 12 December 1810. The novel was published on or about 2 October 1811 and advertised in the *Political Barometer* on 11 November 1811. See *Dictionary of American Biography* 13:48–49. All citations from the novel will be from the completed text, *The Asylum; or, Alonzo and Melissa. An American Tale, Founded on Fact,* 2 vols. (Poughkeepsie: Nelson, 1811), and will be given parenthetically.

47. Bradford Perkins, *Prologue to War: England and the United States, 1805–1812* (Berkeley: University of California Press, 1961), 234.

48. Reported in the *Independent Chronicle,* 16 August 1810.

49. Cited in Perkins, *Prologue to War,* 238.

50. Ibid., 223.

51. See Drew McCoy, *The Elusive Republic: Political Economy in Jeffersonian America* (Chapel Hill: University of North Carolina Press, 1980), esp. 86–90.

52. Perkins, *Prologue to War,* 226.

53. Reported in the *Northern Whig,* 5 December 1809.

54. *Annals of Congress,* 11th Cong., 2nd sess., 798.

55. Ibid., 768, 887.

56. Reported in the *Boston Patriot,* 13 January 1810.

57. *Northern Whig,* 26 December 1809.

58. *Alexandria Daily Gazette, Commercial and Political,* 7 June 1810; George Grennell Jr., *An Oration Pronounced at Northampton, on the Anniversary of American Independence, 1811* (Northampton, Mass.: Printed by William Butler, 1811), 19; William Bostwick Banister, *An Oration Delivered at Newburyport . . .* (Newburyport, Mass.: Allen, 1809), 15.

59. Banister, *Oration Delivered at Newburyport,* 16.

60. *Alexandria Daily Gazette,* 3 May 1810.

61. Robert Hartshorne Bowne to Hil[lesi?] Shaller, 3 March 1808, Bowne Letterbook, vol. 1, 314–15, New-York Historical Society.

62. William Jones to Mssrs. Thomas Mullett and J. J. Evans, 2 October 1811, Jones and Clark Papers, letters, folder 9, Historical Society of Pennsylvania.

63. William Jones to David Lenox, 29 January 1811, Jones and Clark Papers, letters, folder 9.

64. Edward Gernon to Richard Gernon, 1 September 1808, Gernon and Keating Papers, Historical Society of Pennsylvania.

65. Edward Gernon to Richard Gernon, 12 June 1809, Gernon and Keating Papers.

66. Thomas Haskell, "Capitalism and the Origin of the Humanitarian Sensibility, Part 2," in *The Antislavery Debate: Capitalism and Abolitionism As a Problem in Historical Interpretation,* ed. Thomas Bender (Berkeley: University of California Press, 1992), 151.

67. *Annals of Congress,* 11th Cong., 1st sess., 724.

68. *Alexandria Daily Gazette,* 20 December 1809.

69. *Northern Whig,* 25 May 1810.

70. *Alexandria Daily Gazette,* 18 December 1809. See Agnew, *Worlds Apart,* esp. 189–90.

71. *Columbian Centinel,* 3 January 1810.

72. *Republican Crisis,* 11 November 1806.

73. Richard Price, *Observations on the Importance of the American Revolution, and the Means of Making It a Benefit to the World* (1785; reprint, Amherst, N.H.: Cushing, 1805), 57.

74. Benjamin A. Markley, *An Oration Delivered on 4th July, 1809 . . .* (Charleston: Hoff, 1809), 5, 6.

75. Charles Glidden Haines, *An Oration, Pronounced at the Request of the Republican Citizens of Concord* (Concord: I. and W. R. Hill, 1811), 14.

76. For a discussion of how later nineteenth-century thinkers portrayed American capitalism as a balanced alternative to European excess, see Dorothy Ross, *The Origins of American Social Science* (Cambridge: Cambridge University Press, 1991), 65–66, 121–22, 202–3, 387–88.

77. Michael Gardiner, *The Dialogics of Critique: M. M. Bakhtin and the Theory of Ideology* (London: Routledge, 1992), esp. 66.

78. Cited in Charles Sellers, *The Market Revolution: Jacksonian America, 1815–1846* (New York: Oxford University Press, 1991), 138–39.

79. John R. Nelson Jr., *Liberty and Property: Political Economy and Policymaking in the New Nation, 1789–1812* (Baltimore: Johns Hopkins University Press, 1987), 153–61; McCoy, *Elusive Republic,* 217–48; Ann Douglas, *Feminization of American Culture* (New York: Knopf, 1977), 50–51; Merrill D. Peterson, *Thomas Jefferson and the New Nation* (New York: Oxford University Press, 1970), 514–15. But Peterson also charges the embargo with damaging the economy for the following twenty-five years (917).

80. Jefferson to Col. David Humphreys, 20 January 1809, Jefferson Papers, Library of Congress, reel 71, no. 32843.

81. Jefferson to Philadelphia Democratic Republicans, 25 May 1808, Jefferson Papers, reel 67, no. 31480.

82. Samuel Harrison to Jefferson, 28 May 1808, Jefferson Papers, reel 67, no. 31494.

83. Jefferson to Thomas Leiper, 21 January 1809, Jefferson Papers, reel 71, no. 32853, p. 2.

84.  Charles Brockden Brown, *An Address to the Congress of the United States on the Utility and Justice of Restrictions upon Foreign Commerce* (Philadelphia: Conrad, 1809), 41. Subsequent citations will be given parenthetically in the text.

85.  "Protection to the Manufacturers of Cotton Fabrics," *Annals of Congress*, Appendix to the 14th Cong., 1st sess., 1671.

86.  *Annals of Congress*, 14th Cong., 1st sess., 1334.

87.  "Protection to the Manufacturers of Cotton Fabrics," Appendix to the 14th Cong., 1st sess., 1668.

88.  Selah North, *An Oration Delivered at Goshen, July 4th, 1817* (Hartford: Bolles, 1817), 12–13.

89.  *Annals of Congress*, 18th Cong., 1st sess., 1858.

90.  Jonathan Maxcy, *A Discourse Delivered in the Chapel of the South-Carolina College, July 4th, A. D. 1819*, 2nd ed. (Columbia, S.C.: Printed at the State Gazette Office, 1819), 15.

91.  Samuel Putnam Waldo, *The Tour of James Monroe, President of the United States, through the Northern and Eastern States, in 1817* (Hartford: Andrus, 1819), 226–27. On Monroe's sentimental nationalism, see Waldstreicher, *In the Midst of Perpetual Fetes*, 298–302.

92.  *Boston Commercial Gazette*, 14 July 1817.

93.  *Niles' Weekly Register*, 7 June 1817, 239.

94.  *Boston Commercial Gazette*, 14 July 1817.

95.  Ibid., 7 August 1817.

96.  Steven Watts, *The Republic Reborn: War and the Making of Liberal America, 1790–1820* (Baltimore: Johns Hopkins University Press, 1987), esp. 6–10, 101–7, 151–60.

97.  North, "Oration Delivered at Goshen," 12.

98.  Richard Price, *Observations on the Importance of the American Revolution, and the Means of Making It a Benefit to the World* (1785; reprint, Amherst, N.H.: Cushing, 1805), 58.

99.  Daniel Raymond, *Thoughts on Political Economy* (Baltimore: F. Lucas Jr., 1820), 123.

100.  Ross, *Origins of American Social Science*, 66.

101.  *The Female Marine*, 10th ed. ([Boston?]: Printed for the Proprietor [N. Coverly Jr.?], 1816); *The Surprising Adventures of Almira Paul* (Boston: N. Coverly Jr., 1816). Subsequent citations, unless otherwise noted, will be from these editions. As Daniel A. Cohen notes, the "tenth edition" of *The Female Marine* is the most complete of eight that have come down to us, many in fragmentary form. See " 'The Female Marine' in an Era of Good Feelings: Cross-Dressing and the 'Genius' of Nathaniel Coverly, Jr.," *Proceedings of the American Antiquarian Society* 103, part 2 (October 1993): 369. Cohen gives a more extended reading of these texts in his introduction to *The Female Marine and Related Works*, ed. Daniel Cohen (Amherst: University of Massachusetts Press, 1997), 1–45.

102.   "Lucy Brewer (1793–?) was the first woman to write about her experiences in a disguise autobiography," states *The Oxford Companion to Women's Writing in the United States,* ed. Cathy Davidson and Linda Wagner-Martin (New York: Oxford University Press, 1995), 223.

103.   Cohen, " 'Female Marine,' " 365.

104.   "Lucy West," in *The Awful Beacon to the Rising Generation of Both Sexes* (Boston: N. Coverly Jr., 1816), 60. Subsequent citations will be given parenthetically in the text.

105.   Steven Watts, *The Republic Reborn: War and the Making of Liberal America, 1790–1820* (Baltimore: Johns Hopkins University Press, 1987), 170. For an opposing view, stressing the resourcefulness of early Americans, see Joyce Appleby, *Inheriting the Revolution: The First Generation of Americans* (Cambridge: Harvard University Press, 2000), esp. chapters 3 and 4.

106.   Fredric Jameson, *The Political Unconscious: Narrative As a Socially Symbolic Act* (Ithaca: Cornell University Press, 1981), 83.

107.   Ralph Waldo Emerson, *The Collected Works of Ralph Waldo Emerson,* ed. Alfred Ferguson et al. (Cambridge: Harvard University Press, 1971–), 2:81.

108.   David M. Robinson, *Emerson and the Conduct of Life: Pragmatism and Ethical Purpose in the Later Work* (Cambridge: Cambridge University Press, 1993), 18, 26.

109.   Ralph Waldo Emerson, "Compensation," in *Collected Works,* 2:70. For the nineteenth-century use of oceanic metaphors to imagine a liberal order, see Ross, *Origins of American Social Science,* 65–66 and 121–22.

CHAPTER 4.   *Exchange Values*

1.   Peter Temin, *The Jacksonian Economy* (New York: Norton, 1969), 156–65; Gary Browne, "Eastern Merchants and Their Southwestern Collections during the Panic and Deflation, 1837–1843," *Southern Studies* 19 (1980): 315, 321. Assessments of the panic's greater severity include Bray Hammond, *Banks and Politics in America, from the Revolution to the Civil War* (Princeton: Princeton University Press, 1957), 529; Douglass North, *The Economic Growth of the United States, 1790–1860* (Englewood Cliffs, N.J.: Prentice-Hall, 1961), 202; Sean Wilentz, *Chants Democratic: New York City and the Rise of the American Working Class, 1788–1850* (New York: Oxford University Press, 1984), 299–301; Samuel Rezneck, "The Social History of an American Depression, 1837–1843," in *Business Depressions and Financial Panics: Essays in American Business and Economic History* (Westport, Conn.: Greenwood, 1968), 75–98. Edward Balleisen offers a deft summary of both views. See "Navigating Failure: Bankruptcy in Antebellum America," Ph.D. diss., Yale University, 1995, 1:79–108.

2.   *Merchants' Magazine and Commercial Review* 2, no. 3 (March 1840): 216.

3. Ibid. 1, no. 1 (July 1839): 45, 46.

4. Ibid. 1, no. 6 (December 1839): 515.

5. *Graham's Magazine* 28, no. 5 (May 1841): 239. A similar association appeared in a story titled "Wall Street" in the lady's magazine *The Artist* (April 1843), which described "the whirlpool which engulpfs [*sic*] most of the fortunes thrown up by the continuous torrent of business which sweeps over a mighty continent" (72).

6. *Congressional Globe, Appendix,* 25th Cong., 1st sess., 175.

7. Ibid., 169.

8. *Richmond Enquirer,* 9 June 1837.

9. "The Moral of the Crisis," *United States Magazine and Democratic Review,* October 1837, 115, 114. Subsequent citations will be given parenthetically in the text.

10. "Harry O'Blank," *Godey's Lady's Book,* December 1837. Citations will be given parenthetically in the text.

11. John Ashworth, *"Agrarians" and "Aristocrats": Party Political Ideology in the United States, 1837–1846* (London: Royal Historical Society, 1983), 50, 111–13.

12. *Annals of Congress,* 25th Cong., 1st sess., 155.

13. Michael Rogin, *Fathers and Children: Andrew Jackson and the Subjugation of the American Indian* (New York: Knopf, 1975), 251–52, 267, 274–75; Michael Gilmore, *American Romanticism and the Marketplace* (Chicago: University of Chicago Press, 1985), esp. 21–34; Marvin Meyers, *The Jacksonian Persuasion: Politics and Belief* (Stanford: Stanford University Press, 1957), 22–23; Fred Somkin, *Unquiet Eagle: Memory and Desire in the Idea of American Freedom, 1815–1860* (Ithaca: Cornell University Press, 1967), 6–7.

14. Philip Hone, *The Diary of Philip Hone, 1828–1851,* ed. Bayard Tuckerman, 2 vols. (New York: Dodd, Mead, 1889), 1:264. Citations will be given parenthetically in the text.

15. *Congressional Globe,* 26th Cong., 1st sess., 799. Subsequent citations from this debate will be given parenthetically in the text.

16. On the association of debt and moral "stain," see Toby Ditz, "Shipwrecked; or, Masculinity Imperiled: Mercantile Representations of Failure and the Gendered Self in Eighteenth-Century Philadelphia," *Journal of American History* 81 (1994): 71.

17. George Forgie, *Patricide in the House Divided: A Psychological Interpretation of Lincoln and His Age* (New York: Norton, 1979), 50–53.

18. Ralph Waldo Emerson, *The Journals and Miscellaneous Notebooks of Ralph Waldo Emerson,* ed. William Gilman et al., 16 vols. (Cambridge: Harvard University Press, 1960–82), 7:327. Subsequent citations (abbreviated *JMN*) will be given parenthetically in the text.

19. Ralph Waldo Emerson, *The Letters of Ralph Waldo Emerson,* ed. Ralph Rusk and Eleanor Tilton, 10 vols. (New York: Columbia University Press, 1939–95), 2:86. Subsequent citations (abbreviated *L*) will be given parenthetically in the text.

20. Ralph Waldo Emerson, "Man the Reformer," in *The Collected Works of Ralph Waldo Emerson,* ed. Alfred Ferguson et al. (Cambridge: Harvard University Press, 1971–), 1:148, 147.

21. Mary Cayton, *Emerson's Emergence: Self and Society in the Transformation of New England, 1800–1845* (Chapel Hill: University of North Carolina Press, 1989), 51–54, 180, 228; Gilmore, *American Romanticism,* 18–34; Carolyn Porter, *Seeing and Being: The Plight of the Participant Observer in Emerson, James, Adams, and Faulkner* (Middletown, Conn.: Wesleyan University Press, 1981), 91–118; Christopher Newfield, *The Emerson Effect: Individualism and Submission in America* (Chicago: University of Chicago Press, 1996), 156, 161–70. In a section titled "The Morning after the Earthquake: Emerson and the Depression of 1837," B. L. Packer sees the panic as grist for Emerson's spiritual allegory. See *Emerson's Fall: A New Interpretation of the Major Essays* (New York: Continuum, 1982), 95–102.

22. Information about Emerson's finances has been drawn from his account books, in the collection of the Houghton Library, Harvard University. References are to the first three ledgers: Ledger 1 (January 1836–February 1840), Ledger 2 (February 1840–December 1844), and Ledger 3 (January 1845–May 1849). Entries (abbreviated LDG) will be cited parenthetically in the text, by book and page number. Occasionally, Emerson numbered the pages himself; where he did not, I have continued the pagination.

23. For the estimate of inflation from the antebellum period to the twenty-first century, see Balleisen, "Navigating Failure," 1:41.

24. Ralph Rusk, *The Life of Ralph Waldo Emerson* (New York: Columbia University Press, 1949), 250–51.

25. William Emerson to Ralph Waldo Emerson, [12?] December 1836, Houghton Library.

26. For an account of William's total indebtedness as of 1839, see William Emerson to Ralph Waldo Emerson, 1 July 1839, Houghton Library.

27. William Emerson to Ralph Waldo Emerson, 31 May 1838, Houghton Library.

28. William Emerson to Ralph Waldo Emerson, 9 August 1839, Houghton Library.

29. See William Emerson to Ralph Waldo Emerson, 17 September 1838, Houghton Library.

30. "A Modell of Christian Charity," *Winthrop Papers,* ed. Stewart Mitchell, 5 vols. (Boston: Massachusetts Historical Society, 1929–47), 2:244.

31. *The Early Lectures of Ralph Waldo Emerson,* ed. Stephen Whicher, Robert Spiller, and Wallace Williams, 3 vols. (Cambridge: Harvard University Press, 1964–72), 2:197. Subsequent citations (abbreviated *EL*) will be given parenthetically in the text.

32. *The Correspondence of Emerson and Carlyle,* ed. Joseph Slater (New York: Columbia University Press, 1964), 176. Subsequent citations (abbreviated *E&C*) will be given parenthetically in the text.

33. Karen Halttunen, *Confidence Men and Painted Women: A Study of Middle-Class Culture in America, 1830–1870* (New Haven: Yale University Press, 1982), 157, 163–67.

34. *Congressional Globe, Appendix,* 26th Cong., 1st sess., 796.

35. Ibid., 692.

36. *Richmond Enquirer,* 9 May 1837. See also Balleisen, "Navigating Failure," 1:139.

37. *Morning Courier and New York Enquirer,* 8 April 1837.

38. *New York Herald,* 22 April 1837. Bennett's designation of the New Orleans firm is in error here. It was Barrett and Co.

39. David Leverenz, *Manhood and the American Renaissance* (Ithaca: Cornell University Press, 1989), 47.

40. In *Woman's Fiction: A Guide to Novels by and about Women in America, 1820–1870* (Ithaca: Cornell University Press, 1978), Nina Baym argues that antebellum women writers often imagined independence as a rejection of the competitive marketplace. See esp. pp. 40, 47–49. My reading will emphasize the more market-friendly elements in some of these texts.

41. Elizabeth Oakes Smith, "Characterless Women," *Graham's Magazine* 21, no. 4 (October 1842): 199.

42. L. E. Penhallow, "The Failure," *Godey's Lady's Book,* January 1838, 40.

43. Timothy Shay Arthur, *Riches Have Wings; or, A Tale for the Rich and Poor* (New York: Baker and Scribner, 1847), 8.

44. "Autobiography of Ferret Snapp Newcraft, Esq.," *United States Magazine and Democratic Review,* May 1838, 175–76.

45. "Extracts from the Private Diary of a Certain Bank Director," *United States Magazine and Democratic Review,* July 1838, 419.

46. "London Fashionable Chit-Chat," *Atkinson's Casket* 12, no. 5 (May 1837): 234.

47. C. H. Butler, "The Bankrupt's Daughters: A Tale of New York," *Graham's Magazine* 26, no. 2 (August 1844): 56.

48. Marcus Byron, *Herbert Tracy; or, The Trials of Mercantile Life, and the Morality of Trade* (New York: John Riker, 1851), 78, 166.

49. Frederick Jackson, *The Victim of Chancery; or, A Debtor's Experience* (pub. by the author; printed by John Trow, 1841), 66.

50. Arthur, *Riches Have Wings,* 118.

51. "Leaves from a Lawyer's Port-Folio. Number Seven. The Victim," *The Casket and Philadelphia Monthly Magazine* 27, no. 1 (July 1840): 19.

52. S. A. Hunt, "The Wife. A Tale of the Hard Times," *Arthur's Magazine* 2 (November 1844): 225.

53. John Howard Payne, "The Uses of Adversity," *The Ladies' Companion,* August 1837, 174.

54. "Passages in the Life of Timothy Jenkins, Esquire," *The New-Yorker*, 1 July 1837, 226.

55. "The Broken Merchants. A Tale of the Troubles of 1837," *The Ladies' Companion*, June 1837, 60. Subsequent citations will be given parenthetically in the text.

56. Epes Sargent, *Wealth and Worth; or, Which Makes the Man?* (New York: Harper, 1842), 43. Subsequent citations will be given parenthetically in the text.

57. Mary Ryan, *Cradle of the Middle Class: The Family in Oneida County, New York, 1790–1865* (New York: Cambridge University Press, 1981), 153.

58. On the economic activities of mid-nineteenth-century heroines, see Frances Cogan, *All-American Girl: The Ideal of Real Woman-Hood in Mid-Nineteenth-Century America* (Athens: University of Georgia Press, 1989), 212–55. For Jacksonian women forced to become entrepreneurs, see Joyce Appleby, *Inheriting the Revolution: The First Generation of Americans* (Cambridge: Harvard University Press, 2000), 96–99.

59. Arthur, *Riches Have Wings*, 175.

60. Butler, "Bankrupt's Daughters," 56.

61. T. S. Arthur, *The Debtor's Daughter; or, Life and Its Changes* (Philadelphia: Peterson, 1850), 65. Subsequent citations will be given parenthetically in the text.

62. T. S. Arthur, *The Two Merchants; or, Solvent and Insolvent* (Philadelphia: Burgess and Zieber, 1843), 23. Subsequent citations will be given parenthetically in the text.

63. Eliza Follen, *Sketches of Married Life* (Boston: Hilliard, Gray, 1838), 113. Subsequent citations will be given parenthetically in the text.

64. Michel Foucault, *Discipline and Punish*, trans. Alan Sheridan (New York: Vintage, 1979), 195–209. See also Richard Brodhead, *Cultures of Letters: Scenes of Reading and Writing in Nineteenth-Century America* (Chicago: University of Chicago Press, 1993), 13–47.

65. Susan Warner, *Queechy*, 2 vols. (New York: Putnam, 1852). Citations will be given parenthetically in the text.

66. Ann Douglas, *The Feminization of American Culture* (New York: Knopf, 1977), 162–63.

CHAPTER 5.  *The Discipline of Whitman's Art*

1. Stuart Blumin, *The Emergence of the Middle Class: Social Experience in the American City, 1760–1900* (New York: Cambridge University Press, 1989).

2. E. P. Thompson, *The Making of the English Working Class* (New York: Pantheon, 1964), 9.

3. Richard Maurice Bucke, *Walt Whitman* (1883; reprint, New York: Johnson Reprint, 1970), 99; Betsy Erkkila, *Whitman the Political Poet* (New York: Oxford University Press,

1989), 10; Henry David Thoreau, quoted in Gay Wilson Allen, *The Solitary Singer: A Critical Biography of Walt Whitman,* rev. ed. (New York: New York University Press, 1967), 204; Jerome Loving, *Walt Whitman: The Song of Himself* (Berkeley: University of California Press, 1999), 205; Horace Traubel, *With Walt Whitman in Camden,* 9 vols. (1908; reprint, New York: Rowman and Littlefield, 1961–96), 2:84. See also Ezra Greenspan, *Walt Whitman and the American Reader* (Cambridge: Cambridge University Press, 1990), 127–28; M. Wynn Thomas, *The Lunar Light of Whitman's Poetry* (Cambridge: Harvard University Press, 1987), 12, 16, 27–33; Newton Arvin, *Whitman* (1938; reprint, New York: Russell and Russell, 1969), 13–14; Jerome Loving, "The Political Roots of *Leaves of Grass,*" in *A Historical Guide to Walt Whitman,* ed. David Reynolds (New York: Oxford University Press, 2000), 100, 109–13; and David Reynolds, *Walt Whitman's America: A Cultural Biography* (New York: Knopf, 1995), 105–6, 149–50.

4. R. J. Morris, *Class, Sect and Party: The Making of the British Middle Class, Leeds, 1820–1850* (Manchester: Manchester University Press, 1990), 120.

5. Bruce Laurie, *Artisans into Workers: Labor in Nineteenth-Century America* (New York: Hill and Wang, 1989), 12.

6. Reynolds, *Walt Whitman's America,* 450.

7. Erkkila, *Whitman the Political Poet,* 48.

8. Thomas, *Lunar Light,* 78.

9. Bruce Laurie, " 'Spavined Ministers, Lying Toothpullers, and Buggering Priests': Third-Partyism and the Search for Security in the Antebellum North," in *American Artisans: Crafting Social Identity, 1750–1850,* ed. Howard Rock, Paul Gilje, and Robert Asher (Baltimore: Johns Hopkins University Press, 1995), 105. See also Michael B. Katz, "Social Class in North American Urban History," *Journal of Interdisciplinary History* 11 (1981): 597–98.

10. Bucke, *Walt Whitman,* 43. On Whitman's "conservative radicalism," see Kerry Larson, *Whitman's Drama of Consensus* (Chicago: University of Chicago Press, 1988), xxiii; and Denis Donoghue, *Connoisseurs of Chaos: Ideas of Order in Modern American Poetry* (New York: Macmillan, 1965), 28. Arvin calls Whitman the poet of "middle-class culture" (*Whitman,* 2–3).

11. Sean Wilentz, *Chants Democratic: New York City and the Rise of the American Working Class, 1788–1850* (New York: Oxford University Press, 1984), 363. All newspaper citations in this paragraph are reprinted in the *New York Tribune,* 30 April 1850.

12. *New York Tribune,* 20 December 1850; 26 December 1850; 11 March 1851; 12 December 1850; Iver Bernstein, *The New York City Draft Riots: Their Significance for American Society and Politics in the Age of the Civil War* (New York: Oxford University Press, 1990), 77. On industrial congresses, see Laurie, *Artisans into Workers,* 102–3.

13. *New York Tribune,* 4 April 1850; 8 August 1850; 10 April 1850; 26 December 1850.

14. 30 April 1850. On the tailors' riot, see Wilentz, *Chants Democratic,* 377–81; and *New York Tribune,* 6 August 1850.

15. John Ashworth, *"Agrarians" and "Aristocrats": Party Political Ideology in the United States, 1837–1846* (London: Royal Historical Society, 1983), 94; Charles Sellers, *Market Revolution Jacksonian America, 1815–1846* (New York: Oxford University Press, 1991), 13–14; Erkkila, *Whitman the Political Poet,* 27, 41, 95; Wilentz, *Chants Democratic,* 94, 102.

16. *New York Tribune,* 26 July 1850; 4 August 1851.

17. Ibid., 13 February 1851.

18. Ibid., 26 December 1850.

19. Ibid., 26 December 1850, 19 July 1850.

20. Ibid., 14 August 1850. On the retreat to individualist solutions to labor problems advocated by land reformers, see Eric Foner, *Politics and Ideology in the Age of the Civil War* (New York: Oxford University Press, 1980), 72–73.

21. *New York Tribune,* 6 August 1850; 24 April 1850; 19 August 1848; 21 August 1850. See also John Commons et al., *History of Labour in the United States,* 4 vols. (1918; reprint, New York: Kelley, 1966), 1:507.

22. *New York Tribune,* 21 August 1850.

23. Ibid., 20 June 1850.

24. Bernstein, *Draft Riots,* 86–99; Wilentz, *Chants Democratic,* 383–86. See also Commons et al., *History of Labour,* 1:560.

25. *New York Herald,* 13 November 1854; 16 November 1854; 19 December 1854.

26. *New York Times,* 16 January 1855; *New York Herald,* 23 December 1854; 9 January 1855; *New York Times,* 11 January 1855; *New York Herald,* 22 December 1854.

27. *New York Herald,* 9 January 1855; *New York Times,* 16 January 1855; *New York Herald,* 22 December 1854; 30 December 1854; *New York Times,* 16 January 1855; *New York Herald,* 27 December 1854; 23 December 1854.

28. *New York Times,* 11 January 1855; *New York Herald,* 22 December 1854; 16 January 1855; 8 January 1855.

29. *New York Tribune,* 30 December 1854; *New York Times,* 6 February 1855.

30. *In Re Walt Whitman,* ed. Horace Traubel, Richard Maurice Bucke, and Thomas B. Harned (Philadelphia: McKay, 1893), 33; Richard Stott, *Workers in the Metropolis: Class, Ethnicity, and Youth in Antebellum New York City* (Ithaca: Cornell University Press, 1990), 141, 142.

31. *New York Times,* 5 January 1855; Elizabeth Blackmar, *Manhattan for Rent, 1785–1850* (Ithaca: Cornell University Press, 1989), 214; J. G. A. Pocock, "The Mobility of Property and the Rise of Eighteenth-Century Sociology," in *Theories of Property: Aristotle to the Present,* ed. Anthony Parel and Thomas Flanagan (Waterloo, Ontario: Wilfred Laurier University Press, 1979), 147. See also Kenneth Scherzer, *The Unbounded Com-*

*munity: Neighborhood Life and Social Structure in New York City, 1830–1875* (Durham, N.C.: Duke University Press, 1992), 19–24.

32. Anthony Giddens, *The Class Structure of the Advanced Societies* (New York: Harper and Row, 1973), 182; *Brooklyn Daily Eagle,* 16 March 1847, in *Whitman As Editor of the Brooklyn Daily Eagle,* ed. Thomas Brasher (Detroit: Wayne State University Press, 1970), 29; *New York Aurora,* 9 April 1842, in *The Collected Writings of Walt Whitman. The Journalism,* ed. Herbert Bergman et. al (New York: Peter Lang, 1998–), 1:105; Stott, *Workers in the Metropolis,* 133.

33. Allen, *Solitary Singer,* 116; Katz, "Social Class," 600; Michael Katz, Michael Doucet, and Mark Stern, *The Social Organization of Early Industrial Capitalism* (Cambridge: Harvard University Press, 1982), 133–34, 141, 154; Stephan Thernstrom, *Poverty and Progress: Social Mobility in a Nineteenth-Century City* (Cambridge: Harvard University Press, 1964), 117–18. On the distinctions between the use- and exchange-value of working-class homes, see Katz et al., *Social Organization,* 134–36.

34. Antonio Gramsci, *An Antonio Gramsci Reader: Selected Writings, 1916–1935,* ed. David Forgacs (New York: Schocken, 1988). All citations will be given parenthetically in the text. On Gramsci's discussion of intellectuals, see also Leonardo Salamini, *The Sociology of Political Praxis: An Introduction to Gramsci's Theory* (London: Routledge and Kegan Paul, 1981), 109–14; Anne Sassoon, *Gramsci's Politics,* 2nd ed. (Minneapolis: University of Minnesota Press, 1987), 134–50; James Martin, *Gramsci's Political Analysis: A Critical Introduction* (London: Macmillan, 1998), 44–64; Walter Adamson, *Hegemony and Revolution: A Study of Antonio Gramsci's Political and Cultural Theory* (Berkeley: University of California Press, 1980), 143–44; and Joseph Femia, *Gramsci's Political Thought: Hegemony, Consciousness, and the Revolutionary Process* (London: Oxford University Press, 1981), 130–33. For critiques of Gramsci's analysis of intellectuals, see Roger Simon, *Gramsci's Political Thought: An Introduction,* rev. ed. (London: Lawrence and Wishart, 1991), 98; and T. J. Jackson Lears, "The Concept of Cultural Hegemony: Problems and Possibilities," *American Historical Review* 90 (1985): 572.

35. Martin, *Gramsci's Political Analysis,* 50.

36. James Joll, *Antonio Gramsci* (New York: Viking, 1977), 123–24; Renate Holub, *Antonio Gramsci: Beyond Marxism and Postmodernism* (London: Routledge, 1992), 167.

37. John Higham, *From Boundlessness to Consolidation: The Transformation of American Culture, 1848–1860* (Ann Arbor, Mich.: William J. Clements Library, 1969), 15–28. Iver Bernstein discusses the importance of consolidation to the antebellum labor movement in *Draft Riots,* 76–78.

38. All citations from the first edition of *Leaves of Grass* are from the facsimile prepared by Clifton Joseph Furness (New York: Columbia University Press, 1939). Hereafter, I will give page and line numbers parenthetically. Citations of the poetry will include page

numbers from the original edition, followed by line numbers, as provided in *Walt Whit-man's Leaves of Grass: The First (1855) Edition,* ed. Malcolm Cowley (New York: Viking Compass, 1961).

39.  For a discussion of how Whitman intended his balance of "pride and sympathy" as a solution to the nation's political ills, see Erkkila, *Whitman the Political Poet,* 94, 116.

40.  Thomas, *Lunar Light,* 58.

41.  Whitman, *The Collected Writings of Walt Whitman, Notebooks and Unpublished Prose Manuscripts,* ed. Edward Grier, 6 vols. (New York: New York University Press, 1984), 1:56.

42.  On Whitman's "eighteenth-century view of commerce," see Erkkila, *Whitman the Political Poet,* 37–38. All citations from Smith's *The Theory of Moral Sentiments* are from the Glasgow edition, edited by D. D. Raphael and A. L. Macfie (Indianapolis: Liberty Fund, 1984), and will be cited parenthetically in the text. References include the book, chapter, section, paragraph, and page numbers.

43.  For a discussion of approval and sympathy in Smith, see Patricia Werhane, *Adam Smith and His Legacy for Modern Capitalism* (New York: Oxford University Press, 1991), 39–40.

44.  On Smith's agrarian capitalism, see David McNally, *Political Economy and the Rise of Capitalism: A Reinterpretation* (Berkeley: University of California Press, 1988), 228–30, 233. On mirrors in Smith's moral economy, see Elizabeth Hinds, *Private Property: Charles Brockden Brown's Gendered Economics of Virtue* (Newark: University of Delaware Press, 1997), 72–73. Kerry Larson discusses the importance of face-to-face encounters in Whitman, in *Whitman's Drama of Consensus,* xvi.

45.  Werhane, *Adam Smith,* 49–52.

46.  David Waldstreicher, *In the Midst of Perpetual Fetes: The Making of American Nationalism, 1776–1820* (Chapel Hill: University of North Carolina Press, 1997), 117–26.

47.  Erkkila, *Whitman the Political Poet,* 125.

48.  *New York Tribune,* 15 April 1850; 13 February 1851; 26 December 1850; *New York Tribune,* 13 February 1851; 17 January 1851. For the attitudes of northern workers toward slavery, see Foner, *Politics and Ideology,* 57–93; John Jentz, "Artisans, Evangelicals, and the City: A Social History of Abolition and Labor Reform in Jacksonian New York" (Ph.D. diss., City University of New York, 1977), 244–56, 269, 277–80; Bernard Mandel, *Labor: Free and Slave; Workingmen and the Anti-Slavery Movement in the United States* (New York: Associated Authors, 1955), 61–95, 116–30, 134–54; and Bruce Laurie, *Working People of Philadelphia, 1800–1850* (Philadelphia: Temple University Press, 1980), 63–65. For Whitman's views on antislavery, see Reynolds, *Walt Whitman's America,* 117–20, 123–25; Martin Klammer, *Whitman, Slavery, and the Emergence of Leaves of Grass* (University Park: Pennsylvania State University Press, 1995); Christopher Beach, *The Politics*

*of Distinction: Whitman and the Discourses of Nineteenth-Century America* (Athens: University of Georgia Press, 1996), 59, 63–65, 72–80. For Whitman's use of slavery in "I Sing the Body Electric," see Klammer, *Emergence of Leaves of Grass,* 141–48; Erkkila, *Whitman the Political Poet,* 125–27; Beach, *Politics of Distinction,* 68–72; and Thomas, *Lunar Light,* 32.

49. Thomas, *Lunar Light,* 18. See also Erkkila, *Whitman the Political Poet,* 4; and Greenspan, *Walt Whitman,* 109–10.

50. Thomas, *Lunar Light,* 25. See also Larson, *Whitman's Drama of Consensus,* 42.

51. Donoghue, *Connoisseurs of Chaos,* 43, 39, 26; Joseph Conrad, *Heart of Darkness,* ed. Robert Kimbrough (New York: Norton, 1971), 4. On the links between "Crossing Brooklyn Ferry" and commerce, see Thomas, *Lunar Light,* 105–9. Thomas, however, argues that Whitman desires to escape commerce rather than to purify it. On Whitman's alienation in the poem, see also Michael Moon, *Disseminating Whitman: Revision and Corporeality in Leaves of Grass* (Cambridge: Harvard University Press, 1991), 105–10. All citations from the 1856 edition of *Leaves of Grass,* published by Fowler and Wells, will be given parenthetically in the text. Citations will include both the line numbers from the original edition (Brooklyn: 1856) and those (where applicable) from *Leaves of Grass: A Textual Variorum of the Printed Poems,* ed. Sculley Bradley (New York: New York University Press, 1980), vol. 1.

52. Jean-Joseph Goux, *Symbolic Economies: After Marx and Freud* (Ithaca: Cornell University Press, 1990), 13, 14. One of Whitman's admirers, Nellie Eyster, confirmed the power of the Marxian paradigm in a letter to Whitman in 1871: "I was permitted a *long look* into the wonderful mirror of your creation, where I saw the reflex of *your* soul, and felt the influence of your divining power. . . . Life held grander possibilities to me from that hour" (Traubel, *Walt Whitman in Camden,* 1:34–35).

53. Quoted in Ed Folsom, *Walt Whitman's Native Representations* (Cambridge: Cambridge University Press, 1994), 121.

54. *Hunt's Merchants Magazine* 3 (July–December 1840): 17; 13 (November 1845): 408.

55. *New York Herald,* 11 November 1857; *New York Times,* 11 November 1857; *New York Herald,* 11 November 1857; 13 November 1857; 15 November 1857.

56. *New York Herald,* 22 November 1857; *New York Times,* 13 November 1857; *New York Herald,* 15 November 1857.

57. Dion Boucicault, *The Poor of New York* (New York: Samuel French, 1857), 2.1, p. 13.

## CHAPTER 6. *Class Acts*

1. In addition to the works cited below, recent studies of the antebellum middle class include Richard Bushman, *The Refinement of America: Persons, Houses, Cities* (New

York: Knopf, 1992); Carroll Smith-Rosenberg, *Disorderly Conduct: Visions of Gender in Victorian America* (New York: Knopf, 1985), esp. 129–64; Ann Douglas, *The Feminization of American Culture* (New York: Knopf, 1977); Paul Johnson, *A Shopkeeper's Millennium: Society and Revivals in Rochester, New York, 1815–1837* (New York: Hill and Wang, 1978); Sacvan Bercovitch, *The Rites of Assent: Transformations in the Symbolic Construction of America* (New York: Routledge, 1993); Burton Bledstein, *The Culture of Professionalism: The Middle Class and the Development of Higher Education in America* (New York: Norton, 1976); Stuart Blumin, *The Emergence of the Middle Class: Social Experience in the American City, 1760–1900* (New York: Cambridge University Press, 1989); and T. J. Jackson Lears, *Fables of Abundance: A Cultural History of Advertising in America* (New York: Basic Books, 1994). For "consensus historians," see Louis Hartz, *The Liberal Tradition in America: An Interpretation of American Political Thought Since the Revolution* (New York: Harcourt, Brace, 1955); and Richard Hofstadter, *The American Political Tradition and the Men Who Made It* (1948; reprint, New York: Knopf, 1970).

2. Blumin, *Emergence of the Middle Class,* 146–79; Elizabeth Blackmar, *Manhattan for Rent, 1785–1850* (Ithaca: Cornell University Press, 1989), 100–4, 106–8. On urban discipline, see Paul Boyer, *Urban Masses and Moral Order in America, 1820–1920* (Cambridge: Harvard University Press, 1978), 67–107. For "bourgeois republic," see Charles Sellers, *The Market Revolution: Jacksonian America, 1815–1846* (New York: Oxford University Press, 1991), 364–94. Cindy Sondik Aron discusses postbellum anxiety in *Ladies and Gentlemen of the Civil Service: Middle-Class Workers in Victorian America* (New York: Oxford University Press, 1987), 32.

3. Boyer, *Urban Masses,* 59, 96–97; R. J. Morris, *Class, Sect and Party: The Making of the British Middle Class, Leeds, 1820–1850* (Manchester: Manchester University Press, 1990), 249. On the diffuseness of the antebellum "middle class," see Boyer, 60–61.

4. Edward Balleisen, "Navigating Failure: Bankruptcy in Antebellum America," Ph.D. diss., Yale University, 1995, 2:461.

5. August Bolino, *The Development of the American Economy,* 2nd ed. (Columbus, Ohio: Merrill, 1966), 87; Douglass North, *Growth and Welfare in the American Past: A New Economic History* (Englewood Cliffs, N.J.: Prentice-Hall, 1966), 111; Alfred Chandler Jr., *The Visible Hand: The Managerial Revolution in American Business* (Cambridge, Mass.: Belknap, 1977), 81–121; James Huston, *The Panic of 1857 and the Coming of the Civil War* (Baton Rouge: Louisiana State University Press, 1987), 3; Edwin Burrows and Mike Wallace, *Gotham: A History of New York City to 1898* (New York: Oxford University Press, 1999), 659–73.

6. Nathaniel Hawthorne, *The House of the Seven Gables* (Columbus: Ohio State University Press, 1965), 38. A number of studies have treated antebellum (and Victorian) bankruptcy. See James Ciment, "In Light of Failure: Bankruptcy, Insolvency and Financial

Failure in New York City, 1790–1860" (Ph.D. diss., City University of New York, 1992); Barbara Allen Mathews, " 'Forgive Us Our Debts': Bankruptcy and Insolvency in America, 1763–1841" (Ph.D. diss., Brown University, 1994); and Balleisen, "Navigating Failure." For a British perspective, see Barbara Weiss, *The Hell of the English: Bankruptcy and the Victorian Novel* (Lewisburg, Pa.: Bucknell University Press, 1986).

7. Huston, *Panic of 1857,* 20; Burrows and Wallace, *Gotham,* 845; Jerome Mushkat, *Fernando Wood: A Political Biography* (Kent, Ohio: Kent State University Press, 1990), 77. See also Charles Calomiris and Larry Schweikart, "The Panic of 1857: Origins, Transmission, and Containment," *Journal of Economic History* 51 (1991): 807–34; *New York Herald,* 10 November 1857; *New York Times,* 11 November 1857; 12 November 1857.

8. See, for example, *Hunt's Merchants' Magazine and Commercial Review,* December 1857, 667 and January 1858, 20; *The Bankers' Magazine and Statistical Register,* November 1857, 409–10 and February 1858, 601; and *The New Englander,* November 1857, 715; Raymond Williams, *The Long Revolution* (1961; reprint, Westport, Conn.: Greenwood, 1975), 65. Henry Nash Smith argues that many writers of the 1850s sought to allay a widespread anxiety that he links with upward mobility. See "The Scribbling Women and the Cosmic Success Story," *Critical Inquiry* 1 (1974): 58.

9. R. G. Dun and Co. Collection, Baker Library, Harvard University Graduate School of Business Administration. All volumes cited in this chapter are New York City credit reports. French: vol. 189, p. 226; Casse: vol. 227, p. 399; Hecht: vol. 226, p. 251.

10. R. G. Dun and Co. Collection, Parsons and Schoonmaker: vol. 227, p. 400K.

11. Summarizing the evidence, Edward Balleisen estimates the business failure rate in the 1840s and 1850s at 40 to 50 percent. See "Vulture Capitalism in Antebellum America: The 1841 Federal Bankruptcy Act and the Exploration of Financial Distress," *Business History Review* 70 (1996): 476. See also Tony Freyer, *Producers Versus Capitalists: Constitutional Conflict in Antebellum America* (Charlottesville: University Press of Virginia, 1994), 65; and Christopher Clark, *The Roots of Rural Capitalism: Western Massachusetts, 1780–1860* (Ithaca: Cornell University Press, 1990), 217, whose figures fall within that range. In a study of Poughkeepsie, New York, Clyde and Sally Griffen found that, between 1845 and 1880, 32 percent of the firms reported on by R. G. Dun and Co. lasted three years or less, with only 14 percent lasting twenty years or more. See *Natives and Newcomers: The Ordering of Opportunity in Mid-Nineteenth-Century Poughkeepsie* (Cambridge: Harvard University Press, 1978), 104. In communities confronting special strains, the toll could be much higher. Peter Decker estimates that between one-half and two-thirds of all San Francisco merchants in the 1850s failed—a rate that affected many New York firms with ties to the city. See *Fortunes and Failures: White Collar Mobility in Nineteenth-Century San Francisco* (Cambridge: Harvard University Press, 1978), 92. Michael Katz, Michael Doucet, and Mark Stern remark that in the nineteenth-century Canadian city of Hamil-

ton, Ontario, small entrepreneurs "failed in business with extraordinary frequency." The failure rate for antebellum capitalists in Hamilton was at least 37 percent (*The Social Organization of Early Industrial Capitalism* [Cambridge, Massachusetts: Harvard University Press, 1982], 376, 33). In an essay on nineteenth-century American artisans, Bruce Laurie puts the failure rate closer to "two-thirds to three-quarters of master mechanics," with many experiencing "serial failures" (" 'Spavined Ministers, Lying Toothpullers, and Buggering Priests': Third-Partyism and the Search for Security in the Antebellum North," in *American Artisans: Crafting Social Identity, 1750–1850,* ed. Howard Rock, Paul Gilje, and Robert Asher [Baltimore: Johns Hopkins University Press, 1995], 102). By contrast, the most recent national figures (1998) put the overall failure rate at seventy-six per ten thousand firms, up from seventy-four per ten thousand in 1990. See *Statistical Abstract of the United States, 2000* (Washington, D.C.: U.S. Census Bureau, 2000), table no. 877, p. 549. The 90 percent failure rate appears in Alonzo Tripp's *The Fisher Boy* (Boston: Whittemore, Niles and Hall, 1857), 17. Clark cites a claim in the *Massachusetts State Record and Year Book of General Information, 1848* that 97 percent of those entering business with a ten-thousand-dollar credit would have lost twice that amount within twenty-five years. See *Roots of Rural Capitalism,* 217. For more general assessments of the effects of bankruptcy during this period, see Freyer, *Producers versus Capitalists,* 10, and Freyer, *Forums of Order: The Federal Courts and Business in American History* (Greenwich, Conn.: JAI, 1979), 9.

12. John Tebbel, *A History of Book Publishing in the United States,* 4 vols. (New York: Bowker, 1972–81), 1:209, 210; *New York Evening Post,* 24 October 1856; Tebbel, 1:425, 426.

13. R. G. Dun and Co. Collection, Norton: vol. 188A, p. 94; Hewett: vol. 188A, p. 98; Smith: vol. 226, p. 201Z.

14. Hershel Parker, *Herman Melville: A Biography* (Baltimore: Johns Hopkins University Press, 1999), 1:650; Tebbel, *History of Book Publishing,* 1:212; *New York Herald,* 28 October 1857; Mary Kelley, *Private Woman, Public Stage: Literary Domesticity in Nineteenth-Century America* (New York: Oxford University Press, 1984), 147. See also Michael Gilmore, *American Romanticism and the Marketplace* (Chicago: University of Chicago Press, 1985); Idem, "Hawthorne and the Making of the Middle Class," in *Rethinking Class: Literary Studies and Social Formations,* ed. Wai Chee Dimock and Michael Gilmore (New York: Columbia University Press, 1994), 215–38. For a more optimistic reading of panic literature, see Ann Fabian, "Speculation on Distress: The Popular Discourse of the Panics of 1837 and 1857," *Yale Journal of Criticism* 3 (1989): 127–42.

15. Margaret Hunt, *The Middling Sort: Commerce, Gender, and the Family in England, 1680–1780* (Berkeley: University of California Press, 1996), 14, 20; Theodore Koditschek, *Class Formation and Urban-Industrial Society: Bradford, 1750–1850* (Cambridge: Cam-

bridge University Press, 1990), 207–8; Balleisen, "Vulture Capitalism," 509–10; Sondik Aron, *Ladies and Gentlemen*, 32. See also Blumin, *Emergence of the Middle Class*, 8–12; Mary Ryan, *Cradle of the Middle Class: The Family in Oneida County, New York, 1790–1865* (New York: Cambridge University Press, 1981), 150–53; John Smail, *The Origins of Middle-Class Culture: Halifax, Yorkshire, 1660–1780* (Ithaca: Cornell University Press, 1994); Leonore Davidoff and Catherine Hall, *Family Fortunes: Men and Women of the English Middle Class, 1780–1850* (Chicago: University of Chicago Press, 1987); John Gilkeson, *Middle-Class Providence, 1820–1940* (Princeton: Princeton University Press, 1986); Arno Mayer, "The Lower Middle Class As a Historical Problem," *Journal of Modern History* 47 (1975): 409–36; and Gary Kornblith, "Self-Made Men: The Development of Middling-Class Consciousness in New England," *The Massachusetts Review* 26 (1985): 461–74.

16. R. G. Dun and Co. Collection, vol. 341, p. 130.

17. Ibid., vol. 190, p. 400B. Bishop's credit report begins in the same volume, on p. 396. Citations will be given parenthetically.

18. Azel Roe, *Like and Unlike* (New York: Carleton, 1862). Unless otherwise noted, after the initial entry, citations for each novel will be given parenthetically in the text.

19. Beulah Hirst, "Love and Luxury," *Graham's Magazine* 52 (January 1858): 17–29.

20. T. S. Arthur, "Don't Be Discouraged," *Ways of Providence; or, "He Doeth All Things Well"* (Philadelphia: Lippincott, Grambo, 1851).

21. For an examination of the relation between women's shoplifting and late-nineteenth-century market conditions, see Elaine Abelson, *When Ladies Go A-Thieving: Middle-Class Shoplifters in the Victorian Department Store* (New York: Oxford University Press, 1989).

22. Azel Roe, *Looking Around* (New York: Carleton, 1865), 128.

23. Azel Roe, *To Love and to Be Loved* (New York: Appleton, 1851).

24. Richard Kimball, *Undercurrents of Wall-Street: A Romance of Business* (New York: Putnam, 1862).

25. Azel Roe, *James Montjoy; or, I've Been Thinking* (New York: Appleton, 1850).

26. T. S. Arthur, *Trial and Triumph; or, Firmness in the Household* (Philadelphia: Peterson, 1855).

27. Marion Harland (Mary Terhune), *Phemie's Temptation* (New York: Carleton, 1869).

28. See Nina Baym, *Woman's Fiction: A Guide to Novels by and about Women in America, 1820–1870* (Ithaca: Cornell University Press, 1978), 197–207. Mary Kelley discusses Harland's subversiveness in *Private Woman, Public Stage*, esp. 192–96.

29. Ann Stephens, *Fashion and Famine* (New York: Bunce, 1854).

30. Toby Ditz, "Shipwrecked; or, Masculinity Imperiled: Mercantile Representations

of Failure and the Gendered Self in Eighteenth-Century Philadelphia," *Journal of American History* 81 (1994): 66.

31. Charles Smith, *George Melville* (New York: Clark, 1858).

32. Azel Roe, *True to the Last; or, Alone on a Wide, Wide Sea* (New York: Derby and Jackson, 1858).

33. George William Curtis, *Trumps* (New York: Harper, 1861), 341.

34. John Jones, *The City Merchant; or, The Mysterious Failure* (Philadelphia: Lippincott, Grambo, 1851).

35. Mary Townsend, *The Brother Clerks: A Tale of New Orleans* (New York: Derby and Jackson, 1857).

36. Karl Marx and Friedrich Engels, *The German Ideology, The Marx-Engels Reader,* ed. Robert Tucker (New York: Norton, 1972), 138.

37. Davidoff and Hall, *Family Fortunes,* 229.

38. Sellers, *Market Revolution,* 364–95.

39. Van Buren Denslow, *Owned and Disowned; or, The Chattel Child, a Tale of Southern Life* (New York: Dayton, 1857).

40. On the "depravity" of the poor, see Ryan, *Cradle of the Middle Class,* 148–49, 109–16; Boyer, *Urban Masses,* 85–94; Christine Stansell, *City of Women: Sex and Class in New York, 1789–1860* (New York: Knopf, 1986), 63–75.

41. Ned Buntline, *The Mysteries and Miseries of New York: A Story of Real Life* (New York: Berford, 1848). Citations are by book and page, all in the same volume.

42. George Foster, *New York by Gas-Light: With Here and There a Streak of Sunshine* (New York: Dewitt and Davenport, 1850).

43. David Reynolds, *Walt Whitman's America: A Cultural Biography* (New York: Knopf, 1995), 103–5; Wilentz, *Chants Democratic,* 300–301.

44. George Foster, *New York in Slices: By an Experienced Carver* (New York: Graham, 1849), 44.

45. Augustine Duganne, *The Tenant-House; or, Embers from Poverty's Hearthstone* (New York: DeWitt, 1857).

46. Azel Roe, *How Could He Help It? or, The Heart Triumphant* (New York: Derby and Jackson, 1860).

47. On the Pennsylvania Hall riot, see Sam Bass Warner, *The Private City: Philadelphia in Three Periods of Its Growth* (Philadelphia: University of Pennsylvania Press, 1968), 130–36; and Gary Nash, *Forging Freedom: The Formation of Philadelphia's Black Community, 1720–1840* (Cambridge: Harvard University Press, 1988), 277.

CHAPTER 7. *Infinite Systems*

1. Gordon Wood, "Conspiracy and the Paranoid Style: Causality and Deceit in the

Eighteenth Century," *William and Mary Quarterly* 39 (1982): 440. For "infinite system," see Adam Smith, *The Theory of Moral Sentiments,* ed. D. D. Raphael and A. L. Macfie (Indianapolis: Liberty Fund, 1984), I.iii.2.9, p. 59.

2. Quoted in Richard Hofstadter, *Social Darwinism in American Thought,* rev. ed. (New York: Braziller, 1955), 60. See also Robert Wiebe, *The Search for Order, 1877–1920* (New York: Hill and Wang, 1967), 21, 43.

3. James Huston, *The Panic of 1857 and the Coming of the Civil War* (Baton Rouge: Louisiana State University Press, 1987), 36, 35, 40, 36.

4. Carroll Wright, *Industrial Depressions: The First Annual Report of the United States Commissioner of Labor* (1886; reprint, New York: Kelley, 1968), 63, 78, 79, 291, 292.

5. Ralph Waldo Emerson, *The Conduct of Life,* vol. 6, *The Complete Works of Ralph Waldo Emerson,* 14 vols. (Boston: Houghton, Mifflin, 1883). Citations, by title and page, will be given parenthetically in the text.

6. Carlyle to Emerson, 29 January 1861, *The Correspondence of Emerson and Carlyle,* ed. Joseph Slater (New York: Columbia University Press, 1964), 533–34.

7. The journal entry can be found in *The Journals and Miscellaneous Notebooks of Ralph Waldo Emerson,* ed. William Gilman et al., 16 vols. (Cambridge, Mass.: Belknap, 1960–82), 5:332–33.

8. For a discussion of submissiveness and Emersonian liberalism, see Christopher Newfield, *The Emerson Effect: Individualism and Submission in America* (Chicago: University of Chicago Press, 1996), esp. 22–26. Where Newfield sees submissiveness throughout Emerson's career—an effect, he maintains, of market ideology—I stress the gradual development of a market ethic in tandem with the growth of the market itself. By 1860, for Emerson, such market ethics had fully matured.